GENESIS

Books by Dr. Boice

Witness and Revelation in the Gospel of John
Philippians: An Expositional Commentary
The Sermon on the Mount
How to Live the Christian Life (originally, *How to Live It Up*)
Ordinary Men Called by God (originally, *How God Can Use Nobodies*)
The Last and Future World
The Gospel of John: An Expositional Commentary (5 volumes in one)
"Galatians," in the *Expositor's Bible Commentary*
Can You Run Away from God?
Our Sovereign God, editor
Our Savior God: Studies on Man, Christ and the Atonement, editor
Does Inerrancy Matter?
The Foundation of Biblical Authority, editor
Making God's Word Plain, editor
The Epistles of John
The Parables of Jesus
The Christ of Christmas
The Minor Prophets: An Expositional Commentary (2 volumes)
Standing on the Rock
The Christ of the Open Tomb
Foundations of the Christian Faith (4 volumes in one)
Christ's Call to Discipleship
Transforming Our World: A Call to Action, editor
Ephesians: An Expositional Commentary
Daniel: An Expositional Commentary
Joshua: We Will Serve the Lord
Nehemiah: Learning to Lead
The King Has Come
Romans (4 volumes)
Mind Renewal in a Mindless Age
Amazing Grace
Psalms (3 volumes)
Sure I Believe, So What?
Hearing God When You Hurt
Two Cities, Two Loves
Here We Stand: A Call from Confessing Evangelicals, editor
Living by the Book: The Joy of Loving and Trusting God's Word
Acts: An Expositional Commentary

GENESIS

An Expositional Commentary

Volume 3

Genesis 37–50

JAMES MONTGOMERY BOICE

Baker Books

A Division of Baker Book House Co
Grand Rapids, Michigan 49516

© 1987, 1998 by James Montgomery Boice

Published by Baker Books
a division of Baker Book House Company
P.O. Box 6287, Grand Rapids, MI 49516-6287

Previously published by Zondervan Publishing House

Printed in the United States of America

Library of Congress Cataloging-in-Publication Data

Boice, James Montgomery, 1938–
    Genesis : an expositional commentary / James Montgomery Boice.
        p. cm.
    Originally published: Grand Rapids : Zondervan, 1987.
    Content: v. 3. Genesis 37:1–50:26
    ISBN 0-8010-1163-9 (cloth)
    1. Bible. O.T. Genesis—Commentaries. I. Title.
BS1235.3.B63   1998
222'.1107—dc21   98-16993

For current information about all releases from Baker Book House, visit our web site:
http://www.bakerbooks.com

To God,
who in all things
works for the good of those
who love him

Contents

Preface

Several years ago Dr. D. A. Carson, research professor of New Testament at Trinity Evangelical Divinity School, wrote a book called *The Gagging of God: Christianity Confronts Pluralism*. It was a masterful analysis of our postmodern world and an exploration of how Christians can speak of the grace of God in Christ to a generation that has rejected the very categories with which we speak. Our contemporaries have no place for the Bible's truth claims, and if we tell them that God loves them and has a wonderful plan for their lives—well, why not? They are worth loving; they are entitled to it, in fact. And they have some wonderful plans for their lives too. As far as Jesus being the Savior is concerned, that is all right also, as long as we do not deny that there are other equally valid saviors and do not maintain that Jesus has any meaningful claims on our lives.

What Carson argues is that, in order to be effective witnesses to Christ in our age, we will have to go back to the Bible and learn to present our case as the Bible itself does. We will need to begin with the doctrine of God as Creator, explaining who he is and what he has done; explain how human beings are created in God's image and are therefore responsible to God for what they do; how we have fallen from that high calling and intent; and how we now need someone to rescue us from ruin. We must trace the narrative line of the Bible, through Abraham, Moses, David, and the other great Old Testament figures up to the climactic appearance and work of Jesus Christ.

In other words, we must recognize that our world is as spiritually ignorant and pagan as the world into which the gospel of God's grace, both in its Old Testament and New Testament forms, first came. And we must present our message as the Bible did and does. We have an excellent example of this in the New Testament in the way the apostle Paul argued Christianity's case before the pagan philosophers in Athens (Acts 17:2–31).

All of which is to say, there is no better or needful time for anyone to be studying the Book of Genesis than the present.

When I first began to preach on Genesis nearly twenty years ago, I was fascinated with the various competing theories of creation and such issues as the antiquity of man and the extent of the flood. Many Christians were struggling with such matters in those days. Today, however, I am impressed with the fact that our need to know Genesis and appropriate both its message and evangelistic method is far deeper. We need to think about God, a reality that is absent far too often even in evangelical churches, and we need to know about ourselves as fallen yet able to be redeemed.

So study Genesis! Start at the beginning of everything! You will find that your understanding of the Christian faith will be wonderfully and deeply enriched and that your ability to talk about Christ and the gospel will be significantly enhanced.

I am greatly indebted to Baker Book House, which has expressed interest in reissuing these volumes after their having been out of print for several years, and for issuing them in an improved format to match my commentaries on *Psalms, Acts, Romans,* and *Ephesians.* My prayer, as with everything I write, is that the teaching in these volumes may exist to the glory of God, because, as the apostle Paul said in summing up his teaching in Romans, at the end of the eleventh chapter:

> For from him and through him and to him are all things.
> To him be the glory forever! Amen.

Paul might well have been writing about the Book of Genesis.

James Montgomery Boice
Philadelphia, Pennsylvania
July, 1998

121

A Man for All Seasons

Genesis 37:1–2

Jacob lived in the land where his father had stayed, the land of Canaan.

This is the account of Jacob.

Joseph, a young man of seventeen, was tending the flocks with his brothers, the sons of Bilhah and the sons of Zilpah, his father's wives, and he brought his father a bad report about them.

If there was ever a man for all seasons, it was Joseph, the favored son of the patriarch Jacob, whose story begins in the thirty-seventh chapter of Genesis. Joseph's life spanned the social spectrum of the ancient world. Raised as the future heir of the wealthy Jewish patriarch, he fell into slavery in a far-off Gentile land but later rose to a position of prominence as second in command only to Pharaoh. He was loved and hated, favored and abused, tempted and trusted, exalted and abased. Yet at no point in the 110-year life of Joseph did he ever seem to get his eyes off God or cease to trust him. Adversity did not harden his character. Prosperity did not ruin him. He was the same in private as in public. He was a truly great man.

This is one reason why Genesis tells so much about him. The story of Abraham is a long and most important story in Genesis. But the story of Joseph equals it in the number of chapters (fourteen chapters each) and excels it in length (by 25 percent). Genesis 37–50 is a masterpiece of historical narration. It is a striking characteristic of this story that nothing bad is ever reported about Joseph. Like all people he most certainly had a sinful nature, but we are not told of any outward expressions of it. As a result, we are free to respond to and love him as perhaps no other character in the Bible except the Lord Jesus Christ.

Yet, strikingly, Joseph does not figure much in the New Testament—as Abraham and Moses do, for example. We have more spoken words of Joseph than any other Old Testament character. Yet he is never once quoted in the New Testament. In fact, Joseph is mentioned in only four New Testament passages: in John 4:5 (which says that Jacob had given Joseph a plot of ground near Sychar in Samaria, a fact not mentioned in Genesis); in Acts 7:9–14 (where Joseph's story is briefly told by Stephen as part of his recital of Jewish history before the Sanhedrin); in Hebrews 11:21–22 (where he is included among the Old Testament heroes of the faith); and in Revelation 7:8 (which speaks of twelve thousand servants of God from the tribe of Joseph in the latter days). Jesus does not refer to Joseph. Except for a few scattered references throughout the Old Testament, we are forced to interpret Joseph's story from the narrative itself.

A Type of Christ

One of the most striking features of the life of Joseph is the number of points at which he is a type of Jacob's greater son, the Lord Jesus Christ. Abraham is a type of God the Father who offered up his only begotten Son. Isaac typified the passive obedience of the Son himself. Joseph exemplifies the life and ministry of Christ at many points. Henry Morris is unhappy with attempts to define parallels between Joseph's life and the life and ministry of Christ, noting correctly that "the New Testament nowhere speaks of Joseph as a Type of Christ."[1] But Morris is almost the only commentator who is uneasy about these parallels.

Franz Delitzsch, one of the great old commentators, wrote that we may without hesitation look upon the history of Joseph as a "type of the pathway . . . of Christ, from lowliness to exaltation, from slavery to liberty, from suffering to glory."[2]

John Peter Lange, another commentator, lists these parallels: "the jealousy and hatred of Joseph's brethren; the fact of his being sold; the fulfillment of Joseph's prophetic dreams in the very efforts intended to prevent his exaltation; the turning of his brothers' wicked plot to the salvation of many, even of themselves, and of the house of Jacob; the spiritual sentence pronounced on the treachery of the brethren; the victory of pardoning love; Judah's suretyship for Benjamin; his emulating Joseph in a spirit of redeeming resignation;

Jacob's joyful reviving on hearing of the life and glory of his favorite son, whom he had believed to be dead."[3]

Blaise Pascal, author of the famous *Pensées*, wrote:

> *Christ Prefigured by Joseph:* Innocent, beloved of his father, sent by his father to see his brothers, is sold for twenty pieces of silver. Through this he becomes their lord, their savior, savior of strangers and savior of the world. None of this would have happened but for their plot to destroy him, the sale, and their rejection of him.
>
> In prison Joseph, innocent between two criminals. Jesus on the cross between two thieves. He prophesies the salvation of the one and the death of the other, when to all appearances they are alike. Christ saves the elect and damns the reprobate for the same crime. Joseph only prophesies, Jesus acts. Joseph asks the man who will be saved to remember him when he comes in glory. And the man Jesus saves asks to be remembered when he comes into his kingdom.[4]

In more recent days, M. R. DeHaan has used more than twenty pages to trace some of these parallels in *Portraits of Christ in Genesis*.[5] The prize for this approach is taken by Arthur W. Pink. He traces 101 parallels in the last sixty-eight pages of his thought-provoking *Gleanings in Genesis*.[6]

Model for Christians

Joseph is valuable not only as a portrait of Christ but also as a model for Christians wanting to lead a godly life. He is an encouragement, since his steadfast trust in God and persistence in the right eventually lead to his triumph and vindication.

Joseph's triumph was the triumph of faith. In Genesis, eight main characters illustrate the function of faith in the unfolding of the Christian life. Adam, the first who believed God and was justified by grace through that belief, illustrates the *nature* of faith; he believed God's unsupported word about the saving work of the Messiah (Gen. 3:15, 20). Abel, who offered God a better sacrifice than his brother Cain did (Heb. 11:4), illustrates the *basis* of faith; he believed that God would save his people through the death and shed blood of the Redeemer who was to come. Enoch, a preacher of righteousness, illustrates the *walk* of faith; he walked closely with God in an age when almost no one else did (Gen. 5:21–24). Noah, the builder of the ark in which eight people were saved from the great flood, illustrates the *perseverance* of faith; he kept on with the task of constructing the ark for 120 years, when most people would have been laughing at him and all eventually lost interest in his "folly" (Heb. 11:7).

Abraham, the greatest of all faith models, illustrates the *obedience* of faith; he obeyed God even to the point of sacrificing his son (Gen. 22:1–18). Isaac, turning from his own desires to accept the overpowering will of God, illustrates the *power* of faith; he trembled violently, but he was converted by what

God was doing in his life (Gen. 27:33). Jacob, who went his own way for so many years, illustrates the *discipline* of faith; God stayed with him during those years and eventually brought him to the point of personal surrender (Gen. 32:24–29). Joseph, who rose from slavery to a position of power, illustrates the *triumph* of faith; he never wavered until his early dreams were fulfilled and God had indeed placed him on an earthly throne (Gen. 41:41–43).

The greatest single characteristic of Joseph was his absolute faithfulness to God under all circumstances, and it is through this that God worked to exalt him so highly. Joseph never yielded to that saying: "When in Rome, do as the Romans do." In Egypt Joseph might have been tempted to do this. He was far from home with little chance of ever seeing his father or other family members again. He had been deprived of family pleasures. If he had been like many professing Christians today, he might have said, "I am far from home and nobody is ever going to see what I do. I will take my pleasure where I can, and I will do whatever it takes to advance my position." Joseph never said that. He knew that he was God's child and that his responsibility was to live for and be faithful to God, regardless of what should come into his life.

Joseph never complained.

Joseph never compromised.

As a result, Joseph never lost his power before God. Throughout his life God continued to reveal the future to him through dreams, and God continued to guide him no less when he was in Potiphar's prison than when he was beside the monarch's throne. God was always the chief and determining reality in Joseph's life.

What a triumphant perspective that gives to God's people! David also had it. In David's youth the Philistines were ravaging in the country, and their military hero, the giant Goliath, was defying God's armies. David asked why no Israelite had gone out to kill him, and the soldiers answered by telling him how mighty a champion Goliath was. Even Saul said, "You are not able to go out against this Philistine and fight him; you are only a boy, and he has been a fighting man from his youth" (1 Sam. 17:33).

This did not move David, because he had his eyes on God. He replied, "Your servant has been keeping his father's sheep. When a lion or a bear came and carried off a sheep from the flock, I went after it, struck it and rescued the sheep from its mouth. When it turned on me, I seized it by its hair, struck it and killed it. Your servant has killed both the lion and the bear; this uncircumcised Philistine will be like one of them, because he has defied the armies of the living God. The LORD who delivered me from the paw of the lion and the paw of the bear will deliver me from the hand of this Philistine" (vv. 34–37).

This is what Joseph's thinking was like. God was at the center of his thinking, and because his was a great God, he was able to triumph through faith in any circumstances. One commentator says,

From the example of this dreamer who became a doer we may learn how:
To overcome envy
To face adversity
To resist illicit sexual advances
To plan for the future
To forgive those who wrong us
To dispel doubts about forgiveness
To have faith in God's promises
To recognize the sovereignty of God, even in the wrongs done to us by others.[7]

Since Joseph is never reported as having done anything wrong and since he triumphed abundantly in these and many other adverse circumstances, he is an outstanding model of true godly living—second only to the example of Jesus Christ.

The Hand of God

There is another thing about the story of Joseph that we must highlight in this introduction. Joseph's story is a great example, perhaps the chief example in all the Bible, of the benevolent providence of God, the doctrine spelled out in Romans 8:28: "We know that in all things God works for the good of those who love him, who have been called according to his purpose."

The remarkable thing about God's providence in the story of Joseph's life is that God used such little things as links in the chain of circumstances by which he was to exalt Joseph to be the prime minister of Egypt and eventually save millions of people from starvation during the seven-year famine. These circumstances were as insignificant as the wonderful coat that led his brothers to hate him, or the dreams of Joseph that intensified their hatred. They were as wonderful as his being sold to Potiphar, the captain of the guard, or his being imprisoned with the cupbearer and baker of the king of Egypt, one of whom would be alive two years later to remember how Joseph had interpreted his dream while in the prison and suggest that Joseph might be the one to tell Pharaoh the meaning of his dream. When these things are happening, we seldom realize how important they are. But looking back, we can see that God was at work—often when we were least aware of his working.

Let me give you a personal example. Among my resources in preparing for this study was a tape entitled "Joseph in Prison," a sermon preached in 1951 by Donald Grey Barnhouse, a former pastor of Tenth Presbyterian Church. In this sermon, Barnhouse said he had recently taken part in a series of meetings in western Pennsylvania and told how they had come about. He told a story of remarkable circumstances.

It seems that some years before, a certain doctor had done medical work at the University of Pennsylvania and began to attend Tenth Presbyterian Church with his wife and young son. The doctor and his wife became Christians through hearing Barnhouse preach and then grew in faith during the years of the doctor's further training, internship, and residency. The family was caught up in World War II.

When the war was over, the family settled in McKeesport, Pennsylvania, where the doctor established a surgical practice. They joined a church; he taught a Bible class. Then he persuaded his minister to invite Barnhouse to his city for a series of meetings. The invitation broadened to include the members of the ministerial union of McKeesport, and eventually the meetings grew to fill the largest church in town. Barnhouse marveled at how a medical student had walked into a Philadelphia church one Sunday and as a result of that, ten or twelve years later, multitudes of people in McKeesport were hearing the gospel and hundreds were being blessed.

This is the way Barnhouse's story ended. But there is more, which he could not know, but which continued as the circumstances guided by God unfolded. That doctor and his wife had a son who attended Tenth Presbyterian Church with them while they lived in Philadelphia. During the meetings to which Barnhouse referred, this son, now thirteen years old, had an intensifying of his call to the ministry. Unknown to Barnhouse, these meetings had a formative influence on his understanding of what the ministry should be. He went to high school with this call in mind, then college and seminary, always making choices regarding his plan of study on the basis of this perceived call to Christian service. Seminary was followed by study abroad.

The young minister then went to Washington, D.C., and took a position with *Christianity Today* magazine. There were some problems with the magazine in those days, and some of the staff spent a Saturday afternoon talking them over with a former associate editor, Dr. Frank E. Gaebelein. In an aside comment during that conversation, Gaebelein asked the doctor's son what he wanted to do with his life. Did he want to continue doing editorial work for a magazine, or did he look forward to doing something else? The doctor's son replied that he had been training for the ministry and expected God to call him to a city church.

That was the end of the conversation. But, as it happened, Gaebelein was traveling to Philadelphia the next day to preach in Tenth Presbyterian Church, where the pulpit had recently become vacant. He was met at the train station by a member of the pulpit committee. "Have you found a minister for your church yet?" he asked. When he was told the committee had not, Gaebelein replied that he thought he had the man; he recommended the doctor's son. Thus, in 1968—seventeen years after the meetings in McKeesport at which Barnhouse's story broke off, and nearly thirty years after the doctor's conversion—this son was called to the pastorate of Barnhouse's own church in Philadelphia.

I am that son. That doctor was my father. This is my story. How small the circumstances. Yet how intricately God used them to accomplish his own perfect plan!

That is why we must never chafe against circumstances God brings to us. We call them "mere circumstances" and treat them lightly. But they are not "mere circumstances." They are God's weaving of the tapestry of our lives. The important thing for every believer is to be living in the light of God's presence, knowing that his or her life is being guided by God's hand. You may look at your life and see dark threads and wonder how God can possibly use those threads to produce a thing of beauty. But you should look to the life of Joseph and remember that God uses even the wrath of men to praise him.

122

Joseph's Early Years

Genesis 37:3-4

Now Israel loved Joseph more than any of his other sons, because he had been born to him in his old age; and he made a richly ornamented robe for him. When his brothers saw that their father loved him more than any of them, they hated him and could not speak a kind word to him.

The story of Joseph, found in Genesis 37–50, begins with the statement: "This is the account of Jacob," Joseph's father (Gen. 37:2). The first part of that sentence—"This is the account of . . ."—should be familiar to anyone who has been studying the Book of Genesis carefully, for it is the eleventh time a phrase like this has occurred. It is also the last time it will occur. These phrases mark significant divisions in Genesis, so this statement in Genesis 37:2 introduces the beginning of the last section of this volume.[1]

It is a characteristic of these phrases that in the course of the unfolding of Genesis a mere historical sequence of names gives way to parallel presentations. That is, the progression from Adam to Noah to Noah's three sons—Shem, Ham, and Japheth—gives way to contrast between "Shem, Ham and Japheth" in general, on the one hand (10:1), and "Shem," the son through whom the promised line was extended, on the other (11:10). Similarly, we have parallel accounts of the descendants of Abraham's sons, Ishmael (25:12) and Isaac (25:19). At this point in Genesis there is an obvious contrast between the descendants of Esau, enumerated in Genesis 36, and the story of Joseph, the son of Jacob, which concludes the book.

What a contrast it is! On the one hand, there are the numerous sons, families, chiefs, and kings who came from Esau—all the hosts and powers of the Idumean nation. Genesis 36 lists five sons of Esau, twenty-seven chiefs, and eight kings. On the other hand, the "account of Jacob" begins: "This is the account of Jacob. Joseph, a young man of seventeen. . . ."

If we were to choose as the world chooses, which of us would not stand with the line of kings and the rising power of the Edomites? Yet this is not where the hope of the human race lay. Let the world have its great chiefs and mighty kings. The choice of God was with the family of Jacob, and the hope of salvation of that family was with seventeen-year-old Joseph. The chiefs of Edom were numerous and wealthy. Joseph was godly. The kings of Edom were powerful. Joseph had his eyes on the Lord.

It is along the line of Jacob's seed and through the instrumentality of God's work in Joseph that the entire stream of sacred history is now to flow. It is this line alone that God will bless. Consequently, although other branches of the human family will occasionally come into the story for the effect they will have on the children of Israel, we find the phrase "this is the account of . . ." only once more (Num. 3:1) before it is used to introduce us to the Messiah and the founder of that last, new branch of the family of God's redeemed children: "a record [account] of the genealogy of Jesus Christ the son of David, the son of Abraham" (Matt. 1:1).

Joseph's Childhood

Joseph, the one who was to be used so wonderfully in preserving his family and others during the time of great famine, is introduced to us as "a young man of seventeen," as we have seen. Though his story begins at this point, we already know something about the formative events of his childhood.

Joseph was the first son of Jacob's favorite wife, Rachel, for whom Jacob had been willing to work fourteen years. Jacob had one other wife and two concubines—his wives' servants—but he had not sought them. Jacob loved Rachel. Apparently he had loved her from the moment he had first laid eyes on her at the well of Haran after having crossed the desert from Canaan on his flight from Esau. He did not consider it arduous work to labor first for seven years and then (after he had been tricked by being wedded to Leah) for another seven years to have Rachel. The story says that these "seemed like only a few days to him because of his love for her" (Gen. 29:20). Joseph was no doubt particularly cherished as a result of having been born to the one Jacob loved so intensely.

When Joseph was still a young child—the youngest in a family of what was now eleven children—Jacob and his clan returned to Canaan. This was no peaceful journey. The family's move was in haste, and Joseph probably would have remembered the quick decisions and then the rapid flight on the back of a racing camel, resting behind or in the arms of his mother. He would have remembered the confrontation with his domineering grandfather, Laban, and the relief that would have spread over his people when Laban's men finally put their arms down and went back to Haran.

Then there would have been the renewed anxiety when news came that Esau, his father's brother, was coming toward them with four hundred soldiers. How could Joseph forget the evening of preparations as the company was at first divided into camps and then was spread out in many bands going across the desert to meet Esau. He would have remembered how afraid he was as everyone was sent ahead—perhaps to their deaths—and he was left alone with his mother by the river Jabbok. Only his father remained behind to pray and, unbeknown to Joseph, wrestle with God's angel.

On the next day Jacob limped across the river to lead his family to Esau, and Joseph must have been impressed with his father's new bearing. "What's wrong with you, Father?" Joseph must have asked. Jacob would have told him how God sent his angel to wrestle him to submission. What an impression these things must have made on that young mind! How real God must have seemed to Joseph during those traumatic days!

But his was not a godly family. At least, his brothers were not godly. Joseph would have seen their rough ways and looked on in amazement as the story of their murder of the Shechemites unfolded. Shechem, the son of Hamor, who ruled the land in which they were living, had violated Joseph's sister Dinah; and the brothers, particularly Simeon and Levi, had used a ruse to destroy that entire people. Jacob said that their murderous actions had made the family "a stench" to the peoples of the land (Gen. 34:30).

Immediately after this, Jacob took the family to Bethel, where God had first appeared to him when he ran away from home because of Esau's anger. Jacob had told his family: "Get rid of the foreign gods you have with you, and purify yourselves and change your clothes. Then come, let us go up to Bethel, where I will build an altar to God, who answered me in the day of my distress and who has been with me wherever I have gone" (Gen. 35:2–3).

Joseph was about thirteen years old at the time, and he must have been profoundly impressed as Jacob showed him the spot where the great ladder had come down from heaven and touched the earth and led the family as they entered into a new covenant with the covenant-keeping God. One commentator writes, "It may be that this was the turning point of his life. Such events make deep impressions on young hearts. As they stood together on that hallowed spot, and heard again the oft-told story, and clasped each other's hands in solemn covenant, the other sons of Jacob may have been unmoved spectators; but there was a deep response in the susceptible heart of the lad, who may have felt, 'This God shall be my God for ever and ever; He shall be my Guide, even unto death.'"[2]

Shortly after this, three deaths shook the family. First, Deborah, Rebekah's aged nurse, died and was buried under a great oak at Bethel. She had been a link to the past when Joseph's grandmother, Rebekah, whom he had never seen, first came across the desert to be Isaac's bride. Second, his own mother died. Rachel was expecting another child, but the birth was difficult and Rachel died shortly after giving birth to Benjamin, whom she wanted to call Ben-Oni ("son of my trouble"). Joseph gained a brother, whom he came to love very much, but he lost the most important person in his life. A short while later, the third death occurred. Isaac, Joseph's grandfather, died and was buried in the cave of Machpelah near Mamre, where Abraham, Sarah, and Rebekah had been buried before him. This was the tomb of the patriarchs. It must have made a profound impression on Joseph, for he returned to it twenty-seven years later to bury his own father, Jacob (Gen. 49:29–50:14).

These events made Joseph what he was. It is impossible to recount them without emphasizing the importance of similar things on the young of all ages. We can never exaggerate the importance of childhood events. So whenever it is within our power we must see that these events are inducements to godliness or, when it is not within our power to change them, that we react to them as believers in the goodness and sovereignty of God and thus demonstrate the transforming reality of God in human life. Character is formed at a young age. Who knows but that God is forming the character of tomorrow's Christian leaders in your home, church, Bible school, or school classes?

There is also this application. You may yourself be a youth, as Joseph was. Like Joseph, you may have lost a mother at a young age or you may be surrounded by godless brothers or sisters. But you have heard the gospel and have known the reality of God's living presence in your life. If so, cling to him. Stand by God. Determine to do nothing that will dishonor God or hinder you in a life of faithful and moral service for him. If you do, you will find that God will stand by you and will use you in even greater ways than you can imagine at this stage of your pilgrimage.

Birth of Bitterness

The story of Joseph's being hated and sold into slavery by his brothers begins with the story of his dreams in Genesis 37:5. But even before this there was trouble. The problem is that Joseph was his father's favorite son. This has been interpreted by some commentators as improper favoritism on Jacob's part,[3] but this was not the real problem.

Earlier, in Genesis 35:22, we are told that Reuben, Jacob's firstborn, "slept with his father's concubine Bilhah" and that "Israel heard of it." This was an offense for which Reuben lost not only his father's favor but also his birthrights as the firstborn son. Since Reuben had forfeited his rights, Jacob exercised his sovereign choice and appointed Joseph his heir. This is the true meaning of what we have long called Joseph's "coat of many colors" (KJV).

"Coat of many colors" is an unfortunate mistranslation. The Hebrew words that are so translated are generally thought to be uncertain, since the key word *kethoneth* (a "tunic") is followed by the word *passim* (which should mean "ankles" or "wrists"). This has been construed as meaning "many colored" or "richly ornamented." But it is more likely that it means exactly what it says, namely, that Joseph's coat extended to his ankles and wrists. Most tunics were sleeveless and stopped at the knees; they were worn by working men. A long-sleeved, tailored garment was worn by one who did not have to work. So when Joseph appeared in this coat, his brothers recognized it as a sign of his father's choice of Joseph to be a manager, one preeminent over them.

This is also the explanation of the notation that Joseph brought Jacob "a bad report" about the brothers (v. 2). This has been construed as tattling, which we dislike. But Joseph was not so much a talebearer as a truth-teller. It was his responsibility to report to his aging father what was actually going on.

There is one other detail that adds to this picture. It was noted in the previous chapter that there is very little reference to Joseph in the New Testament—only four verses in all. But one of these tells us a fact that we would not know merely from reading Genesis, and it is of interest here. In John 4:5, in the middle of the account of Jesus' meeting with the woman of Samaria at Jacob's well near Sychar, we are told that the well was "near the plot of ground Jacob had given to his son Joseph." The only ground we know that Jacob ever owned was near this place (see Gen. 33:19). So it would seem Jacob had also indicated that Joseph was to be his heir by formally giving him the only plot of ground he owned in Canaan. It was because of this sovereign and *justified* "favoritism" that Joseph's brothers "hated him and could not speak a kind word to him" (Gen. 37:4).

This really means that the brothers hated Joseph because he was not like them. They stood for treachery, murder, and incest. He stood for truth. So as long as he was present, his virtue exposed their vice. In the end they determined to rid themselves of this.

Martin Luther remarked on this tendency: "The same perversity is also today running through all ranks in the church, state and home. For all men are grumbling against those who remind them of what is right, and they are indignant against those who reprove faults and sins, even enormous public sins. One must not oppose anyone but allow everyone to do what he likes! One man makes his rank a pretext for his impudence, another his wealth, another his country or parents, and for these reasons one is supposed to connive at their sins and disgraceful conduct. 'I occupy a magistracy,' they say, 'therefore my rank is to be treated with consideration. I am a citizen of Wittenberg or Nuernberg, and therefore I rightly claim more for myself than a guest or a stranger.' On the other hand, those who are modest and remain within the limits of duty and the laws are regarded with hatred by all. The very same thing happened to excellent Joseph in the household of Jacob."[4]

Hated without a Cause

We can say the same of Jesus, of whom Joseph is a type. Jesus too was loved by his Father. He too stood for truth. He was the heir of the vast domains of his Father. But in spite of the beauty, joy, love, peace, and integrity that were always transparent in his speech and actions, he was hated by his own brothers according to the flesh and was eventually given over to death at their hands.

I think of Jesus' entry into Jerusalem on what we call Palm Sunday. He did not come on a warhorse to impose his will on a beaten and captive people, as many conquerors have entered Jerusalem both before his time and since. He came, as Zechariah prophetically described it:

> Rejoice greatly, O Daughter of Zion!
> Shout, Daughter of Jerusalem!
> See, your king comes to you,
>   *righteous* and having salvation,
>   *gentle* and riding on a donkey,
>   on a colt, the foal of a donkey.
>
> Zechariah 9:9, my emphasis

Righteous! Gentle! Yes, and all other good things besides! Yet within the week the crowds were provoked by the leaders of the nation to cry out, "Crucify him! Crucify him!" Why did they hate the Son of God? It was because he was not like them. He was hated without a cause in him. The cause was in the people, in their hearts. It was directed against anyone who called their wickedness into question.

F. B. Meyer commented on this:

Do you know by sad experience what Joseph felt beneath those Syrian skies? Do the archers shoot at you? Are you lonesome and depressed and ready to give up? Take heart! See the trampled grass and the snapped twigs; others have gone this way before you. Christ your Lord suffered the same treatment from his own. Go on doing right, in nothing terrified by your adversaries. Be pitiful and gentle, forgiving and forbearing. Be specially careful not to take your case into your own hands, demanding redress in imperious and vindictive tones. If you are servants, forbear to answer back. Give your backs to the smiters and your cheeks to them that pluck off the hair. Avenge not yourselves, but rather give place unto wrath. Put down your feet into the footprints of your Savior, who left an example that we should follow him. He did no sin, neither was guile found in his mouth; and yet, when he was unjustly reviled, he reviled not again; when he suffered beneath undeserved contumely and reproach, he did not even remind the perpetrators of the righteous judgment of God, but was dumb as a lamb, and threatened not, and committed himself to him that judgeth righteously."[5]

We know what happened. Joseph was kept through the days of human hatred and was at last exalted to the second highest position in Egypt. Jesus was betrayed, tried, and crucified; but he was raised from the dead and today sits upon the throne of the universe. Are you suffering? If you suffer with him, you will also reign with him. Are you hated? The Lord said, "Blessed are those who are persecuted because of righteousness, for theirs is the kingdom of heaven" (Matt. 5:10).

123

Joseph and His Brothers

Genesis 37:5–24

Joseph had a dream, and when he told it to his brothers, they hated him all the more. He said to them, "Listen to this dream I had: We were binding sheaves of grain out in the field when suddenly my sheaf rose and stood upright, while your sheaves gathered around mine and bowed down to it."

His brothers said to him, "Do you intend to reign over us? Will you actually rule us?" And they hated him all the more because of his dream and what he had said.

Then he had another dream, and he told it to his brothers. "Listen," he said, "I had another dream, and this time the sun and moon and eleven stars were bowing down to me."

When he told his father as well as his brothers, his father rebuked him and said, "What is this dream you had? Will your mother and I and your brothers actually come and bow down to the ground before you?" His brothers were jealous of him, but his father kept the matter in mind.

Now his brothers had gone to graze their father's flocks near Shechem, and Israel said to Joseph, "As you know, your brothers are grazing the flocks near Shechem. Come, I am going to send you to them."

"Very well," he replied.

So he said to him, "Go and see if all is well with your brothers and with the flocks, and bring word back to me." Then he sent him off from the Valley of Hebron.

When Joseph arrived at Shechem, a man found him wandering around in the fields and asked him, "What are you looking for?"

He replied, "I'm looking for my brothers. Can you tell me where they are grazing their flocks?"

"They have moved on from here," the man answered. "I heard them say, 'Let's go to Dothan.'"

So Joseph went after his brothers and found them near Dothan. But they saw him in the distance, and before he reached them, they plotted to kill him.

"Here comes that dreamer!" they said to each other. "Come now, let's kill him and throw him into one of these cisterns and say that a ferocious animal devoured him. Then we'll see what comes of his dreams."

When Reuben heard this, he tried to rescue him from their hands. "Let's not take his life," he said. "Don't shed any blood. Throw him into this cistern here in the desert, but don't lay a hand on him." Reuben said this to rescue him from them and take him back to his father.

So when Joseph came to his brothers, they stripped him of his robe—the richly orna-mented robe he was wearing—and they took him and threw him into the cistern. Now the cistern was empty; there was no water in it.

T hose who lived through the Nazi era (or even those who only read of it) are aware of human cruelty. But even without the Nazi era there is enough reminder of what William Wordsworth called "man's inhumanity to man" in our newspapers and TV news to cure anyone a belief in man's essential goodness. We know of sufficient per-versions, mutilations, atrocities, and multiple murders to assure us that our age is as barbaric as any in history.

In spite of this sad exposure, we are still moved by the story of the cruelty of Jacob's resentful sons to their brother Joseph. One writer says, "We read of very cruel actions performed by the degenerate sons of Adam; but it is not easy to find a parallel in history to the cruel intentions, and to the cruel conduct of Joseph's brethren. Cain was of that wicked one, and slew his brother, and has left a name of infamy to all the generations of mankind. But where shall we find nine men conspiring at once to kill a brother? a brother whose amiable qualities deserved their warmest love? a brother who tenderly loved them, and was in the very act of showing his love to them at the time when their fury broke loose upon him? Joseph put himself to much trouble to find out his brethren, that he might inform himself and his father of their welfare; but they took advantage of his love to wreak their hatred upon him, as if they had been devils in flesh and blood, rather than patriarchs in the church."[1]

This statement is not too harsh. Indeed, it seems impossible to be too harsh in our judgments on these men. The only thing that restrains our judgment is the realization that others acted (and we could have acted) in a similar fashion toward the Lord Jesus Christ when he came from heaven to seek us.

Root of Bitterness

In Hebrews the author of that deep study warns us about allowing a "bitter root" to grow up in our lives "to cause trouble and defile many" (Heb. 12:15). It is a good warning, for it is precisely this that turned the sons of Jacob into would-be fratricides. At the beginning they probably did not have their hearts set on Joseph's murder. But they envied him, and envy eventually gave way to hatred that gave way to a plot against his life.

The text says, "His brothers were jealous of him" (Gen. 37:11), a judgment Stephen echoed in his great speech before the Sanhedrin (Acts 7:9). Envy (or jealousy) means "ill will occasioned by another's good fortune." It involves superiority in the one envied and resentment by the person who envies. It is terribly destructive. The Bible says, "Envy rots the bones" (Prov. 14:30). James wrote, "Where you have envy and selfish ambition, there you find disorder and every evil practice" (James 3:16).

The chief reason is that envy is an angry resistance to God's decrees. Consequently it is ultimately resentment of God and hatred of him. This is the essential issue in the matter of Joseph's dreams. The brothers had envied him before this, as the narrative says. They envied him for his good qualities, which revealed their evil ones, and because of his father's choice of Joseph to assume the rights of the firstborn. But this was not merely resentment of these circumstances. Ultimately God is responsible for circumstances; so the brothers' envy was essentially a resentment of what God had done and was doing, as the dreams show.

Joseph's first dream was about grain. He dreamed that he and his brothers had been working in the fields binding sheaves of grain when suddenly his sheaf rose and theirs gathered around his and bowed down. It did not take a seer to interpret this. (The dream was not as subtle as the dream Pharaoh was to have later on.) This dream meant that at some future time the brothers, all but one of whom were older than Joseph, would bow down to Joseph. Naturally they resented it.

The second dream was like the first. Joseph saw the sun, moon, and eleven stars bowing down to him. Obviously this involved his parents as well as his brothers, which his father recognized. Jacob said, "What is this dream you had? Will your mother and I and your brothers actually come and bow down to the ground before you?" (v. 10).

We may argue here that Joseph was not very wise to tell such dreams. He may have been naive. But whether he was unwise and naive or whether—which is quite likely—he sensed a God-given responsibility to make a divine revelation such as this known, the point is that the brothers hated the dreams as much as they hated Joseph for relating them. The text says,

"They hated him all the more because of his dream and what he had said" (v. 8). That is, they hated his testimony, and they hated the dreams themselves.

This suggests that what they really hated were God's decrees regarding Joseph's and their lives and therefore that they hated God for them. Otherwise why get upset about a dream? If a child has a dream that reveals how the child hopes to be important some day, regardless of how foolish the dream is, the proper course is to ignore the specifics while encouraging the child to apply himself or herself and thus live up to the goal of the dream if possible. One does not hate a child for dreams, however self-centered or bizarre. Since the brothers did hate Joseph, the implication is that they were actually taking the dreams seriously, as perhaps actually revealing what God might do, and they were hating God for it. Later on, they saw Joseph coming toward them and said, "Come now, let's kill him and throw him into one of these cisterns and say that a ferocious animal devoured him. Then we'll see what comes of his dreams" (v. 20). This put them against God and thus revealed their folly as well as their malice toward their younger brother.

Beware of envy. Donald Grey Barnhouse wrote, "How unfortunate that many are not willing to take the place which God has assigned them in this world! When a man is covetous and envious, he is saying, 'God, I am not satisfied; you didn't give me what I want!' Such a man would dethrone God, and re-deal the events and possessions of life so that little *he* would be exalted."[2]

Shoot of Bitterness

Another step in the brothers' unjustified antagonism to Joseph is hatred, which we have already mentioned, since it grows out of envy. Yet we must mention it separately, because it is envy's bitter shoot. Indeed, it is so closely connected with envy that we should probably say that envy is itself a form of hatred and that hatred in the fullest sense is inevitable once jealousy has taken root in the heart.

The narrative tells us three times that Joseph's brothers hated him: in verse 4: "When his brothers saw that their father loved him more than any of them, they *hated* him and could not speak a kind word to him"; in verse 5: "Joseph had a dream, and when he told it to his brothers, they *hated* him all the more"; in verse 8: "His brothers said to him, 'Do you intend to reign over us? Will you actually rule us?' And they *hated* him all the more because of his dream and what he had said" (my emphasis).

If the dreams were from God, as the brothers may have suspected and perhaps feared, they indicated that God had elected Joseph to certain earthly favors. Joseph was not like them. He was godly while they were godless; they hated him for that. But here, in addition, we find them hating him because God had chosen him for a position of special future prominence.

This reminds us of what the Lord Jesus Christ said to his disciples in John 15. He had been reminding them of his election of them, saying that they had not chosen to be his disciples but rather that he had chosen them. Then he continued, "If the world hates you, keep in mind that it hated me first. If you belonged to the world, it would love you as its own. As it is, you do not belong to the world, but I have chosen you out of the world. That is why the world hates you" (John 15:18–19). These verses contain the same two principles: hatred for being different and hatred for being chosen. They tell us that the situation is the same today as it was in Joseph's generation.

If by the grace of God you are different from the ungodly people around you—and "by grace" is the only way you ever can or will be different—then the world will hate you as the brothers hated Joseph. If you show by your conduct that you have been chosen out of your past wicked state and have been directed to obey and love God, then the world will also hate you for your election to godliness. What you must take care of is seeing that the root of bitterness—envy—does not produce the shoot of bitterness—hatred—in your own life. On the contrary, you must live as Joseph lived and trust God to care for you even in life's injustices and deprivations.

Fruit of Bitterness

This leads to a third point. As the story shows a root of bitterness leading to a shoot of bitterness, so also does it show the fruit of bitterness, which in this case is the tangible act of reaching out to kill a brother. In Galatians 5:19–23 we read of the "fruit of the Spirit" contrasted with the "acts of the sinful nature." The fruit of the Spirit is "love, joy, peace, patience, kindness, goodness, faithfulness, gentleness and self-control." The acts of the sinful nature are "sexual immorality, impurity and debauchery; idolatry and witchcraft; hatred, discord, jealousy, fits of rage, selfish ambition, dissensions, factions and envy; drunkenness, orgies, and the like." Paul does not mention murder in this second list, but he mentions two items we have already spoken of, namely, envy and hatred. He could have listed murder also.

Attempted murder was the fruit of bitterness in the lives of these brothers. Jacob had sent Joseph to find his other sons and bring him word of them, and Joseph had searched for them—from Hebron to Shechem to Dothan. It was a journey of four or five days. So Joseph clearly cared for his brothers, just as his father did.

When the brothers saw him coming, they said, "Here comes that dreamer! Come now, let's kill him and throw him into one of these cisterns and say that a ferocious animal devoured him. Then we'll see what comes of his dreams."

Then Reuben intervened, suggesting that they could avoid the shedding of blood by *merely* throwing him into a cistern. Reuben hoped to be able to come back and rescue Joseph and restore him to his father, perhaps seeking to make up for the dishonor he had caused his father by sleeping with the concubine Bilhah (Gen. 35:22). Reuben's plan misfired. Joseph was sold to Midianite traders as a slave.

It would be wonderful if we could say that the only place an action like that ever happened was in the Old Testament or among the deniers of Christ. But unfortunately, envy and hatred leading to vicious actions have also been found within the church of Christ. We find an example in Philippians, where the apostle Paul, writing from prison in Rome, alludes to the strife present in the church of his day: "It is true that some preach Christ out of envy and rivalry, but others out of goodwill. The latter do so in love, knowing that I am put here for the defense of the gospel. The former preach Christ out of selfish ambition, not sincerely, supposing that they can stir up trouble for me while I am in chains" (Phil. 1:15–17). Paul is not complaining. He is actually rejoicing. But his words reveal that there were Christians in Rome who preached the gospel in a way designed to cause trouble for Paul the prisoner.

Paul was the greatest intellectual of the early Christian church. He was a great ambassador for the gospel. He above all people should have been honored and protected by all possible means. But instead, and perhaps for these same reasons, Paul was resented, and efforts were expended to make his situation in Rome more difficult.

I believe that Paul very likely lost his life as the result of the actions of these trouble-making Christians. There is little information from the early church era about the circumstances of Paul's death, but such information as exists suggests that envy led some Christians to denounce Paul and, as a result of their denunciation, Paul and perhaps others were executed under Nero.[3]

Envy and strife caused trouble in those days. So do they cause trouble today. Not necessarily in death, but in the declining impact of the gospel of Christ upon our society and world. Never in the history of the world have the opportunities to proclaim the gospel been greater. Yet never has the believing church been more irrelevant or more divided. We have money. We have talent. There are opportunities for spreading the gospel through all modern means of mass communication. Yet the evangelical churches seem unable to take full advantage of them.

The Mind of Christ

We need what Joseph exhibited in his day and what Paul speaks of in Philippians 2: the mind of Christ. Paul writes:

Do nothing out of selfish ambition or vain conceit, but in humility consider others better than yourselves. Each of you should look not only to your own interests, but also to the interests of others. Your attitude should be the same as that of Jesus Christ:

> Who, being in very nature God,
> > did not consider equality with God
> > > something to be grasped,
> but made himself nothing,

> taking the very nature of a servant,
>   being made in human likeness.
> And being found in appearance as a man,
>   he humbled himself
>   and became obedient to death—
>   even death on a cross!

Philippians 2:3–8

We live in a sinful world. Envy is all too real. Envy leads to hatred and hatred to overt evil acts, even against our brothers and sisters in the faith. It is a root of bitterness, which, when it has flowered, defiles many. Christ is the cure for envy. His mind is in his people, and it will produce the Spirit's fruit rather than the acts of sinful natures.

124

Who Grieves for Joseph?

Genesis 37:25–35

As they sat down to eat their meal, they looked up and saw a caravan of Ishmaelites coming from Gilead. Their camels were loaded with spices, balm and myrrh, and they were on their way to take them down to Egypt.

Judah said to his brothers, "What will we gain if we kill our brother and cover up his blood? Come, let's sell him to the Ishmaelites and not lay our hands on him; after all, he is our brother, our own flesh and blood." His brothers agreed.

So when the Midianite merchants came by, his brothers pulled Joseph up out of the cistern and sold him for twenty shekels of silver to the Ishmaelites, who took him to Egypt.

When Reuben returned to the cistern and saw that Joseph was not there, he tore his clothes. He went back to his brothers and said, "The boy isn't there! Where can I turn now?"

Then they got Joseph's robe, slaughtered a goat and dipped the robe in the blood. They took the ornamented robe back to their father and said, "We found this. Examine it to see whether it is your son's robe."

He recognized it and said, "It is my son's robe! Some ferocious animal has devoured him. Joseph has surely been torn to pieces."

*Then Jacob tore his clothes, put on sackcloth and mourned for his son many days.
All his sons and daughters came to comfort him, but he refused to be comforted. "No,"
he said, "in mourning will I go down to the grave to my son." So his father wept for him.*

There is a white space in my Bible
between verses 24 and 25 of Genesis 37. To understand this chapter, we must
put the despairing, begging cries of Joseph in that space. Verse 24 says that
the brothers "took [Joseph] and threw him into the cistern." The next verse
continues, "As they sat down to eat their meal. . . ." Nothing is said in Genesis
37 of any complaint by Joseph. But in Genesis 42:21, in the midst of a scene
that took place twenty-two years later, the brothers remembered this earlier
moment and confessed, "Surely we are being punished because of our
brother. We saw how distressed he was when he pleaded with us for his life,
but we would not listen; that's why this distress has come upon us." It is a
statement that Joseph was begging for his life from the cistern and that the
brothers would not listen to him.

In fact, it was worse than that. These hard-hearted scoundrels actually sat
down to eat, enjoying their meal while their younger brother cried out to
them.

I find this profoundly moving and rich in comfort for those who, like
Joseph, may have suffered much injustice and indifference. Have you experienced human cruelty? Does no one seem to care that you are suffering?
Are others indifferent to the damage being done to you? Do they even tram-
ple on the bruises? If so, you can identify with Joseph as he cried out from
the pit to his brothers. I hope that you will also be able to identify with him
as he learned, through this and other times of suffering, to commit his ways
to God, who hears the cries of his afflicted people and always moves to rescue
and restore them in due time.

"No One Cares"

The worst thing about being in trouble, as Joseph was, is to find that no
one cares, which is usually the case in this sinful world. When you are at the
top of the pyramid and everything is going well, most people *do* care. That
is why the rich are flattered and the famous are sought after. But lose your
money—lose your position or job or reputation or good appearance—and
immediately people begin to pass by on the other side of the avenue. They
refuse your invitations. They ignore your phone calls. No one wants to know
what you are suffering.

The world is notorious for its indifference. Several years ago newspapers
carried the story of a young woman who was murdered on the streets of New
York City while at least thirty people in nearby apartment houses heard her

cries, looked out at the tragedy unfolding beneath them—and did nothing. Shortly after that, a story came from the Midwest about a young woman who gave birth to a baby on the sidewalk of a poor area of the city while a dozen people watched from inside a cozy corner tavern—and did not even bring her in. As I say, the world is notorious for its indifference. But what shall we say of the indifference of Christians? What about Christian husbands who are insensitive to the frustration and bruised feelings of their wives? Or parents who cannot hear the hurt cries of their children? Or neighbors who cannot see the despairing glances of those who are perhaps even looking to them for help?

I write this chapter as an encouragement to those who are suffering primarily from indifference. But it is a message that cuts two ways. It is a message for those suffering, but it is also a message for those who are insensitive to what others are enduring, particularly if they are contributing to the problem—as they often are.

Let me ask you, what has been the saddest moment of your life? I would guess that it is not a moment in which you yourself suffered some injustice, though you may have suffered many of them; but rather a moment when you heard the cry of some despairing soul and were indifferent to him or her. And it weighs on you!

I think of the effect of this sin on the brothers. F. B. Meyer writes, "Year passed after year; but the years could not obliterate from their memories that look, those cries, that scene in the green glen of Dothan, surrounded by the tall cliffs, over-arched by the blue sky, whose expanse was lit up by a meridian sun. They tried to lock up the skeleton in their most secret cupboard, but it contrived to come forth to confront them even in their guarded hours. Sometimes they thought they saw that agonized young face in their dreams, and heard that piteous voice wailing in the night wind. The old father, who mourned for his son as dead, was happier than were they, who knew him to be alive. One crime may thus darken a whole life. There are some who teach that God is too merciful to punish men; yet he has so made the world that sin is its own Nemesis—sin carries with it the seed of its own punishment. And the men who carry with them the sense of unforgiven sin will be the first to believe in a vulture forever tearing out the vitals, a worm that never dies, fire that is never quenched."[1]

Another writer concludes, "A physicist could compute the exact time required for his [Joseph's] cries to go twenty-five yards to the eardrums of the brothers. But it took twenty-two years for that cry to go from their eardrums to their hearts. . . . Let me plead with you not to eat while some Joseph is crying because you are unyielding and hard. Before it is too late, listen, and make things right."[2]

Insult Added to Injury

We think that nothing could be worse than Joseph's brothers coldly eating their midday meal while Joseph cried out to them for life. But a careful reading suggests that there may have been something even crueler than this. Although the brothers were indifferent to Joseph's plight, I suggest they were not silent. I believe that they actually mocked him, thus adding insult to the injury they were inflicting.

I know that the text does not say this specifically, just as it does not record Joseph's cries from the pit. But when the brothers had seen Joseph coming toward them on his errand from Haran, they said to each other, "Here comes that dreamer! . . . Let's kill him and throw him into one of these cisterns and say that a ferocious animal devoured him. Then we'll see what comes of his dreams" (v. 20). This tells us what was in their hearts and on their lips as Joseph came to them. How could they not have said something like this as they fell upon the lad, stripped him of his ornamented tunic, and cast him into the cistern? Joseph would have protested, "What are you doing? Why are you doing this?"

They must have answered, "So you think you're better than we are, do you? You think you're going to rule over us, that we're going to bow down to you? We'll see who'll bow down to whom!"

"Try dreaming in the pit, little brother!"

"What do your dreams tell you now, pet?"

"If you think you're so holy, why don't you try praying to God now and see if he'll come and get you out of there?"

I also observe the hypocrisy of the brothers in thinking of themselves as fairly decent fellows. I notice the comments of Judah in this respect. Judah was probably the most disreputable character of this bad lot. (The next chapter tells a distasteful story about him.) He was undoubtedly among those who hatched the plot to throw Joseph into the pit to die. But when he saw the Midianite merchants coming and realized that he could make money by selling Joseph to them as a slave, he announced his change of plan by the most disgusting speech in the whole story: "What will we gain if we kill our brother and cover up his blood? Come, let's sell him to the Ishmaelites and not lay our hands on him; *after all, he is our brother,* our own flesh and blood" (vv. 26–27, my emphasis). What hypocrisy! What evil covered over by a sanctimonious speech! Unfortunately, this is the way people speak today even when they are committing the most despicable atrocities.

If you have been the victim of such insults, you are aware of how Joseph felt. You can identify with him. What you must also know is that, despite appearances, God has not abandoned you. He knows what is happening and will deliver you in due time.

Too Little Too Late

There is one other element that was unknown to Joseph but might have increased his anguish if he had known of it: Reuben was plotting to save him. Knowledge of Reuben's plans might have increased his anguish, not because a plan to help would have been unwelcome in itself, but because it was so evidently ineffective. It was a classic case of too little being done too late.

Reuben had indulged his sensual appetites by sleeping with his father's concubine Bilhah, for which he presumably lost his birthright. But indulgence in one sin does not necessarily mean indulgence in another and, as Calvin says, we are taught by this that "the characters of men are not to be estimated by a single act, however atrocious, so as to cause us to despair of their salvation."[3] Reuben apparently cared for Joseph and thus plotted from the beginning to save him. First, he counseled against his murder: "Let's not take his life. . . . Don't shed any blood" (vv. 21–22). Next, he planned to go away and come back secretly to rescue Joseph from the pit. The story says that he wanted to take him back to his father, perhaps to atone in part for his wrong against Jacob. But while Reuben was gone, the Midianite merchants came along and Joseph was sold to them. When Reuben returned, all he could do was bewail the situation: "The boy isn't there! Where can I turn now?" (v. 30).

As I say, Joseph did not know what Reuben was planning. But if he had, it might have added to his grief. Could he not have protested, "Reuben, you mean well, but what you have planned is not good enough. You want to rescue me in secret, as it were. But what I need is an up-front ally. I need someone to stand beside me and fight off the brothers. You want to help, but because you are not forthright about it, you have failed and are implicated in this great injustice."

Have you known a situation like that? Have you taken a stand in some moral situation, suffered for doing right, and then had someone come to you afterward and say, "You were right in what you did. I admire you for it." But they did not stand with you when you needed it, when it might have made a difference.

God Grieves for Joseph

I have spent enough time examining the brothers' treatment of Joseph, showing parallels to those who are ill-treated today. I want to spend the remainder of this study showing the comfort a knowledge of God and his ways gives in such situations. I entitled this chapter "Who Grieves for Joseph?" I now answer, Certainly not the brothers! And certainly not the world to which he was thrown by their callous actions; the Midianites did not care for Joseph. Even Reuben's grief was less impressive than it should have been, since he was at least partially to blame in the tragedy. The only person who did grieve for Joseph was his aged father Jacob, who mourned with a grief that could not be comforted: "Then Jacob tore his clothes, put on sackcloth and mourned for his son many days. All his sons and daughters came to comfort him, but he refused to be comforted. 'No,' he said, 'in mourning will I go down to the grave to my son.' So his father wept for him" (vv. 34–35).

I want you to see that you have such a father, your Father in heaven, and that he grieves for you in your trouble even more than Jacob grieved for his beloved son Joseph. What can we say about this heavenly Father?

First, we can say that *God does indeed care for us,* even when others do not. In this story the care and grief of Jacob are contrasted with the cruelty and indifference of the brothers. In a similar way, the care of God is contrasted with the indifference of the world in our situations. The Greeks were unwilling to believe this of God, for in their philosophical understanding God had to be unmoved and unmovable. They argued that if God could be moved by any human situation, however tragic, then to that extent we who live through such tragedies would have power over him. To the Greeks this was impossible. God must be the Unmoved Mover. This may make good philosophy, but it is not the teaching of the Bible concerning God. God loves! God grieves! God agonizes over the distress and sorrow of his children. Jesus wept over the unbelieving city of Jerusalem (Luke 19:41).

When we go through difficult times, not knowing why they have come or why God is permitting them, we are tempted to believe that God does not care, that he is indifferent. But we are taught otherwise. Jesus said:

> Look at the birds of the air; they do not sow or reap or store away in barns, and yet your heavenly Father feeds them. Are you not much more valuable than they? . . . And why do you worry about clothes? See how the lilies of the field grow. They do not labor or spin. . . . If that is how God clothes the grass of the field, which is here today and tomorrow is thrown into the fire, will he not much more clothe you, O you of little faith?
>
> Matthew 6:26, 28, 30

The apostle Peter wrote, "Cast all your anxiety on him because he cares for you" (1 Peter 5:7).

Second, we can say that *God comforts in sorrow,* even when others speak cruel words or mock our misfortune. I do not know at what point in his long life David wrote the beloved Twenty-third Psalm, so I do not know what might have been on his mind as he composed its various parts. But I do know that David suffered periods of great abuse, when former friends and even members of his family turned against him. His own son Absalom tried to remove him from the throne. When David was driven from Jerusalem, his capital city, Shimei of Benjamin cursed him. These verbal spear thrusts must have wounded David deeply. But David found comfort in the Lord. Was this in his mind as he wrote:

> Even though I walk
>> through the valley of the shadow of death,
> I will fear no evil,
>> for you are with me;
> your rod and your staff,
>> they comfort me.
>
> Psalm 23:4

As I say, I do not know if this was what David was thinking about as he composed this great psalm. But I know that this has been the experience of many who have gone through the dark valleys of life. God has a special way of meeting us and providing comfort in those valleys.

Third, as I have suggested several times already, God not only cares and comforts, *he also preserves us and reaches out to save us in his own proper time.* He does this effectively. Reuben wanted to save Joseph, but his plan misfired. He was not ready with the right actions at the right time. With God it is different. His actions are always right actions, and they always come at precisely the right moment. He did this for Joseph. At the right moment God caused the Midianite merchants to pass by. At the right moment he saw that Joseph was sold to Potiphar, the captain of Pharaoh's guard. At the right moment God caused Joseph to be sent to prison to meet and help Pharaoh's chief cupbearer. At the right time God lifted Joseph to the pinnacle of power in Egypt. I do not know when that right moment is for you. But God knows, and you will find he is never too early or too late.

My daughter Jennifer went through a difficult period of growing up, in part because she was in the youngest class in a new school. I noticed that she took a great deal of comfort from books about the trials of other children. Early in the week when I first worked on this study I came home from work and gave her a big hug and greeting, and she told me with some warmth that I was just like Sir Willoughby.

"And who is Sir Willoughby?" I asked.

"He is the father of the Willoughby children in my book, *The Wolves of Willoughby Chase,*" she answered. She then told me the story—how Sir Willoughby Green had left his children with a governess to go off on a trip, how he had supposedly been lost in a shipwreck at sea, how the governess and her cronies had then taken over the Green estates and made life miserable for the children, and how the father had at last returned to set things right for them.

Jennifer read me the last part, in which the father returns unexpectedly, exclaiming, "What in the devil is going on here? And what have you done with my house?" The wicked governess was then punished and the children rescued.

That is just a story, of course. But you and I do have such a heavenly Father. He is not indifferent; he does care. He is not ineffective; one day he will return in power and judgment after he has first accomplished his own perfect purpose in our lives.

125

God's Man in Egypt

Genesis 37:36

Meanwhile, the Midianites sold Joseph in Egypt to Potiphar, one of Pharaoh's officials, the captain of the guard.

Chapter 37 of Genesis ends by recounting how the Midianites to whom Joseph's brothers had sold him brought him to Egypt where he was in turn sold to a high Egyptian official named Potiphar.

It must have been a dreadful experience for Joseph. Slavery is dreadful under any circumstances. But here was a young man, only seventeen years of age, who only a short time before had been the appointed heir of a devoted and loving father. He was serving his father in seeking out news of his brothers, for whom he deeply cared, when they had suddenly turned on him, had threatened to kill him, and then had sold him into slavery. And now he was sold again, becoming the most menial of slaves in a land he had never visited and in which he did not know the language.

God was with Joseph even in such circumstances as these. And Joseph knew it! His assurance that God was with him and was accomplishing his own perfect will in his life sustained him and gave him a remarkable peace even in Egypt. We have a hymn that says:

> Peace, perfect peace, with sorrows surging round?
> On Jesus' bosom naught but calm is found.
>
> Peace, perfect peace, with loved ones far away?
> In Jesus' keeping we are safe and they.
>
> Peace, perfect peace, our future all unknown?
> Jesus we know, and he is on the throne.
>
> Peace, perfect peace, death shadowing us and ours?
> Jesus has vanquished death and all its powers.

This was Joseph's story. Joseph had been burdened with sorrows, torn from loved ones, plunged into an uncertain future with the prospects of an early death both real and frightening. But he knew God and could therefore lie down with the certainty that God would watch over him even in his sleep. And he would rise for the next day's work knowing that God would bless him and make himself known to others through Joseph's testimony.

We hate slavery. But who would not rather be the slave Joseph in Egypt in the presence of God than the brothers with his blood-stained coat and their lies and burdened consciences?

An Ancient Country

The Egypt to which Joseph was transported by the Midianites and in which he was sold again was a very ancient country. Scholars are divided as to the dates of the beginning of the first Egyptian dynasty, opinions ranging widely from approximately 5500 to 3100 B.C.[1] But even by the latest of these dates, which seems increasingly to be the prevailing view, Egypt had been a large and thriving kingdom for upward of a thousand years before Joseph arrived there.

Egyptian chronologies list thirty-one dynasties from this early beginning to the Greek domination of Egypt as a result of Alexander the Great's conquests. The fifteenth of these thirty-one dynasties was already under way in Joseph's period. There had been an Old Kingdom, with the fourth through sixth dynasties (c. 2613–c. 2181 B.C.), an Intermediate Period, with the seventh through tenth dynasties (c. 2181–c. 2040 B.C.), a Middle Kingdom, with the eleventh through fourteenth dynasties (c. 2133–c. 1603 B.C.), and the beginnings of a Second Intermediate (or Hyksos) Period, which overlapped the Middle Kingdom and included the fifteenth through seventeenth dynasties (c. 1720–c. 1567 B.C.).

It is assumed that Joseph and his family entered Egypt during the Hyksos Period, since the Hyksos were Semitic and would be rulers among whom a Semite like Joseph would naturally rise to a position of prominence. If the family of Joseph arrived in Egypt early in this period, the 430 years of living in Egypt would bring the Exodus into the time of Rameses II, who would have been the pharaoh of the exodus.

Egypt was extraordinarily wealthy in these years. There are several reasons. First, the land was exceptionally fertile due to the yearly inundation of the Nile, which brought rich topsoil to the valley and delta regions. Practically anything would grow in Egypt. Due to the plentiful Nile water and long days of sunshine, almost any field would produce two plentiful crops each year. The Egyptians were therefore self-sufficient in corn, wheat, barley, fruit, vegetables, apples, olives, dates, pomegranates, and other edibles.

Second, the land was rich in natural resources. Fish filled the river and waterfowl were plenteous along the river's banks. Thick-stemmed papyrus plants provided fiber for paper, baskets, matting, sandals, boat building, and other purposes. Game could be found in the desert. The fine mud of the river provided an inexhaustible supply of clay for building blocks and pottery. From the cliffs bordering the river the people took fine limestone and sandstone for the mason, and the sculptor could find harder stone such as alabaster and porphyry at no great distance. Copper came from the eastern desert and the Sinai. Gold was plentiful in upper Egypt, Nubia, and Arabia. The Nile offered easy transport.

But the greatest reason for Egypt's prosperity in these early centuries was that the country had no real enemies. Egypt was protected by the desert anyway. But in this period there were just no nations of any real size to threaten her. Later the Hyksos became such a power. After them the Sea Peoples also became dangerous. The eighteenth dynasty, which drove the Hyksos out, developed an army to do so. But before this there was very little in the way of military force—just the immediate police-type troops who surrounded the pharaoh—and as a result, the efforts that might have gone into military operations went instead into the enrichment of the country.

The Egyptians excelled in mathematics and architecture, which built on mathematical principles. One can sense it today, standing before the great pyramids of Gizeh, built in the fourth dynasty. The construction of these colossal monuments represents a brilliant flowering of the ancient mind. The pyramids were more than seven hundred years old when Joseph entered Egypt.

One Egyptologist writes: "In the Cairo Museum you may stand in the presence of the massive granite sarcophagus which once contained the body of Khufu-onekh, the architect who built the Great Pyramid of Gizeh. . . . Let us in imagination follow this early architect to the desert plateau behind the village of Gizeh. It was then bare desert surface, dotted only with the ruins of a few small tombs of remote ancestors. The oldest stone masonry construction at that time had been erected by Khufu-onekh's great-grandfather. Only three generations of architects in stone preceded him. . . . There probably were not many stone masons, nor many men who understood the technique of building in stone as Khufu-onekh took his first walk on the bare Gizeh Plateau, and staked out the ground plan of the Great Pyramid. Conceive, then, the dauntless courage of the man who told his surveyors to lay out the square base 755 feet on each side! . . . He knew it would take nearly two and a half million blocks each weighing two and one-half tons to cover this square of thirteen acres with a mountain of masonry 481 feet high."[2]

The building of these pyramids was a remarkable work by ancient man. So was the construction of the capital cities of Memphis, Abydos, and Thebes with their palaces and temples. The first portions of the great temples at Karnak had been built before Joseph entered Egypt. The Sphinx had been carved. Some of the pyramids may even have begun to show the effects of the passing of the years.

A Pagan Country

The Egypt Joseph entered was an ancient and advanced nation then, as I have indicated. But it was a debased and pagan nation too. So far as its religion was concerned, it was the most ignorant and polytheistic nation of the ancient world.

For many years, largely as the result of widespread adoption of the theory of evolution in Western lands, students of religion have placed polytheism at a somewhat early point on an imagined scale of historical religious development. According to this understanding, primitive man was largely animistic. That is, he imagined objects to be controlled by fearful spirits thought to dwell in them, and he worshiped them. After this came polytheism, a more detached and slightly more elevated religious understanding. From polytheism came monotheism. After monotheism came a philosophical monotheism. The highest point, according to this theory, would be a form of ethical humanism or ethical Christianity, depending on the viewpoint of the theorist.

Today, however, thanks to the many years of archaeological and comparative religions studies, the evolution of religion from a primitive animism can no longer be assumed. Serious Bible students now look to archaeology and to the findings of anthropology and comparative religions to support the contrary biblical claims. According to the Bible, polytheism as practiced by the Egyptians is not a step up from animism but is actually several steps downward from monotheism. Hence, the religion of Egypt in Joseph's day is to be viewed as something degenerate from true worship.

One of the great Viennese anthropologists, Wilhelm Schmidt, has shown that the religions of the hundreds of isolated tribes in the world today are not primitive in the sense of being original and that there is every reason to postulate the existence of some form of monotheism behind them. According to Schmidt, the tribes have a memory of a "High God," who is no longer worshiped because he is not feared. In fact, he is not to be feared. So instead of sacrificing to him, tribesmen concern themselves with the need to appease the evil and frightening spirits of the jungle.

Commenting on these and other findings, Robert Brow writes, "Their research suggests that tribes are not animistic because they have continued unchanged since the dawn of history. Rather, the evidence indicates degeneration from a true knowledge of God. Isolation from prophets and religious books has ensnared them into sacrificial bribery to placate the spirits instead of joyous sacrificial meals in the presence of the Creator." Brow shows that "an original monotheism gives an explanation of many historical facts which are very intractable on the evolution of religion hypothesis."[3]

This is exactly what the Bible teaches, and the state of ancient Egyptian religion is an example of the Bible's perspective. In Romans 1, the apostle Paul wrote of man's departure from God and the resulting debasement of his religious conceptions:

> Since the creation of the world God's invisible qualities—his eternal power and divine nature—have been clearly seen, being understood from what has been made, so that men are without excuse. For although they knew God, they neither glorified him as God nor gave thanks to him, but their thinking became futile and their foolish hearts were darkened. Although they claimed to be wise, they became fools and exchanged the glory of the immortal God for images made to look like mortal man and birds and animals and reptiles.
>
> verses 20–23

This is a perfect description of Egypt's religion. In fact, there is no country that better illustrates Paul's judgment in all the ancient world.

The gods of Egypt were clustered around the three great natural forces of Egyptian life: the Nile, the land, and the cloudless sky with its brilliant and perpetual sun.

Osiris was one of the chief gods of Egypt, and he was first of all god of the river Nile. In upper Egypt, Hapimon and Tauret were also Nile gods. Nu, the god of life in the river, was also associated with it. Geb was god of the land. But he was closely connected with Nepri, the grain god; Anubis, the guardian of the fields; and Min, the deity of harvests and crops. Animal gods and goddesses were linked to the land: Apis, the bull god, who was worshiped primarily at Memphis; Hathor, the cow; Sekhmet, who was worshiped in the form of a lion; Khnum, the ram; Sobek, the crocodile.

Egypt was noted for its skills in medicine, so there were numerous gods of healing: Amon and Horus, as well as others already mentioned. There was Thoth, the ibis-headed god of wisdom, writing, and invention; Serapis, whose cult lasted even into the Christian era until it finally came to an end in the fourth century; and Imhotep. The sky god was Shu, who ruled the atmosphere. The sky goddess was Nut. With them were the bird gods, Horus and Month. Greatest of all was the sun god Ra, who was thought to be embodied in the reigning pharaoh. Centuries later, after the people of Israel had fallen into slavery and the true God, Jehovah, had sent Moses to demand that Pharaoh let the people go, it was against these false and ineffective gods that the ten plagues were directed.[4]

When in Egypt . . .

"When in Rome, do as the Romans do." The gist of that saying could have been spoken to Joseph in these early years, telling him that since he was in Egypt and would have to stay in Egypt, he might as well do as the Egyptians did and adopt Egypt's religion and morality. After all, the Egyptians were doing quite well by their religion. They worshiped hundreds of gods, and these gods had blessed them. They were the wealthiest nation on earth. Their architecture, medicine, and mathematics were the marvel of their day. Above all, Joseph should assume the mind of a slave and do whatever was necessary to get by. He should work only as hard as he was required to work, and he should take his pleasure wherever he could find it.

This was not the way Joseph responded to his slavery, and his advance in Egypt was due to his rejecting such advice. Joseph retained two great things in Egypt: his character and his awareness of God's presence.

F. B. Meyer writes, "Though stripped of his coat, he had not been stripped of his character."[5] Joseph's fellow slaves may have told him, "You don't have to work as hard as you're doing, and you don't have to live a moral life. No one back home will ever know what you do. Let go! Enjoy yourself!" But Joseph was not living an upright life because he was afraid his family might see him or find out if he did not. He was living an upright life because he was an upright man. He was no less moral in the loincloth of the slave than he was in the richly ornamented robes given to him by his father. A bit of doggerel says:

> It isn't the style nor the stuff in the coat,
>   Nor the length of the tailor's bill;
> It's the stuff in the chap inside the coat
>   That counts for good or ill.

Also, Joseph was constantly aware of God's presence. In fact, it is this that gave him his character and kept him on track even when surrounded by polytheistic religion, immorality, and bad advice. When you read Joseph's story, do you ever notice that his speech is constantly filled with references to God?

When Potiphar's wife propositioned him, Joseph replied, "How then could I do such a wicked thing and sin against *God?*" (Gen. 39:9, my emphasis).

When Joseph had been thrown into prison and the chief cupbearer and the chief baker of Pharaoh had dreams and related them, Joseph instantly replied, "Do not interpretations belong to *God?*" (Gen. 40:8, my emphasis).

When he appeared before Pharaoh and Pharaoh asked for an interpretation of his dream, Joseph responded, "I cannot do it, . . . but *God* will give Pharaoh the answer he desires" (Gen. 41:16, my emphasis). When he interpreted the dream, Joseph began by saying, "*God* has revealed to Pharaoh what he is about to do" (v. 25; cf. vv. 28, 32, my emphasis).

When he saw his brothers later and revealed himself to them, Joseph explained the past events by noting, "It was to save lives that *God* sent me ahead of you. . . . *God* sent me ahead of you to preserve for you a remnant on earth and to save your lives by a great deliverance. So then, it was not you who sent me here, but *God*" (Gen. 45:5, 7–8, my emphasis).

Joseph said of his sons Ephraim and Manasseh, "They are the sons *God* has given me here" (Gen. 48:9, my emphasis).

At the very end Joseph replied to his brothers, "Don't be afraid. Am I in the place of *God*? You intended to harm me, but *God* intended it for good to accomplish . . . the saving of many lives" (Gen. 50:19–20, my emphasis).

His last words were, "I am about to die. But *God* will surely come to your aid and take you up out of this land. . . . *God* will surely come to your aid, and then you must carry my bones up from this place" (Gen. 50:24–25, my emphasis).

God! God! God! God! This was the dominant theme in Joseph's speech and life, and it is this that made him what he truly was: God's man in godless Egypt. May that same awareness make you God's true man or woman wherever his own wise plan has placed you.

126

Man's Man in Canaan

Genesis 38:1-25

At that time, Judah left his brothers and went down to stay with a man of Adullam named Hirah. There Judah met the daughter of a Canaanite man named Shua. He married her and lay with her; she became pregnant and gave birth to a son, who was named Er. She conceived again and gave birth to a son and named him Onan. She gave birth to still another son and named him Shelah. It was at Kezib that she gave birth to him.

Judah got a wife for Er, his firstborn, and her name was Tamar. But Er, Judah's firstborn, was wicked in the LORD's sight; so the LORD put him to death.

Then Judah said to Onan, "Lie with your brother's wife and fulfill your duty to her as a brother-in-law to produce offspring for your brother." But Onan knew that the offspring would not be his; so whenever he lay with his brother's wife, he spilled his semen on the ground to keep from producing offspring for his brother. What he did was wicked in the LORD's sight; so he put him to death also.

Judah then said to his daughter-in-law Tamar, "Live as a widow in your father's house until my son Shelah grows up." For he thought, "He may die too, just like his brothers." So Tamar went to live in her father's house.

After a long time Judah's wife, the daughter of Shua, died. When Judah had recovered from his grief, he went up to Timnah, to the men who were shearing his sheep, and his friend Hirah the Adullamite went with him.

When Tamar was told, "Your father-in-law is on his way to Timnah to shear his sheep," she took off her widow's clothes, covered herself with a veil to disguise herself, and then sat down at the entrance to Enaim, which is on the road to Timnah. For she saw that, though Shelah had now grown up, she had not been given to him as his wife.

When Judah saw her, he thought she was a prostitute, for she had covered her face. Not realizing that she was his daughter-in-law, he went over to her by the roadside and said, "Come now, let me sleep with you."

"And what will you give me to sleep with you?" she asked.

"I'll send you a young goat from my flock," he said.

"Will you give me something as a pledge until you send it?" she asked.

He said, "What pledge should I give you?"

"Your seal and its cord, and the staff in your hand," she answered. So he gave them to her and slept with her, and she became pregnant by him. After she left, she took off her veil and put on her widow's clothes again.

Meanwhile Judah sent the young goat by his friend the Adullamite in order to get his pledge back from the woman, but he did not find her. He asked the men who lived there, "Where is the shrine prostitute who was beside the road at Enaim?"

"There hasn't been any shrine prostitute here," they said.

So he went back to Judah and said, "I didn't find her. Besides, the men who lived there said, 'There hasn't been any shrine prostitute here.'"

Then Judah said, "Let her keep what she has, or we will become a laughingstock. After all, I did send her this young goat, but you didn't find her."

About three months later Judah was told, "Your daughter-in-law Tamar is guilty of prostitution, and as a result she is now pregnant."

Judah said, "Bring her out and have her burned to death!"

As she was being brought out, she sent a message to her father-in-law. "I am pregnant by the man who owns these," she said. And she added, "See if you recognize whose seal and cord and staff these are."

At first reading it is strange and even a bit distasteful to come from Genesis 37, in which the story of Joseph has just gotten under way, to Genesis 38 with its flashback to the sins of Joseph's elder brother Judah in Canaan. For one thing, it is parenthetical. We want to move ahead to see how Joseph fared in Egypt as a slave to Potiphar. Also, the chapter deals with sexual sins, and it is hard to see how these can be edifying. One commentator, who never thinks much of such stories, describes the chapter as being "entirely unsuited to homiletical use, much as the devout Bible student may glean from [it]."[1]

Yet there are good reasons for Genesis 38 to be exactly where it is. First, it is part of *Jacob's* story, which we have already been told these chapters contain (Gen. 37:2). As soon as Joseph is mentioned, we think that the interest of the author has therefore passed to him, since our interest naturally shifts in that direction. But this is not the way the author of Genesis thought. He tells us, "This is the account of Jacob." Then he proceeds to give us Jacob's story, which includes the story of Judah. Much of the action of these years centers on Joseph, since he is the one through whom the family actually moved to Egypt and by whom their lives and the lives of many others were spared. Still, this is Jacob's story (including Judah), and Jacob will come in again later to bless Joseph's sons and prophesy the future of the developing tribes of Israel.

Second, the chapter shows why the period of Egyptian slavery was necessary for the chosen people. In Canaan the descendants of Abraham were inter-marrying with the people of the land and were therefore in danger of being entirely swallowed up by Canaan's culture. The Jews would be preserved as a separate people in Egypt, since the Egyptians disliked foreigners, particularly shepherds (Gen. 46:34).

However, in my judgment, the chief reason why Genesis 38 is included at this point is to provide a contrast to the story of Joseph's conduct in the house of Potiphar, which is related in the next chapter. Genesis 39 tells of Joseph's upright conduct when propositioned by Potiphar's wife. From a human per-spective Joseph had much to gain by this dalliance; and if he refused, he had much to lose. He was in Egypt and could be expected to do as the Egyptians. Nevertheless, he recognized sin as sin and refused to have anything to do with it: "No one is greater in this house than I am. My master has withheld nothing from me except you, because you are his wife. How then could I do such a wicked thing and sin against God?" (Gen. 39:9). By contrast, Judah is in Canaan and has nothing to gain from his dalliance except possibly a few moments of pleasure. But he sins! He goes to an apparent prostitute with as much ease as a person today might hail a taxi.

If Joseph was God's man in Egypt, as we described him previously, Judah was certainly man's man in Canaan. He was in the Land of Promise, but he was as unlike God as the pagans who surrounded him.

The Sins of Judah

The story begins with a time reference, noting that it was "at that time" that Judah left his brothers and went down to Adullam, where he married Shua's daughter. The reference is to the time at which Joseph was sold to the Midianites, which means the events of the chapter must have taken place in the twenty-two-year period between the sale of Joseph and the departure of Jacob's family for Egypt. (There were thirteen years before Joseph's pro-motion to prime minister, followed by seven years of plenteous crops and two years of famine. It is a tight fit, but the events can be squeezed in.)

Apparently Judah went to Adullam shortly after the sale of Joseph, possibly because he could not face the great and undiminishing grief of his father Jacob for Joseph (Gen. 37:34–35). There Judah married a Canaanite woman and had a son by her—Er—whom he gave in marriage to Tamar at approx-imately the age of sixteen or seventeen. After Er's death Judah gave his second son Onan to Tamar, which would be in the nineteenth or twentieth year of this period. This leaves two or three years for the remaining events: a year in which Tamar is returned to her father's house, Tamar's seduction of Judah, and the birth of Tamar's twin sons.[2] If this is proper timing, the events of the chapter fill the years in which Joseph's family remained in Canaan and thus bring us to the next major event in their lives, namely, the migration to Egypt, which took place when Joseph was thirty-nine.

Judah is guilty of three sins in this chapter, and they are progressive. That is, each is related to the one before it and is worse. First, *Judah married an unbelieving or pagan wife*. She is not named, but she was the daughter of Shua of Adullam and is identified as a Canaanite. Her character was presumably passed on to her sons, two of whom God put to death for their wickedness (vv. 7, 10).

It is a sad thing, but many Christian failures can be traced to a marriage to an unbelieving partner. Some years ago I counseled a girl who was on the verge of such a marriage. The man was not a Christian. She was well aware of it. Still she so much wanted to get married that she decided to go ahead with the wedding in spite of my warnings and the advice of her friends. She hoped that he would become a Christian through her testimony. Actually the effect was largely the other way. The girl dropped out of church, moved, made new friends, and eventually was lost to our fellowship. Years later I encountered her. I would not have known her except that she identified herself to me. She looked much older and was obviously unhappy. She poured out her story. Before I left she confided, "I hate to admit it, but you were absolutely right. I should never have married him."

The Bible forbids the marriage of a Christian to a non-Christian. "Do not be yoked together with unbelievers. For what do righteousness and wickedness have in common? Or what fellowship can light have with darkness?" (2 Cor. 6:14). For that reason I never knowingly marry a Christian to an unbelieving person.

"But what about dating?" a young person asks. "Is it possible to date an unbeliever?" I am unwilling to answer this as categorically as I do the question of marrying an unbeliever, because some have undoubtedly become Christians in the process of dating a Christian and the marriages that have resulted have clearly been of God. Yet it is dangerous business, and it requires a strong Christian in the relationship. It requires one who is mature enough not to let romantic interests outstrip his or her Christian interests and who will not even take steps toward marriage (including talking about it) until it is clear that the prospective partner is a genuine and growing follower of the Lord Jesus Christ.

A young person must remember that friendship is the prelude to courtship and courtship is the prelude to marriage, and that somewhere along the line (preferably earlier rather than later) the Christian must be certain of the salvation of the other person. To fail in this is to invite disaster. It is sometimes the case (since God is gracious) that an unbelieving husband or wife will at last be converted by the testimony of the believing spouse. But generally this is not without many years of sorrow and suffering on the Christian's part. It is almost always the case if the marriage involves the believer's knowing disobedience.

Broken Promises

Second, *Judah was unfaithful to his most solemn commitments*, which is not surprising since in his marriage he was first unfaithful to God. The specific incident involved the marriage of Tamar to his sons Er and Onan. According to the custom of the day, if an older brother died without having produced children, it was the responsibility of the next oldest brother to marry the widow and thereby raise up an heir to his brother. That is, the first son of the new marriage would be considered the older brother's son and would preserve his name and be entitled to receive his inheritance. This is called a levirate marriage, from the Latin word *levir*, meaning "brother-in-law." Apparently it was a widespread obligation in antiquity, where maintaining family lines held great importance. It is incorporated into the Mosaic law in Deuteronomy 25:5–10 (cf. Matt. 22:23–28).

This situation prevailed in the case of Tamar. Judah had obtained her to be the wife of his firstborn Er, whom the Lord later put to death for his wickedness. According to the custom, she was then given to Onan, the second son. He agreed to marry Tamar, but he did not want to raise up an heir to his brother, no doubt believing that, if he did not, the privileges of the inheritance would pass to himself. He interrupted his acts of intercourse to avoid impregnating Tamar. The Lord judged this as serious wickedness and put him to death also.

At this point Tamar should have been given to Judah's third son, Shelah, which Judah actually acknowledged: "Live as a widow in your father's house until my son Shelah grows up" (v. 11). But Judah's words were deceptive. He did not want his third son, Shelah, to marry Tamar, "for he thought, 'He may die too, just like his brothers'" (v. 11). As a result, as time went by it became apparent that Judah had forgotten his obligation to Tamar. She was back with her father and, as the saying goes, it was "out of sight, out of mind" for Judah.

Immoral Actions

The longer Judah lived in Canaan, the more he was becoming like the people of the land. In fact, he was becoming worse than the Canaanites, to judge from the sequel to our story. He was actually becoming quite immoral. The story tells us that when Tamar realized that Judah had no intention of giving her Shelah as her husband, she worked out a plan in which she could become pregnant by Judah himself. First, she took off her widow's clothing and instead dressed in the bright apparel of a shrine prostitute. (Cultic prostitution was a common thing in Canaan even at that early date. It continued on to plague Israel during the nation's later years.) Next, Tamar seated herself near the entrance to the town (or shrine) of Enaim, where she expected to meet Judah as he passed by on his way to Timnah for the shearing of his sheep.

As Judah passed by he saw Tamar and, thinking she was a prostitute, asked to sleep with her.

She asked for compensation, and he promised to give her a young goat from his flock. "Will you give me something as a pledge until you send it?" she inquired.

"What pledge should I give you?" he asked.

Tamar asked for his seal, its cord, and the staff in his hand. When he agreed, she allowed him to sleep with her and she became pregnant by him. Afterward she quickly returned to her father's house and put on her widow's clothing again. Naturally, when Judah sent his friend Hirah the Adullamite to redeem his pledge, Tamar was nowhere to be found. He was forced to let the matter rest.

About three months later Tamar was discovered to be pregnant, and the matter was brought to Judah's attention. He proscribed the most extreme penalty: "Bring her out and have her burned to death!" (v. 24).

However, Tamar sent the pledge items to Judah, saying, "I am pregnant by the man who owns these. See if you recognize whose seal and cord and staff these are" (v. 25).

At this point Judah recognized, if not her innocence, at least the fact that she was more in the right than he was: "She is more righteous than I, since I wouldn't give her to my son Shelah" (v. 26). Tamar was saved and later gave birth to twin boys, Perez and Zerah, the former becoming an ancestor of the Lord Jesus Christ (cf. Matt. 1:3; Luke 3:33).

Grace Abounding

There are a number of important applications to this story, as most commentators have recognized. First, it is a lesson about sin, for it shows how one sin inevitably leads to another and how at last most sins are found out. (Of course, at the final judgment every sin will be exposed and all facts known.) Judah's sin of marrying an unbelieving woman led to his breaking his obligation to Tamar and eventually to his easy morality. Moreover, it affected others. No doubt his wife's corruption was passed on to his sons. His sin with Tamar eventually involved her in public disgrace and great danger.

Do not think, if you are tempted to sin (as Judah was or in some other way), that you will escape sin's consequences. Sin has tentacles, and you will be entangled in them. David's sin with Bathsheba (adultery) led to sin against Uriah (murder), and the outworking of the evil eventually affected the whole nation.

Yet, great as Judah's sin was, it is evident that God also worked in the situation for good, since from this incest came Perez, one of the ancestors of the Lord Jesus Christ. Is it not strange that Christ should trace his ancestry through this illicit son of Judah rather than through Joseph, who is so much like Christ and is so dominant in the final portions of the Book of Genesis?

"Strange!" says one commentator. "Nay, not more strange than that he should have compassion on that other woman of Canaan, who in the days of his flesh wrestled with him, and refused to let him go, until he blessed her. That in his genealogy he should be mixed up with human sorrow and human sin, is a fitting type of his being, when he comes, a man of sorrows—a friend of publicans and sinners—calling not the righteous but sinners to repentance. This blot upon his escutcheon—this bar-sinister across his crest—this blight in his family tree—this taint of heathenism and of harlotry in his ancestral blood—is ordained of set purpose. It is ordained to abase the lordly pride and pomp of lineage of the most renowned—to put a mockery on earth's highest glory. It is ordained also to mark the grace and condescension of the Most High, who gives his holy and beloved Son—that Son most freely consenting—to be one of our unclean and guilty race and to come—all holy and righteous as he is in himself—into personal contact and conflict with its guilt and its uncleanness, 'his own self bearing our sins in his own body on the tree, that we being dead to sins, should live unto righteousness' (1 Peter 2:24)."[3]

Luther said that the story of Judah and Tamar was included in Genesis for two purposes: first, to rebuke presumption, and second, to challenge despair. It rebukes presumption in that if Judah—who was an ancestor of the Lord Jesus Christ and was instructed, as he must have been, in the religion of his father Jacob and of his ancestors Isaac and Abraham—if he sinned so easily in going to Tamar, then any of us can likewise sin, regardless of our background, privileges, or training. We must confess our sinful natures and stay close to God, from whom alone the strength to resist temptation comes.

The story challenges despair, because in the midst of this great sin we nevertheless see the great mercy of God. Luther wrote, "The church of God has great need of these examples. For what would become of us? What hope would be left for us if Peter had not denied Christ and all the apostles had not taken offense at Him, and if Moses, Aaron and David had not fallen? Therefore, God wanted to console sinners with these examples and to say: 'If you have fallen, return; for the door of mercy is open to you. You, who are conscious of no sin, do not be presumptuous; but both of you should trust in my grace and mercy.'"[4]

The Bible says, "Where sin increased, grace increased all the more" (Rom. 5:20). It was true in Judah and Tamar's day, and it is true in our time also. Nothing is better calculated to draw us to the source of such unmerited favor.

127

The Women in Jesus' Family Tree

Genesis 38:26–30

Judah recognized them and said, "She is more righteous than I, since I wouldn't give her to my son Shelah." And he did not sleep with her again.

When the time came for her to give birth, there were twin boys in her womb. As she was giving birth, one of them put out his hand; so the midwife took a scarlet thread and tied it on his wrist and said, "This one came out first." But when he drew back his hand, his brother came out, and she said, "So this is how you have broken out!" And he was named Perez. Then his brother, who had the scarlet thread on his wrist, came out and he was given the name Zerah.

There are women in every generation of Jesus' family tree, of course. But it is interesting that in the genealogy of Jesus that begins the New Testament (Matt. 1:1–17) there are references to four women whom you would not normally expect to find there: Tamar, whose story is told in Genesis 38 and who is the reason for looking at the women in this study; Rahab, the prostitute of Jericho, who hid the spies at the time of the Israelite conquest; Ruth, the Moabitess, who has a book of the Old Testament named after her; and Bathsheba, who is not mentioned

899

in the genealogy by name but is identified simply as the one who "had been Uriah's wife" (v. 6).

It is remarkable that *any* women are included in the list, because it was not the custom to mention women in genealogies. None of the great genealogies of Genesis mention women (Genesis 5, 10, 11, 36, 46; the ungodly line of Genesis 4 mentions Lamech's wives and daughter). Neither do the genealogies of 1 Chronicles (chaps. 1–4), Ezra (chaps. 2, 8, 10) or Nehemiah (chaps. 7, 11, 12), or the lesser genealogies of Numbers 3 or Ruth 4. Yet in Matthew's genealogy four women are mentioned within the space of just four verses.

Even more remarkable is the fact that these women were relatively unknown, were Gentiles, and (in three of the four cases) were notoriously sinful at one time of their lives. If we had been looking for notable women to include in Jesus' family tree, we would not have picked these. We would have glanced down the list of the many devoted and believing women leading up to the birth of Jesus Christ and would have chosen people like Eve, Sarah, Rebekah, or Leah. That would be a female portion of a family tree worth citing. We would be proud of such an ancestry. But no! The Holy Spirit, who inspired the writing of the Gospels, did not lead Matthew to mention these women. Instead, he chose Tamar, Rahab, Ruth, and Bathsheba. Something as unexpected and remarkable as that should lead us to look into the matter more closely.

Sinful Women

The first thing we must deal with is that three of the four women are characterized by having been notoriously sinful. Ruth is an exception, but we must remember that even she, being a Moabitess, was under the curse of the Mosaic law (Deut. 23:3).

We have reviewed *Tamar's story*. At the end of Genesis 38 Judah confesses that "she is more righteous than I, since I wouldn't give her to my son Shelah" (v. 26). But this does not mean that Tamar was righteous, only that Judah was worse. Tamar certainly reflected the morals of her Canaanite upbringing when she judged it acceptable to play a prostitute and thus become with child by her father-in-law, Judah. She had a righteous cause. But the rightness of the cause did not justify the methods she used to achieve it.

Rahab's story is told in Joshua 2 and 6, where she is identified as a prostitute (Josh. 2:1; 6:17, 25). She hid the two Jewish spies because she believed the Lord had given the land of Canaan to the Jewish people. Thus, she was spared in the destruction of Jericho. Rahab married Salmon, a descendant of Perez, who was one of the twin sons of Tamar. She was the mother of Boaz, who married Ruth (Matt. 1:3–6; Ruth 4:18–21).

The last of these four women, *Bathsheba*, has a particularly sinful story. It is not greatly lessened by the fact that the sin of David, who committed adultery with her, was greater. From the roof of his palace David saw Bathsheba bathing. He sent to find out who she was. Then, when he was told she was the wife of Uriah the Hittite, instead of dropping the matter, he sent for her and then slept with her. When it was discovered that she was pregnant, he had Uriah killed and married Bathsheba. The son she was carrying died, but a later son, Solomon, succeeded David on the throne of Israel.

In each of these three cases (Ruth being an exception) there is notorious sin. But these are nevertheless the very persons who are taken into the genealogy of the sinless Lord Jesus Christ. Why? It is, as Martin Luther said, so that "no one should be presumptuous about his own righteousness or wisdom, and no one should despair on account of his sins."[1]

Although the women in Jesus' family tree were guilty of great sins, they were at the same time, though sinners, saved by God's grace. This is an encouragement. Luther wrote, "These matters are set forth for our consolation. Great saints must make great mistakes in order that God may testify that he wants all men to be humiliated and contained in the catalog of sinners, and that when they have acknowledged and confessed this, they may find grace and mercy. . . . To be sure, one must beware of sins; but if anyone has fallen, he should not become despondent on that account. For God has forbidden both despair and presumption, turning aside to the left hand and to the right. There should be no presumption on the right and no despair on the left. One must stay on the royal road. The sinner should not abandon his confidence in mercy. A righteous man should not be proud. For 'the Lord takes pleasure in those who fear him and in those who hope in his mercy' (Ps. 147:11)."[2]

Jew and Gentile

The sinfulness of the women in Jesus' family tree is not the most remarkable thing about them, however. In my judgment what is most surprising is that they were all Gentiles. Tamar and Rahab were Canaanites. Ruth was a Moabitess. Bathsheba, though not explicitly said to be so, was presumably a Hittite since she was married to Uriah, who was a Hittite.

What an encouragement to Gentiles! We remember that when the woman of Samaria wanted to debate Jesus about the proper place of worship—"Our fathers worshiped on this mountain, but you Jews claim that the place where we must worship is in Jerusalem"—Jesus replied, "Salvation is from the Jews" (John 4:20, 22). That is, salvation came through the nation of Israel, which produced the Messiah, and included incorporation into that people prior to the death and resurrection of Christ and the expansion of the gospel proclamation to the gentile nations. Yet it was also indicated from the beginning that Gentiles were to be included in the scope of God's saving grace.

The Jewish people trace their ancestry to Abraham. But what happens immediately after Abraham's time? Isaac's bride is Rebekah, who comes from Abraham's people then living in Haran—an important point. She was not a *descendant* of Abraham.

Jacob takes sisters Leah and Rachel, the daughters of Laban, as his wives. They were not descendants of Abraham either. In fact, their father was a particularly pagan man.

Judah married a Canaanite, who was the daughter of Shua, and fathered Perez by Tamar, who was also a Canaanite.

Joseph married an Egyptian woman and had two sons, Manasseh and Ephraim, fathers of two of the tribes of Israel, by her.

Salmon married Rahab.

Boaz married Ruth.

David had Solomon by Bathsheba.

In fact, though there probably were some, it is impossible to name one Jewish woman—with the exception of the Virgin Mary—in all this long line of the ancestors of the Lord Jesus Christ. Those mentioned are all Gentiles. Donald Grey Barnhouse observed this and wrote: "In all the ancestry of Jesus Christ, which is faithfully recorded as the son of David, the son of Abraham, there is not one daughter of Israel mentioned in the list of his grandmothers, but three Gentile harlots and the adulterous Gentile wife of David. Why did God's providence guide matters in this way? The answer is surely in the fact that the church of Jesus Christ is called his bride, and that we, for the most part, are Gentiles. All of these incidents of anointed kings disobeying the commandment of God and taking Gentiles to wife are indicating that the Lord Jesus Christ himself would turn to all the families of the world, and that the church of Jesus Christ would include not merely the physical sons of Abraham, but the Gentiles."[3]

I am glad these women are included. In Ephesians Paul writes that the Gentiles were "foreigners to the covenants of the promise, without hope and without God in the world" (Eph. 2:12). And so we were! But in the inclusion of these gentile women in Jesus' family tree we discover that the mercy of God is not limited to one nation, but is for all who will identify with God's work of redemption through the Savior.

By Faith . . . Rahab

Still we must be identified with the Savior, which is the next point. Tamar, Rahab, Ruth, and Bathsheba were sinners who were also Gentiles. But they were not saved simply because they were sinners or Gentiles. They were saved by becoming worshipers of Jehovah and by looking forward to that Redeemer whom God had promised would come through the line into which they were incorporated.

It is true that we are not told explicitly of the faith of Tamar or Bathsheba, though their faith certainly was or came to be in the God of Israel. But faith is explicit in the case of Ruth and Rahab. Ruth's story is well known. She was a Moabitess who had been married to the son of a Jewish woman named Naomi. Naomi had gone to Moab during a period of severe famine in Israel and had taken her sons with her. But the sons had died. So when Naomi decided to return to her own land, Ruth, her daughter-in-law, determined to go along. Ruth and Naomi had become close friends. But more important than that, Ruth had learned from Naomi during the years they were together and had come to worship Naomi's God.

At first Naomi tried to persuade Ruth to remain in Moab, but Ruth would have none of it. She replied, "Don't urge me to leave you or to turn back from you. Where you go I will go, and where you stay I will stay. Your people will be my people and your God my God. Where you die I will die, and there I will be buried. May the LORD deal with me, be it ever so severely, if anything but death separates you and me" (Ruth 1:16–17).

This moving entreaty and literary gem contains seven statements, which together constitute a vow Ruth never broke: (1) she asked Naomi to stop urging her to return to the people and gods of Moab; (2) she promised to go wherever Naomi went and (3) to live wherever Naomi lived; (4) she claimed Naomi's people as her people and (5) Naomi's God as her God; (6) she affirmed that these decisions would be true for life; and (7) she appealed to God as witness that her vow was sincere and permanent.

And what was the high point of these statements? It was commitment to the God of Israel: "Your God [will be] my God." She came to this through a process: first, coming to love Naomi; second, coming to identify with Naomi's people, the Jews; finally, coming to worship Naomi's God. But whatever the process, the chief element in her decision was commitment to Jehovah. So I repeat, Ruth was saved not merely because she was a sinner, as all of us are, or a Gentile. She was saved because she became a worshiper of Jehovah and looked forward to that Redeemer whom he had promised to send.

And what of Rahab, whose faith is even more evident? Rahab is mentioned in Hebrews 11 in that great listing of the heroes and heroines of the faith: "By faith the prostitute Rahab, because she welcomed the spies, was not killed with those who were disobedient" (Heb. 11:31).

Joshua had sent two spies to look over the land of Canaan, especially the region around Jericho. They stayed overnight in Rahab's house. Word came to the king that they were there. But when he sent soldiers to arrest the two spies, Rahab hid them while sending the soldiers off on a false pursuit. Then she returned to the spies, saying:

I know that the LORD has given this land to you and that a great fear of you has fallen on us, so that all who live in this country are melting in fear because of you. We have heard how the LORD dried up the water of the Red Sea for you when you came out of Egypt, and what you did to Sihon and Og, the two kings of the Amorites east of the Jordan, whom you completely destroyed. When we heard of it, our hearts melted and everyone's courage failed because of you, for the LORD your God is God in heaven above and on the earth below. Now then, please swear to me by the LORD that you will show kindness to my family, because I have shown kindness to you. Give me a sure sign that you will spare

the lives of my father and mother, my brothers and sisters, and all who belong
to them, and that you will save us from death.

Joshua 2:9–13

The spies told her to take her relatives into her house and identify it by
means of a scarlet cord placed in the window, through which she later permitted them to escape. So it was. When the walls of Jericho collapsed, the
portion containing the house of Rahab was left standing and she and her
relatives were spared. Her testimony is that the God of Israel was the true
God—of "heaven above" and of "earth below"—and that he had given them
"this land."

Hope for All

I find these stories of the women in Jesus' family tree a source of hope to
all who may have greatly sinned or, for one reason or another, may be far
from the gospel. They affirm that the door of salvation has been flung open
to Gentiles as well as Jews, to sinners as well as self-styled saints. You will not
be saved if you stand outside the door. You must enter. But you *may* enter;
that is the point. It is Jesus Christ, the Savior, who declares, "Whoever comes
to me I will never drive away" (John 6:37).

Do not say that the invitation to come is for others. It is for you, whoever
you may be. You may be a great sinner, as Bathsheba was. Bathsheba lived in
Israel at a time of great spiritual advantage. In the whole history of Israel there
was never a more glorious period than during the reign of King David. Israel
was at the peak of its development. God was honored. The worship of God
was carefully conducted. The law had been promulgated. The Psalms and
other portions of the Old Testament were being written.

Bathsheba had the knowledge that would have been prevalent at that time.
Yet when David looked her way and called her to him, she apparently went
willingly, for not a single protest is recorded in all of Scripture. Certainly
Bathsheba was a sinner. Yet salvation was for her. No doubt she, along with
David, repented of her sin and worshiped Jehovah the more.

You may not only be a great sinner, as Bathsheba was. You may also be an
ignorant sinner, as Tamar must have been. In one sense, ignorance lessens
the gravity of the sin. But in another sense, it makes the condition of the sinner even more hopeless. Tamar lived at a time when *little* was known of the
true God. There was no Bible. The only knowledge the patriarchs had of God
was what he had chosen to give them through a succession of visions, and
they did not always remember those too well. What would Judah have known
of the true God of his fathers, the God of Abraham, Isaac, and Jacob? Probably
very little. We can hardly imagine that he would have taught much even of
this very little bit to Tamar. Tamar's state was about as hopeless as a person's

state could be. Yet God brought her into the line of the Messiah and doubtless led her to a real and growing faith in him.

Ruth was an upright woman, the only one of the four. But she was a member of an outcast people. You may be poor and despised like Ruth. It is no matter. Salvation is for you as well. You can say as well as Ruth did, "Your people will be my people and your God my God."

Finally, you may be all alone, like Rahab. Charles Haddon Spurgeon, that great Baptist preacher, had a sermon on Rahab in which he took note of the difficulties that might have hindered her faith, emphasizing that she was so alone. "She received no instruction from her parents. . . . Her parents were of the condemned race of the Canaanites. They had no faith in God themselves, and could not inculcate it. She did not become a worshiper of Jehovah because the family always had been so. They had no family pew in the sanctuary, no prophet's chamber in the house, no name to keep up amongst the Lord's people. . . . Reflect again that . . . she was not in a believing country. Not only within doors had she none to sympathize with her, but in the whole city of Jericho, so far as we know, she was the only believer in Jehovah. . . . Remember, too, that . . . her means of knowledge were very slender; and, therefore, the food of her faith was comparatively scant."[4]

Rahab had so little, yet she received everything. She stood alone, yet she stood with Jehovah and therefore found, not only Jehovah but the people of Jehovah besides.

Let nothing keep you from Jesus. The devil will tell you that you are too sinful or too far off or too ignorant. Do not listen to the devil. Listen to Jesus. Believe his promise. Become even closer to him—as his spiritual sister or brother—than those who were in his family tree.

128

Favored by God and Man

Genesis 39:1–6

Now Joseph had been taken down to Egypt. Potiphar, an Egyptian who was one of Pharaoh's officials, the captain of the guard, bought him from the Ishmaelites who had taken him there.

The LORD was with Joseph and he prospered, and he lived in the house of his Egyptian master. When his master saw that the LORD was with him and that the LORD gave him success in everything he did, Joseph found favor in his eyes and became his attendant. Potiphar put him in charge of his household, and he entrusted to his care everything he owned. From the time he put him in charge of his household and of all that he owned, the LORD blessed the household of the Egyptian because of Joseph. The blessing of the LORD was on everything Potiphar had, both in the house and in the field. So he left in Joseph's care everything he had; with Joseph in charge, he did not concern himself with anything except the food he ate.

D uring the last thirty years of the nineteenth century the most popular American author was Horatio Alger (1834–1899). He wrote 109 books that have been authenticated as his, and these sold about thirty million copies by conservative estimates. Alger's young boy heroes have been compared to those of Charles Dickens (1812–1870).

But Alger was nowhere near the stature of Dickens as a writer. His characters are all alike, whereas those of Dickens are as varied and as interesting as life itself. Alger's stories have one plot; Dickens's plots are multiple and amazingly complex. Above all, Alger has none of the great themes of social awarenesses that are so commendable in the English writer. What is it, then, that made Horatio Alger's books so popular—books like *Ragged Dick, Luck and Pluck,* and *Tattered Tom*—or made characters like Richard Hunter, John Oakley, Harry Redmond, and Luke Walton virtually household names for half a century?

The answer is "the American dream." It was Alger's contention (and the sole plot of his books) that in America it is possible by sheer hard work and personal integrity to rise from whatever low position into which one may have been born to a place of influence and wealth. Alger's books are all rags-to-riches stories.

Prospered by the Lord

It is probably the rags-to-riches aspect that makes the story of Joseph so appealing. But there is an enormous difference between Joseph and the Alger heroes. The Alger heroes get ahead by pluck and hard work. Although Joseph was certainly hardworking, the chief emphasis of his story is not on hard work but rather on the fact that the Lord whom he served was prospering him.

This is the dominating theme of Genesis 39, where it is repeated seven times. In verse 2 we are told that although Joseph had been taken to Egypt and sold to Potiphar, one of Pharaoh's officials, "*the* Lord *was with Joseph* and he prospered." Verse 3 tells us that "his master saw that *the* Lord *was with him* and that *the* Lord *gave him success* in everything he did." In verse 5 we read, "From the time he [Potiphar] put him in charge of his household and of all that he owned, *the* Lord *blessed the household* of the Egyptian because of Joseph." Again, "*the blessing of the* Lord was on everything Potiphar had."

At this point the story of Potiphar's wife's temptation of Joseph intervenes, and we learn how he was falsely accused and then unjustly imprisoned. But in spite of these great wickednesses, at the end of the chapter the theme is precisely the same. Verses 20 and 21 say, "While Joseph was there in the prison, *the* Lord *was with him.*" Verse 23 declares, "The warden paid no attention to anything under Joseph's care, because *the* Lord *was with Joseph and gave him success* in whatever he did."

We can see the difference between this and the Alger stories. Joseph was successful, not because he moved from rags to riches, because in this portion of his story at least he was moving from riches to rags. He was successful because the Lord was with him in all his circumstances.

It is an aspect of God's blessing on Joseph at this time that others, especially Potiphar, were blessed for his sake. Indeed, we might argue that Joseph's blessing was chiefly their prosperity since he (for the time being at least) was not particularly prospered.

This is a theme that greatly interested Martin Luther, for he was convinced that the world's blessings are not for the world's sake but for the sake of the people of God who live in it. Luther pointed to Laban, who confessed that he had been prospered because of God's blessing on his nephew Jacob: "If I have found favor in your eyes, please stay. I have learned by divination that the LORD has blessed me because of you" (Gen. 30:27). Luther believed that Germany would have been in a "most wretched plight" were it not for the gospel, which had been recovered during the Reformation period. Luther stated, "The world cannot boast of being worthy of its physical life for even one moment, but that on account of the gospel, baptism, and the forgiveness of sins God bounteously bestows all things even on [our] most wicked and worst enemies."[1]

Luther said that the world does not acknowledge or believe this. But it is interesting that in this case at least, one unbeliever did: Potiphar. He was closest to the situation and saw that God was with Joseph and was the source of his success (v. 3). Thus, Joseph's life brought praise to Jehovah from an important officer in a pagan realm. Has your life had that effect on the ungodly? It can have the opposite effect. Paul reminded the Jews that because of them "God's name [was] blasphemed among the Gentiles" (Rom. 2:24).

Favored by Potiphar

Potiphar did not only notice that Joseph was blessed by God and therefore praise God because of him, he decided that if the Lord was favoring Joseph, then it was to his advantage also to favor Joseph. The text says, "When his master saw that the LORD was with him and that the LORD gave him success in everything he did, Joseph found favor in his eyes and became his attendant" (vv. 3–4). In my judgment this is where Joseph comes closest to being a true type of Christ, for it is said of our Lord in reference to his early years, "Jesus grew in wisdom and stature, and in favor with God and men" (Luke 2:52).

I notice that, as in the case of Jesus, this happened over a considerable period of time. The reference to Jesus states that he "*grew* in wisdom and stature, and in favor with God and man." In Genesis growth is skillfully indicated by the accumulating references to Joseph's success. The progression is something like this: (1) God prospered Joseph when he was just a menial slave; (2) Joseph moved to Potiphar's house, possibly being brought there from a different slave building when it was discovered that he did his work well; (3) Potiphar, the master, noted that God was with Joseph; (4) Potiphar promoted him to be his personal attendant and put him in charge of the entire household; (5) the estate now prospered under Joseph's hand, including matters that concerned both the house and the field; (6) Potiphar therefore withdrew from all management of his affairs and instead left everything to Joseph. How long did this process of recognition and advancement take? Well, Joseph was seventeen years old when he was sold into slavery. He was thirty years old when Pharaoh promoted him (Gen. 41:46), and he had been in prison two years before that (Gen. 41:1). Subtracting seventeen and two from thirty leaves eleven. It took eleven years for the full measure of the blessing of God upon Joseph to be recognized.

This is an important point. One area in which many Christian young people fail is to suppose that advancement flowing from the blessing of God must come quickly. I confess that this is sometimes the case. God sometimes does advance us quickly, at least as quickly as we are capable of advancing without having success go to our heads and lead us astray. But normally success takes time. We must not be unduly impatient.

That is why we must get our priorities straight. Notice that both in the case of the Lord Jesus Christ and in the case of Joseph the favor of God is obtained before human favor. Human approval and the advancement that goes with it are often good things, certainly things to be desired. But they are not good if they are obtained before God's favor or instead of it. We must strive to please God and be blessed by God above everything. At times this will produce setbacks, as it did in Joseph's case as a result of the advances of Potiphar's wife. An unsaved boss once fired his secretary because she refused to type letters saying that merchandise had been shipped when it had not been. But later he called the secretary back and gave her a job as a cashier, a post for which a person of integrity was needed.

The conclusion is that we must serve God first of all and that we must be willing to do this for a lifetime.

Hard and Faithful Service

What emerges from this is a Christian approach to success in which we, first, please God and seek his blessing and, second, do this over a long period of time. But we are not to think that our service is Godward only, still less that it is to be exerted in merely "spiritual" rather than "practical" ways. It should also be evident from these verses that, whatever Joseph did, he certainly did not neglect the interests of his master and he worked zealously to be sure that those interests were furthered. In other words, God blessed Joseph through Joseph's own hard work.

How did Joseph get to the position he later came to occupy? I can imagine that in the beginning he was at quite a disadvantage. He did not know the language of Egypt. He did not know the ways of the Egyptians. Much of the Egyptians' commerce, art, industry, and medicine would have been completely new to him. What did he do? Some slaves would have played dumb, reasoning that if they gave the appearance of not understanding or knowing how to do something, they would not be required to do it. But this could not be the way Joseph reacted. Instead of holding back, playing dumb, and doing as little as he could, Joseph plunged ahead to learn the language, master the trades, and acquire management skills. It must have taken long hours and genuine interest, but Joseph kept at it. Joseph could not have been a clock-watcher. If he were living in our time, we would have found him working extra hours and taking courses at night in order to expand his capacities.

Extra effort must have become a habit that hung on after Joseph's promotion. Luther reasoned that Joseph must have been the first to get out of bed in the morning and must have spent the early hours determining what had to be done and in making assignments specifying who was to accomplish these tasks. Joseph did not wait for the servants to do their duties of their own accord. Moreover, after their tasks were completed, Joseph must have inspected the work to make sure it had been done properly. Luther said, "Accordingly, Joseph was not only good and chaste, and not only diligently poured out prayers to God for his master, for the king, and for the whole land of Egypt, but he was also a most vigilant overseer and manager of the domestic tasks."[2]

Is this not our responsibility as well? Paul wrote to the common workers of his day: "Slaves, obey your earthly masters with respect and fear, and with sincerity of heart, just as you would obey Christ. Obey them not only to win their favor when their eye is on you, but like slaves of Christ, doing the will of God from your heart. Serve wholeheartedly, as if you were serving the Lord, not men, because you know that the Lord will reward everyone for whatever good he does, whether he is slave or free" (Eph. 6:5–8).

This prescribes duties to employees, because it tells those who work for others that they are to serve as if they are serving Christ (which, in a sense, they are) and to do everything possible to further the prosperity of their bosses or company. This is also a message to managers to trust, honor, respect, and advance those who are faithful employees. In this Potiphar was eminently wise, while many of today's (even Christian) employers are foolish.

God or Man

Favored by God and man! This was Joseph's story for the first eleven years of his life in Egypt. But attention to the whole story compels us to acknowledge that Joseph's circumstances did not continue along this line forever. Joseph pleased Potiphar. But unfortunately, he also pleased Potiphar's wife, and the plans she had for him were neither God's nor her husband's. Up to this point it had been God first, followed by favor with man. But suddenly it was God *or* man, and Joseph, like all true men of God, determined to walk with God whatever it might cost him.

This reminds us of the patriarch Enoch, whose story is told in three different passages of the Bible: Genesis 5:21–24; Hebrews 11:5; and Jude 14–15. Jude tells us that Enoch was a preacher who lived in the time before the flood and who preached against the ungodliness of his generation. "Enoch, the seventh from Adam, prophesied about these men: 'See, the Lord is coming with thousands upon thousands of his holy ones to judge everyone, and to convict all the ungodly of all the ungodly acts they have done in the ungodly way, and of all the harsh words ungodly sinners have spoken against him.'"

The passage says Enoch had a message of judgment that centered on the ungodliness of his contemporaries. The text uses the word "ungodly" four times. It was a true message, since his was a particularly wicked culture, but the message was also unpopular.

Genesis tells the secret of Enoch's success in such a dismal time, and in this it reminds us of Joseph. Genesis 5:21–24 says, "When Enoch had lived 65 years, he became the father of Methuselah. And after he became the father of Methuselah, Enoch walked with God 300 years and had other sons and daughters. Altogether, Enoch lived 365 years. Enoch walked with God; then he was no more, because God took him away."

These verses use the phrase "Enoch walked with God" twice, thereby highlighting what was obviously the chief characteristic of his long and faithful life. This was an age in which hardly anyone else was walking with God. Certainly his ungodly cousins (Irad, Mehujael, Methushael, Lamech and his sons), of whom we read in Genesis 4, were not. Like Joseph, Enoch lived in a time and place when sin was ascendant. People were undoubtedly saying, "Why should you stand apart? Why should you think you're better than other people? Come down off your high horse! Do what others do!" Enoch did not yield to that argument because, like Joseph, he was walking with God and this was the most important factor in his life. As long as he was walking with God, well—not *everyone* was sinning. As long as he was standing for righteousness, others might stand for righteousness too.

But it is for the last passage about Enoch that I review his story. We find it in Hebrews 11:5: "By faith Enoch was taken from this life, so that he did not experience death; he could not be found, because God had taken him away. For before he was taken, he was commended as one who pleased God." Enoch pleased God! So did Joseph, even when that meant displeasing those who were around him.

As long as you and I are in this world, we must serve God first and hope that in pleasing him and receiving his blessings we also please men and women and find their favor. Joseph pursued this course and obtained this result for eleven years. For most of us this is the story of a lifetime. But let us observe that there are times when it is not possible to serve or please both God and man. When that happens, we must be clear in our minds that we are to please God first of all and then actually choose for him whatever the consequences. Enoch was undoubtedly despised by his contemporaries; he was certainly ridiculed. Joseph was unjustly slandered and wrongly imprisoned; for the space of two years he was forgotten. But these men stood for God and were vindicated in due time.

We need a generation of men and women like that today. We need Christians who serve humanity as they serve Jesus, but who serve Jesus above all and listen for his commendation: "Well done, good and faithful servant! You have been faithful with a few things; I will put you in charge of many things. Come and share your master's happiness!" (Matt. 25:23).

129

When Temptation Comes

Genesis 39:6–12

Now Joseph was well-built and handsome, and after a while his master's wife took notice of Joseph and said, "Come to bed with me!"

But he refused. "With me in charge," he told her, "my master does not concern himself with anything in the house; everything he owns he has entrusted to my care. No one is greater in this house than I am. My master has withheld nothing from me except you, because you are his wife. How then could I do such a wicked thing and sin against God?" And though she spoke to Joseph day after day, he refused to go to bed with her or even be with her.

One day he went into the house to attend to his duties, and none of the household servants was inside. She caught him by his cloak and said, "Come to bed with me!" But he left his cloak in her hand and ran out of the house.

Charles Durham, a pastor from Kansas, begins his book *Temptation: Help for Struggling Christians* with an interesting illustration.

Several hundred years ago on the island of Cape Hatteras, off the shore of North Carolina, there were men whose business it was to get ships to run aground on the shoals just off the island. These men were "wreckers" who made their living gathering up the parts and cargo of such ships. With a lighted lantern fastened to the head of an old nag, a horse, these men of Nag's Head—for that was the name of their village—walked up and down and back and forth. Out at sea in the darkness of the mid-Atlantic night, ships that were searching for a passage past the islands would mistake that bobbing light for the stern light of a ship they supposed had found safe passage. They would turn inland and run aground on Diamond Shoals. In the morning the wreckers would come and gather the timber for new houses, utensils for their kitchens, and money for their purses. It was a thriving business. In fact, even now visitors to Nag's Head will be shown old houses built and furnished with the material taken from the more than twenty-three hundred ships that perished off this coast either by accident or treachery.[1]

When people first hear about the Nag's Head wreckers they are shocked and indignant. But they would be far more shocked and indignant if they would realize that we are constantly faced by even more malicious spiritual wreckers.

Traditionally the church has spoken of three types of wreckers. The first is the world, which means not the earth globe or even the people who inhabit the earth, but rather the world system, including its morality and values. It is against this spiritual wrecker that the apostle Paul warns in Romans 12:2: "Do not conform any longer to the pattern of this world, but be transformed by the renewing of your mind. Then you will be able to test and approve what God's will is—his good, pleasing and perfect will."

The second type of wrecker is the flesh. It tempts us wrongly to indulge what are otherwise right and normal appetites. We are to spurn the flesh.

The last of these three wreckers stands behind the others and uses them to his advantage. He is the devil, the great enemy of souls. The apostle Peter describes him as a "roaring lion looking for someone to devour" (1 Peter 5:8). Peter says that we are to "resist him, standing firm in the faith, because you know that your brothers throughout the world are undergoing the same kind of sufferings" (v. 9).

A Common Temptation

That last verse is particularly important when we speak of temptation, because one of the devil's techniques is to convince the unwary that the temptation they are facing is something utterly without parallel in the entire history of the race. The devil will say, "No one has ever been tempted as you are being tempted. If they had been, they would have yielded long ago. If they knew what you are going through, they would understand. No one will blame you for doing what you obviously have to do." But that is the devil speaking, not God! The Word of God brands such counsel as lies and the one who speaks them as "the liar" (cf. 1 John 2:22). Whatever temptation we are facing is also being faced by our "brothers throughout the world." Moreover, "No temptation has seized you except what is common to man. And God is faithful; he will not let you be tempted beyond what you can bear. But when you are tempted, he will also provide a way out so that you can stand up under it" (1 Cor. 10:13).

Here is where the temptation of Joseph by Potiphar's wife speaks so powerfully. For whatever else this encounter, recorded in just six verses of Genesis 39, has to teach us, it certainly teaches that temptation is common to mankind. You and I face nothing that has not been faced by others before us. Moreover, we face nothing that has not already been overcome by others—by thousands, perhaps millions, of God's people. Our calling is not to excuse our disobedience or failure. It is to conquer temptation, as Joseph did.

This incident from Joseph's life is so common that it is not too much to suggest that it has probably been played out thousands of times and in countless places this very weekend, perhaps even among people you know. Joseph had come to a position of prominence in Potiphar's house and was noticed after a while by Potiphar's wife. The woman was of a kind who is out to "get her man" regardless of whom he may be married to or of what his moral standards consist. This woman was covetous, for she took covetous notice of Joseph (v. 7). She was shameless, for she accosted him directly: "Come to bed with me!" (v. 7). She was persistent and scheming, for she repeated her invitation more than once and even arranged to have the house empty of the other servants on the final occasion (vv. 11–12).

Joseph did not succumb to this temptation. He resisted her, first by words and then afterward by actual physical flight. In this he followed the injunction Paul was later to give to those in his day, saying, "Flee from sexual immorality" (1 Cor. 6:18).

A Strong Temptation

In the next two chapters we are going to consider the secret of Joseph's success against this temptation and then what to do if we fall into sin through temptation. But before we consider Joseph's victory we need to see that it really was a strong temptation. There are several factors that made it particularly dangerous and made Joseph's victory all the more significant.

First, it was a *natural* temptation in the sense that it appealed to a right and normal appetite. There is a valuable distinction at this point between temptations that are natural in the sense of appealing to a proper appetite and those that are unnatural. A temptation to murder is not natural. True, it is a natural outcome of the hostility to and hatred of others that lie not far below the surface of every human heart, but hostility and hatred are not in themselves either proper or natural. They are perversions through sin of what we were meant to be. Stealing is also unnatural in this sense, though it comes to sinful persons naturally. So is the giving of false testimony and the failure to love the Lord our God with all our hearts, minds, souls, and strength. But as I say, a temptation to sexual sin (as was the case here) is natural in the sense that it appeals to a right, proper, and even God-given appetite or desire. But notice: even though it was natural, it was not right in this case. To have yielded would have been sin; Joseph was right to turn from it.

A decade or more ago, when the so-called playboy philosophy was a new thing, a debate took place in Lubbock, Texas, between William S. Banowsky, then minister of the Broadway Church of Christ, and Anson Mount, one of the founding editors and then public affairs manager for *Playboy*. From *Playboy*'s side it was an attempt to gain publicity and diffuse religious opposition. But in the course of the debate Mount revealed some interesting things about the playboy philosophy. He said that man is capable of evil but is basically good. He said that human pleasure is good by definition. He said that human welfare and happiness are the greatest good. Most of all, his points were that sex is natural, what is natural is good, and therefore it is good to have sex under almost all conditions. Mount was against "legalism," "Puritanism," and objective moral standards.[2]

All this was probably being said to Joseph by Mrs. Potiphar. But if Potiphar's wife did not say it, Joseph could certainly have thought it out for himself. "Joseph, you are now twenty-seven years old. You are not a child anymore, and you certainly have a man's rather than a child's appetites. You have been a slave for ten years. You're unmarried; you are lonely. Don't you have a right to a sexual relationship? This is your chance, your opportunity. Maybe God is even putting it in your way. Certainly it can't be wrong if it feels good. There is nothing more natural than that you should have a relationship with this attractive and infatuated woman."

The problem with these arguments is that they are setting one good thing against another, as the devil tried to do when he tempted Jesus. They set a natural instinct against purity and the revealed will of God. Sex is natural, but it is not to be indulged in under all circumstances or with all partners. It is a gift to be enjoyed within marriage, where it becomes a cement to bind the marriage together and permit two people to grow in the fullest measure of commitment to each other.

Second, the temptation that Joseph faced was a strong temptation because it came to him *when he was away from home*. One commentator writes, "A good home acts as a restraining influence on the behavior of its children. But once they are away from home, emancipation may lead them to throw caution to the wind and succumb easily to the sinful charms of a wicked culture, especially if the person's piety is merely conventional. The veneer of civilization is so thin that voyagers just ten miles out to sea often throw off moral restraint to indulge their immoral appetites."[3]

Why is it that professing Christian young people go away to college and there fall into living with a boyfriend or girlfriend, which they would never have done while at home? Why will a man on a business trip do what he would probably resist doing in his hometown? Why will Christians compromise their speech and actions at parties in a way that they would not in everyday circumstances? The reason is the individual's low view of God. They may profess to believe in God and may actually think of themselves as good (or at least normal) Christians. But what they really have is a tribal view of God. They think of God as the god of their local (but distant) family or hometown or workaday world, and not the one, universal God of all times and places. Let me put it clearly. God is as much at the office party as he is in your workroom. He is as present in your college town as your hometown. He is as present in a brothel as in church. God is omnipresent, present everywhere.

Joseph had such a God, and it is that truth above all else that saved him in the evil day. He was not concerned with the so-called gods of Egypt. He served Jehovah! So he replied to Mrs. Potiphar, "How then could I do such a wicked thing and sin against God?" (v. 9).

The third factor that made this temptation so strong for Joseph is that it came from *an important woman*. She was a godless woman, of course, and wicked. Had she succeeded in seducing Joseph, it probably would have been neither the first nor the last of her extramarital affairs. But though godless and wicked, Mrs. Potiphar was nevertheless important as the world counts importance, and Joseph could not have failed to see that she would be as valuable an ally, if accepted, as she would be an enemy to be feared if he refused her.

F. B. Meyer puts it like this: "It seemed essential to Joseph to stand well with his master's wife. To please her would secure his advancement. To cross her would make her his foe and ruin his hopes. How many would have reasoned that, by yielding only a moment, they might win influence which they could afterwards use for the very best results! One act of homage to the devil would invest them with power which they might then use for his overthrow. This is the reasoning of policy, one of the most accursed traitors in man's heart. It is this policy which leads many to say, when tempted to do wrong by master, or mistress, or foreman, or chief customer, 'I did not care for it, or wish it. I yielded because my bread depended on it; I did not dare offend them.'"

Meyer concludes, "The only armor against policy is FAITH that looks to the long future, and believes that in the end it will be found better to have done right and to have waited for the vindication and blessing of God. Well was it for Joseph that he did not heed the suggestions of policy: had he done so, he might have acquired a little more influence in the home of Potiphar; but it could never have lasted—and he would never have become prime minister of Egypt, or had a home of his own, or have brought his boys to receive the blessing of his dying father."[4]

Fourth, Joseph encountered the temptation *after an important promotion*. It was not when Joseph was struggling to reach the top, moving by degrees from his position as a new and menial slave to becoming Potiphar's personal attendant and business manager. It was afterward, when he might have told himself, "Joseph, you have reached the top now. All your hard work has paid off. Now is the time to relax and enjoy the fruits of the position you have won." Indeed, he might have said that the interest of his master's wife was natural and now rightly his because of his achievement.

Beware of temptation when you think you have arrived! Temptation came to David when he was in his fifties, after he had unified the kingdom, expanded his borders, and brought peace to many of the regions around. And when was our Lord tempted? It was immediately after he had received John's baptism and had heard the voice from heaven saying, "This is my Son, whom I love; with him I am well pleased" (Matt. 3:17). Indeed, the devil even used that divine testimony in his temptation, for he began by casting doubt upon the very words the Lord had just heard: "*If you are the Son of God,* tell these stones to become bread" (Matt. 4:3, my emphasis).

Beware of temptation when you have achieved a victory!

Beware when you have just led someone to the Lord!

Beware when you have completed some difficult assignment and are now taking some needed and well-deserved rest. Paul did not consider himself to have finished his spiritual warfare until he was on the verge of martyrdom: "I have fought the good fight, I have finished the race, I have kept the faith. Now there is in store for me the crown of righteousness, which the Lord, the righteous Judge, will award to me on that day—and not only to me, but also to all who have longed for his appearing" (2 Tim. 4:7–8).

Fifth, the temptation was strong because it came to Joseph *repeatedly*. This is one of the devil's chief strategies—to come again and again, as he did to Jesus. He knows that we are weak. If we are Christians, we have some knowledge of what is right and what is wrong. Moreover, we have the presence of the Holy Spirit within to warn us of Satan's advance and turn us from evil. When temptation comes we often react quite properly, saying, "This is a violation of the standards of the Word of God. I cannot do that and be a Christian." But then the devil comes back, using one argument after another, and eventually he wears us down. This is what Potiphar's wife was trying to do in Joseph's case. She constantly sought him out, asked him to spend time with her, and then propositioned him. Alexander Pope stated it well when he wrote:

> Vice is a monster of so frightful mien
> As to be hated needs but to be seen;
> Yet seen too oft, familiar with her face,
> We first endure, then pity, then embrace.

The final factor that made this temptation strong for Joseph was that it seized *the perfect opportunity*. The text says that it came on a day when he was about his duties in the house. Only he was there—he and Mrs. Potiphar. "None of the household servants was inside. She caught him by his cloak and said, 'Come to bed with me!' But he left his cloak in her hand and ran out of the house" (vv. 11–12). Many have fallen into sin because it came to them when no one seemed to be around, and the circumstances, as we say, "were right": "No one will know," the sinner has told himself. "I have been in the will of God for a long time; here is a point where I can step out briefly, then step back in. No one will know anything about it but myself."

No one? No one but the person with whom you sin—who may often speak of it. And God, who will not hold blameless those who sin against him!

All or Nothing

In the next chapter we will look at the ways in which Joseph resisted Potiphar's wife. But to those who are facing this or any other temptation, let me say: Do not wait until the next chapter to deal with it. Deal with it now.

What should you do? Joseph did a number of things, but in the final analysis—several other approaches to the woman having failed—Joseph did what should always be done anyway in the face of temptation to fleshly sin: he fled from it. He left his cloak behind and ran from the home. There was no easy way, you see. He had tried to reason with the woman, to no avail. He had tried to avoid her; that had failed. Here was a situation where it was all or nothing, and Joseph gave it all, thereby choosing the path that led to prison rather than the path that led to sin. I love the King James language at this point. The King James Version says at verse 12, "He left the garment in her hand, and fled, and got him out." Nobody else was going to *get him out*. If he was to remain pure, he was going to have to get out of there himself. And he did! That is why we still read his story and admire him, while so many others, who have had equal opportunities but have gone the way of the world, have been forgotten.

If you are in Joseph's situation, do as he did, regardless of the cost. Flee fornication, choose God, and stand for righteousness.

130

Sin against Man, Sin against God

Genesis 39:6–12

Now Joseph was well-built and handsome, and after a while his master's wife took notice of Joseph and said, "Come to bed with me!"

But he refused. "With me in charge," he told her, "my master does not concern himself with anything in the house; everything he owns he has entrusted to my care. No one is greater in this house than I am. My master has withheld nothing from me except you, because you are his wife. How then could I do such a wicked thing and sin against God?" And though she spoke to Joseph day after day, he refused to go to bed with her or even be with her.

One day he went into the house to attend to his duties, and none of the household servants was inside. She caught him by his cloak and said, "Come to bed with me!" But he left his cloak in her hand and ran out of the house.

Apart from the Bible, an important authority for one small area of my life is the late James Fixx, the author of popular books on running. His most widely circulated book is *The Complete Book of Running*, in which he has a section describing some of the mental quirks that happen in a race. He writes, "When we race, strange things happen

919

to our minds. The stress of fatigue sometimes makes us forget why we wanted to race in the first place. In one of my early marathons I found myself unable to think of a single reason for continuing. Physically and mentally exhausted, I dropped out of the race. Now I won't enter a marathon unless I truly want to finish it. If during the race I can't remember why I wanted to run in it, I tell myself, 'Maybe I can't remember now, but I know I had a good reason when I started.' I've finally learned how to fight back when my brain starts using tricky arguments."[1]

This was not the exact situation with Joseph, of course; he remembered his reasons for wanting to serve God even in the temptation. But it is the case with many. We need to have our reasons in mind before temptation comes, so that if we find ourselves unable to remember our reasons later, we will at least remember that we have reasons for obeying God and live in response to them rather than surrender to our passions.

"A Rose by Any Other Name . . ."

The first thing Joseph had clearly in his mind is that sin truly is sin. He called it wickedness: "How then could I do such a wicked thing and sin against God?" (Gen. 39:9).

This is an important starting point, because one of the devil's tricks in his campaign to promote sin and limit godliness is to call sin something other than what it is and thus make it sound less objectionable and perhaps even desirable. This is true of almost any sin. Unjustified hostility and temper are called "self-expression" or "letting it all hang out." Because it is "good" to express yourself, letting it all hang out becomes a justification for every type of ill-mannered, inconsiderate, and openly destructive behavior. Pride is reinterpreted as "self-esteem." Gluttony is called "the good life." Coveting is trying to "improve yourself" or "get ahead." The worst of these efforts is to rename sin in the matter of sexual relationships. Perversions, which are condemned so directly and fiercely in the Bible, are called "an alternative lifestyle." Fornication is "experimentation." Adultery is "an attempt to cure a lackluster marriage."

The problem with these attempts to justify sin by renaming it is that they conflict with reality. By that I mean, call it what you will, sin is still sin and it will operate destructively as sin regardless of your nomenclature.

The national press has reported an example of this in the case of Margaret Mead, the renowned anthropologist, whose work *Coming of Age in Samoa* was used to justify and promote much of the so-called sexual revolution of recent decades. Mead arrived in Samoa in 1925 as a twenty-three-year-old Columbia University graduate student. She spent two and a half months learning the language. Then she made a study of the lifestyle and behavior of Samoan adolescent females. She worked with sixty-eight girls, but most of her data was collected from the twenty-five who made regular trips to her rustic office to tell stories of their apparently innocent sexual escapades under the blue skies and palm trees. Mead was convinced that the terrible teenage years were not a problem in Samoa, and she credited this to the island's supposed sexual permissiveness. "Free love promotes nonviolence" was her conclusion.

This was what many people back in the United States wanted to hear, of course, and as a result her book was soon hailed as a classic. Mead's conclusions were frequently cited by such prominent scholars as Bertrand Russell and Havelock Ellis. The book became the greatest-selling anthropology book in history.

Now all this has been challenged. Derek Freeman, an Australian anthropologist writing for Harvard University Press *(Margaret Mead and Samoa: The Making and Unmaking of an Anthropological Myth)*, has charged: (1) sex out of wedlock was illegal at the time of Mead's research, not accepted, as Mead claimed; (2) Samoan society has always been intensely competitive, not relaxed and easygoing, as she stated; and (3) psychological disturbances like hysteria and compulsive behavior are commonplace, giving rise to high rates of assault, homicide, and rape, which Mead denied. Some anthropologists suggest that Samoan culture could have changed in the fifty years between Mead's visit and Freeman's research. But Freeman replied that accounts of rape were reported regularly in a Samoan newspaper in Mead's vicinity during her stay.

How did this renowned anthropologist come to such erroneous conclusions? Freeman suggests that the girls Mead interviewed may have fooled her by making up stories of love in the afternoon, perhaps indulging their own sexual fantasies. He claims that the Samoans are fond of such inventions because they serve as "a respite from the severities of their authoritarian society." Mostly Freeman accuses Mead of having reached her conclusions before she did her research and of using false or doctored evidence to support them.

Another writer, George Leonard, used his position as senior editor of *Look* magazine to promote the sexual revolution during the 1960s. In 1970 he wrote, "A society that considers most good feelings immoral and bad feelings moral perpetuates the ultimate human heresy: an insult, if you will, to God and his works." But today Leonard has changed his tune. In a 1983 publication, *The End of Sex*, he argues that the sexual revolution has not done what its proponents claimed it was doing. It has not enhanced sex; instead, it has only cheapened love. He speaks like a writer of one of the biblical books when he says, "I have learned that there are no games without rules."[2]

This is what Joseph knew and what all truly godly people sort out in their minds before temptation comes to them. Sin is not just "an alternative lifestyle," "innocent experimentation," or "merely letting it all hang out." Sin is wickedness, and it remains so regardless of what we rename it.

Wrong against Others

The second thing Joseph had straight before temptation came to him is that sin generally (if not always) hurts others. Indeed, this was the part of his argument that he developed at greatest length in replying to Mrs. Potiphar. Joseph said, "With me in charge . . . my master does not concern himself with anything in the house; everything he owns he has entrusted to my care. No one is greater in this house than I am. My master has withheld nothing from me except you, because you are his wife. How then could I do such a wicked thing and sin against God?" (vv. 8–9).

In these verses Joseph acknowledges three things: (1) he had arrived where he was because of Potiphar and therefore had a moral debt to Potiphar to honor his trust; (2) Potiphar had not given his wife to Joseph even though he had given him authority over everything else in the house; (3) Mrs. Potiphar was her husband's wife, which placed moral obligations on her as well as on Joseph. To sin with her would mean harming her as well as harming Potiphar.

How strongly people resist acknowledging sin's harm! Luis Palau, the well-known Latin American evangelist to whom God has given an effective ministry on three continents (South America, North America, and Europe), bemoans the American tendency to regard sin as "just a little thing" and ignore its effects. He says, "If you think it is 'just a little thing,' come to Latin America and see what we are going through down here. Most of the countries are miserably poor. In some countries seventy percent of the population is illegitimate. There is a terrible nothingness in the structure of society in that part of the world because of sexual immorality."[3]

I see the same thing in the United States. I see the results of promiscuity: venereal disease (syphilis, gonorrhea, herpes) that has now reached epidemic proportions, AIDS (Acquired Immunodeficiency Syndrome) that has decimated and terrified the homosexual community, illegitimate birth, and abortions (now one and a half million annually). But I also see less obvious things: broken homes, frustrated males and females groping after lasting relationships, and a generation of confused, wandering, and wounded children. Above all I see it in the children. We are destroying our children. Are we to think that God will hold us guiltless for what we are doing to these innocents?

"I only wanted to be happy," someone will say. What do you think God will reply to that? Do you think your personal happiness is an excuse for the harm you are inflicting on others?

"I couldn't help it," says another. Indeed!

"Don't worry about the children; they can take care of themselves," says a third. Jesus said, "If anyone causes one of these little ones who believe in me to sin, it would be better for him to have a large millstone hung around his neck and to be drowned in the depths of the sea. Woe to the world because of the things that cause people to sin! Such things must come, but woe to the man through whom they come!" (Matt. 18:6–7).

When you look at a charred mountainside covered with the burned waste of trees that once beautified the location and provided homes and coverings

for animals, you abhor a careless attitude toward fire. So also should the
charred waste of human lives cause us to hate and turn from sin.

Offense against God

In addition to seeing sin as sin and as something that is always harmful to
other human beings, Joseph saw that sin is an offense against God. Like David
later on—who prayed after his sin with Bathsheba, "Against you, you only,
have I sinned and done what is evil in your sight" (Ps. 51:4)—Joseph recognized that, however great an offense his sin might be to other people, it was
far more offensive to God. This is the point of emphasis in his reply to Mrs.
Potiphar. It is the key verse, the last thing he mentions: "How then could I
do such a wicked thing and sin against God?" (v. 9).

This verse needs to be taken in each of its parts, and each part needs to
be assimilated into our own thought and practice. The first important word
is "I." How could *I*—*I* who have known the true God and have been the ben-
eficiary of his grace, *I* who have been taught the difference between right
and wrong, *I* who have been redeemed from sin by the precious blood of
Jesus Christ—how could *I* do such a wicked thing and sin against God? If
that *I* does not come home to you with great force—reminding you that you
have been bought with a price and that you are therefore now not your own
but rather a new creature in Christ, whose calling and duty now is to live for
and serve him—if that, as I say, does not come home to you with great force,
what right do you have even to think you are a Christian? In what respect
are you any different from the sinful, devil-serving world that surrounds you?

There is also the word "do." How could I *do* such a thing? As long as the
temptation to sin is merely in the mind and the sin itself is not performed,
there is room for victory. Indeed, there is room for perfect victory, for the
temptation itself is not sin. But what if I *do* sin? Ah, then the battle is lost,
and I have denied my profession of faith as well as denying Christ. I must
not do it. How could I, who know Christ, *do* such a wicked thing against God?

Again, it is a "wicked thing" that I am being tempted to do. This brings
me back to the first point of this chapter, which is recognizing that sin is sin
and that it is terrible. I ask, "Have you no proper sense of pride, you who are
a child of the King?" There is an expression in French, *"noblesse oblige."* It
means, "Good breeding imposes obligations." That is true humanly speaking,
but how much truer it is spiritually. If we are Christ's, we must live righteous
lives. The apostle John says, "If we claim to have fellowship with him yet walk
in the darkness, we lie and do not live by the truth. But if we walk in the light,
as he is in the light, we have fellowship with one another, and the blood of
Jesus, his Son, purifies us from all sin" (1 John 1:6–7).

The last word in this classic protest against wickedness is "God." How could
I sin against *God*? Yes, that is the bottom line. Offending other human beings
is bad, but I might excuse myself. "They deserved it," I might say. But God?

God, the Righteous One? God, who is altogether good and loving? God, the Just? I cannot offend against God by acting wickedly.

A Practical Discipline

The concluding point in this analysis is that, having settled these matters in his mind before the temptation ever came to him, Joseph did not hesitate to put them into practice. He did this in three ways.

First, he let his position be known. That is, he spoke about it. We have already seen that Joseph must have spoken of his faith to Potiphar, for Potiphar perceived that "the LORD [Jehovah] was with him [Joseph] and . . . gave him success in everything he did" (Gen. 39:3), and he could not have known that unless Joseph had told him about his father's God. Now Joseph also spoke of his faith to Mrs. Potiphar, confessing that the greatest hindrance to his sinning was the character of the God he worshiped. Do you talk about your faith openly? Talking about God and your relationship to him will not keep you from sinning in itself, but it will make it harder for you to do so. In fact, it may keep you out of the place of temptation, for those who want to sin will not want you around to spoil sin for them.

Second, Joseph kept busy. That is, he did not merely talk about righteousness and against sin; he also practiced righteousness and avoided sinning. One commentator writes: "Work can keep us from mischief. A seminary professor said that God calls some men to the ministry in order to keep them out of jail. A Turkish proverb points out, 'Men are usually tempted by the devil, but the idle man positively tempts the devil.' If the devil finds a man idle, he'll try to give him some work to do."[4] A friend of mine who works with the inner-city street people of Los Angeles provides his converts with this formula for succeeding with the Lord: (1) pray and read your Bible daily; (2) go to church and meet with other Christian people more than two times each week; and (3) ask your pastor for a job and get busy for God. It is hard to say which of those three points is more important in a given case.

Finally, Joseph put his principles into practice by running from sin when that became necessary. If he had not had his principles straight before Mrs. Potiphar accosted him, he might have paused to try to think through the matter, and his delay would have been fatal. But he had already thought through them and had decided that he would have to avoid this woman at all costs. Would that all God's people were so set against sin! What misery would be avoided! What victories for righteousness would be won!

131

What If I Do Sin?

Genesis 39:6–12

Now Joseph was well-built and handsome, and after a while his master's wife took notice of Joseph and said, "Come to bed with me!"

But he refused. "With me in charge," he told her, "my master does not concern himself with anything in the house; everything he owns he has entrusted to my care. No one is greater in this house than I am. My master has withheld nothing from me except you, because you are his wife. How then could I do such a wicked thing and sin against God?" And though she spoke to Joseph day after day, he refused to go to bed with her or even be with her.

One day he went into the house to attend to his duties, and none of the household servants was inside. She caught him by his cloak and said, "Come to bed with me!" But he left his cloak in her hand and ran out of the house.

In the last two chapters we looked at the temptation that came to Joseph in the matter of Potiphar's wife and the secret of Joseph's life that kept him from sin. Considered as history, his is a great and uplifting victory. It is recorded in the annals of heaven as well as in the pages of the Word of God.

But we do not read the story of Joseph's triumph only as past history. We also read it as the story of a Christian man in an ungodly environment, much

925

like ourselves, and we inevitably compare ourselves to him. In some situations that comparison is favorable. We too have been victorious over temptation by the power of God. Unfortunately, in other situations that comparison is unfavorable, and we are filled with shame as we recollect our past failures. It may be worse than that. We may be bogged down in this or some other great failure, and we may think that Joseph's story therefore has no bearing on us. He stood in the time of temptation. We have fallen. We are therefore tempted to give up in our efforts to live a pure life and instead sin more, as if what we do from this time on does not matter.

To deal with this problem I want to interject a study of Psalm 51 at this point. It is a digression as far as subject matter is concerned; but since it deals with a similar situation in the life of King David, it is not really a digression in the flow of our thought. It tells us what to do if we do *not* stand like Joseph, if we do sin.

Confession of Sin

The Fifty-first Psalm is introduced as "A psalm of David. When the prophet Nathan came to him after David had committed adultery with Bathsheba." Therefore it is a psalm arising out of the blackest period of David's life. Joseph had run from sin when Potiphar's wife had propositioned and later tried to trap him. But David did not run. Quite the contrary! When he saw Bathsheba bathing on the roof of her home in Jerusalem, he sent to find out who she was. And then, when he had been told that she was the wife of Uriah the Hittite, instead of letting the matter drop immediately he invited Bathsheba over to the palace and committed adultery with her. After that, when he was told that she was pregnant, he arranged to have her husband killed in battle so he could marry her.

It was nearly a year after this that the prophet Nathan came to David with a story designed to expose the king's guilt. This produced a remarkable repentance on the part of David. Psalm 51 is the result. In it David confesses his sin and shows through the development of the psalm how confession leads to full restoration on the part of the truly repentant soul. The psalm has four parts: (1) confession of sin, (2) cleansing by faith in an atoning sacrifice, (3) creation of a new spirit within, and (4) witnessing to what God has done.

The first section of this psalm, in which David confesses his sin, has two parts: first, the basis upon which the confession is made, namely the mercy of God; and second, the confession itself. The first part deals with God's mercy and is a preface or preamble to the psalm. It refers to the mercy of God three times:

> Have *mercy* on me, O God,
>   according to your *unfailing love;*
> according to your *great compassion.*

verse 1

On this basis David prays, "Blot out my transgressions. Wash away all my iniquity and cleanse me from my sin" (vv. 1–2).

Now and then as I speak to people who do not know the Lord, I get a reaction from them that is something like this: "Don't speak to me of God's mercy. I don't want mercy from God. All I want is justice. I just want God to be fair to me and give me what I deserve." I suppose a person has a right to think that way. But what a person who says that generally does not realize is that the justice of God will never vindicate the sinner, but will only condemn him. The Bible says, "There is no one righteous, not even one; there is no one who understands, no one who seeks God. All have turned away, they have together become worthless; there is no one who does good, not even one" (Rom. 3:10–12). It says, "The wages of sin is death" (Rom. 6:23). The one who wants justice from God will receive that: a just judgment that will send him or her to hell. It is not justice that we want from God; it is mercy.

David does not come to God on the basis of God's justice. He does not even come on the basis of something he can do to earn God's favor. He bases his approach solely on what he knows to be the character of God. What is God's character? It is "mercy," "unfailing love," and "compassion." This is the God who comes when we are lost in sin, giving his Son for us and opening our blind eyes by the Holy Spirit so we might believe on Jesus and be saved.

Moreover, the reason God has revealed himself to us in this way, assuring us of his mercy, is that we might be kept from sinning. What son is it that will best obey his parents and do what is right? A son to whom the father says, "I see that you're going out into the street to play with the boys, and I know you may get into trouble. Well, I want you to know that if I ever find out about it, I'll thrash you good!"

Will it be that child, or the child whose father says to him, "Now look, we live in a big city, and in the city there are many temptations. There is even a street gang in our neighborhood, and you may be tempted to form your allegiance with the gang and not with your family. When you do something wrong or when you get into trouble, you'll be tempted to run to them. Never forget that your home is where you belong. Gangs will come and go, but you'll always be a member of this family. So no matter what you do, whether you break a window or steal something or get into trouble with the police, whatever it may be, I want you to come home to me and tell me first, because I'm on your side, and we'll make whatever restitution needs to be made and face the consequences together. You belong to this family, and I love you."

Which son is going to lead the most exemplary life? Obviously the second one. Parents who will raise their children in this way will receive fruit in their lives that a person who threatens them will never see. This is how God deals with us. The God who is all righteousness, before whom no impure person can stand, is also the God of mercy, who comes to us in Christ and assures us of forgiveness for our sins even before we do them.

Charles Spurgeon has a good comment on this portion of the psalm. "While I regarded God as a tyrant, I thought sin a trifle; but when I knew him to be my father, then I mourned that I could ever have kicked against him. When I thought that God was hard, I found it easy to sin; but when I found God so kind, so good, so overflowing with compassion, I smote upon my breast to think that I could ever have rebelled against one who loved me so, and sought my good."[1]

Having reminded himself of the mercy of God, David proceeds to an honest and forthright confession of his sin. Already, even in speaking of God's mercy, he has spoken of his "sin," "iniquity," and "transgressions" (vv. 1–2). Now he elaborates further.

> For I know my transgressions,
>   and my sin is always before me.
> Against you, you only, have I sinned
>   and done what is evil in your sight,
> so that you are proved right when you speak
>   and justified when you judge.
> Surely I was sinful at birth,
>   sinful from the time my mother conceived me.
>
> verses 3–5

It should be unnecessary to stress that sin should be confessed. But it must be stressed simply because confession comes so hard to human nature. It is even hard to confess wrongdoing to another human being. Look into your own life and examine how hard it is for you to tell another person, "I am sorry I have done such and such." How many times have you done that in the last week? How many times in the last year? And when you have asked yourself that question, continue the examination by demanding: "How many times *should* I have asked forgiveness during the last week? How many times *should* I have asked forgiveness during the last year?" You will find that one of the hardest things you have ever faced has been saying "I am sorry" to another person. But if it is hard to say that to another human being, who also sins as we do, how much more difficult is it genuinely to confess sins to God! Yet we must. There is no substitute for an honest, forthright, total confession of sin. There is no cleansing without it. We must learn to say with David, "I know [acknowledge] my transgressions, and my sin is always before me."

We are often like Adam. He sinned along with his wife in eating of the fruit of the tree of the knowledge of good and evil. But when God came to him in the garden demanding, "Have you eaten from the tree that I commanded you not to eat from?" (Gen. 3:11), Adam did not confess his transgression. Instead he began to shift the blame to other people and eventually to God himself. He said, "The woman you put here with me—she gave me some fruit from the tree, and I ate it" (v. 12).

It was the same with Cain. Cain killed his brother. But when God came demanding, "Where is your brother Abel?" Cain answered, "I don't know. Am I my brother's keeper?" (Gen. 4:9).

And what about Abraham? Abraham lied about his wife, Sarah, saying she was his sister, because he feared that the men of the Negev would kill him for her. When he was found out he excused himself, saying that it was not an outright lie: "Besides, she really is my sister, the daughter of my father though not of my mother; and she became my wife" (Gen. 20:12).

This is not how David prayed. David acknowledged his sin, laying it out and confessing it utterly. This is the significance of verse 4: "Against you, you only, have I sinned." Many commentators have pointed out that this was not strictly true. David had sinned against Bathsheba and against Uriah, her husband. He sinned against the armies of Israel, who lost their battles during the time of David's sin. He sinned against the nation. But in the sight of the perfection and majesty of God, David knew that these wrongs fell into relative insignificance. The greatest of all problems with sin is that it is an offense against God. It would make a vast difference in many lives if people could only see this. David did see it. Therefore, he did not try to cover sin up, but confessed it, saying, "Against you, you only, have I sinned."

Another aspect of David's confession is his acknowledgment that it is not only that he sinned once, but that his whole nature was permeated with sin: "Surely I was sinful at birth, sinful from the time my mother conceived me" (v. 5). This verse says nothing about sex being wrong. This is the way it has been interpreted in some sectors of the Roman Catholic Church as the result of an asceticism that became a goal of Catholic piety during the early and late Middle Ages. But this is not what David is talking about. He is saying that there was never a moment in his life when he was free from sin and no part of his being escaped sin's contamination. It is the same with us. By ourselves we have never done anything to please God; everything we have done is contaminated by sin. But God can cleanse us. He can begin a work that will enable us to live victoriously.

Cleansing

The second part of David's psalm of repentance deals with cleansing from sin through faith in an atoning sacrifice. But this idea is hidden from many by the imagery with which David prays.

> Cleanse me with hyssop, and I will be clean;
> wash me, and I will be whiter than snow.

verse 7

Why does David use this imagery? Why does he pray that he might be cleansed "with hyssop"? Well, hyssop was a little plant that grew throughout the ancient Near East and was used in the sacrifices of the temple. The hyssop plant was broken off at the stem and was then bound to a short stick with a scarlet cord, making a brush. The first biblical use of this implement was on the occasion of the first Jewish Passover, when the people of Israel were about to leave Egypt for their own land. The instructions for the observance of the Passover said:

> Select the animals for your families and slaughter the Passover lamb. Take a bunch of hyssop, dip it into the blood in the basin and put some of the blood on the top and on both sides of the doorframe. Not one of you shall go out the door of his house until morning. When the LORD goes through the land to strike down the Egyptians, he will see the blood on the top and sides of the doorframe and will pass over that doorway, and he will not permit the destroyer to enter your houses and strike you down.
>
> Exodus 12:21–23

Later the same kind of brush was used to sprinkle those who offered sacrifices at the temple, to sprinkle lepers when they had been cleansed, and to carry out other rites of purification.

When David prayed, "Cleanse me with hyssop," he had this in mind. Therefore he was not merely confessing his need of forgiveness. He was also acknowledging that the only means of his cleansing was the shed blood of an innocent sacrifice offered in his place. In this he looked forward to Jesus, the perfect and sufficient sacrifice, whose blood washes away the people's sin.

It is on this same basis that the author of 1 John tells us, "If we claim to be without sin, we deceive ourselves and the truth is not in us. If we confess our sins, he is faithful and just and will forgive us our sins and purify us from all unrighteousness" (1 John 1:8–9).

A New Creation

Having confessed his sin and been cleansed from it, David prays that God will renew him supernaturally. He says:

> Create in me a pure heart, O God,
>   and renew a steadfast spirit within me.
> Do not cast me from your presence
>   or take your Holy Spirit from me.
> Restore to me the joy of your salvation
>   and grant me a willing spirit, to sustain me.
>
> verses 10–12

The word "create" in this verse is the powerful Hebrew verb *bara'*, used in the first verse of Genesis for God's creation of the world out of nothing and in verse 27 of that same chapter for the creation of Adam in God's image. It is an action that only God can take. Consequently, when David prays, "Create in me a pure heart," he is actually saying, "Create a pure heart *out of nothing*." It is not a matter of God merely reforming David, for there is nothing in him out of which a genuinely pure heart could be formed. He is all sin: "Surely I was sinful at birth, sinful from the time my mother conceived me." Where there was nothing but filth before, David wanted God now to make a pure heart. Where there was nothing but a depraved and rebellious mind, David wanted God to create a willing spirit.

That is what we all need. It is an important part of dealing with sin that we confess it and experience the cleansing of God on the basis of Christ's atoning sacrifice. But in addition to this we need to be remade if we are to keep from sin and live to God. A great problem with many Christians is that they seem to be satisfied continuing to live as they always have, even at times much as they lived before they became believers. What we need is the creation of a new heart and its constant renewal.

Communicating God's Praise

There is one more point to this psalm, and it concerns the result of the work that is done in us when we come to God for cleansing and renewal. The result is praise to God. It comes through the breaking of our spirit. This is what David says:

> The sacrifices of God are a broken spirit;
> a broken and contrite heart,
> O God, you will not despise.
>
> verse 17

It is due to this inward humbling or breaking of what was before a haughty spirit that David could now perceive a future period of usefulness in spite of his sin: "Then I will teach transgressors your ways, and sinners will turn back to you" (v. 13). As long as we think our lives are pretty good apart from God and we are doing pretty well at living up to some set of moral standards, no great victory is given to God. But when we know we are sinners and we have been rescued from sin and renewed in spirit solely by the mercy of God, then glory goes to him and we are happy to be witnesses.

Too often we bring our lives to God as if they were tumblers partially filled with dirty water. We think the water is clean, and we are proud of the fact that the glasses are almost full. God needs to dump the dirty water out and fill us with his purity.

Just before Christ's crucifixion, a woman came to him with an alabaster box of ointment. We are told that when she had broken it, the ointment flowed out and the whole house was filled with the odor. If our spirits are really broken, as God wants them to be, there will arise from us an odor so sweet that it will fill whatever place we go to and will bring praise to God, whom we serve and worship.

On earth our praise will be only the tuning of the orchestra. At our best there will be discordant sounds. But to those who can hear them, the sounds of the instruments will be an anticipation of the symphony. And the day will come when the former adulterer, the former drunkard, the former hypocrite, the former materialist will meet in God's presence and have nothing but praise for him who called them out of darkness into his marvelous light.

132

It's a Bad, Bad World

Genesis 39:13–20

When she saw that he had left his cloak in her hand and had run out of the house, she called her household servants. "Look," she said to them, "this Hebrew has been brought to us to make sport of us! He came in here to sleep with me, but I screamed. When he heard me scream for help, he left his cloak beside me and ran out of the house."

When his master heard the story his wife told him, saying, "This is how your slave treated me," he burned with anger. Joseph's master took him and put him in prison, the place where the king's prisoners were confined.

Genesis 39:13–15, 19–20

O n the north shore of Lake Geneva in Switzerland, not far from the delightful tourist town of Montreux, stands the Castle of Chillon. It is a fine example of a medieval Swiss fortress, and it is often visited by tourists because they cannot fail to see it as they pass close by along the lakeshore. The fame of Chillon, however, does not derive from its romantic island setting, reached only by a drawbridge, nor from its double battlements facing the land, nor its rustic but magnificent public halls or armory. It is known chiefly because of a poem written about it by the colorful romanticist Lord Byron. The poem is called "The Prisoner of Chillon."

933

The real prisoner of Chillon was probably not as tragic a figure as Byron made him out to be, but he was a real person. His name was François Bonivard (1493–1570), and he was imprisoned during the Protestant Reformation. Today visitors can descend to the dungeon where Bonivard was kept from 1532 to 1536. It is below ground and only slightly above the water level of the lake, which laps against the outside wall. To this day the dungeon has a chilling atmosphere and is a dreadful place. To reach it the tourist makes his way from an inner courtyard down to an antechamber, which in turn leads to the first of several prison rooms, one leading into another. At last the visitor steps across a threshold where a solid oak or iron door once stood and enters the slightly curving dungeon. The floor retains the irregular shapes of the island granite upon which the chateau is constructed. Along its center are seven stone columns, which support the rooms above. On one of these, the second, is an iron ring to which Bonivard was fettered.

One looks at that column with its dreadful ring and senses that, whatever liberty Byron may have taken with the facts of the case, he was certainly realistic in his description of the breaking of the human spirit under such inhuman conditions. Upon Bonivard's release by the Bernese, who wrested control of the castle from the Duke of Vaud, the broken prisoner explains, in Byron's words,

> My very chains and I grew friends,
> So much a long communion tends
> To make us what we are:—even I
> Regained my freedom with a sigh.

Why Bother to Be Good?

I do not know if it was into a prison like this that Joseph was eventually cast as a result of the passionate desire and then passionate hatred Potiphar's wife had for him. But if not, it was probably worse. We know that at the beginning of his imprisonment Joseph was treated quite badly. The author of Genesis does not discuss Joseph's condition in telling the story, but we find a description of his treatment in Psalm 105. The psalm tells of Joseph's plight in Egypt, saying,

> They bruised his feet with shackles,
>   his neck was put in irons.

> verse 18

So far as we know, François Bonivard was not chained by his neck. But Joseph was bound both by neck and ankles as he awaited either eventual execution or a slow physical decline by reason of his captivity.

But what made Joseph's imprisonment so terribly bruising is that it was utterly, unequivocally, uncompromisingly unjust. Indeed, it was worse than

that. It was the precise opposite of what Joseph should have received for his
steadfast refusal to commit fornication with his master's wife.

It was the opposite of what he should have received from Potiphar. There
is a cynical saying in contemporary life that "the husband (or wife) is always
the last to know." But it is hard to think that Potiphar could have been totally
unsuspecting of his wife's infidelities. There is nothing in the story to make
us think that this was the first time Mrs. Potiphar had made advances to
another man or even to another slave. In fact, the opposite is the case. She
was so shameless, so direct, and so persistent that we can only think there
must have been a succession of these romances. They would have been known
to the servants. (Perhaps this is why we do not read of them saying anything
when the lady of the house first made her slanderous lie against Joseph.) The
woman's sin must have been known to or at least suspected by Potiphar.

But Potiphar was a man in a high position, and people in high positions
have to keep up pretenses. Sin is no less prevalent on the Main Line than it
is in the ghetto. But among "good people" sin is covered up, and Potiphar
may well have been covering it up before this. It is true that the text says "he
burned with anger" (v. 19). But there are different kinds of anger, and he
may have been as angry with the situation or with the fact that it had become
public as he was angry with Joseph. At any rate, if he had really believed his
wife's story, he probably would have had Joseph killed. As it was, he merely
placed him in prison—a special prison "where the king's prisoners were confined" (v. 20).

What are we to suppose Joseph thought of that? I doubt if he was thinking
much about the quality of the prison. No doubt he was thinking about prison
itself and about how unjust it was for him to be confined there. If Potiphar
had investigated the situation and had been convinced on the basis of the
available testimony that Joseph was guilty as charged, then he should have
had Joseph killed, even though the penalty would have been based on an
erroneous judgment. But if Potiphar did not believe Joseph was guilty, then
he should not even have confined him to prison. He should have declared
him innocent and permitted him to continue performing his duties—or at
least transferred him to another equally honorable post.

Joseph felt this injustice from his human master. But he must have felt an
even greater injustice from God. That is whom Joseph was really serving after
all! True, he was serving Potiphar. But Joseph was doing what the apostle Paul
was later to advise the slaves of his day to do: "Whatever you do, work at it
with all your heart, as working for the Lord, not for men, since you know
that you will receive an inheritance from the Lord as a reward. It is the Lord
Christ you are serving" (Col. 3:23–24). Joseph had been serving God, and it
was precisely God who had let him get into prison.

Joseph had been serving God all his life. In Canaan he had done it through
serving his father, Jacob. He had given his father true reports when his brothers were practicing wickedness. When his father had sent him to find his

brothers and bring back word of them, he had carried out the assignment, even when it meant the much longer and possibly even dangerous trip from Shechem to Dothan. Joseph had been a model son. But what had it gotten him? His brothers hated him, threw him into a cistern, and then sold him into slavery.

In Egypt he had tried again. It was no fun being a slave, especially if you had been your father's favorite and heir before the slavery. But Joseph accepted this and applied himself to becoming the best slave possible. He had succeeded! He rose through the ranks, became Potiphar's personal attendant, and eventually was given responsibility for managing all the household. Moreover, when the master's wife disclosed her own immoral character, Joseph had resisted the wrong even to the point of running from the house when there was no other way to avoid her. Should God not reward that kind of virtue? If there is a God and if this is a moral universe, why should slander be listened to? Why should lies be believed? Why should men be allowed to do what is wrong and make righteous people suffer? Why do bad things happen to good people?

F. B. Meyer puts it personally: "Was it any use, then, being good? Could there be any truth in what his father had taught him of good coming to the good, and evil to the bad? Was there a God who judgeth righteously in the earth? You who have been misunderstood, who have sown seeds of holiness and love to reap nothing but disappointment, loss, suffering, and hate—*you* know something of what Joseph felt in that wretched dungeon hole."[1]

Victory in the Mind

I suppose we all know something of what Joseph felt in that Egyptian prison. But I wonder if we also know what Joseph *knew*. For of course, knowing what Joseph knew was the secret to victory in this distressing situation. It is what made Joseph become increasingly tender and kind through adversity rather than becoming bitter. Joseph knew three things.

First, Joseph knew that since he was being slandered and persecuted for righteousness' sake rather than for anything evil he had done, *suffering proved that he was God's man* and not a product of this present evil world. It is what Jesus had in mind when he spoke of suffering for righteousness' sake:

> Blessed are those who are persecuted because of righteousness, for theirs is the kingdom of heaven.
>
> Blessed are you when people insult you, persecute you and falsely say all kinds of evil against you because of me. Rejoice and be glad, because great is your reward in heaven.

Matthew 5:10–12

Jesus meant that those who follow him and live like him can be happy in persecutions, because the persecutions revealed that they are truly his followers and heirs of his kingdom.

This is directly opposite to the kind of feelings Joseph could have had. Joseph could have said, "Things are going badly for me in spite of the fact that I have been trying to live a good life. That must mean that God does not care for people like me, or else that there is no God." He would have become bitter if he had thought like that. Instead, he must have reasoned that persecution actually proved that he was God's servant and that he was living for him.

Second, since Joseph had faith in the sovereignty and wisdom of God, which his whole life demonstrates, he must have known that *suffering was being used by God to mold his character*. God had been doing it already. He must have seen how his years as a slave had deepened and matured him. Why should he think that it would be otherwise now? Was God not using persecution to perfect him just as he uses it to perfect all believers? In the wisdom of God, persecution is often the means by which believers are helped along the road to practical holiness and thereby made a little more like Jesus.

The apostle Peter knew this. He had known it personally, and he had seen it in the lives of his converts. Hence, when he wrote his first letter to those in Asia who were experiencing persecution, he said: "In this you greatly rejoice, though now for a little while you may have had to suffer grief in all kinds of trials. These have come so that your faith—of greater worth than gold, which perishes even though refined by fire—may be proved genuine and may result in praise, glory and honor when Jesus Christ is revealed" (1 Peter 1:6–7). Peter was saying that persecution is like one of the small crucibles used in ancient times by a refiner to purify the most precious metals. It is the experience by which God removes dross from the lives of his children and purifies true faith.

Billy Graham tells of a friend who went through the Great Depression, losing a job, a fortune, a wife, and a home. He was a believer in Jesus Christ, and he tenaciously held to his faith even though he was naturally depressed and cast down by circumstances. One day in the midst of his depression he stopped to watch some men doing stonework on a huge church in the city. One was busy chiseling a triangular piece of stone. "What are you going to do with that?" he asked. The workman stopped and pointed to a little opening near the top of the spire. "See that little opening up there near the top?" he said. "Well, I'm shaping this down here so that it will fit in up there." The friend said that tears filled his eyes as he walked away from the workman. For it seemed that God had spoken to him personally to say that he was shaping him for heaven by the ordeal through which he was passing.

The third truth that Joseph must have known and clung to during his imprisonment was that *persecution allows the believer to show the supernatural strength of his master*. If everything is going well with you and you rejoice, what makes you different from unbelievers? Nothing at all! They also (usually) rejoice when circumstances are favorable. If you are able to rejoice when things are not favorable, however, then Jesus Christ may be clearly seen in you and the supernatural power of the Christian faith is made manifest. Persecution is the dark background for the supernatural radiance of Christ's life.

Again this truth is best illustrated by a story. Mr. and Mrs. Arthur Matthews and their daughter Lilah were the last missionary family of the China Inland Mission to leave China after the communist takeover at the end of World War II. During their last two years in China they suffered great persecution. For the better part of those two long years they lived in a small room, where their only furniture was a stool. They could not contact their Christian friends for fear of subjecting them to reprisals for befriending aliens. Their funds were cut off by the government except for the smallest trickle. The only heat they had came from a small stove, which they lit only once each day to boil rice for dinner. Indeed, the fuel was made by Mr. Matthews from the refuse the animals deposited around the streets. For a time the couple submitted to the treatment stoically, asking all the while that God would soon deliver them from China.

At last a turning point came in their outlook. They realized that Jesus had come from heaven, not merely submitting to the will of his Father, but delighting in it. And they saw that their own experience was comparable. It was an opportunity for the radiance of joyful obedience to be manifested in them and one in which their conduct could be a supernaturally effective witness. After this they came to rejoice and even to sing hymns. They came to accept the privilege of suffering for the sake of Christ with as much joy as they later had when they learned of their pending deliverance.

It was a similar knowledge of the opportunities afforded by persecution that taught Hugh Latimer to cry out to Nicholas Ridley as they were both led to the stake in Oxford, England, in 1555, "Be of good comfort, Master Ridley, and play the man; we shall this day light such a candle by God's grace in England as (I trust) shall never be put out." Latimer was right. The behavior of believers was then and still is a great testimony to God's grace.

For Righteousness' Sake

But *be sure that when you are persecuted it is for righteousness' sake*, which was the case with Joseph, and not for being a nuisance, being fanatical, or—need I say it?—for wrongdoing. Jesus Christ himself is our model.

When Jesus came to earth he exposed the evil of the world, and men hated him for it. Before Christ came, people seemed to be able to get away with hypocrisy, dishonesty, selfishness, lying, greed, and a long list of other vices by pointing out that others were like themselves and that they were better than others in some respects. When Christ came, these vices were revealed for what they were, just as the filth of a sewer is revealed by thrusting a strong light into one of its openings. Many men who saw and heard Christ hated this exposure of their true natures and killed him for exposing them.

In a similar way, people today will hate any exposure of their evil that comes from the evidences of the righteousness of Christ in his followers. That is why Jesus said, "No servant is greater than his master. If they persecuted me, they will persecute you also. If they obeyed my teaching, they will obey yours also. . . . If I had not come and spoken to them, they would not be guilty of sin. Now, however, they have no excuse for their sin. He who hates me hates my Father as well" (John 15:20–23).

Let me ask this question: Is there anything in your conduct that reveals Christ's righteousness? Is Jesus Christ seen in your character? I know that we are living in a country that has adopted many Christian values, tolerance being among them, and so has risen to a level where persecutions are not likely to be what they were in the early Christian centuries. But it is also true, I fear, that much of our Christianity has sunk to a level where it is hardly noticed. The world has become tolerant of us, but we have become far more tolerant of the world.

Have you ever put the principles of Christ's righteousness into action in your home, job, or business? You might say, "I am up against a situation in my factory that is so rotten and has been going on so long, that if I did the righteous thing, I'd be fired." Once a man came to Tertullian who had exactly that problem. His business interests had been conflicting with his loyalty to Jesus Christ. He ended by saying, "What can I do? I must live."

"Must you?" Tertullian asked. If it came to a choice between righteousness and a livelihood in Tertullian's day, the believer was expected to choose righteousness.[2]

133

Prospering in Prison

Genesis 39:20–23

*But while Joseph was there in the prison, the L*ORD *was with him; he showed him kind-*
ness and granted him favor in the eyes of the prison warden. So the warden put Joseph
in charge of all those held in the prison, and he was made responsible for all that was
done there.

Genesis 39:20–22

Several years ago the young adult min-
istry of Tenth Presbyterian Church held a retreat at which they played a game
of "Tenth Presbyterian Church Trivia." I do not know all the questions that
were on that particular test, but afterward a number recounted one trivia
question about me. The question asked: What are the points of Dr. Boice's
favorite sermon?

I did not know I had a favorite sermon before that. But I learned that my
favorite sermon was on commitment and was entitled "This People, This
Place." It spoke of a people among whom one has a sense of being called to
minister and a place to which one has a special call of God. It emphasized
that both of these commitments were to be lifelong. The points were: (1) people
before programs, (2) place before promotion, and (3) permanence. The text

was the thirty-second chapter of Jeremiah, in which God exhibited exactly that commitment on behalf of his people, the Jews, and his city, Jerusalem. The conclusion was that God prospers the work of one who is committed for the long haul.

I do not know if it is entirely appropriate to speak of Joseph's commitment to place during his years in prison—since he was not committed voluntarily. But Joseph had that kind of commitment even when he was not in prison and, having it, he was blessed everywhere.

Earlier in Genesis 39 we read that "the LORD was with Joseph" and "gave him success in everything he did" (vv. 2–3, 5). In these verses, although the circumstances have changed, the story nevertheless remains the same: "But while Joseph was there in the prison, *the LORD was with him;* he showed him kindness and granted him favor in the eyes of the prison warden. So the warden put Joseph in charge of all those held in the prison, and he was made responsible for all that was done there. The warden paid no attention to anything under Joseph's care, because *the LORD was with Joseph* and *gave him success in whatever he did*" (Gen. 39:20–23, my emphasis).

Character before Career

When we read these verses in terms of God's blessing and Joseph's success, we think naturally (and, I believe, rightly) of the fact that Joseph rose to a position of authority in the prison. In this, his course was parallel to his earlier rise from being a menial slave to being a personal attendant and manager for Potiphar.

But Joseph's real success was greater than that. There is an unforgettable school motto that illustrates what I mean. The motto of Harvard University, where I did my undergraduate study, is *Veritas*, which means "truth." The University of Basel, in Switzerland, which I attended some years later, has *Fundamentum Christos* for its motto; it means "Christ is the foundation." But the motto I have in mind comes from the Stony Brook School on Long Island, where I attended high school. Stony Brook's motto is "Character before Career." This means it is far more important to develop integrity, morality, and godliness in students than merely to equip them for outstanding careers.

It is along these lines that we are to note Joseph's achievement, in my judgment. True, he did rise from being merely another prisoner to being one to whom the warden entrusted everything. But that was not too big a thing after all. He was still a prisoner; his fate was still uncertain. What was important was the way in which his character grew during his imprisonment. In similar circumstances another man might have become quite harsh, bitter, or withdrawn. Not Joseph! Joseph continued to develop those good traits that already characterized him.

I notice two things particularly. Joseph continued to think about God and, indeed, to orient his entire life around the reality of God's character. We saw this at the beginning of our studies. "The greatest single characteristic of

Joseph was his absolute faithfulness to God under all circumstances, and it is through this that God worked to exalt him so highly. Joseph never yielded to that saying: 'When in Rome, do as the Romans do.' In Egypt Joseph might have been tempted to do this. He was far from home with little chance of ever seeing his father or other family members again. He had been deprived of family pleasures. If he had been like many professing Christians today, he might have said, 'I am far from home and nobody is ever going to see what I do. I will take my pleasure where I can, and I will do whatever it takes to advance my position.' Joseph never said that. He knew that he was God's child and that his responsibility was to live for and be faithful to God, regardless of what should come into his life.

"Joseph never complained.

"Joseph never compromised.

"As a result, Joseph never lost his power before God. Throughout his life God continued to reveal the future to him through dreams, and God continued to guide him no less when he was in Potiphar's prison than when he was beside the monarch's throne. God was always the chief and determining reality in Joseph's life."[1]

It is the same at this stage of Joseph's story. The verses that end chapter 39 contain no words of Joseph. But in the next chapter, when the cupbearer and baker of the king of Egypt are introduced and shortly afterward tell Joseph their dreams, Joseph's first words (almost his first recorded words in prison) are: "Do not interpretations belong to God? Tell me your dreams" (Gen. 40:8). We might have expected him to have been thinking about himself and to have said, "Don't get mixed up with dreams, boys. I had a dream once, and when I told my brothers about it they hated me and sold me into slavery. I'm here because of dreams." But Joseph was not thinking about himself. He was thinking about God, and he was strengthened in this regard because of his imprisonment. Dreams? The interpretations of dreams belong to God. Joseph saw everything in the light of God's existence.

I said that the words "Do not interpretations belong to God?" were *almost* Joseph's first recorded words from prison. That is because there is one sentence before that. I note now that it is also important in showing an aspect in which Joseph's character was growing. The text says, "When Joseph came to them the next morning he saw that they were dejected. So he asked Pharaoh's officials who were in custody with him in his master's house [the prison], 'Why are your faces so sad today?'" (vv. 6–7). These words tell us that Joseph continued to be strengthened in his interest in and concern for other people, when he could have been morosely and exclusively concerned about himself.

"Character before Career." None of us would ever willingly choose to go to prison, and I am sure that Joseph did not relish his imprisonment either. But it was not all bad. Prison strengthened character in Joseph, and he was to show that character when he was later exalted to the first place beside the pharaoh's throne.

The Weeping Prophet

I think of another biblical character who prospered in prison, "the Weeping Prophet." Jeremiah prophesied in Jerusalem at the end of the history of the southern kingdom, and his message—though extended over many decades throughout the long years of his life—was always the same: Jerusalem will be destroyed for its sin by the Babylonians. This was unpopular, of course. But it was not until the end of his ministry, shortly before the city was overthrown, that Jeremiah was imprisoned. The story tells us that during a lull in the fighting, when the Babylonian army had withdrawn from Jerusalem to engage the army of the pharaoh of Egypt attacking from the south, Jeremiah started to leave the city to attend to family business in the tribal area of Benjamin. He was accused of deserting to the Babylonians and was arrested. Then, without benefit of trial, he was beaten and confined in the house of Jonathan the secretary, which had been made into a prison. The text says, "Jeremiah was put into a vaulted cell in a dungeon, where he remained *a long time*" (Jer. 37:16, my emphasis).

We might think that an experience like this, especially after so long and fruitless a ministry, might have modified the prophet's message. He might have told himself, "Jeremiah, you are not getting anywhere except prison by this useless warning of the people. Why not stop it? Why not change your tune?" Actually, the opposite occurred. After this long imprisonment, when King Zedekiah finally sent for him and inquired privately, "Is there any word from the LORD?" Jeremiah abruptly replied, "Yes, you will be handed over to the king of Babylon" (v. 17).

Prison did not weaken Jeremiah. Prison strengthened his witness, and he continued to express it to the very end, when the city fell.

Samson and Delilah

Samson regained his physical strength while in prison. He was the twelfth of the judges listed in the Book of Judges and the most colorful. But Samson had a weakness for women and was finally betrayed by Delilah of the Philistines. After many entreaties he told her that the secret of his strength was in his hair. She had it cut off while he slept. Then, when the Philistine soldiers fell upon him, they overpowered him, put out his eyes, and took him to Gaza, where they bound him in bronze shackles and set him to work grinding grain. In prison Samson's hair grew long again and his strength returned. His sense of the Lord's presence and his desire to serve him utterly also returned. When a party was given for the Philistine god Dagon, Samson was brought out and mocked. He asked God to strengthen him once more to allow him to take a justified revenge on the Philistines. Leaning on the great pillars that supported

Dagon's temple, Samson brought the roof of the temple down so that, as the text says, "He killed many more when he died than while he lived" (Judg. 16:30).

Prison strengthened Samson physically and probably also strengthened his resolve to serve God.

On the Lord's Day

I think also of two New Testament examples of prosperity in prison. First, the apostle John on Patmos. We are not told much about the reason for John's imprisonment, but it is hard to doubt that it was for the sake of his faithful witness to Christ's gospel. When he introduces himself about midway through the first chapter of Revelation, it is as "your brother and companion in the suffering and kingdom and patient endurance that are ours in Jesus." He adds that he "was [imprisoned] on the island of Patmos because of the word of God and the testimony of Jesus" (v. 9).

What happened to John on Patmos? He tells us that he heard a loud voice, saying, "Write on a scroll what you see and send it to the seven churches: to Ephesus, Smyrna, Pergamum, Thyatira, Sardis, Philadelphia and Laodicea" (Rev. 1:11). When John turned around to see who was speaking to him, he saw a vision of the glorified Jesus standing among seven golden lampstands that represented the seven churches. The text says that he was

> dressed in a robe reaching down to his feet and with a golden sash around his chest. His head and hair were white like wool, as white as snow, and his eyes were like blazing fire. His feet were like bronze glowing in a furnace, and his voice was like the sound of rushing waters. In his right hand he held seven stars, and out of his mouth came a sharp double-edged sword. His face was like the sun shining in all its brilliance
>
> verses 13–16

John had seen Jesus before in the days of his flesh, but he had never seen anything like this. It was like Moses seeing the back of God as he passed by the cave where Moses had been placed, or like Isaiah catching his vision of the Lord high and lifted up, when his glory filled the temple. John says that when he saw the risen Lord in his glory he "fell at his feet as though dead" (v. 17). It required something like a resurrection to restore John to service.

Imprisonment did not destroy John. Imprisonment strengthened his perception of Jesus and enabled him to write the magnificent, climactic book of the Bible.

A Strengthened Ministry

Prison strengthened Joseph's character, Jeremiah's witness, Samson's physical prowess, and John the evangelist's perception. I conclude by noting that in the case of the apostle Paul, being in prison strengthened his ministry.

Paul had been in prison before. In 2 Corinthians 6:5 he speaks of more than one imprisonment, and we know of several ourselves through reading the Book of Acts. He was imprisoned at Philippi, where God used Paul and Silas's witness to save the Philippian jailer. He was interred at Jerusalem and was incarcerated for two years at Caesarea. But it is chiefly Paul's imprisonment in Rome that concerns us here. For God richly blessed that time of imprisonment and gave Paul success in writing his great prison epistles (Philippians, Colossians, 2 Timothy, Philemon) and in leading many to the Lord.

In an earlier study I pointed out that Paul's imprisonment in Rome was made much worse by the envy of others who were supposed to be proclaiming the same gospel he was. He spoke about them in Philippians: "It is true that some preach Christ out of envy and rivalry, but others out of good will. The latter do so in love, knowing that I am put here for the defense of the gospel. The former preach Christ out of selfish ambition, not sincerely, supposing that they can stir up trouble for me while I am in chains" (Phil. 1:15–17). Apparently some of this ill will roused the authorities against Paul and eventually contributed to his martyrdom.[2]

How did the things that happened to the apostle result in the spread of the gospel? The first answer is that through them Paul was able to bear a remarkable witness to the Praetorian Guard. In Philippians 1:13 Paul writes, "It has become clear throughout the whole palace guard and to everyone else that I am in chains for Christ." We must visualize the scene at this point. Paul is imprisoned in Rome, chained to a Roman guard. Ever since his arrest in Jerusalem he had been chained to a guard, except for the moments on the ship carrying him to Rome. He is now in care of the picked troops who guard the emperor. Paul has some freedom of action. He may have visitors. For a while he lived in a private home. But always there was the guard.

What did Paul do in this situation? He might have complained: "This is unjust; Roman law is slow; this soldier represents all that Rome stands for, and I cannot bear the sight of him." But this was never Paul's way. He himself was a soldier for Christ, and the man at the end of the chain represented a person for whom Christ died. Paul bore a witness. And he bore witness, not only to this soldier, but to the one who replaced him for the second watch and the one who replaced him for the third watch and so on throughout the days and years. In this way, in time, Paul reached most of the imperial guard.

There is another way in which Paul's suffering for Christ served to advance the gospel. It had an effect on other Christians. Paul says, "Because of my chains, most of the brothers in the Lord have been encouraged to speak the word of God more courageously and fearlessly" (Phil. 1:14). Christians moved from fear to boldness through Paul's example. They learned to testify.

Paul's words about the spread of the gospel through suffering reveal the effect of his life upon non-Christians and upon believers. Non-Christians became Christians. Believers were emboldened to preach the gospel. If these

things are to be true in your life, you must let suffering draw you closer to
the Lord. It can do the opposite; it can draw you away. It can embitter your
heart and produce a complainer in you where there should be a victorious
Christian. All too often Christians are like the man described by Epictetus,
one of the pagan philosophers: "I am in sore straits, O Lord, and in misfortune; no one regards me, no one gives me anything, all blame me and speak
ill of me." Epictetus asks, "Is this the witness that you are going to bear, and
is this the way in which you are going to disgrace the summons which he gave
you?" (*Discourses*, I, xxix).[3]

It was entirely the opposite in the case of the men I have mentioned: Paul,
John, Samson, Jeremiah, and first of all Joseph. They drew close to God, and
God prospered them even in their prisons.

134

"I Had a Dream"

Genesis 40:1–22

Some time later, the cupbearer and the baker of the king of Egypt offended their master, the king of Egypt. Pharaoh was angry with his two officials, the chief cupbearer and the chief baker, and put them in custody in the house of the captain of the guard, in the same prison where Joseph was confined. The captain of the guard assigned them to Joseph, and he attended them.

After they had been in custody for some time, each of the two men—the cupbearer and the baker of the king of Egypt, who were being held in prison—had a dream the same night, and each dream had a meaning of its own.

When Joseph came to them the next morning, he saw that they were dejected. So he asked Pharaoh's officials who were in custody with him in his master's house, "Why are your faces so sad today?"

"We both had dreams," they answered, "but there is no one to interpret them."

Then Joseph said to them, "Do not interpretations belong to God? Tell me your dreams."

So the chief cupbearer told Joseph his dream. He said to him, "In my dream I saw a vine in front of me, and on the vine were three branches. As soon as it budded, it blossomed, and its clusters ripened into grapes. Pharaoh's cup was in my hand, and I took the grapes, squeezed them into Pharaoh's cup and put the cup in his hand."

"This is what it means," Joseph said to him. "The three branches are three days. Within three days Pharaoh will lift up your head and restore you to your position, and you will put Pharaoh's cup in his hand, just as you used to do when you were his cupbearer. But when all goes well with you, remember me and show me kindness; mention me to Pharaoh *and get me out of this prison. For I was forcibly carried off from the land of the Hebrews, and even here I have done nothing to deserve being put in a dungeon."*

When the chief baker saw that Joseph had given a favorable interpretation, he said to Joseph, "I too had a dream: On my head were three baskets of bread. In the top basket were all kinds of baked goods for Pharaoh, but the birds were eating them out of the basket on my head."

"This is what it means," Joseph said. "The three baskets are three days. Within three days Pharaoh will lift off your head and hang you on a tree. And the birds will eat away your flesh."

Now the third day was Pharaoh's birthday, and he gave a feast for all his officials. He lifted up the heads of the chief cupbearer and the chief baker in the presence of his officials: He restored the chief cupbearer to his position, so that he once again put the cup into Pharaoh's hand, but he hanged the chief baker, just as Joseph had said to them in his interpretation.

A striking feature of the Book of Jonah is the variety of circumstances God used to accomplish his will in the life of the rebellious prophet. At the beginning of the story, following Jonah's disobedience in setting out for Tarshish instead of going to Nineveh, God intervened with things as great as the violent storm that threatened to destroy the ship in which Jonah was sailing and the great fish that swallowed him after he had been thrown overboard. But there were other details: the decision of the captain to bring Jonah up on deck at precisely the time the sailors were casting lots to see who was responsible for their trouble, that the lot fell on Jonah, and the calming of the water after he had been thrown overboard. Then, at the end of the story, God was still at work in the appearance of the quickly growing vine, the small worm that attacked it, and the arrival of the scorching wind from the desert. In all these circumstances, some great, some small, God was at work to direct the life and form the character of his servant.

It was the same in the case of Joseph, with the important exception that he was not resisting but was patiently submitting to the will of God. From the earlier moments of his youth until he reached the age of thirty, God was at work in his life through a series of circumstances that eventually raised him from the status of an imprisoned slave to that of prime minister of Egypt.

Chain of Circumstances

It is worth thinking back over these circumstances. The first was the special love of Joseph's father, Jacob, which provoked the resentment and hostility of the youth's eleven brothers. The text says, "Now Israel loved Joseph more than any of his other sons, because he had been born to him in his old age; and he made a richly ornamented robe for him. When his brothers saw that their father loved him more than any of them, they hated him and could not speak a kind word to him" (Gen. 37:3–4). That hatred would eventually lead to Joseph's being sold into slavery to the Midianites through whom he was eventually brought to Egypt.

The second significant circumstance was his dreams foretelling the bowing of his brothers and parents to himself. This was the chief catalyst to the murderous anger of his brothers, for they responded, "Do you intend to reign over us? Will you actually rule us?" (Gen. 37:8). They hated him even more because of his dreams, the story informs us.

When the brothers finally fell on Joseph and threw him into the abandoned cistern it was with the intention of murdering him. But again God intervened in circumstances, causing the caravan of Midianite traders to pass by. And did he not also intervene through the ruthless but selfish thinking of Judah, who said, "What will we gain if we kill our brother and cover up his blood? Come, let's sell him to the Ishmaelites and not lay our hands on him; after all, he is our brother, our own flesh and blood" (Gen. 37:26–27)? Through these selfish acts and "chance" occurrences Joseph was brought to Egypt, where God used him to save many people during the years of famine.

Nobody else had this purpose. The characters all had their own purposes. "Many are the plans in a man's heart, but it is the LORD's purpose that prevails" (Prov. 19:21). Years later Joseph was to speak about that purpose, saying, "You intended to harm me, but God intended it for good to accomplish what is now being done, the saving of many lives" (Gen. 50:20).

In Egypt the intervention of God in Joseph's circumstances continued. In a manner entirely apart from his own control he was purchased by Potiphar, the captain of Pharaoh's palace guard. Then, after he had risen to a position of prominence and favor in Potiphar's household, he was accused of attempted rape by the evil wife of Potiphar and was thrown into prison.

These all seemed to be evil circumstances designed (if they had a design) for Joseph's ruin. But God was still working, and even these downward steps were actually forward steps to the throne.

Genesis 40 introduces us to a last set of happenings before Joseph's exaltation. It tells us:

> Some time later, the cupbearer and the baker of the king of Egypt offended their master, the king of Egypt. Pharaoh was angry with his two officials, the chief cupbearer and the chief baker, and put them in custody in the house of the captain of the guard, in the same prison where Joseph was confined. The captain of the guard assigned them to Joseph, and he attended them.
>
> Genesis 40:1–4

Isn't that remarkable! Joseph is at the lowest point of his career, to judge from outward circumstances. We would say, "If ever a man was abandoned both by God and man, it is surely Joseph in Potiphar's prison. He will never emerge from that dungeon alive." But God had not forgotten Joseph, and he now intervened again by turning the heart of the king against his chief cupbearer and baker so that these two high officials were brought to the very prison in which Joseph was confined. Although it took several years (cf. Gen. 41:1), it was through this contact that Joseph was finally lifted from the prison to the palace.

All this was for Joseph's sake, though he could not have been fully aware of it at the time. What about you? Is God not also working out the circumstantial details of your life? One commentator writes correctly, "God directed everyone from king to jailer as easily as you set a watch or wind its spring. How sinful, therefore, for a Christian to worry or fret. God moves the very stars in their orbits to work his will, and he rules the passions of men and the decisions of those in authority to accomplish what he had planned."[1]

That is why Christians should not fret at the loss of a job, a flat tire, a bout of unexpected sickness, or whatever. God is God, and "we know that in all things God works for the good of those who love him" (Rom. 8:28).

What about Dreams?

Years before this, Joseph had dreamed two dreams foretelling a day in which his family would bow down to him. Now we are told of a second pair of dreams. Both the cupbearer and the baker of the king of Egypt had a dream forecasting what was to happen to each of them individually.

The first to disclose his dream was the cupbearer. To most of us a title like "cupbearer" or "baker" suggests a common servant—one who either poured wine at the pharaoh's table or worked in the kitchens. But this is not the idea at all. Thomas Chaucer was the son of the famous early English poet Geoffrey Chaucer, author of *The Canterbury Tales*. He was a member of Parliament and four times speaker of the House of Commons. He is said to have fought at Agincourt under Henry V. I mention him because he rose to considerable eminence at the English court and served as Chief Butler of England to both Henry V and Henry VI. Chief Butler was an honorary title bestowed on a high nobleman who was close to the king. It was the same with the chief cupbearer and chief baker of the king of Egypt. These were not servants. They were noblemen of high station. It has been suggested, no doubt rightly, that they held their titles in reference to the role they played in ceremonies involving the worship of the Egyptian god Horus. They would bear the wine and carry the ceremonial bread to be used in such ceremonies.

The chief cupbearer told his dream, in which he had seen a vine containing three branches. These branches budded, blossomed, and produced clusters of grapes. He was holding Pharaoh's cup in his hand in this dream. So he reached out and took the grapes, squeezed them into Pharaoh's cup, and put the cup in his hand.

Joseph interpreted this dream as showing that Pharaoh would restore the cupbearer to his old position within three days.

At this point the chief baker was encouraged to tell his dream. He had dreamed that he was carrying three baskets on his head and that the topmost basket contained baked goods for Pharaoh. But the birds were eating them from the basket.

Joseph explained this dream by saying that within three days Pharaoh would remove the baker from the prison, behead him, and hang his body on a tree, where the birds would eat away his flesh.

What are we to think of these dreams? Or of the freedom of God to speak through dreams generally? We begin by noting that God was certainly in these dreams both in the giving of them and in the giving of their interpretation to Joseph. Moreover, God is involved in all the dreams of this story. He gave and fulfilled Joseph's initial dreams about the time his brothers and father would bow to him (Gen. 37:5–7, 9; cf. 43:26, 28). Later he gave Pharaoh his dreams about the seven plentiful years and the seven years of famine and enabled Joseph to interpret them (Genesis 41). We may want to argue, as many modern-day psychologists would, that dreams are reflections of subconscious desires and frustrations: Joseph's aspirations to excel over his brothers, the cupbearer's sense of his innocence and the baker's fears related to his own guilt, Pharaoh's justified concern about a recurring pattern of good years and bad years for Egyptian agriculture. But even if these were secondary causes of the six dreams, God was certainly the first cause, since each of them actually did forecast what was to happen. In Isaiah God cites his ability to predict the future as proof that he alone is God and no other (cf. Isa. 41:21–24).

This does not mean that God always speaks in dreams or even that he does so at all in our day. It is worth noting, for example, how little significance dreams have in the Bible. The Bible is a big book covering many thousands of years of history. But there are only three places in the Bible where dreams figure prominently. In the Old Testament they are restricted to Genesis and Daniel. In the New Testament people sometimes had visions, as John did on the island of Patmos. But strictly speaking, there are only six dreams, and all these occur in Matthew.

Did these reveal the future? Yes. But largely at a time when the Scriptures of the Old and New Testament had not been given. This was clearly the case in Genesis; and with Daniel the dreams were part of the revelation that God was then giving. We are wise to conclude that today dreams are not revelations from God, though they may be accurate reflections of our own subconscious states. For a true and trustworthy revelation we are to turn to Scripture alone, *Sola Scriptura*.

"Revealer of Secrets"

Significantly, the emphasis of this chapter is not on the psychological phenomenon of the dreams but on the interpretation of them by Joseph. This is noteworthy in regard to interpreting the dreams of both the cupbearer and the baker.

Joseph replied to the cupbearer directly and boldly. We see it even before the dream was told to him. When the two noblemen disclosed that they were sad because there was no one to interpret their dreams, Joseph immediately replied, "Do not interpretations belong to God? Tell me your dreams" (v. 8). After he had heard the cupbearer's dream it was the same thing. Joseph said, "The three branches are three days. Within three days Pharaoh will lift up your head and restore you to your position, and you will put Pharaoh's cup in his hand, just as you used to do when you were his cupbearer" (vv. 12–13). Joseph knew God and knew that he knew God. Moreover, he had such confidence in this knowledge that he fully expected God to make his counsels known to him in regard to his being able to interpret the cupbearer's dream.

How powerful that man is who knows and knows that he knows! There is a saying, which I believe comes from the Far East, that goes:

> He who knows not and knows not that he knows not
> is a fool; shun him.
> He who knows not and knows that he knows not
> is a child; teach him.
> He who knows and knows not that he knows
> is asleep; awake him.
> He who knows and knows that he knows
> is a wise man; follow him.

Joseph fit the last category. He knew and he knew that he knew. As a result he was not only wise but powerful, yes, powerful even while in prison.

This is what made Jeremiah the most powerful man in Israel even while he was incarcerated. It is why King Zedekiah sought him out.

It is what gave Samson his power.

It was knowledge of God and of what was right that made John the Baptist strong. Herod was king; yet Herod feared John. He feared to let him live and yet feared to kill him.

Knowing that he knew the true gospel made Paul strong.

Knowing gave John the Evangelist his power.

Martin Luther was strong because he knew what the Word of God taught, regardless of the opinions of popes or councils to the contrary. He bestrode the Europe of his day like a colossus, declaring, "Here I stand; I can do no other; God help me."

All Christians are to be like these men. Donald Grey Barnhouse wrote, "Today, God speaks through his written Word, and the Holy Spirit reveals the truth to his own. This is why we are to speak as the oracles of God (1 Peter 4:11). Let every believer understand that he is responsible to set forth the truth which he has seen and heard (1 John 1:3). If you know the depths of truth, you are to speak with finality of the truth revealed by the Holy Spirit through the Word."[2]

There is a special lesson in Joseph's interpretation of the dream of Pharaoh's baker. The baker's dream was not favorable. Joseph said, "The three baskets are three days. Within three days Pharaoh will lift off your head and hang you on a tree. And the birds will eat away your flesh" (vv. 18–19). Here we see the *courage* of Joseph. Although it was difficult, particularly in a case where the interpretation concerned the life of one who had become his friend, he was not afraid to deliver the whole counsel of God.

I wish all believers had this courage. In fact, I will narrow my concern and say that I wish all ministers had it. How many there are who are willing to preach the cupbearer's sermon but are unwilling to preach the baker's sermon! They are afraid to stand before a congregation and say that they are members of Adam's fallen race, under the curse of God's broken law, and that if they had what was coming to them, they would all end up in the hell that God has prepared to punish sinners. They are afraid to say that God has appointed but one mediator between God and man, the man Christ Jesus, and that if they are not united to him by saving faith, they will perish miserably. They preach that God loves sinners, but they will not preach that God hates sin. They preach about heaven, but they will not warn about hell. If we are to be faithful to God, we must preach all that God reveals. God will deal severely with those who know these truths but allow people to perish without warning them of his judgment.

Salvation from the Lord

I started this study with a reference to the story of Jonah, and I return to it now for one final point. At the close of the second chapter of that book, at the end of his prayer from within the great fish, Jonah utters a sentence that might well be termed the theme verse of the entire Word of God: "Salvation comes from the LORD" (Jonah 2:9). This too is in Joseph's story.

After he had interpreted the dream of the cupbearer, showing that he would soon be restored to his position as Pharaoh's honored officer, Joseph said something that was quite human: "When all goes well with you, remember me and show me kindness; mention me to Pharaoh and get me out of this prison. For I was forcibly carried off from the land of the Hebrews, and even here I have done nothing to deserve being put in a dungeon" (vv. 14–15). Some commentators criticize Joseph for this, arguing that he should not have appealed in this way to a clear unbeliever but should instead have left his case before God. I do not agree with them. For one thing, I am sure Joseph did present his case to God. For another, there is nothing wrong with doing whatever is humanly possible to avoid difficulty and improve one's condition. If Joseph had possessed access to an Egyptian court, he would have been entirely justified in appealing to it against the injustice of his imprisonment. Paul later did the same thing in his appeal to Caesar from his imprisonment at Caesarea.

But for Joseph, deliverance was not to come in this fashion. As I say, there was nothing wrong with his asking the cupbearer to remember him when he was restored to Pharaoh's favor. Yet deliverance did not come from the grateful memory of a pagan butler (who was actually ungrateful) but from God.

It may be that way in your life. You may be trying to extricate yourself from difficulty by every means at your disposal and may have found that everything you do is unavailing. In your case, as it was with Joseph, deliverance may have to come directly from God. Why? I do not know the whole answer to that question. But I do know that when we are helped by another person we are naturally grateful to that person and see him or her as the cause of our good fortune. But when we have failed in all human ways and are then delivered by God, we are filled with a holy awe of God and find ourselves to be deeply delighted in him. That end may be worth many years of suffering.

135

Forgotten!

Genesis 40:23

The chief cupbearer, however, did not remember Joseph; he forgot him.

I begin this study by asking you to look, not at Genesis 40:23, which is our text, but at the white space in your Bible between that verse and the verse that begins chapter 41. What would you say if you were commissioned to write a statement to fill up that space? It would not be easy to do, because between the end of chapter 40 and the beginning of chapter 41 we have the real maturing of Joseph. What is equally important, we have a lesson that every believer needs to learn in order to live a victorious Christian life.

The clue to what happened in the white space comes from Genesis 40:14–15, where Joseph did a very human thing. Joseph had interpreted the dream of the chief cupbearer of the king of Egypt to show that at the end of three days he would be restored to his position as one of the highly honored noblemen of Pharaoh. But he added, "When all goes well with you, remember me and show me kindness; mention me to Pharaoh and get me out of this prison. For I was forcibly carried off from the land of the Hebrews, and even here I have done nothing to deserve being put in a dungeon."

We can almost hear the chief cupbearer's reply. "Yes, yes," he must have said. "Of course I'll remember you. It's very fine what you're able to do with dreams. Very talented. Very talented."

But the three days passed, the cupbearer was returned to favor, and the chapter ends: "The chief cupbearer, however, did not remember Joseph; he forgot him" (v. 23).

Then the next chapter starts, "When two full years had passed . . ." (Gen. 41:1).

Two full years! Joseph had asked to be remembered. In circumstances like these it would have been natural for Joseph to surround himself by a wall of bitterness and rebellion. But Joseph did not grow bitter. Instead he grew increasingly mellow as he waited for the deliverance God was to bring.

Soul in Iron

There is an interesting history of translations of a verse from Psalm 105 that concerns this period of Joseph's life. It is the verse referred to earlier in this book that says, "They bruised his feet with shackles, his neck was put in irons" (v. 18). The second part of that verse says quite clearly that Joseph's *neck* was put in irons. That is, he was fettered to his cell by an iron collar, at least at the beginning, before he was favored by the prison warden. But for some reason, when the Hebrew Old Testament was translated into Greek (the Septuagint) the word for "neck" was rendered by the word *psyche*, which means "soul." That was the first mistake. Then, when the great Jerome came to do his Latin translation, for some reason he inverted the subject and object of the sentence and instead of saying, "His soul was laid in iron," he said, "Iron entered into his soul." After that the expression passed into the English prayer book and became a proverb.[1]

Well, the phrase is a translation error. But if there was ever a felicitous mistranslation, this is it. For the phrase well describes how a cruel fetter placed upon the body can in time seem to be placed on your soul, and after that of having entered your soul. You begin by trusting God in the affliction. But after a while, the monotony of the struggle wears you down and you begin to take on some of the rust of the manacle. You are like the horse that pulls the plow. The work is the same every day. So is the food! You begin to think that life is oats and hay on Monday, hay and oats on Tuesday, oats and hay on Wednesday, and so on throughout the weeks and years.

I imagine that this was in danger of happening to Joseph, though by the grace of God it did not. F. B. Meyer has a section in his study of Joseph in which he imagines Joseph's joy when the chief cupbearer promised to remember him after he had been delivered from prison. The cupbearer probably said, "If you're right and I get out of here and back to a position of favor with Pharaoh, you'll certainly hear from me. I'll give you a place as one of the servants who works for me, either in the palace or in the fields. You can count on me." Joseph would have taken heart at that. When the day of the cupbearer's release came, Joseph would have walked with him to the door of the prison and would have caught a glimpse of blue sky as the door opened to permit the nobleman to leave and then closed again.

Joseph would have gone back to his duties. Later that day when the door opened again Joseph would have run to it thinking that the cupbearer had spoken to Pharaoh, secured his pardon, and had now come to release him. But it was something else.

The next time the door opened, Joseph ran to it again. Once more it was something else; it was not the nobleman.

Meyer imagines that Joseph began to make excuses. "No doubt the butler had had to receive the congratulations of his friends; arrears of business had perhaps accumulated in his absence, and now engrossed his attention; many things had probably gone wrong which required time and pains to set right; or perhaps he was waiting for a good opportunity to urge the claims of his prison friend on the king."[2] For days Joseph would have run to the door every time it opened. But then he only walked to the door without running. At length he looked to the door without going to it. At last he did not even look up. It was useless to hide from himself what he had long suspected. Human hopes had disappointed him. The cupbearer had forgotten. Two long years passed thus.

For many people, more than two years have passed in this condition. They are not in a literal prison, but they are in a prison of circumstances. They are trapped by life. For some this means going to the same dull jobs day after day and perhaps enduring the same abuse and mistreatment of nagging bosses as they add up the same columns of figures or try to sell the same merchandise on the same dull shelves. For others it means the same problems. They deal with people, and they feel that there is not an objection, complaint, or criticism that they have not heard a hundred times before. There were times when they looked to some coworker or superior to help them. "I know you're going to get a promotion," they might have said. "Remember me when all goes well with you." When that coworker was moved up the organizational ladder and they went to the office party that was to tell their friend good-bye, they caught a glimpse of blue sky. They told God, "That's what I want. That's the position for me." But then the friend went off, the months passed, and it became obvious that they had been forgotten.

That can embitter a person. It could have grated on Joseph. But Joseph's two forgotten years did not embitter him. On the contrary, they steadied and deepened his character. Disappointment and monotony do not have to make you rebellious. Instead of the iron entering into your soul, the iron can enter your backbone and you can be made compassionate and trusting at the same time.

This does not happen automatically, of course. It did not happen automatically with Joseph. It happens only when one who is forgotten by man becomes conscious that although forgotten by man, he or she is not forgotten by God and that God is accomplishing his purposes even during the two long years.

The God Who Remembers

It is worth stressing that God does not forget his people, because *we* do forget. We forget others. We forget God. We even forget that God does not forget. As a result we become bitter and do not mature as Joseph did.

I think of the story of Noah alone on the great deep during the year the flood was upon the earth. If ever a man was alone, it was in this case—though Noah did have a wife, his three sons, and his sons' wives with him. The problem was that everything else was gone. A person does not have to be many miles at sea, even in a large ocean liner, to feel dreadfully cut off. But in this case Noah was literally cut off from all others, since they had been drowned by the rising torrents. During those months of bobbing about like a small piece of jetsam, Noah must have wondered whether God had forgotten him, his family, and the animals.

Moreover, Noah was a spiritual man, and he must have wondered about his fate from a spiritual perspective. It is true that he had tried to live a righteous life and had found favor with God in conjunction with his godly walk. But he was still a sinner despite his efforts to live righteously. Who was he to think that he should be spared indefinitely when all around him had perished? Might he not rightly be left to perish after all? Was he not guilty also, like the rest? Could he not also term himself a "chief of sinners"? Noah's very spirituality would have thrust these thoughts upon him. But it was precisely at that point, when he might have believed himself to have been forgotten both by man and God, that we are told: "God remembered Noah and all the wild animals and the livestock that were with him in the ark" (Gen. 8:1). The text uses the word "remember," but it means that God had not forgotten Noah. Despite appearances, God had been remembering Noah all along and was working out his perfect plan for all of them.

I think also of the cry of the believing thief who was crucified with Jesus. He had not been a believer at the start, but he had been won to faith by Jesus' patient endurance and love for others even in the midst of great pain. He said, "Jesus, remember me when you come into your kingdom" (Luke 23:42). Jesus' reply was instantaneous: "I tell you the truth, today you will be with me in paradise" (v. 43). And he was! That man had never felt more forgotten than when he hung on that cross. But Jesus remembered him, and he was with Jesus before the day ended.

Three Lessons

The story of Joseph's being forgotten by Pharoah's chief cupbearer leads to certain lessons, and the first is to *stop trusting in men,* all of whom are ultimately undependable. The Bible says, "Stop trusting in man, who has but a breath in his nostrils. Of what account is he?" (Isa. 2:22). That is, "Why trust a creature who can only live by taking one breath at a time? If he misses only one breath, he dies. Trust God, who is the eternal breath from whom all our little breaths come."

Meyer writes, "We cannot live without human sympathy and friendship. We long for the touch of the human hand and the sound of the human voice. We eagerly catch at any encouragement which some frail man holds out, as a drowning man catches at twigs floating by on the stream. But men fail us; even the best prove to be less able or less willing than we thought. The stream turns out to be a very turbid one when we reach it, in spite of all reports of its sufficiency. 'Cursed be the man that trusteth in man, and maketh flesh his arm, and whose heart departeth from the LORD: for he shall be like the heath in the desert, and shall not see when good cometh; but shall inhabit the parched places in the wilderness, a salt land and not inhabited.'"[3]

At one point Joseph must have hoped in man. But his experience taught him not to trust man, and he was delivered from the bitterness that overtakes many when they do trust others and are disappointed by them.

Have you ever recognized that these silent years are probably the years that made Joseph win out over any incipient revengeful spirit? When we think of revenge we usually think of what Joseph might have done to his brothers at a later date, when he had become the most powerful man in Egypt and they had come into his power unwittingly. We do not have to wait that long in the story—after the seven years of plenty and the first two years of famine. We can see Joseph's unrevengeful spirit almost immediately. What of Potiphar, who had imprisoned him? What of Potiphar's wife, who had accused him unjustly? I can almost hear Potiphar at a later time upbraiding his wife for her wickedness. "You fool," he might have said. "You have made an enemy of the mightiest man in Egypt. What will we be able to do when he decides to move against us?"

"You threw him in prison," she might have retorted. "All I wanted to do was seduce him. You punished him when he had not done anything wrong."

The chief cupbearer might also have been worried. He had promised to remember Joseph, but he had forgotten him and left him in the terrible depths of the prison. Might not Joseph plot revenge against him? Joseph might have taken a well-justified revenge on any or all of these. But he had ceased to trust men, and as a result he was not bitter against them. That is why at the end of the story, when his brothers fear a final retaliation, Joseph says, "Don't be afraid. Am I in the place of God? You intended to harm me, but God intended it for good to accomplish what is now being done, the saving of many lives. So then, don't be afraid. I will provide for you and your children" (Gen. 50:19–21).

Second, allow disillusionment with man to *turn you to the love and faithfulness of God*. Men and women may forget you, but Jesus never will. The Bible says, "If we are faithless, he will remain faithful, for he cannot disown himself" (2 Tim. 2:13). I remind you of some of the hundreds of verses that encourage trust in God.

Proverbs 3:5–6: "Trust in the LORD with all your heart and lean not on your own understanding; in all your ways acknowledge him, and he will make your paths straight."

Psalm 146:3, 5–6: "Do not put your trust in princes, in mortal men, who cannot save. . . . Blessed is he whose help is the God of Jacob, whose hope is in the LORD his God, the Maker of heaven and earth, the sea, and everything in them—the LORD, who remains faithful forever."

Jeremiah 17:5, 7: "Cursed is the one who trusts in man, who depends on flesh for his strength and whose heart turns away from the LORD. . . . But blessed is the man who trusts in the LORD, whose confidence is in him."

Psalm 118:8: "It is better to take refuge in the LORD than to trust in man."

Psalm 56:3: "When I am afraid, I will trust in you."

Psalm 115:11: "Trust in the LORD."

Meyer says, "He [God] may leave you long without succor. He may allow you to toil against a tempestuous sea until the fourth watch of the night. He may seem silent and austere, tarrying two days still in the same place, as if careless of the dying Lazarus. He may allow your prayers to accumulate like unopened letters on the table of an absent friend. But at last he will say, 'O man, O woman, great is thy faith: be it unto thee even as thou wilt.'"[4]

The third and last lesson is to *wait for God*. It is true that God does not always work according to our timetable. When God told the cupbearer through Joseph that he would be released from prison within three days, Joseph must have been encouraged to think that perhaps his deliverance would also be only days away. But God had not told him how long his confinement would last. He only knew that he was to wait on God and that in God's own time the bars of the prison cell would be parted.

In ancient Egypt, perhaps as early as the time of Joseph but certainly long before the Christian era, there was a fable that concerned the mythical bird the Phoenix. The Phoenix was believed to have a life span of five hundred years and to be reborn at the end of that time by returning to its birthplace at Heliopolis. When the Phoenix returned to Heliopolis, it was said to have built a funeral pyre for itself and then to have been consumed on it after it had died. It then arose from the ashes to live for another half-millennium. That was only a myth, of course, though it was actually believed by most persons living in the ancient world and was even used by the early Christian apologists as evidence for the resurrection. But myth or not, it is a picture

of that renewal of spirit and body that always comes to God's people in his
own proper time.

Isaiah understood it:

> Even youths grow tired and weary,
>> and young men stumble and fall;
> But those who hope in the LORD
>> will renew their strength.
> They will soar on wings like eagles;
>> they will run and not grow weary,
>> they will walk and not be faint.

Isaiah 40:30–31

136

Not Just a Dream

Genesis 41:1–40

Then Joseph said to Pharaoh, "The dreams of Pharaoh are one and the same. God has revealed to Pharaoh what he is about to do. The seven good cows are seven years, and the seven good heads of grain are seven years; it is one and the same dream. The seven lean, ugly cows that came up afterward are seven years, and so are the seven worthless heads of grain scorched by the east wind: They are seven years of famine.

"It is just as I said to Pharaoh: God has shown Pharaoh what he is about to do. Seven years of great abundance are coming throughout the land of Egypt, but seven years of famine will follow them. Then all the abundance in Egypt will be forgotten, and the famine will ravage the land. The abundance in the land will not be remembered, because the famine that follows it will be so severe. The reason the dream was given to Pharaoh in two forms is that the matter has been firmly decided by God, and God will do it soon.

"And now let Pharaoh look for a discerning and wise man and put him in charge of the land of Egypt. Let Pharaoh appoint commissioners over the land to take a fifth of the harvest of Egypt during the seven years of abundance. They should collect all the food of these good years that are coming and store up the grain under the authority of Pharaoh, to be kept in the cities for food. This food should be held in reserve for the country, to be used during the seven years of famine that will come upon Egypt, so that the country may not be ruined by the famine."

The plan seemed good to Pharaoh and to all his officials. So Pharaoh asked them, "Can we find anyone like this man, one in whom is the spirit of God?"

Then Pharaoh said to Joseph, "Since God has made all this known to you, there is no one so discerning and wise as you. You shall be in charge of my palace, and all my people are to submit to your orders. Only with respect to the throne will I be greater than you."

Genesis 41:25–40

P̲eople usually do not put stock in dreams, nor should they. Dreams are generally wishful thinking or expressions of fears. In literature the word "dream" is used as an image of something unsubstantial. In Shakespeare's *Tempest*, Prospero compares life to the passing world of spirits, saying, "We are such stuff as dreams are made of" (act 4, sc. 1). A ditty goes,

> Row, row, row your boat
> Gently down the stream;
> Merrily, merrily, merrily, merrily,
> Life is but a dream.

Frenchmen are more cynical. They say, *"Tout songes sont mensonges"* ("All dreams are lies").

Like most people, I remember very few dreams—though we are told we have many every night. But as I write this chapter the last dream I remember comes to mind. I was about to leave for a few weeks of summer vacation with my family, and I dreamed that I was taking them to church on my first Sunday away from Philadelphia. The church looked like a theater. As we entered we had to make way for a very youthful group that was apparently to sing that morning. They were dressed in baby-blue suits and dresses covered with sequins, and they were obviously made up for the stage. The worship service was preceded by a "pre-worship show" that had more of the flavor of Disney World or Hollywood than heaven. When the service began, fountains sprouted, television cameras descended on booms or rose from the floor, and the baby-blue chorus began to sing one of the punk songs of the evangelical subculture. I am sure as I look back on it that my dream reveals much of what I most fear and detest in church life. Needless to say, my family and I never did attend a church like that, and I am even hopeful that none quite as bad as that is in existence.

Sometimes the Bible speaks of dreams in this fashion. In Psalm 73 the writer compares the wicked to "a dream when one awakes," saying that the Lord "will despise them as fantasies" (v. 20).

God of All Circumstances

In Genesis 41 we find a pair of Pharoah's dreams, which Joseph interpreted. These are not like those dreams about which I have been speaking.

In most cases—perhaps all—in which you dreamed or someone else was dreaming, the dreams were only a projection of subconscious fears or desires. This was not the case with Pharaoh. Pharaoh's dreams had been given to him by God, and they were part of that magnificent chain of events by which Joseph, then the brothers, then Benjamin, and finally Jacob and his entire family were brought to Egypt.

The story begins with Joseph in prison two full years after he had interpreted the dreams of the chief cupbearer and the chief baker of the king of Egypt. When Joseph told the chief cupbearer that he would be restored to his position, he added, "But when all goes well with you, remember me and show me kindness; mention me to Pharaoh and get me out of this prison. For I was forcibly carried off from the land of the Hebrews, and even here I have done nothing to deserve being put in a dungeon" (Gen. 40:14–15). When he was restored to his position the cupbearer forgot Joseph, and two years passed. Two years! If the cupbearer had remembered Joseph sooner, Joseph could have congratulated himself on having the foresight to have requested this favor of him. But this is not a story of a man or man's gratitude. It is a story of God's providence. This way God received all the credit and the cupbearer none.

"When two full years had passed, Pharaoh had a dream: He was standing by the Nile, when out of the river there came up seven cows, sleek and fat, and they grazed among the reeds. After them, seven other cows, ugly and gaunt, came up out of the Nile and stood beside those on the riverbank. And the cows that were ugly and gaunt ate up the seven sleek, fat cows. Then Pharaoh woke up.

"He fell asleep again and had a second dream: Seven heads of grain, healthy and good, were growing on a single stalk. After them, seven other heads of grain sprouted—thin and scorched by the east wind. The thin heads of grain swallowed up the seven healthy, full heads. Then Pharaoh woke up; it had been a dream" (Gen. 41:1–7).

Proverbs 21:1 tells us that "the king's heart is in the hand of the LORD; he directs it like a watercourse wherever he pleases." But the dreams of this king were in the Lord's hand just as much as his heart, and they were no more difficult for the Lord to direct than were the dreams of the cupbearer and baker. We learn from this that God is never at a loss to bring about what he desires. We might ponder how it would be possible to get Joseph, the condemned slave, out of the prison and into the palace. We might devise one intrigue after the other, all of which would probably take many years and end in failure. But in a night God sends a dream, and before the next day runs its course Joseph is not only out of the prison and in the palace, but he is the prime minister of Egypt. This truth should be a cause of joy to each Christian: "We know that in *all* things God works for the good of those who love him, who have been called according to his purpose" (Rom. 8:28, my emphasis).

It is worth noting at this point that Pharaoh's dream of the Nile, cattle, and grain is typically Egyptian in flavor and is one more piece of evidence that Moses, who lived in Egypt and knew Egyptian life intimately, wrote Genesis, as the Bible claims he did (cf. Luke 24:27). No Jew ignorant of the life of Egypt could invent a dream like this.

There is further witness to the historicity of these events. In the previous chapter we are told that the third day after the cupbearer and baker dreamed their dreams was Pharaoh's birthday. Several generations ago there were modernists who attacked this portion of Genesis because, so they said, birthdays were not celebrated in Egypt. There is no record of birthdays ever being celebrated there, they said. As far as we know, birthdays are a Persian, not an Egyptian custom. How easy to attack the Bible in this fashion! There are always things mentioned in the Bible for which we do not have independent corroboration, and if one is inclined to put every other source of information above the Bible, it is easy to conclude that the Bible is in error at that point. How dangerous! In this case archaeologists discovered the Rosetta Stone, by which scholars learned to read Egyptian hieroglyphics, and one of the sections of the Rosetta Stone was a decree on the occasion of the celebration of the birthday of a pharaoh. So that argument against the reliability of Genesis died.

The same thing had happened with a word used a little further on in Genesis. After Joseph was made prime minister by Pharaoh he was given a chariot, and those who accompanied him were to go before shouting, "Make way!" (NIV) or "Bow the knee!" (KJV). For a long time scholars were ignorant of the meaning of this word—*'abhrekh* in the Hebrew Bible—and assumed that somehow its use was a mistake. But it has been pointed out that even today in the Near East when a camel driver commands his camel to get down on its knees for mounting or loading, he says *"Ibrekh!"* It is the same word used by Pharaoh almost four thousand years ago.

Joseph and Joseph's God

Pharaoh told these very Egyptian dreams to his court magicians and philosophers, but none of them could interpret them for him. At first glance this seems remarkable to us. When Nebuchadnezzar at a later period of Bible history had a dream and found that his wise men were unable to interpret it, this was not surprising, since he had forgotten the dream. Nebuchadnezzar's magicians, enchanters, sorcerers, and astrologers said that they would interpret the dream if he remembered it. This was not the case with the dream of the pharaoh of Egypt. Pharaoh recalled his dream, but as I said, none of the court wise men would hazard a guess at what was, after all, not all that puzzling.

The real explanation is that God was making the minds of Pharaoh's philosophers blank. On the one hand, he filled the mind of Pharaoh with dreams. On the other hand, with the same ease he removed even the suggestion of an interpretation from those who might naturally be expected to disclose it.

At this point the chief cupbearer of Pharaoh came forward with a confession. He told Pharaoh:

> Today I am reminded of my shortcomings. Pharaoh was once angry with his servants, and he imprisoned me and the chief baker in the house of the captain of the guard. Each of us had a dream the same night, and each dream had a meaning of its own. Now a young Hebrew was there with us, a servant of the captain of the guard. We told him our dreams, and he interpreted them for us, giving each man the interpretation of his dream. And things turned out exactly as he interpreted them to us: I was restored to my position, and the other man was hanged.
>
> Genesis 41:9–13

God was using the cupbearer's experience to bring Joseph's name before Pharaoh, and in a moment the call went out for Joseph to appear in court.

It has been noted that even with a call like this, Joseph took time to shave and change his clothes before approaching Pharaoh. Others have asked how, if Joseph took such care in approaching an earthly monarch, we can be so careless in how we approach God, the Monarch over all. It is a good point, but it is not the emphasis of this passage. The emphasis is on how quickly Joseph was lifted up to stand before Pharaoh and how quickly the challenge to interpret Pharaoh's dream came.

I suppose that there is not a character in all the Bible who experienced such sudden and radical reversals of fortune as did Joseph. One day he was his father's favored son, destined to inherit his authority and wealth; the next day he was cast into a cistern, menaced by death, and then sold into Egypt as a slave. In Egypt Joseph gradually rose to a position of authority in Potiphar's household; but in an instant his affairs were reversed and he found himself set in irons in the prison of the captain of the guard. One day he had hopes of deliverance through his friend the chief cupbearer; but that day was succeeded by many other days of discouragement and despair. Then within hours he was suddenly shaved and clothed and in the court of Pharaoh.

Sudden reversals are difficult for most of us, for our eyes are not constantly on God as Joseph's were. When we experience a sudden reversal for the worse, we are despondent. We think God has abandoned us, and we become bitter. When we experience a sudden reversal for the better, we are arrogant. Instead of thinking that God has abandoned us, we sometimes abandon God in our thinking and become quite secular. It is a rare Christian who can enjoy sudden prosperity and keep his or her spiritual life on course.

Joseph was one of those rare persons. When he was in prison he did not forget God. When the chief cupbearer and chief baker told him why they were troubled, Joseph replied, "Do not interpretations belong to God? Tell me your dreams" (Gen. 40:8). Here, before the mightiest monarch of his day, it is the same thing. Pharaoh told Joseph, "I had a dream, and no one can interpret it. But I have heard it said of you that when you hear a dream you can interpret it."

Joseph shot back, "I cannot do it, but God will give Pharaoh the answer he desires" (Gen. 41:15–16).

Joseph could have been tempted to answer Pharaoh differently. He could have reasoned that Pharaoh knew nothing about the true God and might even be offended by mention of a God other than the various deities of Egypt. Besides, this was Joseph's great opportunity. Assuming that God would give him the interpretation of Pharaoh's dream, would it not be better for him to take credit for the interpretation himself? This would advance his standing in Pharaoh's eyes, facilitate his deliverance from the prison, and gain him opportunity to witness later. Was this a temptation for Joseph? The text gives no indication that it was. For a lesser man perhaps. Not for Joseph! Joseph lived with his eyes on God. So when Pharaoh said he had heard that Joseph could interpret dreams, Joseph immediately replied that God, not himself, would give the interpretation.

At this point Pharaoh told his dream and Joseph explained it. He told of seven years of abundant harvest to be followed by seven years of famine and ended by saying boldly:

> Now let Pharaoh look for a discerning and wise man and put him in charge of the land of Egypt. Let Pharaoh appoint commissioners over the land to take a fifth of the harvest of Egypt during the seven years of abundance. They should collect all the food of these good years that are coming and store up the grain under the authority of Pharaoh, to be kept in the cities for food. This food should be held in reserve for the country, to be used during the seven years of famine that will come upon Egypt, so that the country may not be ruined by the famine.
>
> verses 33–36

The proposal seemed good to Pharaoh, so he appointed Joseph to be in charge of all Egypt. Only in regard to the throne was Pharaoh greater.

Pharaoh and Joseph's God

When Pharaoh placed Joseph in charge of all Egypt, he did so because of two rare qualities in Joseph. The two presuppose each other. First, he noticed that Joseph was "discerning and wise," the very traits Joseph called for in the man to be put in charge of the famine collections in Egypt (vv. 33, 39). This was a recognition of Joseph's character. Second, he noticed that Joseph was one "in whom is the spirit of God" (v. 38). This is the first mention in the Bible of the Holy Spirit's coming upon a man. Later it occurs a great deal (cf. Exod. 31:3–5; 35:30–31) and comes to a climax in God's pouring out his

Spirit upon all believers at Pentecost in fulfillment of Joel 2:28–32 (cf. Acts 2:1–21). Here the Holy Spirit comes upon Joseph to enable him to govern the greatest nation of his time.

In his evaluation of Joseph, Pharaoh immediately perceived that this young man of thirty had something he did not have and that God was its source. This is always the case. When a man or woman is touched by God, that person will inevitably be different from those unconverted people around him or her, and the change will be strikingly for the better. Oh, at first there may be resentment that the one whom God has saved no longer has the same values or does the same things as others, things that fill the mind and time of his or her former companions. They may say, "So-and-so thinks he is too good for us" or "She's making a fool of herself with all this religious nonsense." But in time the criticism gives way to admiration and even to the appointment of such a person to a position of great honor.

Pharaoh saw this supernatural character in Joseph. Moreover, he recognized its source and knew at once that this was the man he needed to guide Egypt in the difficult times ahead.

I wonder if people see that kind of character in us and if they recognize that it is God who has given it to us. The only way we will ever have that character (and the only way that others will ever see it) is if we have our eyes on God in all things. What happens if we see circumstances apart from God? If circumstances bring adversity, we complain and consider the world and those responsible to be unjust. If circumstances bring prosperity, we boast and think that somehow we are ultimately responsible. The one character is whining and unpleasant. The other is arrogant and intolerable. But if we have our minds on God, we see God in circumstances and trust him. Adversity strengthens and mellows us. Prosperity humbles us and draws us even closer to the Lord.

Just a dream? No, rather a dream sent by God.

Just a prison? No, rather an experience that a wise and loving God has deemed necessary for our maturing.

Just a job?

Just a friendship?

Just an accident? No, rather that in which the hand of God is working for our and others' benefit. The Bible says, "Those who honor me I will honor" (1 Sam. 2:30). Learn to honor God in all things and see if he does not advance you even in the eyes of others.

137

Joseph, the Prime Minister

Genesis 41:41–57

*So Pharaoh said to Joseph, "I hereby put you in charge of the whole land of Egypt."
Then Pharaoh took his signet ring from his finger and put it on Joseph's finger. He dressed
him in robes of fine linen and put a gold chain around his neck. He had him ride in a
chariot as his second-in-command, and men shouted before him, "Make way!" Thus he
put him in charge of the whole land of Egypt.*

*Then Pharaoh said to Joseph, "I am Pharaoh, but without your word no one will lift
hand or foot in all Egypt." Pharaoh gave Joseph the name Zaphenath-Paneah and gave
him Asenath daughter of Potiphera, priest of On, to be his wife. And Joseph went throughout the land of Egypt.*

*Joseph was thirty years old when he entered the service of Pharaoh king of Egypt. And
Joseph went out from Pharaoh's presence and traveled throughout Egypt. During the seven
years of abundance the land produced plentifully. Joseph collected all the food produced
in those seven years of abundance in Egypt and stored it in the cities. In each city he put
the food grown in the fields surrounding it. Joseph stored up huge quantities of grain,
like the sand of the sea; it was so much that he stopped keeping records because it was
beyond measure.*

*Before the years of famine came, two sons were born to Joseph by Asenath daughter
of Potiphera, priest of On. Joseph named his firstborn Manasseh and said, "It is because
God has made me forget all my trouble and all my father's household." The second son
he named Ephraim and said, "It is because God has made me fruitful in the land of my
suffering."*

The seven years of abundance in Egypt came to an end, and the seven years of famine began, just as Joseph had said. There was famine in all the other lands, but in the whole land of Egypt there was food. When all Egypt began to feel the famine, the people cried to Pharaoh for food. Then Pharaoh told all the Egyptians, "Go to Joseph and do what he tells you."

When the famine had spread over the whole country, Joseph opened the storehouses and sold grain to the Egyptians, for the famine was severe throughout Egypt. And all the countries came to Egypt to buy grain from Joseph, because the famine was severe in all the world.

The second half of Genesis 41 tells the story of Joseph's investiture as prime minister of Egypt, the position to which we have known from the beginning God had destined him. It is surely a remarkable promotion, the culmination of a rise from slavery to greatness that is perhaps unparalleled in the long history of the human race.

F. B. Meyer speaks of it in moving language: "It was a wonderful ascent, sheer in a single bound from the dungeon to the steps of the throne. His father had rebuked him; now Pharaoh, the greatest monarch of his time, welcomes him. His brethren despised him; now the proudest priesthood of the world opens its ranks to receive him by marriage into their midst, considering it wiser to conciliate a man who was from that moment to be the greatest force in Egyptian politics and life. The hands that were hard with the toils of a slave are adorned with a signet ring. The feet are no longer tormented by fetters; a chain of gold is linked around his neck. The coat of many colors torn from him by violence and defiled by blood, and the garment left in the hand of the adulteress, are exchanged for vestures of fine linen drawn from the royal wardrobe. He was once trampled upon as the offscouring of all things; now all Egypt is commanded to bow before him, as he rides forth in the second chariot, prime minister of Egypt, second only to the king."[1]

The story says that Joseph was thirty years old when he entered Pharaoh's service. He was seventeen when his brothers sold him into slavery. So only thirteen years had passed between the time Joseph was a mere shepherd boy and the day he assumed control of the world's mightiest kingdom.

The Secret of Character

In a sermon on this chapter preached many years ago, Donald Grey Barnhouse noted that "the secret of power is character, but the secret of character is God." This is remarkably demonstrated in the case of Joseph. Here was a man brought in one moment from the dungeon to the palace, where he was presented for the first time to the mightiest monarch of his day. Yet so great and striking was his character that Pharaoh, though a pagan, immediately perceived that Joseph had something he and his highest administrators did not have. It was because of his character that power passed into Joseph's hands. But as I said, it was because of God that Joseph had this character.

During the days of his adversity Joseph had looked to God and had found strength to triumph. Now, having triumphed, he would continue to look to God and go from strength to strength. In the chapters of Genesis that follow, nothing bad is ever said about Joseph. In fact, he is one of the few major characters in the Bible—Daniel is the only other—of whom this can truthfully be said.

The fact that Joseph kept his eyes on God in adversity is remarkable. But even more remarkable is the fact that he kept his eyes on God when he was prosperous. How often promotions ruin people! A man can be a strong witness for God and be wonderfully used by God in the ministry of his local church when he is in some lowly position in his firm. But let him be promoted to vice president, and suddenly he has a new image to keep up. He drops his old friends, moves in with the country club set, and now no longer has time for witnessing, Bible study, or other Christian activities. And his wife keeps pace with his deprovement! She adopts airs and now no longer primarily wants her children to be godly. She wants them to meet the right people and marry those who will promote their careers or social advancement. Many Christians have been impoverished by prosperity. Many have been brought low by promotions.

The same thing happens to nations, too, and this is one reason why the United States of America has ceased to be a godly nation. American was never a truly Christian nation, of course. But there were years in our history when godly people were numerous and exerted an influence beyond their numbers. In those days America stood for morality, and a European statesman was right in the assessment: "America is great because America is good." Unfortunately, that was long ago. Since then America has grown prosperous, and prosperity has ruined us. When we had less, Americans went to church on Sunday and generally tried to practice what was taught there. Now we have money for a vacation home where we spend weekends. Or we take trips in our campers or go golfing at the club. We think we do not need God.

Nor is it much different for those who do not have quite as much money. They may not be wealthy, but they have enough money to be able to do what they want. And in case they do not, our cities and communities feel some deep obligation to "keep the troops entertained" on Sunday. Sunday has become the biggest day of the week for professional sports, and often Sundays are given over to citywide entertainments. In Philadelphia, for example, Sundays have become "Super Sundays" or "Fundays," and God is forgotten.

This is why the morality of the nation has been declining. God is our only source of morality—not the government, not the courts, not the laws. Goodness flows from God. So if we leave God out of our lives, we begin to lose touch with what is good and tear away the fabric of morality strand by strand.

Dr. Barnhouse gives an illustration of this process in the sermon I have just mentioned. In ancient times a country's coins were not minted on the large mechanical presses that we have today. They were made by melting the gold or silver that was to become the coin, pouring a small bit onto a hard mold, then pressing a die containing the image of the ruler or a god onto the metal. Coins made in this way were irregular and had soft, uneven edges. What happened in the ancient world was that people who received these coins would take a sharp knife and carefully peel away some of the excess gold or silver. They would put this in a place where they kept their precious metal peelings, and when they had enough they would melt it down and have another coin. This was so common that in a period of just a hundred years the city of Athens passed eighty laws against trimming its coins, which only proved that everyone was doing it. Today it is almost impossible to find a coin in any museum from which the edges have not been repeatedly trimmed away.

This is what the apostle Paul referred to indirectly when in 1 Corinthians 9:27 he said, "I beat my body and make it my slave so that after I have preached to others, I myself will not be *disqualified* for the prize" (my emphasis). That word "disqualified" is *adokimos*, which was the term used to describe a coin that had been whittled away so badly that it was no longer acceptable. The merchants would not take it anymore. It had to be recalled and reminted.

This is the kind of whittling process that goes on in the individual life when prosperity gets too great and people begin to compromise and then find acceptable those low standards of behavior that would have been a horror years before. As the individual goes down, so does the nation. Soon people do not even expect justice from the courts. The courts become merely a battleground in which special-interest groups fight to get as much as they can or get permission to do whatever they desire to do, no matter how destructive or how ugly.

Joseph was not like this. For that reason he alone, though only one person, was the best thing to happen to the entire nation of Egypt in this period of its history. Joseph was advanced to the highest position of his day. But he did not say, "Well, now I am sitting pretty. Things are going my way. I can farm out the responsibilities that I am supposed to be exercising and enjoy myself thoroughly." Not at all! Joseph had his eyes upon God still. Thus, the next thing we hear him saying, after he had interpreted Pharaoh's dream and had been made prime minister and had been married and had two sons and named them, is: "It is because *God* has made me forget all my trouble and all my father's household" and "it is because *God* has made me fruitful in the land of my suffering" (vv. 51–52, my emphasis). Because he had his eyes on God, Joseph maintained his own personal morality and faithfully executed the responsibility of preparing for the famine.

The point is clear. If you are to live for God, whether in adversity (as Joseph was in adversity for most of the preceding thirteen years) or in prosperity (as he was from this point on), it must be by the power of God in your life.

A Type of Christ

When we first began to study the life of Joseph, I pointed out that this man is a type of the Lord Jesus Christ—even though he is never explicitly referred to as a type of Christ in the New Testament. Many commentators note these parallels, and A. W. Pink alone (who sometimes runs to excess in this kind of thing) lists 101 of them in the final sixty-eight pages of his *Gleanings in Genesis*.[2]

With the exception of one initial acknowledgment that Joseph is a type of Christ, I have generally passed over these parallels, not wanting to digress from the story of Joseph by doing so. But at this point it is hard to refrain from it; for Joseph at the pinnacle of his earthly success causes us to look back over his life, and the review calls attention to Jesus, who, although he was humbled during the days of his flesh, is now highly exalted.

Meyer makes the parallels as follows:

Joseph was rejected by his brethren; Jesus by the Jews, his brethren according to the flesh. Joseph was sold for twenty pieces of silver to the Ishmaelites; Jesus was sold by the treachery of Judas for thirty pieces, and then handed over to the Gentiles. Joseph was cast into prison; Jesus abode in the grave. Joseph in the prison was able to preach the gospel of deliverance to the butler; Jesus went and preached the gospel to the spirits in prison. The two malefactors of the cross find their counterpart in Joseph's fellow-prisoners. Joseph, though a Hebrew by birth and rejected by his own brethren, nevertheless was raised to supreme power in a gentile state, and saved myriads of them from death; Jesus, of Jewish birth and yet disowned by Jews, has nevertheless been exalted to the supreme seat of power and is now enthroned in the hearts of myriads of Gentiles to whom he has brought salvation from death and spiritual bread for their hunger. The very name that Pharaoh gave to Joseph meant "Savior of the world"—our Savior's title. Yes, and we must carry the parallel still further. After Joseph had been for some time ruling and blessing Egypt, his very brethren came to him for forgiveness and help; so in days not far away we shall see the Jews retracing their steps and exclaiming—as thousands are now doing in Eastern Russia—"Jesus is our Brother." So all Israel shall be saved!

We have now, therefore, to think of Jesus as seated on his throne, prime minister of the universe, the interpreter of his Father's will, the organ and executor of the divine decrees. On his head are many crowns; on his finger is the ring of sovereignty; on his loins the girdle of power. Glistening robes of light envelop him. And this is the cry which precedes him, "Bow the knee!" Have you ever bowed at his feet? It is of no avail to oppose him. The tongue of malice and envy may traduce him and refuse to let him reign. But nothing can upset the Father's decree and plan. "Yet have I set my Son upon my holy hill." "At his name every knee shall bow, and every tongue shall confess that he is Lord." Agree with him quickly. Ground your arms at his feet. "Kiss the Son, lest he be angry."[3]

Even though Meyer interprets Joseph's Egyptian name, Zaphenath-Paneah, as "Savior of the world," this is not an interpretation on which scholars are universally agreed. The name has been variously translated as "Abundance of Life," "Revealer of Secrets," "God's Word Speaking Life," and so on. Each of these can be applied to Jesus.

However, in the last generation or so, important work has been done in the area of Egyptian etymology, and this has suggested that the name Zaphenath-Paneah should more accurately be translated "God Speaks and He Lives [or 'Came into Being']." This was suggested first by the German scholar Steindorff in the periodical *Zeitschrift fuer Aegyptische Sprache* (xxvii, 41ff.). It has been picked up in the critical commentaries on Genesis by John Skinner and Gerhard Von Rad, among others.[4] If this is the true meaning of the name given to Joseph by Pharaoh, it is a magnificent testimony to the character of God in Joseph that Pharaoh saw. Joseph had said that the ability to interpret dreams was not his but God's. By giving him his Egyptian name Pharaoh confessed that this was so, adding that everything Joseph was had come about in accordance with God's will and in God's power. What a testimony! God spoke, and he came into being. Oh, that this could be noticed in everyone who has believed in Jesus as Savior!

I have been talking about the parallels between Joseph and Jesus, of course, and in this respect the name is even more appropriate. It must not suggest, as the ancient heretic Arius taught, that there was a time before which Jesus was not. That is contradicted elsewhere. But it does point to Jesus as the very Word of God, the *logos* of John 1:1, 14, through whom all else came into being. It testifies to the power of God the Father. It is in Christ that we see God and hear him as well.

"Go to Jesus"

This brings me to my final point. At the end of Genesis 41 we are told how the seven years of plenty were followed by the beginning of the seven years of famine. We see how the people—who had undoubtedly been warned by Joseph, but who (like most people everywhere) had not planned for the future and had instead consumed their abundance from the seven good years—came to Pharaoh crying out for food. Pharaoh's reply was, "Go to Joseph and do what he tells you" (v. 55).

I make this parallel. Our day is one in which the world's rulers have had disturbing visions of what the future holds. They have looked into the future and have been given dreams of world famine, runaway population growth, exhaustion of the world's material resources, and nuclear war. Even in the most favored countries and in the most favored times the produce of the years of plenty does not seem to be enough to go around, and the specter of want looms darkly just around the corner. This is no accident. The nations have forsaken God, and God is bringing them to the brink of despair.

But despair is not necessary. Disaster is not predetermined. God's man, the Lord Jesus Christ, has come. And just as the great king of Egypt told the starving, worried people of his day to go to Joseph, so does the true King of the universe command men and women everywhere today to "go to Jesus." Are you hungry for spiritual things? He is "the bread of life" (John 6:35). Are you thirsty? Jesus said, "If anyone is thirsty, let him come to me and drink" (John 7:37). In Christ is all the fullness of God (Col. 1:19). He has invited you to come to him: "Come to me, all you who are weary and burdened, and I will give you rest" (Matt. 11:28). "Whoever comes to me I will never drive away" is his promise (John 6:37). The Bible tells us that all who come will receive from him "without money and without cost" (Isa. 55:1).

The last line of Genesis 41 tells us that "the famine was severe in all the world" (v. 57). So also today. If famine has you in its grasp, you must go to Jesus and do what he tells you. You must confess your sin and receive him as your personal Savior.

138

The Gift of Forgetting

Genesis 41:50–52

Before the years of famine came, two sons were born to Joseph by Asenath daughter of Potiphera, priest of On. Joseph named his firstborn Manasseh and said, "It is because God has made me forget all my trouble and all my father's household." The second son he named Ephraim and said, "It is because God has made me fruitful in the land of my suffering."

In the middle of the account of Joseph's investiture as prime minister of Egypt and his subsequent preparation for the years of famine, there is a parenthesis about his domestic circumstances. It tells us that he was given Asenath, daughter of Potiphera, priest of On, as his wife, and that two sons were born to him: Manasseh, which means "forgetting," and Ephraim, which means "doubly fruitful." These verses are important, even though they are a parenthesis, and for that reason I deal with them briefly in this study.

By now we should be vividly aware of the importance of names in the Bible. Adam is the word for "dust" or "earth," for God formed the man from the dust of the earth and breathed into him the breath of life (Gen. 2:7). Eve

976

means "mother" in the sense of "life giver." As Adam said, "She [was to] become the mother of all the living" (Gen. 3:20). Cain means "Here he is!" Seth means "granted" or "given by God." So it goes throughout the early history of the race, as recorded in Genesis. In view of this important symbolism it is not surprising to find Joseph naming his two sons "Forgetting" and "Doubly Fruitful," as testimony to the faithfulness of God in bringing him through the years of suffering to personal fruitfulness. In this study I want to show that Joseph's experience of God's favor, symbolized by the names of his sons, should be the experience of all who know God.

The Gift of Remembering

One of the most rewarding studies of a biblical word applies to the word "forgetting." But before I deal with forgetting in a good sense, as in the name of Joseph's first son, Manasseh, it is useful to think of when not to forget, or forgetting in a bad sense. Humanity's need to remember is the background against which a good forgetting should be considered.

The background, of course, is that men and women easily forget what should be remembered. This is true of human relations; people forget the debt they owe to others. This is even truer in people's relationship to God. Peter says in one place that people are "willfully ignorant" of certain spiritual realities (2 Peter 3:5 KJV), and for that reason the Bible is everywhere filled with poignant appeals to men and women not to forget God or his commandments. A chief complaint against Israel in the Old Testament is that the people have forgotten God. In the great "Song of Moses" recorded in Deuteronomy 32, the lawgiver of Israel declares:

> You deserted the Rock, who fathered you;
> you *forgot* the God who gave you birth.
>
> verse 18, my emphasis

Isaiah said:

> You have *forgotten* God your Savior;
> you have not remembered the Rock, your fortress.
>
> Isaiah 17:10, my emphasis

The theme is strong in Jeremiah:

> A cry is heard on the barren heights,
> the weeping and pleading of the people of Israel,
> because they have perverted their ways
> and have *forgotten* the LORD their God.
>
> Jeremiah 3:21, my emphasis

"This is your lot,
  the portion I have decreed for you,"
    declares the LORD,
"because you have *forgotten* me
  and trusted in false gods."

Jeremiah 13:25, my emphasis

"My people have *forgotten* me."

Jeremiah 18:15, my emphasis

Ezekiel wrote: "Therefore this is what the Sovereign LORD says: Since you have *forgotten* me and thrust me behind your back, you must bear the consequences of your lewdness and prostitution" (Ezek. 23:35).

Because the people repeatedly forgot God, the Old Testament also frequently admonished them to remember him and his benefits. "Praise the LORD, O my soul, and *forget not* all his benefits," wrote David (Ps. 103:2, my emphasis). "*Do not forget* the things your eyes have seen" God do on your behalf, wrote Moses in Deuteronomy 4:9 (my emphasis). "Be careful *not to forget* the covenant of the LORD your God that he made with you," he said later in the same chapter (Deut. 4:23, my emphasis). "*Do not forget* the LORD," says Deuteronomy 6:12 (my emphasis). The author of Ecclesiastes declared, "*Remember* your Creator in the days of your youth" (Eccl. 12:1, my emphasis).

When we are talking about God, the commands of God, or God's great deeds in behalf of his people, it is a gift to remember these items. Not one should be forgotten.

Remembering Sins No More

Against this background of remembering God there is nevertheless a proper place for forgetting, and it is this that brings us close to Joseph's situation. What is it that a believer in God should forget?

The first thing a believer needs to forget is *any sin that has been confessed to God* and has therefore been forgiven by him. We know that if we confess sin, it is forgiven, because God tells us this is the case. In 1 John 1:9 we are told, "If we confess our sins, he is faithful and just and will forgive us our sins and purify us from all unrighteousness." This verse bases our assurance of forgiveness on two things that are found in God's character. First, God is faithful. This has bearing on forgiveness, because it means that God is faithful to his promises to forgive. He tells us that if we confess our sins, he will forgive them. First John 1:9 is itself one of these promises. Second, God is just. This refers to the death of the Lord Jesus Christ, for it is on the basis of his death that God can forgive justly, as Paul writes in Romans 3:26. God justly forgives because Jesus graciously died for sins in our place.

If God has forgiven a sin, the one who believes in Christ and has confessed the sin has no right to bring it up again. It is forgiven, as God says it is.

But the case is even stronger than this. In the Book of Jeremiah God says that he does not merely forgive the believer's sin but actually remembers it no more. The passage has to do with the new covenant and deserves a full quotation.

> "This is the covenant I will make with the house of Israel
>   after that time," declares the LORD.
> "I will put my law in their minds
>   and write it on their hearts.
> I will be their God,
>   and they will be my people.
> No longer will a man teach his neighbor,
>   or a man his brother, saying, 'Know the LORD,'
> because they will all know me,
>   from the least of them to the greatest,"
>   declares the LORD.
> "For I will forgive their wickedness
>   and will *remember their sins no more.*"

Jeremiah 31:33–34, my emphasis

What a remarkable statement this is! It should not be taken in an absolute sense, for if that were the case, it would be opposed to the doctrine of God's omniscience. It would mean that there is something God has ceased to know, some past happening in history that has somehow been erased from his mind. The text cannot mean that and God still be omniscient, as we know he is.

Nevertheless, with that qualification this is still a remarkable statement. For it is undoubtedly meant to contrast with those many other statements that stress God's remembering. God says, "Can a mother forget the baby at her breast and have no compassion on the child she has borne? Though she may forget, *I will not forget* you!" (Isa. 49:15, my emphasis). God says of the wicked, "*I will never forget* anything they have done" (Amos 8:7, my emphasis). In these and other texts God promises to remember everything. And yet, in Jeremiah 31:34 God says he will forget the sins of his people. It means that God will never bring them up against them. God will never say to you, "Remember that sin you committed, that bad thing you did." God will never say that as long as you have come to Christ, confessed the sin, and asked forgiveness for it.

I tell you who will bring it up: the devil. The devil will bring it up, because the devil is a nagger and he will try to hinder your present walk with Christ by a remembrance of past failures. The devil will say, "You don't think that you can possibly live a Christian life, do you? Remember what you did back there! That was terrible! A Christian doesn't do things like that! You had better just give up and not take this Christian thing too seriously! Here, I'll give you something else to do, something more in line with your character."

Let me say it clearly: If you find yourself thinking along those lines, it is not the voice of God you are hearing, but the voice of Satan; and you have no right to listen to it. Of course, if you have not confessed your sin, you must begin there. Sin must be confessed. But if you have confessed it, then you must forget it in the same sense that God has forgotten it. You know it is there. You know what you have done, and the fact of that past failure should keep you closer to God. But you have no right to remember it in the sense of bringing it up like a dog digging up an old bone to gnaw on it. To do that is sheer unbelief. It is to say, "God, I know that you have promised to forgive my sins and forget about them forever. But I am not sure I can really believe that. Are you sure we shouldn't fuss over them a little bit further?"

Oh, the joy of being able to forget about past sins! In hell no one forgets; that is one of the horrors of hell. Do you recall C. S. Lewis's depiction of hell in *The Great Divorce*? He describes it as a place where nobody ever forgets anything and instead remembers every slight, every cruel exchange of words, every harmful act—and where everybody is utterly unforgiving. In heaven all these things are put away, for all has become new. The sins of God's people are truly forgotten and gone.

Forgetting the Past

All this has been preparation for appreciating the text in which Joseph is said to have named his son "Manasseh," since God had made him forget his trouble and his father's household. The subject here is not sin but rather the sorrows and troubles of the past. Joseph was saying that God had enabled him to forget these as well. Again, Joseph did not mean that he literally forgot that he had ever had a father and eleven brothers. In the very next chapter we discover how much he missed them and longed to see them again. He meant rather that God had healed his wounds, suffered as the result of past abuses and disappointments, and had made his life fruitful.

I have known people—I am sure you have too—who have been so obsessed with disappointments or slights that their whole life is warped by them, and they are greatly hindered from living a fruitful life now. They have not allowed God to heal them. Joseph could have been like that. He had certainly had many disappointments. Instead he let the past be past and went on with God.

I think here of the way the apostle Paul put the principle in his description of his goals in the Christian life. He wrote, "Not that I have already obtained all this, or have already been made perfect, but I press on to take hold of that for which Christ Jesus took hold of me. Brothers, I do not consider myself yet to have taken hold of it. But one thing I do: *Forgetting* what is behind and straining toward what is ahead, I press on toward the goal to win the prize for which God has called me heavenward in Christ Jesus" (Phil. 3:12–14, my emphasis).

When Paul wrote that he forgot those things that were behind, what was it exactly that he forgot? Well, it was not his knowledge of the Bible and Christian doctrine, because he had just written a letter that is full of it. Some of the greatest truths of the Christian faith are stated in this very chapter in a striking, brief form. Nor was it a forgetting of God's grace and past mercies, because he had also been talking about them in this letter. He knew that all he had of value in his life was through the grace of God manifested in Christ Jesus. Paul's forgetting was along the same line as Joseph's forgetting. In 2 Corinthians 6:4–10 he spoke of some of the things he had suffered: troubles, hardships, distresses, beatings, imprisonments and riots, hard work, sleepless nights, hunger. Yet God had kept him through those, and he was not willing that a remembrance of those past hardships now should deter his present aspirations for God's service.

I think too that Paul was unwilling to remember past blessings if even these should keep him from attaining the graces of God yet to come. There is an illustration of the opposite attitude in the Old Testament story of God's leading Israel out of Egypt toward the Promised Land. God had provided everything they could possibly have needed for their journey. They had shade by day and light by night. They had water and manna. The time came, however, when the people ceased to look forward to the land God was giving them and instead looked back to their life in Egypt, which they began to think of as having been better. They said, "We *remember* the fish we ate in Egypt at no cost—also the cucumbers, melons, leeks, onions and garlic. But now we have lost our appetite; we never see anything but this manna!" (Num. 11:5–6, my emphasis). The people were dissatisfied and began to hunger for past blessings.

This does not mean that we are not to be thankful for past blessings. If we had been among the people of Israel when they were in Egypt and had been able to buy melons, leeks, onions, garlic, and cucumbers, it would have been quite proper to thank God for them, especially if we had been slaves. It would have been proper years later to remember how gracious God had been. This would have been right. But it would have been wrong to long for these things after God had begun to lead us into new paths and had set new and greater blessings before us.

Unfortunately there have always been leeks-and-garlic Christians. You are one if you are constantly looking to the past. If your Christian testimony is taken up with what God did for you thirty or forty years ago, or if you are constantly talking about the good old days when God's blessing on your life seemed great, then you are looking to the past. You can never do that and move forward. One of my good friends describes old age as the point in life when a person ceases to look forward and looks back. If that is accurate, then there are certainly a lot of old or middle-aged Christians—and I do not mean only in terms of their years. They are living a leeks-and-garlic type of Christianity, and Paul warns against it. He would say, "Look! Past blessings are fine.

We have received them from God's hands; we should be thankful for them. We rejoice in everything that he has done in our lives. But now we must let those things lie in the past and move forward. There can be no progress without this proper forgetting."

Doubly Fruitful

We come, finally, to the second of Joseph's sons, Ephraim, whose name means "doubly fruitful." There must have been times in Joseph's life when he thought—though nothing of this sort is recorded—that he would never be fruitful. He had tried to do good work for Potiphar, but it had all come to nothing. Even his faithfulness in prison came to nothing. He would never have an honorable position. He would never have a home. He would never have a wife. He would never have children. God was training him for very great things in these circumstances, of course. But Joseph did not know that. He could have written over this long period of his life: "Fruitless and unfruitful."

Ah, but God was not finished with him yet! The day came when God transformed his circumstances and made him so fruitful that years later, when his aged father, Jacob, came to reflect on his son's remarkable life, it was Joseph's fruitfulness that particularly grabbed his attention:

> Joseph is a *fruitful* vine,
>   a *fruitful* vine near a spring,
>   whose branches climb over a wall.
> With bitterness archers attacked him;
>   they shot at him with hostility.
> But his bow remained steady,
>   his strong arms stayed limber,
> because of the hand of the Mighty One of Jacob,
>   because of the Shepherd, the Rock of Israel,
> because of your father's God, who helps you,
>   because of the Almighty, who blesses you
> with blessings of the heavens above,
>   blessings of the deep that lies below,
>   blessings of the breast and womb.
>
>   Genesis 49:22–25, my emphasis

It could have been said of Joseph, as it is of the righteous man in Psalm 1, that he did not "walk in the counsel of the wicked or stand in the way of sinners or sit in the seat of mockers." But his delight was "in the law of the LORD," and as a result, he became "like a tree planted by streams of water, which yields its fruit in season and whose leaf does not wither. Whatever he [did] prosper[ed]" (vv. 1–3).

I mention two things in closing. First, it is significant that Joseph named his first son Manasseh ("forgetting") and his second son Ephraim ("doubly fruitful"), rather than doing it the other way around. For no one can really be fruitful until the past is forgotten in the proper sense. If we are living in the past, whether that is the past of unconfessed sin, hurts, suffering, or even old blessings, we will never be completely fruitful in the present. We must let the past be the past, forgetting it, and go on with God.

Second, I notice that Ephraim, being a Hebrew plural of emphasis, does not mean merely "fruitful" (as some commentators have rendered it) but "doubly fruitful," for the one who is blessed by God should go on from strength to strength and from blessing to blessing. This is what Jesus was talking about in John 15 when he used the same image to predict a fruitful spiritual life for his disciples. He said that he had chosen them, as God the Father had clearly chosen Joseph; that he would prune their branches, as God had pruned Joseph during the years of his suffering; that he would nevertheless keep them close to him so that they would remain in him in all circumstances, as God had kept Joseph during the years of his troubles. The result of this would be not merely that they would bear fruit (John 15:4), but that they would bear "much fruit" (vv. 5, 8), "fruit that will last [that is, 'fruit that would remain']" (v. 16).

That is what Jesus has in mind for each of his disciples, that we may be "doubly fruitful" in his service.

139

God and the Conscience Part 1: The Pinch of Want

Genesis 42:1–5

When Jacob learned that there was grain in Egypt, he said to his sons, "Why do you just keep looking at each other?" He continued, "I have heard that there is grain in Egypt. Go down there and buy some for us, so that we may live and not die."

Then ten of Joseph's brothers went down to buy grain from Egypt. But Jacob did not send Benjamin, Joseph's brother, with the others, because he was afraid that harm might come to him. So Israel's sons were among those who went to buy grain, for the famine was in the land of Canaan also.

The human conscience is a very strange thing. Considering how evil men and women are, it is surprising that we have a conscience at all. Yet we do. At times it plagues us. One of my resource books on Genesis points out that since 1811 the U.S. government has been receiving anonymous sums of money as self-imposed fines for a variety of offenses, such as taking army blankets for souvenirs, deliberately failing to put the correct postage on a letter, or cheating on one's income tax. A widow was looking over her late husband's books and discovered that he had cheated the government out of fifty dollars the year before; she promptly mailed a check for that amount to the Treasury. These monies have been placed in a special account named the Federal Conscience Fund, which now totals over three million dollars.[1]

Conscience lies at the heart of William Shakespeare's best-known play, *Hamlet*. During much of the play it restrains Hamlet from bold action. "Conscience doth make cowards of us all," he explains (act 3, sc. 1). On the other hand, it is the device he uses to reveal the guilt of King Claudius of Denmark, who has murdered his father. "The play's the thing wherein I'll catch the conscience of the King," he cries as act 2, scene 2 ends.

George Washington called conscience "that little sparkle of celestial fire." Lord Byron, who needed but seemed to profit little from his conscience, called it "the oracle of God."[2]

But here is the problem. It is true that we have something called conscience that sometimes makes us feel guilty for past wrongdoings. But conscience is often far from overwhelming in its effects, and it is tragically possible for us to kill it or at least put it very soundly to sleep. I mentioned a proper working of conscience in William Shakespeare's *Hamlet*. But one of Shakespeare's most wicked characters is Richard III, and he, though bothered at one time by an accusing conscience—

> My conscience hath a thousand several tongues,
> And every tongue brings in a several tale,
> And every tale condemns me for a villain.
>
> *Richard III*, act 5, scene 3

—nevertheless successfully triumphs over it, so that at the end he is able to call out, "Conscience, avaunt, Richard's himself again!" (act 5, sc. 3).

One man who was obviously struggling to put conscience to rest wrote to the government, saying, "I have cheated on my income tax. I can't sleep. Here is a check for seventy-five dollars. If I still can't sleep, I'll send you the balance."

Sundial of the Soul

What is conscience? One writer has compared conscience to a sundial, which is able to give fairly good time by day when the sun is shining on it but is totally unable to give any kind of time by night. We imagine a boy and a girl on a date, and the girl asks, "What time is it? Mother told me to be home by eleven o'clock." It is pitch black when she says this. The boy says, "Well, here's a sundial. Let's see." He strikes a match and holds it up to the gnomon. "Look, it's only eight-thirty!" If he moves the match around, he can make the sundial read any time he wants. Seven-thirty! Five-thirty! Twelve noon! That is no good, you see. Mother said that her daughter was to be home by eleven o'clock sun time.

Another way of showing why it is inadequate to "let your conscience be your guide," as we say, is that we can wrestle our conscience down. The first time you are tempted to do something you know you should not do, your conscience will thunder, "No!" So of course, you do not do it.

But then you begin to work on your conscience. You talk to it, saying, "Well, I realize that for the reason I had in mind at first it probably was not right for me to do what I wanted to; you were no doubt right to tell me not to. But I've been thinking it over, and I think that although I couldn't do it for the reason I mentioned last week, I could probably do it for this reason. . . ."

Again your conscience says, "No," but not quite as loudly as before.

A week later you try again. "Yes, I understand that neither of those first two reasons was very good. But I think maybe I could do it for this reason. . . ."

Your conscience says, "No"—quietly.

You add, "And here is another reason I've thought of. . . ."

Your conscience says nothing. So you go out and do it.

There is only one way in which conscience can be a sure guide to right conduct, and that is when the light of God's Word is shining on it. When the light of God shines on the sundial of your conscience, you get the right time. But apart from that the conscience is like a trained circus dog. You whistle once, and it will stand up. You whistle twice, and it will roll over. The third time it will play dead.

The Consciences of Joseph's Brothers

In Genesis 42 we come to this matter of the conscience. For in a certain sense the story of Genesis ceases to be merely Joseph's story at this point and becomes largely the story of Joseph's ten brothers as God works through many devices to awaken their nearly dead consciences and bring them to repentance and cleansing. We do not know much about the state of their hearts in the long years leading up to this chapter. But they had been guilty of great wickedness, and they never mentioned God. It is probably right to regard them as having been unsaved men. Therefore, it is through God's work on their consciences that they are actually born again.

In this and the next half-dozen messages we are going to see how God shines upon a darkened conscience, stirs it, and brings repentance.

I have spoken several times of our ability to kill the conscience or at least put it into such a deep sleep that it cannot bother us. But as we begin this chapter we cannot really feel that the consciences of Joseph's brothers were utterly subdued. Dozing perhaps, but fitfully! Wounded, even gravely wounded, but not dead! Why do I say this? It is because of a very strange sentence in verse 1. Genesis 42:1–2 tells us, "When Jacob learned that there was grain in Egypt, he said to his sons, "Why do you just keep looking at each other? . . . I have heard that there is grain in Egypt. Go down there and buy some for us, so that we may live and not die." What is the significance of that question, "Why do you just keep looking at each other?" And what does it have to do with ten men being sent to Egypt to buy grain?

Well, there is a proverb that says: "Never speak of rope in the house of a hangman." We remember when we begin to think about this, that Egypt was the place into which these men—Benjamin had not been among them—had sold Joseph. They had planned to kill him. But when the caravan of Midianite merchants came by on their way to Egypt, Judah said, "Come, let's sell him to the Ishmaelites and not lay our hands on him; after all, he is our brother, our own flesh and blood" (Gen. 37:27). This was done. The Midianites counted out the twenty shekels of silver. Joseph was handed over. The last the brothers saw of Joseph was his anguished face as he was led away in chains with the caravan.

The brothers devised a lie to explain his disappearance to Jacob. They tore Joseph's robe and dipped it in blood, pretending that a wild animal had killed and eaten him. Then they tried to put the incident from their minds. But they could not. We can imagine the furtive glances between them whenever Joseph's name would be mentioned, and we can imagine the weight that must have descended on them whenever the place of their brother's imprisonment was spoken of.

Egypt? . . . Egypt?

Judah must have looked at Reuben, and Reuben at Simeon. Levi must have thrown anguished glances at Zebulun. "Why do you keep looking at each other?" Jacob asked. Egypt? As Shakespeare said, "Conscience doth make cowards of us all."

God's First Weapon

The fact that Joseph's brothers looked guiltily at one another instead of taking decisive steps when the family heard that grain was in Egypt, shows that their consciences were not entirely dead, only asleep, and that fitfully. But if nothing more had happened in this story than the mere mention of Egypt, these men would doubtless have continued on in their own guilty way and would have died unrepentant. This was their way, but it was not God's way. God now moved to awaken them and lead them to repentance.

The first weapon God used was famine. That is, he brought the pinch of material want into their lives so that they could no longer remain outwardly content in Canaan but were forced out of their peaceful backyard pond into new waters. Egypt? That was the last place on earth these brothers would have chosen to go. What if they should meet Joseph? How would they be able to endure the reproachful hatred of that innocent but physically broken slave? Still, there was famine in Canaan, as well as in Egypt. Crops had failed. The livestock were dying. People would die eventually. What should they do? If there was corn in Egypt, they would have to go there or perish—as much as they dreaded the thought of doing so.

There is a saying, "Needs must when the devil drives."

988 God and the Conscience Part 1: The Pinch of Want

It would be better to say, "Needs must when the sovereign God determines." God was determining, and the famine was his first weapon to awaken conscience in these lives.

It is interesting how often we find this principle expressed in the Word of God. One classical passage is in the book of the minor prophet Hosea. Hosea had a wife who proved unfaithful to him, as God had told him in advance she would be. But although she ran away in her unfaithfulness, God continued to deal with her, at times through Hosea himself, and eventually she came back and loved him as at the first. The woman's name was Gomer. In Gomer's case, the first thing God did was to provide for her in spite of her waywardness. She had fallen into a place in life in which the man she was living with could no longer provide for her properly. So God sent Hosea to see that she had food to eat and adequate clothes to wear. She had said,

> "I will go after my lovers,
>   who give me my food and my water,
>   my wool and my linen, my oil and my drink."
>
> Hosea 2:5

But her lovers had failed her, and it was actually Hosea who provided these items.

> "She has not acknowledged that I was the one
>   who gave her the grain, the new wine and oil."
>
> verse 8

This gracious provision by her rejected husband was meant to soften Gomer's heart and bring her back to Hosea, just as God's gracious provision for us is meant to draw us to him. But Gomer would not allow God's bounty to turn her from sin. So next God took away her necessities.

> "Therefore I will take away my grain when it ripens,
>   and my new wine when it is ready.
> I will take back my wool and my linen,
>   intended to cover her nakedness. . . .
>
> I will stop all her celebrations:
>   her yearly festivals, her New Moons,
>   her Sabbath days—all her appointed feasts.
>
> I will ruin her vines and her fig trees,
>   which she said were her pay from her lovers."
>
> verses 9, 11–12

Has God done that in your life? Has he dispatched the specter of deprivation, the pinch of want, to bring you back to him?

Perhaps the famine you are feeling is a famine for the Word of God. Amos prophesied about the same time in Israel's history as Hosea did, and he also spoke of famine, graphically, without Hosea's imagery. He quoted God as saying,

> "I gave you empty stomachs in every city
>> and lack of bread in every town,
>>> yet you have not returned to me. . . .
>
> I also withheld rain from you
>> when the harvest was still three months away. . . .
>
> Many times I struck your gardens and vineyards,
>> I struck them with blight and mildew.
> Locusts devoured your fig and olive trees,
>> yet you have not returned to me. . . .
>
> I sent plagues among you
>> as I did to Egypt."
>
> Amos 4:6–7, 9–10

None of these devices worked. So, says God,

> "The days are coming . . .
>> when I will send [another] famine through the land—
> not a famine of food or a thirst for water,
>> but a famine of hearing the words of the LORD.
> Men will stagger from sea to sea
>> and wander from north to east,
> searching for the word of the LORD,
>> but they will not find it."
>
> Amos 8:11–12

When God tells one of his children something the person does not want to hear, he or she often wishes that God would stop talking. But what if God actually did so? Ah, that is much, much worse. Without physical bread a man or woman may die but live forever. We can live eternally without bread. But what if we are deprived of God's Word? We cannot live at all without that. Jesus said, "Man does not live on bread alone, but on every word that comes from the mouth of God" (Matt. 4:4; cf. Deut. 8:3). To be deprived of that spoken bread is disastrous.

The Lost Son

There is one more great example of this theme in Scripture, but I have held it until now because of its outcome. It tells what should happen when God brings the pinch of want to bear. It is the story of the Prodigal Son.

Jesus said that a certain man had two sons. One day the younger of the two came to him to demand his share of the estate. After the father had divided the inheritance, the boy took off for a far country, where he wasted his wealth in wild living. The story says, "After he had spent everything, there was a severe famine in that whole country, and he began to be in need. So he went and hired himself out to a citizen of that country, who sent him to his fields to feed pigs. He longed to fill his stomach with the pods that the pigs were eating, but no one gave him anything" (Luke 15:14–16).

Fortunately the son's deprived circumstances got through to him, and he came to his senses. He said, "How many of my father's hired men have food to spare, and here I am starving to death! I will set out and go back to my father and say to him: Father, I have sinned against heaven and against you. I am no longer worthy to be called your son" (vv. 17–19). Then, having made his resolution, he put it into practice and went home.

That is what the pinch of want should do to you—if you are in a far country, if you have squandered your wealth in wild living, if you have sinned against both God and man. It should bring you to your senses, send you home, and produce a genuine confession. If it does do that, you will find your heavenly Father ready to receive you and joyfully provide for you again.

In our last study, when we were still in Genesis 41, we saw that God blessed Joseph in Egypt after his many long years of suffering and gave him a son whom Joseph called Manasseh. Manasseh means "forgetting." "It is because God has made me forget all my trouble and all my father's household," Joseph said (Gen. 41:51). Joseph had the gift of forgetting. But the brothers? In their unrepentant state the brothers had no son named Manasseh. There was no forgetting for them. Egypt? . . . Egypt? How could they forget what they had done to their brother? Still, God was working. The famine in Canaan was the first of his increasingly stringent measures designed to return them to himself. After that they too would be able to forget about the past. The far country would be behind them, and they would be together with their father and younger brother again.

The pinch of want is never pleasant, but it is a gift when it brings us to our senses. David said, "Before I was afflicted I went astray, but now I obey your word" (Ps. 119:67). May God awaken our consciences to that same obedience.

140

God and the Conscience Part 2: The Pain of Harsh Treatment

Genesis 42:6–16

Now Joseph was the governor of the land, the one who sold grain to all its people. So when Joseph's brothers arrived, they bowed down to him with their faces to the ground. As soon as Joseph saw his brothers, he recognized them, but he pretended to be a stranger and spoke harshly to them. "Where do you come from?" he asked.

"From the land of Canaan," they replied, "to buy food."

Although Joseph recognized his brothers, they did not recognize him. Then he remembered his dreams about them and said to them, "You are spies! You have come to see where our land is unprotected."

"No, my lord," they answered. "Your servants have come to buy food. We are all the sons of one man. Your servants are honest men, not spies."

"No!" he said to them. "You have come to see where our land is unprotected."

But they replied, "Your servants were twelve brothers, the sons of one man, who lives in the land of Canaan. The youngest is now with our father, and one is no more."

Joseph said to them, "It is just as I told you: You are spies! And this is how you will be tested: As surely as Pharaoh lives, you will not leave this place unless your youngest brother comes here. Send one of your number to get your brother; the rest of you will be

kept in prison, so that your words may be tested to see if you are telling the truth. If you
are not, then as surely as Pharaoh lives, you are spies!"

At the end of the previous study I told the story of the Prodigal Son, who was awakened to his deplorable state by hunger while in a far country. As Jesus told the story, the young man "came to his senses" and said, "How many of my father's hired men have food to spare, and here I am starving to death! I will set out and go back to my father and say to him: Father, I have sinned against heaven and against you. I am no longer worthy to be called your son." The remarkable thing is that he actually did what he said he would do. He "got up and went to his father" and confessed his sin (Luke 15:17–21).

This is what the pinch of want should do to us if God sends it. It should awaken us to our condition and cause us to confess our unconfessed sin. Unfortunately, as we know, physical want does not always have this effect. God often has to apply harsher treatment.

Sticks and Stones

God was to do this with Joseph's older brothers. They had been guilty of a great sin in having sold their younger brother Joseph into slavery. But although they had not been entirely successful in suppressing the memory of this great wickedness—whenever Joseph's name or the name of the country into which he had been sold was mentioned, they could be seen casting furtive, guilty glances at one another (Gen. 42:1)—they had nevertheless suppressed the memory enough so that it was going to take a very harsh and prolonged treatment to elicit a confession. Without the pinch of physical want they would never have gone down to Egypt. They would have gone anywhere else if there had been hope of finding food anywhere other than in Egypt. But even having been forced to Egypt by the famine, they would still never have confessed their sin if God had not used an increasingly hard collection of devices to tighten his grip on them and force their confession to the surface.

The second of these devices—after the pinch of physical want—was the pain of harsh treatment at the hands of Joseph. Before long this was to become harsh treatment of a physical sort; all of them were cast into prison, and one of them, Simeon, was kept in prison. But at the beginning, this harsh treatment came merely in the form of words. The story tells us that when the brothers came down to Egypt to buy grain, Joseph "recognized them, . . . pretended to be a stranger and spoke harshly to them" (Gen. 42:6–7).

"What is so bad about that?" someone asks. "After all, it was just words; words couldn't hurt them." Remember the little childhood jingle:

> Sticks and stones may break my bones,
> But words can never hurt me.

I think that of all the untruths that are foisted onto children, this one about "words never hurting" is perhaps the most unjustified and vicious. It is not that sticks and stones do not hurt. They do. Physical abuse—we can add material want as the result of famine—does hurt us. But it does not hurt nearly so much as harsh words. We can starve to the point of severe malnutrition and recover; we can almost forget the hunger. But words? Harsh words that have been spoken to us are never forgotten. Words cut deeper than any sword, and we usually carry the wounds of words with us to our graves.

I remember a story Dale Carnegie tells on himself in his classic volume *How to Win Friends and Influence People*. Early in the book Carnegie makes the point that criticism of another person is futile because it puts the other person on the defensive and usually makes him want to justify himself. And it is dangerous because it wounds the other's pride, hurts his sense of importance, and arouses resentment. Then Carnegie said this: When he was still very young and was still trying to impress people, he wrote a foolish letter to the American author Richard Harding Davis. A few weeks earlier he had received a letter from someone else with this notation at the bottom: "Dictated but not read." He was impressed with that. It sounded busy and important. So when he wrote to Richard Davis, although he wasn't the slightest bit busy or important, he ended his note with the words: "Dictated but not read." Davis never answered the letter. He merely returned it with this message scribbled across the bottom: "Your bad manners are exceeded only by your bad manners."

Carnegie confessed that he had blundered and probably deserved the rebuke. But he resented and remembered it. In fact, he remembered the hurt so sharply that ten years later when he read in the paper of the death of Richard Harding Davis, the one thing that came to his mind was the insult the author had given him.[1]

It is not only insults that hurt us. Even truth hurts, sometimes even when it is spoken kindly. Not long ago I was doing a study of divorce in which I criticized the increasingly permissive stance of evangelical leaders. Because I was doing that, someone gave me two issues of *Eternity* magazine in which the late columnist Joseph Bayly had said virtually the same thing. He expressed compassion for the hurting divorcee, as any of us should do. But he challenged his readers, especially ministers and other spiritual leaders, to take the plain teaching of the Bible seriously. "Somehow," he said, "we must restore the sacredness of the marriage vows."[2]

That was in the issue for November 1982. In May of the following year Bayly published a letter that had been sent to him in response to the earlier article. It read: "My reaction to the article is one of deep compassion for the angry, frightened, threatened person who wrote it. . . . Certainly the vituperation and the almost hysterical condemnation that characterize this article do not demonstrate the love we are commanded to have for one another. If it does, please don't love me anymore!"[3]

It is clear to anyone who reads the original article and the letter responding to it that the only "angry, frightened, threatened, vituperative, and hysterical" person is the one who wrote the letter. But that aside, the response is vivid evidence of how deeply truth (not to mention an injustice or insult) cuts the mind and conscience.

> Sticks and stones may break my bones,
> But words can never hurt me.

No! Words do hurt. Words work, which is one reason why God uses true words to unsettle us and awaken our consciences.

The Voice of God

Words are what Joseph, under God's leading, used to bring his brothers to their senses. Some writers have been critical of Joseph at this point, suggesting that his decision to conceal his identity and deal harshly with his brothers was wrong and unmerciful. According to these people, Joseph should have made himself known immediately. But people who embrace this type of sentimental, naive romanticism do not get appointed to positions of great authority, such as the one Joseph occupied, nor should they. This was a matter involving a great wrong; it required perceptive and very careful handling.

We must remember that these were hard men. Years before this, when Joseph was just a boy, they had dissembled with the Shechemites, who had defiled their sister Dinah, then massacred the entire village. Their father said they had made him "a stench" to the Canaanites and Perizzites (Gen. 34:30). Reuben had dishonored his father by sleeping with his father's concubine Bilhah (Gen. 35:22). Judah had gone in to his daughter-in-law Tamar, thinking her a prostitute, and had gotten her pregnant (Genesis 38). And then all the brothers together had sold Joseph into slavery (Genesis 37). These were not men a person could treat gently. It took a vigorous shaking by the prime minister of Egypt to unsettle them.

Besides, there is also the matter of Joseph's being God's man. He had been honored more than once as a prophet of God. God had spoken to him, guided him, protected him, kept him from sin. Surely he was not left to his own devices now, but was rather acting as God's agent in awakening the consciences of these brothers. His words were God's voice to them.

Probably this is what we are to understand by the reminder of Joseph's dream about the brothers in verse 9. More than twenty-two years before this, when Joseph had been just a boy, he had dreamed that he and his brothers were in the field binding grain when suddenly his sheaf rose and stood upright and theirs gathered around and bowed down. Again, he dreamed that the sun, moon, and eleven stars bowed to him. This dream was fulfilled for the first time on this occasion when, as we are told, "Joseph's brothers arrived [and] bowed down to him with their faces to the ground" (v. 6). When Joseph saw them bowing, he remembered his dreams. Was that an accident? Could Joseph have remembered his dreams and not have also been reminded that the hand of God was in this business and would be until the end?

Robert Candlish wrote that, in his opinion, if Joseph were left to himself he would have revealed his identity in a moment but that he was restrained by God, who was using him for the salvation of his brothers. "It was the Lord that brought [the dreams] to his remembrance, and Joseph, I am persuaded, recognized the Lord in this. At once he perceives that this affair of his brethren coming to him is of the Lord. It is not a common occurrence; it is not mere casual coincidence. The Lord is here—in this place and in this business; and therefore the Lord must regulate the whole, and fix the time and manner of discovery. If he had been left to himself, Joseph would not have hesitated a moment; his is not a cold or crafty temperament; he is no maneuverer; he would have had all over within the first few minutes. But the Lord restrains him. He is, I doubt not, consciously in the Lord's hand—doing violence to his own nature to serve the Lord's purposes. And much of the interest and pathos of these scenes will be found to lie in the strong working of that nature under the control and guidance of the Lord."[4]

The Play's the Thing

I think, too, that F. B. Meyer is probably right when he suggests that Joseph probably repeated exactly the scene that had taken place at the pit's mouth when his brothers had first fallen upon him years before. This is a hard thing to prove, of course, but it is reasonable.

Although we are not given all the details we might wish in Genesis 37, it is not unreasonable to think that when Joseph's brothers saw him coming toward them in his envied tunic, they probably rushed at him, accusing him of having come to spy out their corrupt behavior and report on them to their father. As I say, we are not told they did this. But it is reasonable to think they may have done so, and if they did, it would explain why Joseph immediately thought of accusing them of the same thing: "You are spies!" (Gen. 42:9, 14). Moreover, if the brothers had accused Joseph of having been a spy for their father, the lad would certainly have protested that he was no spy, that he was only concerned for their welfare—the same thing the brothers were forced to say later: "No, my lord. . . . Your servants have come to buy food. . . . Your servants are honest men, not spies" (vv. 10–11). To carry the parallel a bit further, it is clear that Joseph's being cast into the pit in the earlier story has a parallel in his putting the brothers into prison in the second (v. 17).

This approach to the brothers on Joseph's part would have made a powerful appeal to their consciences. Indeed, it is shortly after their imprisonment that the brothers confess their sin openly for the first time, perhaps themselves suggesting a parallel: "Surely we are being punished because of our brother. We saw how distressed he was when he pleaded with us for his life, but we would not listen; that's why this distress has come upon us" (v. 21).

In the last study, when I first introduced the matter of the conscience and asked about its strengths and limitations, I referred to William Shakespeare's tragedy *Hamlet* because it has so much to say about conscience. That play is worth recalling, because the device that Hamlet used to uncover his murderous uncle's guilt is comparable to what Joseph may have used here. Before the play begins, Hamlet's uncle has murdered his father to gain the crown of Denmark. Hamlet suspects the murder and wants to avenge it. How is he to make sure? Claudius seems to be guilty, but is he? Even after the ghost of Hamlet's father appears and tells him the details of his murder, Hamlet hesitates to strike. What if he should be wrong? What if the king, his uncle, is innocent?

At last he hits upon the idea of a play. A troup of players has come to the castle, and Hamlet arranges to have them perform a play reenacting the details of the murder the ghost had told him about. He calls it "The Mousetrap" and identifies it as the device by which he will catch the king's conscience. When the play is performed, the king is deeply affected. He rises suddenly and rushes from the room. "Give me some light," he says. Later he confesses his fault, though not openly:

> O, my offence is rank, it smells to heaven:
> It hath the primal eldest curse upon't,
> A brother's murder.
>
> Act 3, scene 3

If Joseph was reenacting the scene at the pit, perhaps even repeating to the brothers the words they had hurled at him, which had been indelibly etched in his memory, then it is understandable that the brothers began to come around at this point. Joseph's words were not an unbridled outpouring of invective or cruelty. They were carefully calculated words that proved effective in bringing the brothers to a necessary confession of their sin and so to salvation.

Our Elder Brother

That is why we must never resent or resist the harsh treatment God sometimes gives out as we study his Word or hear it proclaimed from the pulpit. God hates sin. Therefore the Word of God, which reflects his holy character, customarily exposes our sin and calls for repentance. Comfort? Yes, the Bible contains great comfort, and promises too. But the comfort and promises are for those who confess their sin, obey God, and pursue righteousness.

Perhaps these words have been used of God to bring to mind some distant but unconfessed sin in your life. You may almost have forgotten it. But because it is unconfessed, it is offensive in the sight of heaven. God is probing, and he is using words to do it.

"You shall have no other gods before me." Have you put other things, even self, in the place of God?

"You shall not make for yourself an idol in the form of anything in heaven above or on the earth beneath or in the waters below." Have you made an idol of a career, another person, a vice, a virtue? Are you god in your own life?

"You shall not misuse the name of the LORD your God." Have you misused God's name? Have you misused religion itself, as if it were something to advance you rather than express your indebtedness to God?

"Remember the Sabbath day by keeping it holy."

"Honor your father and your mother."

"You shall not murder."

"You shall not commit adultery."

"You shall not steal."

"You shall not give false testimony against your neighbor."

"You shall not covet your neighbor's house. You shall not covet your neighbor's wife, or his manservant or maidservant, his ox or donkey, or anything that belongs to your neighbor" (Exod. 20:2–17). Have you committed these sins? If you have, God is speaking sharply—not diplomatically—at this point. He is telling you to confess those buried sins. Your spiritual life depends on it.

I can make it even clearer than that. If you have not confessed your sin, especially if you have not yet believed on Christ, I tell you that your sin is the sin of Joseph's brothers. You have a brother—he is not afraid to call you brother—who has never been concerned for anything in your case but your good. And what have you done to him? You have accused him of spying out your hidden sins to destroy them. You have driven him from your life. In the person of those who have gone before you in history, you have reviled him, spit upon him, crucified him. You must come to the place where you plead guilty concerning your brother. That is hard. It is painful to make that confession.

But once you confess the sin, you find that Jesus is most gracious. Indeed, he is so gracious that he has already gone to death before you, enduring the cross, so that you might be saved both for this life and for eternity.

141

God and the Conscience Part 3: The Press of Solitude

Genesis 42:17–23

And he put them all in custody for three days.

On the third day, Joseph said to them, "Do this and you will live, for I fear God: If you are honest men, let one of your brothers stay here in prison, while the rest of you go and take grain back for your starving households. But you must bring your youngest brother to me, so that your words may be verified and that you may not die." This they proceeded to do.

They said to one another, "Surely we are being punished because of our brother. We saw how distressed he was when he pleaded with us for his life, but we would not listen; that's why this distress has come upon us."

Reuben replied, "Didn't I tell you not to sin against the boy? But you wouldn't listen! Now we must give an accounting for his blood." They did not realize that Joseph could understand them, since he was using an interpreter.

During the years my wife and I spent in Switzerland we spent all the time I could afford away from my graduate work in the mountains. The high mountains of Switzerland are wonderful at any time of year—in summer when fields of alpine flowers blanket the mountain pastures and small clusters of edelweiss cling to the bare granite peaks and outcroppings, in winter when the peaks, pastures, and even the lower mountain valleys are covered with a thick, silent carpet of snow. But the most wonderful time of all in the mountains is spring. In spring, the hard, harsh grasp of snowy winter weakens and the glories of summer begin to push their way up the rugged valleys to the heights. If you are high in the mountains during that wondrous passage of seasons, you notice that little trickles of water begin to flow beside the paths and roadways. The snow becomes softer, melting. Patches of gray stone or brown earth appear. Here and there deep blue gentian or red alpine roses appear beside the rocks. At last the snow retreats to the most distant heights and warm, restoring breezes sweep over the lush green meadows.

Something like that happens when the Spirit of God begins to blow upon sin-hardened consciences. At first there is a mere trickle of recognition of wrong done. But as the breath of God grows warmer, the trickle becomes a torrent of remorse and confession, the ice of rebellion melts, and the miracle of forgiveness, cleansing, and new life engulfs the tender soul.

This was beginning to happen with Joseph's ten brothers. They had come to Egypt out of sheer necessity, remembering only what they had done collectively to their brother and dreading the possibility that they might meet him in some dark habitat of slaves. Still they were hardened men. It was only as God added the harsh words of Joseph (whom they did not recognize) to the pain of material want that the trickle of confession began. At first it was small. They said, "Your servants were [actually, 'are'] twelve brothers, the sons of one man, who lives in the land of Canaan. The youngest is now with our father, and one is no more" (Gen. 42:13). They meant that as far as they knew, Joseph was probably dead; yet they felt compelled to mention him as their brother. "Joseph . . . our brother!" Earlier, when he had approached them while they were with the sheep at Dothan, he had been "that dreamer" (Gen. 37:19). Now he is "our brother" (Gen. 42:21; cf. v. 13) and even "the boy" (v. 22) or "the child" (KJV).

In the next part of the story the guilty memory of the brothers becomes an open confession for the first time. They say to one another, "Surely we are being punished because of our brother. We saw how distressed he was when he pleaded with us for his life, but we would not listen; that's why this distress has come upon us." Reuben chimes in, "Didn't I tell you not to sin against the boy? But you wouldn't listen! Now we must give an accounting for his blood" (vv. 21–22).

Flight from God

What did God use to bring about this quickening of conscience and confession? He had used the pain of material want to bring the ten brothers (Benjamin had remained at home with his father) to Egypt, where they were particularly vulnerable to God's prodding. He had used Joseph's harsh words to prick their carefully constructed defenses; the words had begun to get through. Now God uses solitude or physical imprisonment to set them apart from life's incessant trivial demands and give them time to awake to his displeasure. The section begins: "He [that is, Joseph] put them all in custody for three days" (v. 17).

Solitude! It is a valuable gift of God even when there is no particularly great sin to be exposed! In solitude people meet God. One of the reasons for the shallowness of much of our modern church life is that we have so little solitude.

One person who protested against this was A. W. Tozer, a great pastor in the city of Chicago. He expressed his concerns in a book called *The Pursuit of God*. Possessions are one thing that keep us from God, wrote Tozer. "There can be no doubt that this possessive clinging to things is one of the most harmful habits in life. Because it is so natural it is rarely recognized for the evil that it is; but its outworkings are tragic."[1]

Nor is it only things that keep us from God. The frantic, busy pace of our lives keeps us from God too, said Tozer. God must be cultivated, and that takes time, he wrote.

> The idea of cultivation and exercise, so dear to the saints of old, has now no place in our total religious picture. It is too slow, too common. We now demand glamour and fast-flowing dramatic action. A generation of Christians reared among push buttons and automatic machines is impatient of slower and less direct methods of reaching their goals. We have been trying to apply machine-age methods to our relations with God. We read our chapter, have our short devotions and rush away, hoping to make up for our deep inward bankruptcy by attending another gospel meeting or listening to another thrilling story told by a religious adventurer lately returned from afar.
>
> The tragic results of this spirit are all about us. Shallow lives, hollow religious philosophies, the preponderance of the element of fun in gospel meetings, the glorification of men, trust in religious externalities, quasi-religious fellowships, salesmanship methods, the mistaking of dynamic personality for the power of the Spirit: these and such as these are the symptoms of an evil disease, a deep and serious malady of the soul.[2]

Solitude is necessary for Christian life and growth under any circumstances. To grow we must spend time with God. We must escape from our slavery to things. We must step aside from the busyness of everyday life. But if this is true for everyone in every spiritual state, it is certainly true of one who is cherishing some distant, unconfessed sin and who is hoping that God has forgotten about it. With such a soul God will at first deal gently. He will bring want or harsh treatment. But then, if these alone do not unearth the fault and lead to confession, God will frequently shut the person up from normal activities—perhaps through sickness or the loss of a job—and reach him or her there. We have a hymn that goes:

> Speak, Lord, in the stillness
> While I wait on thee,
> Hushed my heart to listen
> In expectancy.

It is frequently in the stillness of solitude that we hear that still but persistent small voice of God's Spirit.

Let Conscience Work

We are introduced to the brothers' thoughts only after Joseph had released them from three days' imprisonment and had begun to deal with them again. But although their changing attitudes emerge in response to his prodding, I have no doubt that they merely reflect what had already been building in their minds during the days of confinement. God was at work. Therefore, the ice of their rebellion was melting and the crime of which they were guilty was beginning to work its way toward the surface.

The first thing solitude did was awaken and intensify guilt. "Awaken" may not be the perfect word for what was happening, since the brothers seem to have had some awareness of their guilt throughout the story. But they had done their best to put their guilt to sleep, and it was this at-least-dozing guilt that was now being jarred into consciousness. Moreover, it was being intensified by the brothers' dire circumstances. It was bad enough that they had been harshly received by Joseph and placed in prison. But then, after three days had passed and they had been released, they discovered that the prime minister was confronting them with an even more painful dilemma. He was letting them go home, but he was requiring them to leave one of their number behind as a guarantee that they would return with their youngest brother, Benjamin, as he had requested. Joseph said, "If you are honest men, let one of your brothers stay here in prison, while the rest of you go and take grain back for your starving households. But you must bring your youngest brother to me, so that your words may be verified and that you may not die" (vv. 19–20).

The next line says, "This they proceeded to do" (v. 20).

What understatement! What delicate telling of what must have been a most traumatic moment in their lives! All can go but one. One must stay. Ah, but who was to be that one? Who was to remain behind in the prime minister's prison uncertain of his fate, of whether he would ever be released or ever see his homeland again? I can see the brothers looking at one another with even greater anguish now than when they had looked at one another while still at home with their father Jacob.

Should Reuben stay? Reuben who had dishonored his own father by sleeping with his concubine Bilhah?

Should Judah stay? Judah who had committed incest with his daughter-in-law Tamar?

What about Simeon or Levi, who had taken such cruel and unjustifiable revenge on the unsuspecting citizens of Shechem?

Each of the ten had his own particular sins rising before him like ghosts of days past. But over them all stood the one apparently damning sin of their vicious and utterly unjustified enslavement and possibly murder of their brother. No wonder they said, "Surely we are being punished because of our brother" (v. 21)! No wonder Reuben exclaimed, "Didn't I tell you not to sin against the boy? But you wouldn't listen! Now we must give an accounting for his blood" (v. 22)!

Eventually they settled on Simeon as the one who should remain behind. Perhaps Simeon even volunteered. But whether it was Simeon or some other, each of them knew that he himself had every reason to be incarcerated. Solitude was doing its work. Guilt was intensifying.

Bitter Memory

The second thing solitude did in the lives of these men was refresh their memories. So far as we know, there had never been a time previous to this when the anguish of Joseph had been openly discussed between them. Indeed, the narration itself does not mention it. It is only when their deep guilt has already been forced to the surface that they remember what we had long suspected but had not been told was the case, namely, that Joseph had cried and pleaded for his life but was not heeded. They say, "We saw how distressed he was when he pleaded with us for his life, but we would not listen" (v. 21).

This is just one sentence; it treats the matter briefly. But I am sure that even a quick reading of this sentence makes clear that it was the details of their attack on Joseph and his anguished response that came back to them on this occasion. In the broadest sense, of course, they always remembered what they had done. There was never a moment when they had been able to forget it entirely. Yet now, in silence and with time to recollect that stricken face, those copious tears, that frightened and reproachful final backward glance—these came vividly to their minds and smote them inwardly.

There is a section of *Paradise Lost* in which the great English poet John Milton spoke of conscience awakening the memory of past days for Satan:

> Now conscience wakes despair
> That slumber'd, wakes the bitter memory
> Of what he was, what is, and what must be.
>
> Book 4, line 23

"Bitter memory of what . . . was." That is what makes memory so effective in God's hand. It is not merely recollection of sin in general but the vivid recalling of the specific details of sin—in Satan's case, of "what he was" before his rebellion—that is painful.

There is an example of this in a book by Charles Colson. Those who dislike Colson for his methods when he was in a prominent position politically would think that if Colson had any guilty memories at all, they would concern Watergate or the events associated with it. But that is not what troubles Colson. In a chapter entitled "It Is in Us," meaning "*sin* is in us," Colson tells of a particularly cruel thing he did when as a brand-new marine lieutenant he was leading his platoon of forty grimy, sweating soldiers on a training mission on Vieques Island, a satellite of Puerto Rico. The marines had been instructed not to trade with or buy anything from the impoverished people of the island. But this order was expected to be ignored. Thus, on the second day of maneuvers, when the hot, exhausted platoon suddenly came upon an old man leading a scrawny donkey burdened down under two ice-filled sacks of cold drinks, the men headed toward the old man to buy some.

Suddenly Colson intervened. "Sergeant, take this man prisoner. He is trespassing on government property," he said. The sergeant stared in disbelief but began to carry out the order. "And confiscate the contraband," Colson added. The soldiers cheered as they stole the old man's chilled drinks, which a moment before they would gladly have paid for, and drank them all. After the drinks were gone, the "prisoner" was released and sadly slunk away, probably thankful that he had only lost what was quite possibly his life savings and most certainly his means of livelihood for many months—and not his freedom or his life.

Technically Colson had only been observing the rigors of military law. But now, years later, it is this and not the more spectacular "crimes" of Watergate that comes to his mind when he thinks of past sins. He calls the Vieques Island incident an example of "the sins for which I feel the greatest contrition."[3]

My point is that you and I, all of us, have such disgraceful incidents in our past, and that it is the details of these that come to our minds as God works upon us during our moments of solitude. F. B. Meyer writes, "In early life you may have wronged some man or some woman. You may have taught some young lad to swear. You may have laughed away the early impressions from some anxious seeker, until they fled to return no more. You may not have done your best to save those committed to your care. And now others seem to be treating you as you treated the associates of earlier days. You now are eager for salvation; and you learn the bitterness of being ridiculed, thwarted, tempted and opposed. You recall the past; it flashes before you with terrible intensity. You cry, 'God forgive me! I am verily guilty concerning that soul whom I betrayed or wronged.' And this is the work of the Holy Spirit. Let him have his blessed way with you till you are led by him [to Jesus]."[4]

Let Us Reason

The third thing solitude did for these guilty brothers of Joseph was cause them to reason spiritually. They were not godly men. Indeed, they were probably not even saved men before the events of these chapters. They did not reason spiritually. They thought as most worldlings do, namely: "It's a mechanical world; God does not exist or at least he does not intervene here. In such a world it's every man for himself, and the devil take the hindmost. Who is to say that I've sinned? Who has a right to hold me to an accounting?" Then God did intervene, and suddenly the brothers' tune changed: "Surely we are being punished *because of* our brother. We saw how distressed he was when he pleaded with us for his life, but we would not listen; *that's why this distress has come upon us.* . . . Now we must give an accounting for his blood" (vv. 21–22, my emphasis).

As I say, before this they imagined that they were in an impersonal, immoral universe. Now with their sin before them, they realize that the universe is moral after all—it is God's universe, and every sin must and will have a reckoning.

We must say at this point that it does not necessarily follow that every calamity of life is directly linked to some act of sin on our part. Some have taught this. In fact, this erroneous idea is reflected even by some of those whose views are in the Bible. Job's counselors wanted to explain his misfortune by some previous great act of sin. The Lord's disciples reasoned the same way when they noticed the man who had been born blind: "Rabbi, who sinned, this man or his parents, that he was born blind?" (John 9:2). Jesus replied that although this is a moral universe, the facts are not always so easy to explain as this: "Neither this man nor his parents sinned . . . but this happened so that the work of God might be displayed in his life" (v. 3).

Calamity is not always a proof of past sin. Still, if calamity has come to your life and God has used it (or solitude or whatever) to bring the memory of your wrongdoings to mind, you know that you cannot escape the moral consequences of your sin by quibbles. Never mind that some suffer innocently! Never mind that God works in some suffering merely to bring himself glory! That is not your case. You see the connection. You know you are guilty. You know that God is not letting you escape unscathed. He is buffeting you to bring you to repentance.

I speak here of the effect of solitude to encourage spiritual reasoning. For God uses solitude to "bring us to our senses." He reminds us of the connection between sin and its consequences.

But this is not the only way God causes us to reason spiritually. He causes us to reason about salvation also, saying, "Come now, let us reason together. . . . Though your sins are like scarlet, they shall be as white as snow; though they are red as crimson, they shall be like wool" (Isa. 1:18). I am sure that as the brothers of Joseph thought about their past sins, those sins rose up before them like a horrible bloodred mass. They saw no hope of cleansing. They saw only a just and terrible retribution for their wrongdoing. It is the retribution we will see if we remain unrepentant. "Sin means death!" That is the first great axiom of Christianity. But God, who brought the brothers to see this spiritual connection, continued to work in them so that in time they freely confessed their sins and found salvation through the atoning blood of him who was to come. Christ's blood washed their red sins white. And they became, not merely redeemed men, wonderful as that was, but even revered fathers of the tribes of Israel. Judah, who was among the worst, was one through whom the Savior came.

You may not have committed the sins Judah or any of these others committed, but you have sins of your own. Perhaps God is bringing them to your mind even now. You need to confess them and find salvation through Jesus, the Lamb of God, who takes away the world's sin.

142

God and the Conscience Part 4: The Proof of God's Presence

Genesis 42:24–35

He turned away from them and began to weep, but then turned back and spoke to them again. He had Simeon taken from them and bound before their eyes.

Joseph gave orders to fill their bags with grain, to put each man's silver back in his sack, and to give them provisions for their journey. After this was done for them, they loaded their grain on their donkeys and left.

At the place where they stopped for the night one of them opened his sack to get feed for his donkey, and he saw his silver in the mouth of his sack. "My silver has been returned," he said to his brothers. "Here it is in my sack."

Their hearts sank and they turned to each other trembling and said, "What is this that God has done to us?"

When they came to their father Jacob in the land of Canaan, they told him all that had happened to them. They said, "The man who is lord over the land spoke harshly to us and treated us as though we were spying on the land. But we said to him, 'We are honest men; we are not spies. We were twelve brothers, sons of one father. One is no more, and the youngest is now with our father in Canaan.'

"Then the man who is lord over the land said to us, 'This is how I will know whether you are honest men: Leave one of your brothers here with me, and take food for your starving households and go. But bring your youngest brother to me so I will know that you are not spies but honest men. Then I will give your brother back to you, and you can trade in the land.'"

As they were emptying their sacks, there in each man's sack was his pouch of silver!
When they and their father saw the money pouches, they were frightened.

An instructive combination of ideas in Genesis 42:24 makes a useful introduction to this study. In the first half of that verse we are told that for the first time Joseph began to break down in the presence of his brothers and weep out of his great love for them. His weeping related to God's work in bringing them to a confession of sin, which they had made to one another and which Joseph had heard, though they did not know that he had understood them. In the second half of Genesis 42:24 we are told of an entirely different action. "He [that is, Joseph] had Simeon taken from them and bound before their eyes."

The significance of this combination of ideas is that the brothers were able to see one act and not the other and, seeing only one, had an entirely wrong impression of this Egyptian ruler. When Joseph wept he "turned away from them," so that they could not see his tears. The time for him to reveal himself as their brother had not yet come. Simeon, on the other hand, was bound "before their eyes." To the guilty, stricken brothers this sight would be exceedingly painful—in the same category as Zedekiah's seeing the murder of his sons just before his eyes were put out by Nebuchadnezzar, king of Babylon, against whom he had rebelled (cf. Jer. 52:10–11). The brothers would have judged Joseph to be harsh, vindictive, and unfeeling. Little did they know that beneath his rough ways, intended for their good, there was a heart filled with the most compassionate love for them.

It is often that way in our relationship to God. Sin brings God's harsh treatment, and we see only harsh treatment. We do not see that even this flows from God's love for us. We do not see that God's love and discipline are complementary.

God of Circumstances

At this period of history the capital of Egypt was at Memphis, about ten miles south of the present city of Cairo, and Jacob was presumably still living at Hebron (Gen. 35:27). The distance between these places is about 250 miles. Travel between them would have taken perhaps three weeks, so this must have been a long and difficult journey for the nine remaining brothers. On the one hand, they must have been experiencing a measure of relief. They had been in danger of their lives and had been imprisoned; now they had been released and were on their way home. On the other hand, they were returning without Simeon, who had been required to remain in the prime minister's prison. How would they explain Simeon's incarceration to their father? In

addition, they had been buffeted by God to the point at which they had actually confessed to one another their sin of selling Joseph into slavery.

The brothers must have been relieved yet anxious, grateful yet troubled.
They did not need another shock, another unsettling circumstance. Yet this
is what they received from God as he continued to work on their softening
consciences.

Before these men started for home, the story tells us, Joseph caused each
man's silver to be returned to him in one of his purchased sacks of grain. In
addition, he gave them provisions for their journey. The use of these provisions would have kept them from opening their sacks until well along their
way. But at last, for some reason or another, perhaps because the traveling
provisions ran short, one of the brothers opened his sack and discovered the
money Joseph had returned. What consternation! "My silver has been
returned," he said to the others. "Here it is in my sack."

This caused their hearts to sink, and they turned to each other fearfully.
"What is this that God has done to us?" they asked (v. 28).

Here we must sit up and take notice. This is the first time in the entire
story, beginning with the birth of the first of the sons of Jacob in chapter 29,
that any of Joseph's brothers is said to have mentioned God. As we have seen,
Joseph spoke of God constantly. There is hardly a sentence he utters that does
not have the name of God in it. Not so with these brothers! Not once in all
their story until now have they even uttered the word "God." Now significantly,
as the hand of God tightens around them, they exclaim in anguish, "What
is this that God has done to us?"

This statement is such a significant breakthrough in these lives that it is
worth examining in detail. I ask two questions of it:

1. *What do the brothers mean by this question?* A person who is reading this
casually might think that the answer is obvious. Their silver had been returned
in circumstances that might cause them to be accused of having cheated the
ruler of Egypt. Therefore they might be thought to be saying, "What is God
trying to accomplish by allowing us to fall into such questionable and dangerous circumstances?" or even "*Why* is God allowing us to fall into these circumstances?" I suggest that although these questions may be valid, what the
brothers are really uttering is not so much a question (though it is phrased
that way) as a statement. Actually, for the first time they are acknowledging
that God is controlling a specific, important circumstance of their lives. They
mean: "God has done this! God is not forgetful of our sin, as we had thought!
God has seen it! God remembers it! God is intervening powerfully and directly
in our lives!"

What makes this so significant and particularly relevant to us is that the
circumstance to which they referred was no miracle. When we are far from
God and arrogantly think that God should intervene in our lives to do something we want, we generally have a miracle in mind. Or at least we want God
to work contrary to the normal course of events. This was no miracle, this

finding of their money in their sacks. We know how it happened: Joseph caused it to be put there. And even though the brothers did not know exactly how their money was returned, they certainly did not think it was a miracle. They did not understand it, but the money got there somehow—through some mistake perhaps. What bothered them was not the miraculous but rather the providential nature of the event. It could have been the most insignificant of circumstances. But it was not insignificant to them. However small it was, it was proof that God was present in their circumstances and that he was going to demand a reckoning for their sin regarding Joseph.

I have found evidence of this truth many times in counseling troubled or convicted people. God had been working with them, and as they tell me their stories they often stress some small detail or several small details as evidence of God's working. Looked at coldly, such circumstances are nearly always explainable. An unbeliever would dismiss them as mere accidents. I have learned not to think like this. To some other person they may well appear as accidents, or nothing, but they are the touch of God's hand to the one under conviction. In speaking of them the person is acknowledging that God is working in his life and is accomplishing more than he can see by the circumstances.

2. *What does the brothers' statement concerning God signify?* The answer is that they were coming to grips with the true God at last. In other words, their statement does not only mean that they were recognizing that God was doing something to them ("What is this that God has *done* to us?") but also that they were recognizing that it was God who was doing it ("What is this that *God* has done to us?").

I have pointed out that this is the first moment in the story when any of the brothers refers to God. I do not mean to suggest, however, that in literal fact there was never an occasion on which any one of them ever used God's name. Though it is not recorded for us, I am sure there were hundreds, perhaps thousands of times when one or another of the brothers would refer to God, saying, "God this . . ." or "God that . . ." After all, they were the sons of Jacob, and at Hebron the God of Jacob was a household word. He was the one who had brought Abraham, their great-grandfather, out of Ur. He was the one who had appeared to their father at Bethel and had wrestled with him at Jabbok. God! They knew all about God!

Ah, but they did not! They used the word "God," but that did not mean any more to them than the words "nature" (if they had such a word) or "fate" or "destiny" or "happenstance." God was not real to them. They had been living their lives as if God did not exist or at least did not exist for them personally. So when they say, "What is this that God has done to us?" they are acknowledging the bearing of the true God on their lives for the very first time.

I wonder if you have come to the point at which God has really become *God* to you? You have used his name carelessly. You have joined the babble of the multitudes whose two most popular words today are "My God!"

You have said, "God bless you," and have not understood what you were saying.

You have said, "God knows."

Perhaps—God forgive you—you have used God's name in swearing.

These uses of God's name do not mean that you know God. On the contrary, they are evidence that you probably do not. Who is the God of these expressions? Nobody! He is an entity the unbeliever cannot even begin to define.

I will tell you who God is. God is he who created the heavens and the earth, including you, and to whom you are accountable for every thought, word, deed, and action. He is the God of Abraham, Isaac, and Jacob, who led these fathers out of the corrupt environment of their times and set a new way before them. He is the God who required righteous conduct from the people of Israel and who requires no less from you. He is the one who sent Jesus, his only Son, to die for such sin-ruined prodigals as yourself. He is a God who demands that you turn from sin and place your whole trust for salvation in Jesus and what he has accomplished by dying in your place. He is the God who is working in you now, in the circumstances of your life, to turn you to him.

How do you know that you are beginning to come to grips with the true God of the Bible and not a mere figment of your imagination? It is when you become conscious of sin and are troubled by it. I notice in this story that the brothers' first confession of sin (though only to themselves) and their first genuine awareness of the true God are found together, within the space of just a few verses. It is always that way. You cannot approach the true God without being aware of your sin. You cannot find salvation without confessing that sin.

God's Kindness Leads

There is another point that also comes from these verses, and I cannot skip over it. The point concerns grace. Thus far in the story the interventions of God in the lives of Joseph's brothers to bring them to repentance have all had a rough edge to them. They have issued from grace, since they have been intended for good in the brothers' lives. Still, they have not been the kind of things we would willingly choose for ourselves: the pinch of material want, the pain of harsh treatment, the press of solitude. Here for the first time, in the case of the money being returned in the brothers' sacks, we have something that is purely gracious, that has no rough edges whatever. Joseph simply wanted to give their money back. So far as we can tell he had no ulterior motive. Unlike the situation in chapter 44, when his cup is hidden in Benjamin's sack, Joseph does not send soldiers after the departing brothers. In fact, he never mentions the money again, and his steward even assures the brothers later that he received their payment and that they are not to worry about it.

How difficult it is for unbelievers to fathom grace! In Leviticus 26 there is a verse that speaks of the slightness of that which terrifies the wicked: "As for those of you who are left, I will make their hearts so fearful in the lands of their enemies that the sound of a wind-blown leaf will put them to flight" (v. 36). Proverbs 28:1 goes a step further, showing that a guilty person will sometimes flee from nothing: "The wicked man flees though no one pursues." In Genesis 42 we have the ultimate extension of this principle: fear not merely of a trivial thing or of nothing at all, but fear of what is good. God was doing good to these brothers, returning their money. But because they were not yet in a right relationship to him, they feared even his goodness and turned to each other trembling.

Even so, God was leading by this gracious act as well as by the other circumstances. It was a case of Romans 2:4, which asks the unrighteous, "Do you show contempt for the riches of his kindness, tolerance and patience, not realizing that God's kindness leads you toward repentance?"

How was God's kindness leading? Well, the fact that the money was returned in their sacks (after all the other circumstances of their journey to Egypt) led the nine brothers to the fullest and most open dealings with their aged father to date. Almost all the commentators note how honest and forthright these men were in telling their father what had happened in Egypt. I do not find this to be quite accurate, since they said nothing about what happened to them as a result of their days in solitude—how they came to confess their sin in regard to Joseph: "Surely we are being punished because of our brother. We saw how distressed he was when he pleaded with us for his life, but we would not listen; that's why this distress has come upon us" (v. 21). But even though they did not fully level with Jacob (though they would do so in time as God continued to work on their consciences), they nevertheless did give an accounting that shows progress.

They did not tell of their sins regarding Joseph. But neither did they hide the problem they had gotten themselves into regarding Simeon and Benjamin: "The man who is lord over the land said to us, 'This is how I will know whether you are honest men: Leave one of your brothers here with me, and take food for your starving households and go. But bring your youngest brother to me so I will know that you are not spies but honest men. Then I will give your brother back to you, and you can trade in the land'" (vv. 33–34).

The brothers were not quite fully honest men yet, but they were getting to be. They were beginning to learn what it was like to live by truth and not lies, by honesty rather than deceit.

The second point at which we see progress comes at the end of the chapter. The brothers had explained to Jacob that they would be unable to go back to Egypt without Benjamin, and Jacob protested. For a time he would refuse to let Benjamin go. Then Reuben, who had earlier dishonored his father by sleeping with his father's concubine Bilhah, intervened, pledging his own sons for the safety of Benjamin: "You may put both of my sons to death if I do not bring him back to you. Entrust him to my care, and I will bring him back" (v. 37). Earlier he had served himself; no one else's happiness—not even his father's—was allowed to intrude. Now he put himself and his own family on the line regarding Benjamin.

I say again, as I often have in these studies: I cannot see your heart, and therefore I do not know what it conceals. I do not know whether you are hiding unconfessed sin. I do not know whether God is working through the pinch of want, the pain of harsh treatment, the press of solitude, or the circumstantial proof of his presence to bring some sin to light and lead you to a saving repentance. But I do know this. If God is working (or has worked), there will be confession. Sin will be repudiated. You will be growing in an honest life marked by the highest commitment to truth. And you will be thinking of and working for other people and their happiness rather than your own.

Why? Because Jesus is like that, and this is what Jesus did for you. He did not come to please himself but rather to please others. He did not come to be ministered unto, but to minister and to give his life for many.

143

No One Loves Me, This I Know

Genesis 42:36–38

Their father Jacob said to them, "You have deprived me of my children. Joseph is no more and Simeon is no more, and now you want to take Benjamin. Everything is against me!"

Then Reuben said to his father, "You may put both of my sons to death if I do not bring him back to you. Entrust him to my care, and I will bring him back."

But Jacob said, "My son will not go down there with you; his brother is dead and he is the only one left. If harm comes to him on the journey you are taking, you will bring my gray head down to the grave in sorrow."

Several years ago I did technical work on the use of the word "witness" *(martys)* in the Greek language and looked at some secular Greek authors in that study. One I read carefully was Epictetus, the Stoic philosopher who was once a slave but who lived out the greater portion of his life as a freedman in Rome during the reign of Nero. He wrote of the privilege of bearing a good witness for God and chided those who failed to do so: "What kind of witness do you bear for God? 'I am in sore straits, O Lord, and in misfortune; no one regards me, no one gives me anything, all blame me and speak ill of me.' Is this the witness that you are going to bear, and is this the way in which you are going to disgrace the summons which he gave you?"[1]

When I first read that characterization of the complaining witness by Epictetus I laughed, because it is such an apt description. It is one we have all probably heard hundreds of times: "No one regards me, no one gives me anything, all blame me and speak ill of me." It is how we think when we are feeling sorry for ourselves.

Jacob was feeling sorry for himself when his sons returned from Egypt reporting that they had been challenged by Egypt's prime minister. The prime minister was Joseph, of course. But the brothers did not know this and did not suspect his motives when he accused them of having come to Egypt to spy out the land. He put Simeon in prison and demanded that the next time they should return with their youngest brother, Benjamin, to prove that they were honest men. When Judah, Reuben, and the others told their father they could not go back to Egypt unless Benjamin came with them, Jacob complained about this adverse turn of circumstances: "You have deprived me of my children. Joseph is no more and Simeon is no more, and now you want to take Benjamin. Everything is against me!" (Gen. 42:36). I suppose that if he had known our little song for children, "Jesus Loves Me," he might have twisted it to sing:

> No one loves me, this I know.
> My misfortunes tell me so.

The chapter concludes with Jacob's holding out against what was to become a necessity.

A Sea of Troubles

I think that we are often like Jacob when we complain that everything is against us. And we are just as laughable! Circumstances fail to treat us right, someone says something less than complimentary, we are faced by a difficult decision—and suddenly we feel that nothing has ever gone right for us in our entire lives, and we pout about it. Is that the kind of witness we are going to bear for God? Is this the way we are going to disgrace the summons he gave us?

It should be perfectly evident, as we treat this brief parenthesis in the story of God's working upon the hardened consciences of Joseph's brothers, that I am going to hold up Jacob as a negative example. I am going to say, "Don't be like him!" But before I do that I want to show that, although he was wrong when he said, "*Everything* is against me," he was nevertheless not entirely wrong in recognizing that in a sinful world such as ours at least some things *are* against God's people. True, they are usually not what you and I think of when we are despondent. We feel that "things" are not working out for us, and we should know that "things" really are, since "in all *things* God works for the good of those who love him" (Rom. 8:28). But although "things" (circumstances) are controlled by God and are used by him for our benefit, we nevertheless do have enemies who seek our downfall.

Traditionally the church has spoken of three of these: the world, the flesh, and the devil. The world is not for us. The flesh attacks us from within. The devil would drag us down to hell if he were able. These three opponents are not everything, but they are formidable, and it is good to keep in mind that they are.

When we speak of the world in the sense of its being our spiritual opponent, we are not using the word in reference to the earth (in the sense of the "world globe") or even to the people who inhabit the earth (as in the phrase "the whole world"). We are using it to refer to the "world system" Jesus referred to when he said, "If you belonged to the world, it would love you as its own. As it is, you do not belong to the world, but I have chosen you out of the world. That is why the world hates you" (John 15:19). The world is always "keeping up with the Joneses," "winning through intimidation," "looking out for number one," and otherwise operating according to its own goals and values rather than the values of God. The world is always trying to compel the Christian to be like it. That is why the apostle Paul wrote, "Do not conform any longer to the pattern of this world, but be transformed by the renewing of your mind. Then you will be able to test and approve what God's will is—his good, pleasing and perfect will" (Rom. 12:2).

The flesh is what we carry about in ourselves. "Flesh" does not refer to the soft material that covers our bones and is nourished by the circulation of our blood, any more than "world" refers merely to the earth globe. In the sense in which we are using the word here and in which the Bible uses it when it speaks of the "sins of the flesh," flesh means the earthly nature of man apart from divine influence. Apart from the intervention of grace, the fleshly nature is utterly disposed to sin and is rebellious against God. Paul writes of this nature, saying: "The acts of the sinful nature are obvious: sexual immorality, impurity and debauchery; idolatry and witchcraft; hatred, discord, jealousy, fits of rage, selfish ambition, dissensions, factions and envy; drunkenness, orgies, and the like" (Gal. 5:19–21). Joseph's brothers were such men. They were fleshly. They were governed by a nature that was opposed to God.

The third of the three classic opponents of the Christian is the devil. Peter describes him as "a roaring lion looking for someone to devour" (1 Peter 5:8).

Because the devil is such an imposing enemy and because he has already been introduced to us in Genesis in the story of the serpent's temptation of Eve and Adam, it is somewhat surprising that he has not been mentioned explicitly afterward in Genesis. We are not to conclude from this that he is inactive, however. Certainly the devil was active in the growth of the debauchery (and perhaps spiritualism and demon worship) that preceded the flood. No doubt he was at this point also actively opposing God's chosen people.

We must remember that God had said that he would send a redeemer through the chosen line of Abraham, Isaac, and Jacob but that he had not yet disclosed through which of the twelve sons of Jacob that Redeemer would come. (We do not find that out until Genesis 49.) My guess—I admit it is a guess—is that the devil supposed that Joseph was the one and therefore moved heaven and earth to persecute, corrupt, and, if possible, do away with Joseph. The devil already had the older ten brothers in his pocket, as it were. It was easy for him to turn them against Joseph; he would undoubtedly have had them kill him if God had not intervened to protect and eventually prosper the young man. Actually, as we later learn, the Messiah was not to come through Joseph or his sons but through Judah, whom God was bringing to faith through these incidents. The devil would never have suspected this hard, secular, and sensual man. But in the very next chapter it is Judah who leads the other brothers in putting himself on the line for Benjamin.

Jacob said, "Everything is against me!" He was not right in saying this, as I have indicated. But he would have been right if he had acknowledged these three enemies: the devil, who was no doubt seeking to destroy him as well as Joseph; the world, whose godless values and goals were a constant threat to all of this chosen family; and the sins of his own fleshly nature.

If God Be for Us

Yet how could Jacob say such a thing? True, he was opposed by great enemies. But had he forgotten God? Had he entirely forgotten the one who had appeared to him at Bethel: "I am the LORD, the God of your father Abraham and the God of Isaac. I will give you and your descendants the land on which you are lying. Your descendants will be like the dust of the earth, and you will spread out to the west and to the east, to the north and to the south. All peoples on earth will be blessed through you and your offspring. I am with you and will watch over you wherever you go" (Gen. 28:13–15).

It is having a God like this that transforms opposition for God's people. For it is not that we do not face spiritual enemies. We do! It is rather that we have a God who is greater than any circumstances and all enemies and who promises to be with us, bless us, and keep us through everything.

I think here of that wonderful story involving Elijah's successor, Elisha, and the young man who was Elisha's servant. The story is set in a time of war in which the king of Aram had been fighting against the king of Israel. The Arameans were stronger and would have defeated Israel, except for the fact that God had been revealing the plans of the king of Aram to Elisha, who had in turn been passing them on to Israel's commander. When the Arameans laid a trap, God told Elisha. Elisha told the king of Israel, and the Hebrew armies went another way. This happened so often that the king of Aram suspected a traitor and summoned his officers to demand who was disclosing his plans to the enemy.

The officers told the truth. "None of us, my lord the king, . . . but Elisha, the prophet who is in Israel, tells the king of Israel the very words you speak in your bedroom" (2 Kings 6:12).

When the king heard this he determined to capture Elisha and thus stop him from conferring with the king of Israel. When he learned he was at Dothan—the very place Joseph had gone to find his brothers and had been attacked by them and thrown into a cistern—the king went to Dothan by night and surrounded the city.

The next morning the servant of Elisha got up and went out of the city, probably to draw water from a well for his master's use. There he saw the Aramean armies. He was terrified. We can see him dropping his water jug, running back up the path to the city, bursting through the gates, finding Elisha, and exclaiming, "Oh, my lord, what shall we do?" (v. 15).

Elisha was calm. "Don't be afraid," he answered. "Those who are with us are more than those who are with them" (v. 16). At this point Elisha asked God to open the eyes of the servant, and when God did so the young man saw the hills full of horses and chariots of fire all around Elisha. The end of the story shows how, when the armies of Aram began to move against Elisha, God struck the soldiers with blindness and Elisha led them in their blind state into the armed city of Samaria, where they were captured by Israel's king.

What is it that surrounds us? Is it the world with all its temptations and ensnarements? The flesh with its lusts? The devil with his malicious hatreds and eternal enmity against God? It does not matter: *"Those who are with us are more than those who are with them."*

"But I am in sore straits, O Lord, and in misfortune; no one regards me, no one gives me anything, all blame me and speak ill of me."

"Those who are with us are more than those who are with them."

"But Lord, Joseph is no more and Simeon is no more, and now they want to take away Benjamin."

"Those who are with us are more than those who are with them."

"But I don't see those who are on our side, Lord."

It doesn't matter. *"Those who are with us are more than those who are with them."*

The one who is above all and who is on our side is alone sufficient; and if he is for us, who can be against us?

He who did not spare his own Son, but gave him up for us all—how will he not also, along with him, graciously give us all things? Who will bring any charge against those whom God has chosen? It is God who justifies. Who is he that condemns? Christ Jesus, who died—more than that, who was raised to life—is at the right hand of God and is also interceding for us. Who shall separate us from the love of Christ? Shall trouble or hardship or persecution or famine or nakedness or danger or sword? As it is written:

"For your sake we face death all day long;
    we are considered as sheep to be slaughtered."

No, in all these things we are more than conquerors through him who loved us. For I am convinced that neither death nor life, neither angels nor demons, neither the present nor the future, nor any powers, neither height nor depth, nor anything else in all creation, will be able to separate us from the love of God that is in Christ Jesus our Lord.

                                                              Romans 8:32–39

The Other Seven Thousand

I suspect that at this point Jacob might protest that he did not mean to say exactly what he did say and that his protest was really meant along slightly different lines. He had complained that "everything" was against him. "But," he might say, "I did not really mean that everything was against me. I know that God is for me and will probably work this all out somehow, though I cannot see how he will do it. I did not mean that. What I really meant was that no other human beings are for me. I am trying to do the right thing, but it is dreadfully hard. I am so alone."

Have you ever said that? Have you ever felt that you have seriously tried to serve God and have done so for many years, but that it is difficult? Have you felt that you were the only one trying to hold the line at times? Have you felt that although *everything* may not be against you, at least *no one* is standing with you or serving with you to share the burden?

Elijah felt that. Elijah had been used by God in a magnificent way. He had stood against the wickedness of King Ahab. He had been used of God to declare a rainless period of three years. Then at the end of that time he appeared suddenly to arrange a confrontation with the priests of Baal. Elijah had the false priests build an altar to their god while he built a similar altar to Jehovah. There were to be stones, wood, and offerings, but no fire. The true God was to provide the fire.

Elijah invited the priests of Baal to go first. They sang and chanted and called for fire. But, of course, none came. Elijah taunted them. "Shout louder! . . . Surely he [Baal] is a god! Perhaps he is deep in thought, or busy, or traveling. Maybe he is sleeping and must be awakened" (1 Kings 18:27). Still no fire! At last the prophets of Baal gave up, and Elijah called on Jehovah. Immediately fire fell from heaven and consumed not only the sacrifice but the wood, stones, and soil; it even evaporated the water in a trench around the sacrifice, which Elijah had also constructed and filled. After this the prophets of Baal were killed, and the period of drought in Israel ended.

There are few greater stories of a victory over evil in Israel in the entire Old Testament. We would expect that the triumph would have left Elijah thankful and exhilarated. But this was not the case. Like so many of us after the end of some great struggle of our lives, Elijah felt let down and discouraged. Ahab and his evil wife, Jezebel, threatened to kill him for having killed the false priests, and Elijah had to flee. The next time we see him he is in a cave at Mount Horeb in Sinai, where he had fled for his life.

Elijah prayed to God: "I have been very zealous for the LORD God Almighty. The Israelites have rejected your covenant, broken down your altars, and put your prophets to death with the sword. I am the only one left, and now they are trying to kill me too" (1 Kings 19:10).

He repeated the same self-pitying complaint: "I have been very zealous for the LORD God Almighty. The Israelites have rejected your covenant, broken down your altars, and put your prophets to death with the sword. I am the only one left, and now they are trying to kill me too" (v. 14).

At this point God revealed that he had chosen another king to replace Ahab: Jehu the son of Nimshi. He had chosen another man to help and eventually succeed Elijah as Israel's prophet: Elisha the son of Shaphat. Elijah was to anoint both to these roles. Then God said: "Yet I reserve seven thousand in Israel—all whose knees have not bowed down to Baal and all whose mouths have not kissed him" (v. 18).

Today you may seem to be alone in your determination to live for God in this wicked, spiritually hostile world. You may believe that everything and everyone is against you. But this is not the case. You are not alone. God is with you—he alone is greater than any opponent you may face—and in addition to God himself there are also thousands who have not and will not bow their knees to the pagan gods of our culture. Let that encourage and lift your spirits. Instead of saying, "No one loves me," say:

> Jesus loves me, this I know.
> Forward, then, to battle go.

144

God and the Conscience Part 5: The Pattern of Necessity

Genesis 43:1–14

Now the famine was still severe in the land. So when they had eaten all the grain they had brought from Egypt, their father said to them, "Go back and buy us a little more food."

But Judah said to him, "The man warned us solemnly, 'You will not see my face again unless your brother is with you.' If you will send our brother along with us, we will go down and buy food for you. But if you will not send him, we will not go down, because the man said to us, 'You will not see my face again unless your brother is with you.'"

Israel asked, "Why did you bring this trouble on me by telling the man you had another brother?"

They replied, "The man questioned us closely about ourselves and our family. 'Is your father still living?' he asked us. 'Do you have another brother?' We simply answered his questions. How were we to know he would say, 'Bring your brother down here'?"

Then Judah said to Israel his father, "Send the boy along with me and we will go at once, so that we and you and our children may live and not die. I myself will guarantee his safety; you can hold me personally responsible for him. If I do not bring him back to you and set him here before you, I will bear the blame before you all my life. As it is, if we had not delayed, we could have gone and returned twice."

Then their father Israel said to them, "If it must be, then do this: Put some of the best products of the land in your bags and take them down to the man as a gift—a little balm and a little honey, some spices and myrrh, some pistachio nuts and almonds. Take double the amount of silver with you, for you must return the silver that was put back into the mouths of your sacks. Perhaps it was a mistake. Take your brother also and go back to the man at once. And may God Almighty grant you mercy before the man so that he will let your other brother and Benjamin come back with you. As for me, if I am bereaved, I am bereaved."

It has been years since I have paid much attention to the recruitment slogans of America's armed forces. But as I think over the slogans that have been used in the past and are being used today, what strikes me is the aura of achievement, competence, and control they project. The most established is probably the marines' motto: *Semper Fidelis* ("Always Faithful"). But how about "The Marines are looking for a few good men" or "Join the Navy, see the world"? The army draws its recruits with the slogan "Be all you can be." A recent air force poster shows the cockpit of a modern fighter jet and boasts, "This desk can reach Mach II." The copy underneath says, "But you can handle it!"

The appeal of these posters is their ability to touch our natural desire to manage things or be in control, which is what most of us want deep down in our subconscious. We want a good life, but most of us are willing to endure things that are not so good—so long as we are in control of the situation. We will bear all things, believe all things, hope all things, endure all things—we will willingly submit to great hardships—as long as we are doing the submitting and retain ability to manipulate the difficult circumstances to our ends. Some persons will die for what they believe—if the choice is theirs. The difficulty comes when control of life passes out of our hands and we see ourselves as the one acted upon rather than as the actor. We resist necessity.

Which is one reason why God uses it in awakening the conscience to his demands on a life! As long as we feel we are in control, we think we can keep God and his standards at a distance. When we lose control we are more inclined to acknowledge that it is God's world in spite of everything and that we must ultimately come to terms with him.

The Persistent God

This was the next thing God did in the task of awakening guilt in Joseph's brothers and bringing health and healing to his family. Already it had been a long process. God began by bringing *the pinch of material want* into their circumstances. This want, produced by the famine, dislodged them from their comfortable life in Canaan and brought them to Egypt, where they met Joseph, though they did not know him. Next God subjected them to *the pain of harsh treatment*. They had probably never endured this before, for back in

Hebron everyone would have spoken respectfully to them. They would have been flattered. But in Egypt Joseph accused them of being foreign spies. The third element in God's work of restoration of these men was *the press of solitude*. They were thrown into prison, and it was there in prison, not knowing whether they would be released or forgotten, that their consciences at last began to come vividly alive. It was after their incarceration that they first confessed sin: "Surely we are being punished because of our brother. We saw how distressed he was when he pleaded with us for his life, but we would not listen; that's why this distress has come upon us" (Gen. 42:21).

However, even at this point the brothers had only confessed their sin to one another and not to anyone who had not already known of it. And their confession, genuine as it was, was still without reference to the sovereign God of their fathers. It could merely have meant that history seems to follow a moral course: sin is often exposed, the guilty are punished. It took *proof of God's presence* in the details of the restoration of their money to cause them to bring God into the picture for the first time. "What is this that God has done to us?" was their cry.

Much had been accomplished in these sin-hardened brothers of Joseph, accomplishments vividly detailed in Genesis 42. But there is a proper break between chapters 42 and 43, since, however much had been accomplished, the sin against Joseph would never have been fully brought out into the open, confessed, and then forgiven were it not for the continuing hand of God in the events now narrated. There is no record that the brothers ever mentioned Joseph again once they returned home. They were away from Egypt, the place of their problems. They had grain. Perhaps things could get back to normal, they must have been thinking.

Normal? What they thought normal was actually abnormal in the sense that it was contrary to the prevailing character of God. They thought that a life of covered-over sin could be tolerated. But God would not tolerate it, and he continued to work to bring the hidden sin to light. Robert Candlish wrote of their probable speculations: "Before their stock in hand is exhausted, plenty may have returned to the land of Canaan; and when Egypt's lordly potentate ceases to have the immense power which his command of Egypt's full granaries gives him over a starving world, he may become less tyrannical and more placable, and may be got to consent on easier terms to Simeon's release. But it is otherwise ordered by the Lord. The famine continues to become more severe rather than more mild. The corn brought out of Egypt is eaten up. The patriarch-father himself, as responsible for the household's subsistence, is the first to turn his thoughts to the land of plenty, and the storehouses on the banks of the Nile: 'Go again, buy us a little food' (vv. 1–2)."[1]

What God did at this point was to impose the pattern of necessity upon this family.

The Forms of Necessity

I see three kinds of necessity in verses 1–14. First, there is the necessity of *nature*, expressed in this case by the great famine. Instead of abating, as the brothers may have fondly hoped it would, the famine grew worse. The text says, "Now the famine was still severe in the land" (v. 1).

Famine is a terrible scourge. This famine, recorded in Genesis 41–47, is the earliest documented famine in history. But there were undoubtedly many famines before this time due to the devastating effects of drought, wars, and plant disease; and there have certainly been many since. Famine struck Rome in 436 B.C. and was so severe that many threw themselves into the Tiber River to end their lives. Famine struck England in A.D. 1005. All Europe suffered in 879, 1016, and 1162. Even in the nineteenth century, in spite of the great advances in technology and commerce, hunger afflicted many countries: Russia, China, India, Ireland. Famines continue today. Many perish in India due to malnutrition and accompanying diseases. The worst famine area in our time is in northeast Africa, particularly Ethiopia, where rain has been virtually nonexistent for years. That area may be in the midst of a cycle of drought similar to that which struck Egypt in Joseph's time.

The frightening thing about these famines is that little seems to be able to be done about them. Yet they are only one example of a long list of so-called acts of nature that humble us from time to time. Who has not been awed by the force of a great storm or hurricane, or frightened by the howling fury of a blizzard? Who has not been taken up short by sickness or the inescapable reality of death? These things remind us that we are not sovereign, that God is sovereign. They warn us that we dare not trifle with the great God of nature with whom we have to do.

The second kind of necessity God imposed upon the family of Joseph was *the will of man*, expressed here in the demands of the unrecognized Egyptian ruler. These demands had been made known to Jacob shortly after the brothers had returned from their journey to Egypt: "The man who is lord over the land said to us, '. . . Bring your youngest brother to me so I will know that you are not spies but honest men. Then I will give your brother back to you, and you can trade in the land'" (Gen. 42:33–34). Jacob had refused even to consider letting Benjamin leave home: "My son will not go down there with you; his brother is dead and he is the only one left" (Gen. 42:38). Now he seems to suggest that the brothers might be able to slip down to Egypt without Benjamin: "Go back and buy us a little more food" (Gen. 43:2).

Judah knew better than that. He may have been a sin-hardened man, but he was no fool; he knew that Joseph meant business when he demanded that Jacob's youngest son be brought to him by the brothers on their next visit. Judah would not budge: "The man warned us solemnly, 'You will not see my face again unless your brother is with you.' If you will send our brother along with us, we will go down and buy food for you. But if you will not send him, we will not go down, because the man said to us, 'You will not see my face again unless your brother is with you'" (vv. 3–5).

This kind of necessity confronts us at a different level than the necessity of nature, because at first it does not seem all that inescapable. The will involves people, and we generally think that we can get people to change. A husband has a quality his wife does not like; the wife thinks she can change him. Children think they can change their parents. Employees think their boss can be made to act differently or change his mind in some undesirable requirement. These changes do not always come, and we are therefore forced back on God, who alone is able to transform human beings. Generally we are forced to the conclusion that the changes—if there are any—must occur in us. Thus God awakens us to our own need and leads us to ask him for assistance.

The third kind of necessity imposed upon Joseph's father and brothers was *circumstances*—just the way things were. This is seen in Jacob's protest against Judah's insistence that he could not go down to Egypt again unless Benjamin were brought along. Jacob asked, "Why did you bring this trouble on me by telling the man you had another brother?" (v. 6). This was a petty and unreasonable protest, for, as the brothers pointed out, no one could have anticipated the prime minister's demand. "The man questioned us closely about ourselves and our family. 'Is your father still living?' he asked us. 'Do you have another brother?' We simply answered his questions. How were we to know he would say, 'Bring your brother down here'?" (v. 8). It did not matter in the slightest how this situation had come about. These were the circumstances, and they had to be dealt with as they were. They were inescapable.

So also with many of the circumstances of our lives. We may chafe under them, but our restlessness and protests accomplish nothing. God uses them to change us and sometimes to ferret out problems in our lives.

Changed Lives

Does the pattern of necessity really bring changes? It did in this story. We see two changes: first in Judah, then in Jacob himself.

The change in Judah was an important one, similar to the change already noted in his brother Reuben in the previous chapter. When Jacob had refused to allow Benjamin to go to Egypt with the others, Reuben had intervened to pledge his own sons as security: "You may put both of my sons to death if I do not bring him back to you. Entrust him to my care, and I will bring him back" (Gen. 42:37).

This was extravagant; Jacob would never have killed Reuben's sons. But the sentiment behind the pledge was nevertheless sincere. This is the same concern for Benjamin now seen in Judah's remarks. He says, "Send the boy along with me and we will go at once, so that we and you and our children may live and not die. I myself will guarantee his safety; you can hold me personally responsible for him. If I do not bring him back to you and set him here before you, I will bear the blame before you all my life" (Gen. 43:8–9).

Before this, Judah had been hard and self-centered. Now he is beginning to soften. For the first time in his life he has made someone else's happiness more important than his own. It is significant that he will later lead the plea for Benjamin's life and freedom after Benjamin is accused of having taken the cup of Joseph, which was found in his sack (Gen. 44:1–34).

The greatest changes of all were in Jacob. Earlier in the story he had refused to face necessity, saying that he would never allow Benjamin to be taken to Egypt. He had even complained petulantly, "Everything is against me. . . . Why did you bring this trouble on me by telling the man you had another brother?" (Gen. 42:36; 43:6). Jacob was wrestling against God again as he once did on the banks of the Jabbok on the border of Esau's territory.

But Jacob had learned his lesson then, and the lesson of those earlier days came back to him as he faced up to these God-ordained necessities:

> If it must be, then do this: Put some of the best products of the land in your bags and take them down to the man as a gift—a little balm and a little honey, some spices and myrrh, some pistachio nuts and almonds. Take double the amount of silver with you, for you must return the silver that was put back into the mouths of your sacks. Perhaps it was a mistake. Take your brother also and go back to the man at once. And may God Almighty grant you mercy before the man so that he will let your other brother and Benjamin come back with you. As for me, if I am bereaved, I am bereaved.
>
> 43:11–14

Two names are significant in this place: first, "Israel," which was Jacob's new or covenant name, and second, "God Almighty," to whom the chastened patriarch appeals. When Abram's name was changed to Abraham, the old name was never used again; the new name represented a profound and permanent growth in his character. It has been otherwise with Jacob. His name was changed to Israel at Jabbok, but it is not often after this that his new or covenant name is used. Usually he was thinking and operating much as the old Jacob had done. He was self-centered, self-serving, complaining. However, at this point of the story we see Jacob emerging as Israel, as a "Prince with [or 'one who has been conquered by'] God." In this character he rightly appeals to the sovereign God (God Almighty) for the issue's outcome.

Robert Candlish is incisive at this point.

> The closing declaration, "If I be bereaved of my children, I am bereaved," is, in the view of all the circumstances, an instance of acquiescence in the will of God all but unparalleled. Jacob is now in extreme old age, and he is about to be left alone so far as the companionship of his sons is concerned. When long ago the ten brothers went from home to feed their flocks, Joseph was the comfort of his father's heart—Benjamin being but a child. In his love to the ten

Jacob sends Joseph to Shechem, and Joseph goes on to Dothan and there disappears. Jacob has still Benjamin as well as the ten to comfort him in his being bereaved of Joseph. When the ten are first constrained to go to Egypt for food, Jacob has still Benjamin left to comfort him. But now he is to be literally left alone; Benjamin goes with the rest. And however it may be necessary to put a good face on the mission and send the brothers off with a hopeful blessing, it is for the father a terrible venture. Already Simeon is the tenant of an Egyptian prison. This new embassy in which all the rest join may end in their all sharing Simeon's fate, if not even in a worse catastrophe than that. Jacob consents to the surrender. Leave him Benjamin, and you leave him something to look to and lean on after the flesh. When he gives up Benjamin, what remains? It is all, henceforth, with Jacob an exercise of mere and simple faith, "enduring as seeing him who is invisible."

Let any one imagine the state of Jacob after he has thus sent all his sons away. It is the very triumph of that faith which is "the substance of things hoped for, the evidence of things not seen." Weeks or months must elapse before any tidings can reach him of the good or ill success of this expedition. The vessel that carries such a venture in its bosom may not be heard of till his grey hairs, through weary watching, have become greyer still. His fond eye, dimmed with the bitter tears of age, sees them—scarcely sees them—leaving him perhaps for ever on this earth. He may look on them, he may look on Benjamin, no more on this side of the grave. He has no express promise that he shall. What probable presumption is there that he shall? It is indeed a dark and doubtful prospect. But by God's grace the very extremity of the emergency rouses the old believer to a new venture of faith. He has trusted God before; he will trust him still. "I will trust and not be afraid," is his language. "Though he slay me, yet will I trust him."

And this is the man whom but yesterday we saw thoroughly unmanned, indulging almost in a childish burst of passionate upbraiding against his God as well as against his sons—"All these things are against me." He is like one sunk in the mingled imbecility and obstinacy of helpless dotage. Where is his manly reason? Where is his religious resignation, his shrewd sense, his strong faith? What a change now!

Jacob is himself; he is Israel! The pilgrim of half a century is on his feet again with staff in hand, eye fixed once more on "the city which hath foundations, whose builder and maker is God." This is not his rest; his tent in Canaan is not his home; its dear fellowships are not his portion. All things are not against him, though "all these things," the "things that are seen," may seem to be so. . . .

Thus, a second time, "when he is weak, then is he strong,"—strong in faith, seeing an unseen Lord, leaning on an unseen powerful arm, looking up into an unseen loving face, looking out for an unseen glorious home. Strong in such faith, he can attend to what is urgent in the occasion on hand, going into even its minute business details. He can order his household gravely but cheerfully in a crisis that makes the hearts of the other inmates fail. . . . Calmly committing himself and his way to the God who blessed him at Bethel, led him to Syria and brought him back to Canaan—the God who has guided and guarded him all his life hitherto, the God of whom he can say, "I know in whom I have believed"—he will walk on for the rest of his earthly sojourn, not wearily, not grudgingly, but rejoicingly, hopefully—not weeping always, as if all things were against him—but praising God who makes all things work together for his good.[2]

If you are fighting against the circumstances God has brought into your life, learn that it is useless to wrestle against the God of Jabbok. Allow yourself to be mastered by God and commit your way to him. Praise him, knowing that he will be with you and will bless you to the very end.

145

God and the Conscience Part 6: The Power of True Affection

Genesis 43:15–34

So the men took the gifts and double the amount of silver, and Benjamin also. They hurried down to Egypt and presented themselves to Joseph. When Joseph saw Benjamin with them, he said to the steward of his house, "Take these men to my house, slaughter an animal and prepare dinner; they are to eat with me at noon."

The man did as Joseph told him and took the men to Joseph's house. Now the men were frightened when they were taken to his house. They thought, "We were brought here because of the silver that was put back into our sacks the first time. He wants to attack us and overpower us and seize us as slaves and take our donkeys."

So they went up to Joseph's steward and spoke to him at the entrance to the house. "Please, sir," they said, "we came down here the first time to buy food. But at the place where we stopped for the night we opened our sacks and each of us found his silver—the exact weight—in the mouth of his sack. So we have brought it back with us. We have also brought additional silver with us to buy food. We don't know who put our silver in our sacks."

"It's all right," he said. "Don't be afraid. Your God, the God of your father, has given you treasure in your sacks; I received your silver." Then he brought Simeon out to them.

The steward took the men into Joseph's house, gave them water to wash their feet and provided fodder for their donkeys. They prepared their gifts for Joseph's arrival at noon, because they had heard that they were to eat there.

When Joseph came home, they presented to him the gifts they had brought into the house, and they bowed down before him to the ground. He asked them how they were, and then he said, "How is your aged father you told me about? Is he still living?"

They replied, "Your servant our father is still alive and well." And they bowed low to pay him honor.

As he looked about and saw his brother Benjamin, his own mother's son, he asked, "Is this your youngest brother, the one you told me about?" And he said, "God be gracious to you, my son." Deeply moved at the sight of his brother, Joseph hurried out and looked for a place to weep. He went into his private room and wept there.

After he had washed his face, he came out and, controlling himself, said, "Serve the food."

They served him by himself, the brothers by themselves, and the Egyptians who ate with him by themselves, because Egyptians could not eat with Hebrews, for that is detestable to Egyptians. The men had been seated before him in the order of their ages, from the firstborn to the youngest; and they looked at each other in astonishment. When portions were served to them from Joseph's table, Benjamin's portion was five times as much as anyone else's. So they feasted and drank freely with him.

W hat awakens the human conscience and draws a woman or man to Jesus Christ? In Reformed circles it is customary to say that it is mostly a sense of need occasioned by awareness of sin. We know sin by the law. So we say that a person must first be slain by the law before he can be resurrected by the gospel. That is good theology. Yet in actual experience it is more often the case that an awareness of the great love of God is the decisive factor. John R. W. Stott once polled members of the congregation of All Souls Church, London, and he was startled by this fact. He found that the vast majority were brought to Christ, not by an acute awareness of their sin, as he had supposed, but by the winsome love of Christ displayed in the gospel.

This is not to say that God does not use other means to awaken the conscience and bring us to where we can recognize and respond to his love. We have been looking at some of these other means in the story of God's awakening a sense of sin and bringing repentance in the lives of Joseph's brothers. He had used the pinch of material want, the pain of harsh treatment, the press of an enforced solitude, the proof of his presence in small things, and last of all, the pattern of an ordained necessity. These had shaken the brothers out of their spiritual lethargy and had brought them to confess their sin—at least among themselves. Still there was a sense in which the most effective of God's means were yet to come. In this section of the story God uses the power of a genuine affection to melt their hearts still further.

Law terrifies; it should terrify us even more than it does. But love draws! Johann Staupitz, prior of the Augustinian monastery Martin Luther entered as a young man, said, "God is not angry with you. Do not be angry with him." It was when Luther saw that God had quenched his wrath against him at the cross and was now reaching out to him in love that the future Protestant Reformer was transformed.

Drawn by Love

This is not the first time in the story that Joseph's brothers received a token of Joseph's good favor toward them. On their first visit to Egypt they had purchased grain and had started back to Canaan. But toward the end of their journey—perhaps because they had run out of immediate provisions for their animals—one of the brothers opened his sack and found his silver returned. Later, after they had returned home, each one discovered that his silver had been returned to him. This frightened them. Indeed, it brought them to recognize the hand of God in their circumstances. "What is this that God has done to us?" they cried.

However, as I said when we considered this portion of the story earlier, there is nothing in it to make us think that Joseph's intentions were anything other than absolutely kind. Unlike the situation in chapter 44, where the cup is hidden in Benjamin's sack, Joseph did not send soldiers after the departing brothers to bring them back to Egypt. Nor does he mention their money again. The brothers bring it up, discussing it with Joseph's household steward (Gen. 43:18–23). Joseph never mentions it. So far as he was concerned, the return of their money was an act of pure benevolence. Joseph simply wanted to give their money back. He had no hidden motives.

Something like this occurs again in this part of the story. However, here Joseph's benevolence is even more noticeable and is more stressed.

The story begins with the brothers' fear, the same fear that had gripped them when the return of their silver was discovered. At their father's insistence they had brought double the money on this journey, the first part to pay for the grain already purchased, the second part to pay for a new supply. But when they presented themselves in Egypt and were immediately invited to eat with Joseph at noon, they suspected a plot against them. The text says, "They thought, 'We were brought here because of the silver that was put back into our sacks the first time. He wants to attack us and overpower us and seize us as slaves and take our donkeys'" (v. 18). The complaint was pathetic. Joseph intended only good for them, but they supposed he was hostile. "He wants to enslave us and even take our poor donkeys," they said.

It is when they were in this frame of mind that the benevolence of the prime minister began to be poured out on them. First, they were reassured about their money by Joseph's steward. They explained the situation to him. But he, who presumably knew about and may perhaps even have carried out the former arrangements, replied with irony, "It's all right. . . . Don't be afraid. Your God, the God of your father, has given you treasure in your sacks; I received your silver" (v. 23). They were not to worry about their money anymore.

Second, the steward brought out Simeon. This must have been a cause of great joy for these brothers. Not knowing Joseph's intentions, they may have suspected that his treatment of Simeon would be dishonorable and that he might already have sold him into slavery—in which path they were soon to follow. But no, Simeon had not been enslaved, and now he was no longer even imprisoned. The prime minister was a man of his word. Their brother had been given back to them.

Third, they were given water to wash their feet and food to feed their donkeys. These were signs of respect and great courtesy. They were being treated as friends, not enemies.

Fourth, Joseph arrived and began to speak kindly. He inquired about their health, asking how they were. He asked about their father: "How is your aged father you told me about? Is he still living?" (v. 27). Lastly his gaze settled on Benjamin. "Is this your youngest brother, the one you told me about?" he inquired. When told that he was, Joseph responded, "God be gracious to you, my son" (v. 29). In all this Joseph had been trying to control himself, being deeply moved at the sight of his full brother, whom he had not seen for more than twenty years. On the verge of breaking down, he rushed from the room to weep privately.

Fifth, an elegant feast was spread before the astonished brothers. A day before, they had been on the verge of starvation, which is why they had come to Egypt. Now they were introduced to the bounty of this most favored land. The last line suggests that they enjoyed it. Up to this point they may have been fearful, suspecting evil motives on the prime minister's part. But dining with him broke down their fears. Joseph must have been the kindest of hosts, and they must have warmed to his gracious hospitality. He would have asked questions of them, and they would have replied with what he most wanted to hear—tales of their families and home. This scene is too tender even for the Bible's words. The story says simply, "So they feasted and drank freely with him" (v. 34).

The interesting thing, however, is that the brothers enjoyed the benefits of Joseph's affection without actually knowing who he was. And when the feast was over—perhaps on the next day—the brothers simply prepared to return home, leaving this interesting interlude behind them.

Love for All

This is where the story most becomes an illustration of how millions of men and women respond to the true and even greater benevolence of God. All are recipients of what theologians call "common grace," the provision of God for all persons; yet they fail to acknowledge it or allow it to accomplish the ends for which God dispenses such benevolence. Romans 2:4 speaks of this: "Do you show contempt for the riches of his [that is, God's] kindness, tolerance and patience, not realizing that God's kindness leads you toward repentance?"

If you are not a follower of Jesus Christ, you are in the same position as Joseph's brothers at this point in the story. You have sinned against your elder brother, the Lord Jesus Christ, by denying his claims and refusing his proper lordship over your life. He has used means to awaken you to your need and bring you to an open confession of sin. But you have gone only so far as God's tactics have forced you to go; even though he has been most loving and gracious toward you, you have not acknowledged his hand in these benefits.

I want you to awaken to God's goodness. I want you to see that all you are and all you have are a result of God's common grace to you.

Let me explain it from God's perspective. God does not owe you anything. He does not even owe you a chance at salvation. When Adam and Eve first sinned against him in Eden, God could have judged them harshly and have sent them to hell at once; and if he had done that, he would have been absolutely just in his actions. Adam and Eve would have received nothing more than their proper desserts. If, acting in a different fashion, God had instead allowed them to live and produce offspring until there were literally millions of their descendants spread out over the entire earth to occupy it and pollute it by their abundant acts of idolatry, theft, fornication, hatred, greed, and other forms of sin, and then had brushed them all into eternal torment, God would nevertheless still have been just. No one could fault him. The righteous angels in heaven would still be able to cry out, as they do even today, "Holy, holy, holy is the LORD Almighty; the whole earth is full of his glory" (Isa. 6:3).

God owes us nothing. Yet, as we well know, God did not immediately banish Adam and Eve to hell, nor did he later suddenly consign the masses of mankind to torment. On the contrary, though there is a judgment to come, God has continually poured out his blessings on men and women.

You have received such blessings. Donald Grey Barnhouse writes correctly, "You are not a believer in Christ and yet you are still out of hell. That is the grace of God. You are not in hell, but you are on earth in good health and prosperity. That is the common grace of God. The vast majority of those who read these words are living in comfortable homes or apartments. That is common grace. You are not fleeing as refugees along the highways of a country desolated by war. That is common grace. You come home from your job and your child runs to meet you in good health and spirits. That is common grace. You are able to put your hand in your pocket and give the child a quarter or a half dollar for an allowance. It is common grace that you have such abundance. You go into your house and sit down to a good meal. That is common grace. On the day that you read these words there are more than a billion and a half members of the human race who will go to sleep without enough to satisfy their hunger. The fact that you have enough is common grace. You do not deserve it. And if you think that you do deserve anything at all from

God beyond the wrath which you have so richly earned, you merely show your ignorance of spiritual principles."[1]

Romans 2:4 puts the matter of God's common grace to you and others as a question: "Do you show contempt for the riches of his kindness, tolerance and patience?" The answer is, of course, you do—unless you have repented of your sin and turned back toward God through faith in Jesus Christ. By nature human beings are ungrateful. By nature you show "contempt" for God's kindness. Yet it is precisely this kindness that God is using to bring you to repentance.

I quote Barnhouse again:

> To despise the riches of God's grace is the blackest of all sins. It far outweighs the sins that are a violation of righteousness. Fallen man has a fallen nature. That is why the Lord seemed to overlook the outbreaks of the flesh, knowing man's frame and remembering that he is but dust (Ps. 103:14). You who boast, perhaps, that you are not guilty of the great fleshly sins should realize that the despising of God's goodness is a sin that far transcends an act that might be called a crime under human law.
>
> Why is God so good toward the lost? He declares that the purpose of the riches of his goodness, forbearance and longsuffering is to lead man to repentance; and he further declares that man does not know the object of God's goodness. Is this not a further picture of the state of man by nature? Can it not be seen that the dark ignorance of unbelief has brought a further fruit of ignorance of the grace of God? You are in good health? Why does God permit it? The answer is that he wants you to turn to him and acknowledge his goodness and accept the riches that he has for you. You have other blessings that come from the common grace of God. The purpose of such riches is to cause you to turn about-face and come to him for further blessing.[2]

God's Love Commended

I have spoken of "common grace" in the sense that God's genuine affection has been poured out upon all persons regardless of who they are or what wrongs they may have done. As Jesus said, God "causes his sun to rise on the evil and the good, and sends rain on the righteous and the unrighteous" (Matt. 5:45). Common grace? Yes! But in another sense, it is not at all common. It is most *uncommon*. It is extraordinary, and it leads us to the most uncommon or extraordinary love of all. We find it in Romans 5:6–8: "At just the right time, when we were still powerless, Christ died for the ungodly. Very rarely will anyone die for a righteous man, though for a good man someone might possibly dare to die. But God demonstrates his own love for us in this: While we were still sinners, Christ died for us."

It is "while we were still sinners" that God has done everything for us. Here is love at its fullest. It is while we were still sinners and, in fact, oblivious both to the extent of our sin and to the uncommon kindness of God toward us in all things that God sent his own son, the Lord Jesus Christ, to die for us.

Moreover, God goes to the unheard of length of commending his love to us by this fact. The word *commend* (KJV; "demonstrate," NIV) is used in two ways in the New Testament. It sometimes means "to establish, prove, or make certain." In this sense the death of Christ certainly "proves" God's love for us, the meaning the NIV translators have favored. But "prove" is a cold word. It has the temperature of algebraic axioms and corollaries. It seems remote. The other use of "commend" is "to recommend or set forth in such a manner that the matter appeals to the heart." This surely is the fullness of the meaning here. The death of Jesus Christ proves the reality and demonstrates the nature of God's unfathomable love. But more than that, it commends it to us in such a manner that we will repent of our sin—which left unrepented of keeps us from God—and instead leads us to embrace Jesus Christ as our own personal Savior.

Have you done that? If not, notice that the word "commend" ("demonstrate") is in the present tense ("commends" or "demonstrates") rather than in the past tense ("commended" or "demonstrated"). That is, it is not merely a past happening that today may be forgotten. It is a present reality, as much a force today as it has ever been. It is today—right now—that God is commending his deep and genuine love to you by Jesus' death.

Today you and I may look back at Joseph's brothers and fault them for their ignorance of Joseph's identity and their slowness to repudiate past sin. But if we try, we can find at least some partial excuses for them. Their sin was long past. There was nothing they could do to change its consequences. As far as their recognition of Joseph was concerned, how could they possibly guess that this powerful Egyptian was the despised brother they had last seen as he was led off as a teenager into slavery?

There are no such excuses for us. We know there is God; the Bible says that only fools deny it (Ps. 14:1). We know that all we are and have come from God's hand; the Bible says, "Every good and perfect gift is from above, coming down from the Father of the heavenly lights, who does not change like shifting shadows" (James 1:17). When we stop to think about it, we even know that God sent the Lord Jesus Christ to save us by giving his life in our place. But do we acknowledge this? We do not—unless God awakens our consciences and turns us from our manifest ingratitude.

That is what you must allow God to do for you—if you have not turned from sin previously. You must allow him to turn you to faith in your older brother, the Lord Jesus Christ, who has loved and continues to love you perfectly.

146

God and the Conscience Part 7: The Purge of Self-Confidence

Genesis 44:1–17

Now Joseph gave these instructions to the steward of his house: "Fill the men's sacks with as much food as they can carry, and put each man's silver in the mouth of his sack. Then put my cup, the silver one, in the mouth of the youngest one's sack, along with the silver for his grain." And he did as Joseph said.

As morning dawned, the men were sent on their way with their donkeys. They had not gone far from the city when Joseph said to his steward, "Go after those men at once, and when you catch up with them, say to them, 'Why have you repaid good with evil? Isn't this the cup my master drinks from and also uses for divination? This is a wicked thing you have done.'"

When he caught up with them, he repeated these words to them. But they said to him, "Why does my lord say such things? Far be it from your servants to do anything like that! We even brought back to you from the land of Canaan the silver we found inside the mouths of our sacks. So why would we steal silver or gold from your master's house? If any of your servants is found to have it, he will die; and the rest of us will become my lord's slaves."

"Very well, then," he said, "let it be as you say. Whoever is found to have it will become my slave; the rest of you will be free from blame."

Each of them quickly lowered his sack to the ground and opened it. Then the steward proceeded to search, beginning with the oldest and ending with the youngest. And the cup was found in Benjamin's sack. At this, they tore their clothes. Then they all loaded their donkeys and returned to the city.

Joseph was still in the house when Judah and his brothers came in, and they threw themselves to the ground before him. Joseph said to them, "What is this you have done? Don't you know that a man like me can find things out by divination?"

"What can we say to my lord?" Judah replied. "What can we say? How can we prove our innocence? God has uncovered your servants' guilt. We are now my lord's slaves—we ourselves and the one who was found to have the cup."

But Joseph said, "Far be it from me to do such a thing! Only the man who was found to have the cup will become my slave. The rest of you, go back to your father in peace."

C harles W. Colson has a great insight regarding the Christian life. In his book *Loving God,* the former Special Counsel to President Richard M. Nixon tells of sitting on a platform in the crowded Delaware State Prison, where he had come to address the inmates, and thinking over a life that had brought him to high government service, followed by arrest, conviction, and imprisonment in connection with the Watergate scandal. He thought of the scholarships and honors earned, the legal cases argued and won, the decisions made from high government offices. Then he realized: "It was not my success God had used to enable me to help those in this prison, or in hundreds of others just like it. . . . All my achievements meant nothing in God's economy. No, the real legacy of my life was my biggest failure—that I was an ex-convict. My greatest humiliation—being sent to prison—was the beginning of God's greatest use of my life."[1]

This is a profound insight, because everything in us naturally thinks the other way. We think that our successes, earned by native ability and the hard sweat of our brow, are the great things God must use and recognize—even when they are achieved, as they often are, in violation of his moral laws. It is a great insight when that natural self-confidence is broken and we find ourselves thrown back utterly upon the good mercy of God.

Self-Confidence Broken

For many chapters we have been looking at the work of God in the lives of Joseph's sin-hardened brothers. Twenty-two years before the events of Genesis 44 take place, they had sold their innocent and unsuspecting brother into slavery, and all the years since then they had lived with their terrible secret. No one knew—not Jacob, their father; or Benjamin, Joseph's younger brother; and certainly not their wives or children. But God knew, and he was working in them to expose their sin and bring genuine healing to their lives.

We have seen some of the means God used: physical want, harsh treatment by Joseph, prison, small but unsettling circumstances, the pressure of an ordered necessity, affection. These were important and increasingly effective devices. But although they were working in the sense of softening the brothers' hearts and awakening them to the awareness that God had not abandoned them to their sin but was still with them, they had nevertheless not really brought the brothers to confess their sin openly. The men had not thrown themselves upon the great, unmerited mercies of God. This necessary end God was now to bring about as the result of one swift blow. At the very moment when the brothers must have been congratulating themselves on how well they had done and how easily they had escaped the worst of what they feared lay before them, God suddenly struck like lightning and demolished their self-confidence. It was out of this death of self that they were spiritually reborn.

To understand Genesis 44 we must put ourselves in the brothers' shoes as they started out from Egypt that final morning. They had gone to Egypt with gloomy apprehensions, fueled perhaps by the even gloomier fears of their father. The last time they had been in Egypt the prime minister was suspicious of them. He called them spies and refused to believe their word about their family, particularly their testimony about their youngest brother, Benjamin, who had been left behind in Canaan. More than this, the prime minister demanded proof that they were speaking the truth. They were to bring their younger brother to Egypt, and to make sure they did, he took one of their number, Simeon, and held him behind as a hostage. As they went down to Egypt the second time, they must have wondered if their word would be believed even then, though they had Benjamin with them. They must have wondered if Simeon would be released or even if he was still in the prison and not already sold into slavery elsewhere.

Their fears were ungrounded. Their *word* was proved good and was believed by Joseph. They must have been quite pleased as they departed, telling themselves that it is certainly always a wise course to tell "the truth, the whole truth, and nothing but the truth." Their word had been vindicated.

Moreover, these brothers must have been confident in their *money*. They had paid for grain the first time. Then, although they did not know how the money from that first transaction had found its way back into their sacks, they had possessed enough silver to bring not only that first payment but even a second payment to the prime minister when they eventually returned.

The Bible does not say this, but I imagine they must have been just a bit smug as they counted out their coins in the steward's presence. "Seventy . . . eighty . . . ninety . . . ninety-five . . . ninety-nine . . . a hundred!" There! Paid in full! No one could say that they were not well-established men of this world. They had made a purchase. Their money was good. Not even this rough governor of Egypt could accuse them of dishonesty. I suppose that this time they even demanded a receipt showing that the cash had been paid.

There was a third thing they were confident about: their *integrity*. Never mind that they had once sold their younger brother into slavery and had lived with their lie for two decades. They were "honest men." So when the steward of Joseph's house went after them according to Joseph's orders, accusing them of having stolen his master's silver drinking cup,[2] they were aghast at the suggestion. "Why does my lord say such things?" they questioned. "Far be it from your servants to do anything like that! We even brought back to you from the land of Canaan the silver we found inside the mouths of our sacks. So why would we steal silver or gold from your master's house? If any of your servants is found to have it, he will die; and the rest of us will become my lord's slaves" (vv. 7–9). It takes a great deal of self-confidence to offer to be sold into slavery if any one of a number of a group of people is found to have done something wrong.

Look at these men as the steward begins to search their sacks. Study their faces. Here is Judah, proud of his integrity. Here are Reuben and Levi, confident that their word will again be vindicated. See their confidence grow as the bundles are systematically opened, beginning with the sack of the oldest. Reuben did not take the prime minister's cup. Simeon does not have it. Levi and Judah are guiltless. Dan and Naphtali, Gad and Asher, Issachar and Zebulun are innocent. At last the steward comes to the sack of Benjamin. Who is worried now? Nobody! Benjamin of all persons could not be guilty of wrongdoing; he was not even in on the plot to sell Joseph. The sack is opened. The grain is sifted. Suddenly the bright Egyptian sun flashes on metal. What? Is there something silver in the sack? Slowly the steward draws forth the special cup.

The cup!

How did it get there? No matter! The cup is there in spite of all the men's protestations. Who is guilty? Benjamin? Someone else who had hidden the stolen object in the baggage of the least suspicious person? No matter again! The truth is that they were all guilty of a far more blameworthy sin, and it was that sin that God was now uncovering and for which he was exacting vengeance.

This is stated in a strange way in the story. After the brothers tear their clothes in grief and consternation and return together to Egypt, Judah says to the prime minister, "What can we say to my lord? . . . How can we prove our *innocence?* God has uncovered your servants' *guilt*" (v, 16). What a strange combination: "Our innocence . . . [our] guilt!" How can both properly be uttered in one sentence? The answer, of course, is that the words accurately and poignantly describe the situation. Innocent of the theft of Joseph's cup, they were. But they were also deeply, irrevocably, damnably guilty of the dreadful sin of having sold their brother into slavery. This had now been brought forcefully to light.

"All for Nothing!"

This is what must happen to you if you are to be forgiven your sin and brought to salvation through the work of Jesus Christ. Apart from God's persistent probing of our consciences we are like these brothers before the exposure of their sin. We are guilty of a great sin against God and against our elder brother, Jesus Christ. God is our Creator, and Jesus is our rightful master and Lord. But we have despised their claims and have gone about our lives self-confidently, priding ourselves in our supposed self-righteousness.

Were the brothers men of their word? "So are we! We tell the truth. We do not lie. If God has anything against us, let him come down here and spell it out. Let him confront us with the facts."

Were the brothers confident of their money? "So are we! We are not beggars in this life; we will not be beggars in the life to come. We pay our way. We go to church. We pray occasionally. We give to Christian work or charity. Who can fault us on that? If God finds our work inadequate, let him make a case against us. We will defend ourselves, and he will find that we have done even more than he requires."

Were the brothers confident of their integrity? "We do not come behind in this matter either. No one will ever call me a thief! I have not stolen from other human beings or from God. Let God take note of that. I am innocent."

Are you now? Innocent like Judah or Reuben or the others? Oh, you may be innocent of some small sin for which you pride yourself. You have not done as the publican over there. You fast twice a week. You give tithes of all you possess. Yet you are guilty of great pride before God, and that will condemn you and carry you down to hell unless you repent of it and turn to Jesus Christ as your Savior.

F. B. Meyer has an illustration at this point to show that even Benjamin, the innocent one, needed to be purged of whatever self-confidence he may have had and that even the most "innocent" of persons today likewise needs to be divested of it.

A preacher of the gospel was once speaking to an old Scotswoman, who was commonly regarded as one of the most devout and respectable people in that part of the country. He was impressing on her, her need of Christ. At last, with tears in her eyes, she said, "Oh, sir, I have never missed a Sabbath at the kirk; and I have read my Bible every day; and I have prayed and done good deeds to my neighbors; and I have done all I knew I ought to do. And now do you mean to tell me that it must all go for nothing?"

He answered, "Well, you have to choose between trusting in these and trusting in the redemption which God offers you in Christ. You cannot have both. If you are content to part company with your own righteousness, the Lord will give you his; but if you cling to your Bible-reading and Sabbath-keeping and good deeds, the Lord's righteousness cannot be yours."

It was quite a spectacle, he said afterwards, to see that old woman's face. The cup was found in Benjamin's sack. For some time she sat in silence, her elbows on the table, her face buried in her hands; a great struggle was going on within. At length the tears began to stream from her eyes, and, lifting up her clasped hands to heaven, she cried out, "Oh, my God, they shall all gang for naething! In a moment more she cast herself on her knees and accepted the Lord Jesus as her Savior.

Says Meyer, "It is when the cup is found in Benjamin's sack that he, too, is brought to the feet of Jesus."[3]

Defeat Is Victory

When a person is exposed to this divine logic for the first time, it sounds wrong. It sounds as if a person who has had the experience of the brothers must now be broken psychologically and must be as useless to God and others as a brainwashed prisoner. But God's ways are not our ways, and actually the opposite is the case. It was precisely at this point, when their own self-confidence and self-righteousness were broken—not a moment before—that Joseph's brothers were healed.

Notice what happened. First, their relationship to God was transformed. Before this they had been running from him while covering up their sin. When he had made his presence felt through the return of their money on their first trip to Egypt, they acknowledged that he was at work: "What is this that God has done to us?" (Gen. 42:28). But it was in the form of a question. They still had not openly confessed their sin. In this later story they recognize God's hand again. Only now it is not "What has God done to us?" It is rather: "God has uncovered our sin. God has won the victory."

In my judgment, this is the point in the story at which the brothers are actually born again. Before this they were unregenerate. From this point on they are transformed individuals.

Second, there is a change in the brothers' relationships to others. This is the central thing emphasized, and it is the purpose for which Joseph had constructed his entire strategy. Here the scene of the selling of Joseph into slavery was set up again. The brothers were in a position of relative control and power. Benjamin, the favored of his father, was in jeopardy. What would the brothers do in a situation in which Benjamin's guilt seemed to be established by the discovery of the cup in his sack? The steward said, "Whoever is found to have it will become my slave; the rest of you will be free from blame" (v. 10). Would the brothers save their own worthless skins at their youngest brother's expense? Would they step aside and see Benjamin go off into slavery as long as they could go free? What kind of story would they make up to explain to their aged father why his beloved son Benjamin had not come back to Canaan with them? Would they pretend that a wild animal had devoured *him*?

Thanks to the work of God, none of these thoughts was now in the minds of the brothers. Years before, they willingly sold Joseph. Now there is not one of them who did not wish that the cup had been found in his sack rather than in Benjamin's. And they did not abandon him! When Benjamin was taken back to Egypt, they all returned to Egypt. They were ready to offer themselves as Joseph's slaves. Most impressive of all, when Joseph declared that only the one who had stolen the cup should be retained as a slave, it was Judah—Judah, who twenty years earlier had counseled the sale of Joseph to the Midianites—who offered to remain in Benjamin's place: "Now, then, please let your servant remain here as my lord's slave in place of the boy, and let the boy return with his brothers. How can I go back to my father if the boy is not with me?" (vv. 33–34).

Oh, glorious transformation! Glorious to God, who alone is able to bring life out of death and righteousness to a sin-scarred conscience.

If you are still trying to run from God and turn aside his gracious intervention in your life, learn these two lessons. First, God will always uncover your iniquity. Usually he discloses iniquity in this life. But even if he does not do so here, he will certainly do it in the life to come. The Bible says, "Your sin will find you out" (Num. 32:23). The secrets of all hearts will be disclosed. All hidden things will be brought into the light from darkness. As Meyer says, "There is absolutely no chance of escape for a man, save in the wounds of Jesus; these are the city of refuge into which the pursuer cannot enter, and in which the fugitive is safe."[4] If you have not entered into that city and been cleansed by that blood, do so now while there is yet hope. Jesus stands ready not only to expose but to forgive, not only to condemn but to cleanse and restore to useful service.

Second, learn that it is not what you achieve in this world that matters, but what God in righteousness chooses to do through you. I began this study with an illustration of the purging of self-confidence from the life of Charles Colson. I close with a quotation from him also. "It is not what we do that matters, but what a sovereign God chooses to do through us. God doesn't want our success; he wants us. He doesn't demand our achievements; he demands our obedience. The kingdom of God is a kingdom of paradox, where through the ugly defeat of a cross, a holy God is utterly glorified. Victory comes through defeat; healing through brokenness; finding through losing self."[5]

May God show you that defeat, that brokenness, that loss of self—so that you may enter into that glorious victory through which others are blessed and he alone is glorified.

147

Judah's Plea for Benjamin

Genesis 44:18–34

Then Judah went up to him and said: "Please, my lord, let your servant speak a word to my lord. Do not be angry with your servant, though you are equal to Pharaoh himself. My lord asked his servants, 'Do you have a father or a brother?' And we answered, 'We have an aged father, and there is a young son born to him in his old age. His brother is dead, and he is the only one of his mother's sons left, and his father loves him.'

"Then you said to your servants, 'Bring him down to me so I see him for myself.' And we said to my lord, 'The boy cannot leave his father; if he leaves him, his father will die.' But you told your servants, 'Unless your youngest brother comes down with you, you will not see my face again.' When we went back to your servant my father, we told him what my lord had said.

"Then our father said, 'Go back and buy a little more food.' But we said, 'We cannot go down. Only if our youngest brother is with us will we go. We cannot see the man's face unless our youngest brother is with us.'

"Your servant my father said to us, 'You know that my wife bore me two sons. One of them went away from me, and I said, "He has surely been torn to pieces." And I have not seen him since. If you take this one from me too and harm comes to him, you will bring my gray head down to the grave in misery.'

"So now, if the boy is not with us when I go back to your servant my father and if my father, whose life is closely bound up with the boy's life, sees that the boy isn't there, he will die. Your servants will bring the gray head of our father down to the grave in sorrow. Your servant guaranteed the boy's safety to my father. I said, 'If I do not bring him back to you, I will bear the blame before you, my father, all my life!'

"Now then, please let your servant remain here as my lord's slave in place of the boy, and let the boy return with his brothers. How can I go back to my father if the boy is not with me? No! Do not let me see the misery that would come upon my father."

The literature of this world is filled with many moving speeches, but it is hard to think of one equal in poignancy and power to the plea of Judah for Benjamin recorded in Genesis 44.

The dying discourse of Socrates in Plato's "Phaedo" is moving; at the last, when Socrates dies, the reader often weeps with Phaedo, Crito, and the others. The heart-rending speeches of Shakespeare's tragic King Lear are sad, though ineffective. Years ago I memorized General Douglas MacArthur's farewell address to the U.S. Congress after he had been relieved as commander of the armed forces in the Korean conflict, and I remember how moved I was as I got to the closing lines. MacArthur referred to the military ballad "Old soldiers never die, they just fade away," and concluded: "Like the old soldier of that ballad I now fade away, an old soldier who tried to do his duty as God gave him the light to see that duty. Good-bye." These and other speeches, both real and fictional, are stirring. But it is hard to think of any as poignant or powerful as Judah's.

F. B. Meyer wrote, "In all literature, there is nothing more pathetic than this appeal."[1] H. C. Leupold said, "This is one of the manliest, most straight-forward speeches ever delivered by any man. For depth of feeling and sincerity of purpose it stands unexcelled."[2] Donald Grey Barnhouse called it "the most moving address in all the Word of God."[3]

A Word in Season

Two things that make this plea so moving are the circumstances under which it was spoken and the background of him who spoke it. We remember that Judah, who pleads for his younger brother Benjamin in this chapter, is the same man who had counseled selling his other younger brother Joseph into slavery twenty-two years earlier.

Some writers have tried to excuse Judah here, saying that his earlier advice was meant to save Joseph. They argue that the brothers wanted to kill him but that Judah suggested selling him as a substitute action: Joseph would be a slave, but at least his life would be spared. I do not find that thought in the story. Reuben *did* want to save Joseph. The story says so explicitly in Genesis 37:21–22. All that the story tells us about Judah is that he saw the Midianite traders and counseled making money from the sale of Joseph rather than merely killing him, which was profitless. He was even sanctimonious about it: "What will we gain if we kill our brother and cover up his blood? Come, let's sell him to the Ishmaelites and not lay our hands on him; *after all, he is our brother, our own flesh and blood*" (Gen. 37:26–27, my emphasis).

It is hard to imagine anything more hypocritical and vile than that. Yet in Genesis 44, Judah pleads most movingly for Benjamin. The contrast heightens the poignancy.

Again, there is the desperation of it. This is not the speech of an Athenian Alcibiades, confident of his political status, abilities, or oratorical skill. This is not the great Winston Churchill, who said on one occasion that he spent most of his free time preparing his "impromptu" speeches. This is a man who, along with his brothers, had been buffeted by God as few other persons have been. Joseph had played with him as a cat plays with a mouse, though for worthwhile purposes. Judah had been starved, abused, and imprisoned. He had been shown unexpected favor, as Joseph received him. But then he had been accused of perfidy and had suffered the unmitigated agony of having to stand helplessly by as Joseph's steward uncovered his master's silver cup in the sack of young Benjamin. This man had all the stuffing knocked out of him. His self-confidence was demolished. He was desperate. It is from the nadir of his fortunes that he pleads so eloquently.

Judah's speech has five parts. First, he implores Joseph to grant him a favorable hearing: "Please, my lord, let your servant speak a word to my lord. Do not be angry with your servant, though you are equal to Pharaoh himself" (v. 18). This is a proper courtly opening, containing due recognition of the prime minister's importance in the political life of Egypt and a touch of proper flattery. Still, it is natural and artless. It is evident that the man is earnest to the point of despair.

Second, Judah reminds the governor of the substance and sequence of his past dealings with them. He tells how Joseph had inquired after the brothers' family, asking specifically if their father was still living and if there were any other brothers in the family. When they replied that they had an aged father and one younger brother, adding that they had also lost another young brother years before, Joseph said they were to bring the remaining brother down to Egypt so that he might see him for himself. They had explained the difficulty: "The boy cannot leave his father; if he leaves him, his father will die" (v. 22). But Joseph had insisted: "Unless your youngest brother comes down with you, you will not see my face again" (v. 23). Since all these facts were already known to the prime minister, Judah must have already been succeeding in winning his consent to the discourse.

Third, Judah reports what had taken place when the brothers had returned home from their first journey, facts that Joseph would have had no way of knowing but that were in obvious harmony with what they had told him earlier. He tells how the brothers had explained the prime minister's demand and how their father had protested: "You know that my wife bore me two sons. One of them went away from me, and I said, 'He has surely been torn to pieces.' And I have not seen him since. If you take this one from me too and harm comes to him, you will bring my gray head down to the grave in misery" (vv. 27–29). Judah does not say so, but it is evident that the father at last relented and permitted Benjamin to accompany the others to Egypt. But what pathos! What agony on the part of the old man! It would take a hard ruler to resist Judah's melting account of the old man's distress.

Fourth, Judah comes to the present dilemma: not that Benjamin had been found to have the cup or that the integrity of all the brothers had now come into question and their lives were jeopardized; but rather the threat to the life of the old man whom Judah clearly loved deeply. "So now, if the boy is not with us when I go back to your servant my father and if my father, whose life is closely bound up with the boy's life, sees that the boy isn't there, he will die. Your servants will bring the gray head of our father down to the grave in sorrow" (vv. 30–31).

The fifth and final part of Judah's speech is his personal plea for Benjamin. He explains how he had pledged himself for his younger brother's safety: "Your servant guaranteed the boy's safety to my father. I said, 'If I do not bring him back to you, I will bear the blame before you, my father, all my life!'" (v. 32). He offers to take Benjamin's place and remain in Egypt as the cruel taskmaster's slave: "Now then, please let your servant remain here as my lord's slave in place of the boy, and let the boy return with his brothers. How can I go back to my father if the boy is not with me? No! Do not let me see the misery that would come upon my father" (vv. 33–34).

I do not know what response Joseph would have been hoping for from Judah or the others as he had devised this test earlier in the day. But whatever he had hoped, he could not have desired anything better than this. The brothers not only stood by Benjamin; they pleaded for him. And Judah, who had once counseled selling Joseph into slavery, now offered to become a slave himself if Benjamin could go free.

The Plea of Moses

I have said that there is no more poignant or powerful appeal of one person for another in all literature than this amazing plea of Judah for Benjamin, not even in the Bible. But there are at least similar (and also profoundly moving) examples of this same thing elsewhere in Scripture, and there is a connection between them, as I intend to show.

The first example is the plea of Moses for his people when they made and worshiped the golden calf. Under the direction of Moses the people who had left Egypt had come to Mount Sinai. The Bible says that God descended upon the mountain in the midst of a cloud of smoke and fire. Nevertheless, Moses spent forty days on the mountain receiving the Ten Commandments and other parts of the law.

As the hours turned to days and the days to weeks, the people who were left in the valley gradually overcame their awe of the cloud, smoke, and fire and grew increasingly cynical and impatient. They said to Aaron, Moses' brother, "Come, make us gods who will go before us. As for this fellow Moses who brought us up out of Egypt, we don't know what has happened to him" (Exod. 32:1). They remembered the worship of Apis the bull and Hathor the cow that they had known in Egypt, so they asked Aaron to make an image of Apis or Hathor for them. Aaron took their gold and melted it in the fire, and when he was done he had enough metal to make a small calf. That satisfied the people. So they began to worship the calf, saying, "These are your gods, O Israel, who brought you up out of Egypt" (v. 4). It was not long before this debased and degenerate worship gave place to debased and degenerate living, and the people began to throw themselves into an orgy.

Up on the mountain God was still speaking to Moses. But he knew what was going on in the valley, and he angrily interrupted the giving of the law to send Moses back down to the nation.

How ironic the situation was! And how horrible! God had just given Moses the Ten Commandments. But while God was giving the Ten Commandments, the people of Israel were willfully breaking each one. The commandments say:

> I am the LORD your God, who brought you out of Egypt, out of the land of slavery. You shall have no other gods before me. You shall not make for yourself an idol in the form of anything in heaven above or on the earth beneath or in the waters below. You shall not bow down to them or worship them; for I, the LORD your God, am a jealous God, punishing the children for the sin of the fathers to the third and fourth generation of those who hate me.
>
> Exodus 20:2–5

While God was saying that, the nation he had delivered was making the image and worshiping it in direct violation of the first and greatest of all God's commandments.

When Moses returned to the people, he began to deal with their sin the best he knew how. In seething anger he had smashed the stone tables of the law that God had given him. Now in righteous anger he entered into the camp, rebuked Aaron publicly, and called for all who remained on the Lord's side to stand beside him. The tribe of Levi responded. So at Moses' command the Levites were sent to kill those who had led the rebellion. The Bible says that of the two million people who had come out of Egypt, 1.5 percent (three thousand persons) were slain. Moses called on the rest to reconsecrate themselves to God.

From a human point of view, Moses had dealt with the sin. The leaders were punished. The loyalty of the people was at least temporarily reclaimed. All seemed to be well.

But Moses stood in a special relationship not only to the people but also to God. And God still waited in wrath upon the mountain. What was Moses to do? By this time not all the law had been given, but Moses had received enough of it to know something of the horror of sin and something of the uncompromising righteousness of God. Had God not said, "You shall have no other gods before me"? Had he not promised to punish the children for the sin of the fathers to the third and even the fourth generations? Who was Moses to think that the limited judgment he had begun would satisfy the holiness of almighty God?

On the mountain Moses had said that the people were God's people (Exod. 32:11). But he knew that they were his people also, and he loved them. The night passed, and the morning came on which Moses was to reascend the mountain. He had been thinking during the night. Sometime during the night a way had come to him that might possibly divert the just wrath of God. He had remembered the sacrifices of the Hebrew patriarchs and the newly instituted sacrifice of the Passover. God had shown by these sacrifices that he was prepared to accept an innocent substitute in place of the just death of the sinner. Perhaps God would accept . . . At this point Moses would hardly have voiced his idea, even to himself. But when morning came, with great determination he began to climb the mountain once again. In an agony of love he now prepared to make a most sublime and selfless offer.

Moses reached the top of the mountain and began to speak to God. It must have been in great anguish, for the Hebrew text is uneven and the second sentence that Moses speaks breaks off without ending. The fact is indicated by the presence of a dash in the middle of verse 32. It is a strangled cry, a gasping sob welling up from the heart of a man who is asking to be sent to hell if only it can mean the salvation of the people he had come to love. The Bible says, "So Moses went back to the LORD and said, 'Oh, what a great sin these people have committed! They have made themselves gods of gold. But now, please forgive their sin—but if not, then blot me out of the book you have written'" (vv. 31–32).

Oh, the love of this man Moses! He had seen the sin of Israel. Already they had rebelled against God and against him. They had turned their backs on his good leadership. They would do so again. But still he loved them. He wanted to save them, just as Judah wanted to save Benjamin.

Paul's Example

The second illustration of a self-sacrificing spirit is found in Romans 9. It stands at the beginning of a section of the book in which Paul discusses the present unbelief and future destiny of the Jewish race. Paul was a Jew by birth and education and was proud of his heritage. He agonized at the evident unbelief of the people to whom Christ first came and to whom the gospel had been so long and earnestly preached. Nothing in Paul's experience indicated that there would be a mass turning to the Messiah by the Jews and hence, along with his agony for them, he feared a historical outpouring of God's judgment.

Moreover, as an acute observer of events in Judea and the Roman world, Paul must have observed the rising tide of nationalism spurred on by the Zealots and feared that it was soon to engulf the country and end in terrible destruction. He must also have known of Christ's prophecies concerning Jerusalem. Jesus said,

> When you see Jerusalem surrounded by armies, you will know that its desolation is near. . . . For this is the time of punishment in fulfillment of all that has been written. . . . There will be great distress in the land and wrath against this people. They will fall by the sword and will be taken as prisoners to all the nations. Jerusalem will be trampled on by the Gentiles until the times of the Gentiles are fulfilled.
>
> Luke 21:20, 22–24

In the light of these prophecies and the historical situation, Paul feared for the people and wrote, "I speak the truth in Christ—I am not lying, my conscience confirms it in the Holy Spirit—I have great sorrow and unceasing anguish in my heart. For I could wish that I myself were cursed and cut off from Christ for the sake of my brothers, those of my own race, the people of Israel" (Rom. 9:1–4).

Like Moses, Paul was saying that he could consent to being sent to hell if it would result in the salvation of the sinful, rebellious, unbelieving people he loved.[4]

The Master's Spirit

Now I want to show the connection among all three examples: Judah, Moses, and Paul. The connection is the spirit of Christ, for it is from him—the Savior and master of all three men—that this transformed behavior comes. These men were all born again, and because they were born again they inevitably showed forth the character and love of their Savior.

But oh, how far beyond even these great biblical examples is the Spirit of Jesus himself! Judah was willing to become a slave to save Benjamin, so greatly did he love both him and his father. Moses was willing to be sent to hell for the sake of his people. Paul expressed a willingness to be accursed if it could mean the salvation of those he loved. Yes! But not one of them actually had to do it. And even if they had, they would have been sacrificing themselves only for people very much like themselves. In Jesus' case the sacrifice was made for those basically unlike himself. We are sinners. He is the sinless one. We are unlovely and unloving. Only he possesses that perfect love that reaches out to us when we are in rebellion against him. When Jesus pleaded for us before his Father, he said in effect, "I am willing to be sent to hell to save these sinful, rebellious, unbelieving people."

God replied, "This sacrifice I will accept. You will be cursed for others. My wrath will fall on you rather than on them. On the basis of your sacrifice I will deal mercifully with them. I will save them."

When Judah pleaded for Benjamin, Moses for his people, Paul for the Jews of his day—all three knew or may have hoped that it would not actually be necessary for them to pay the great price mentioned. Even Judah may have thought that the prime minister of Egypt might be merciful and that he would not have to be a slave or that, having become a slave for Benjamin, he might thereafter somehow again procure his liberty. When Jesus pleaded for us, he knew that he would have to pay the full price of our redemption by his death, and still he did not shrink from the cost. Do you know him as your Savior? Have you been won by such love? If you have, he has already cleansed you from all unrighteousness and has given you a spirit formed by his love that is capable of sacrificing even your own well-being for others.

148

"I Am Joseph"

Genesis 45:1–4

Then Joseph could no longer control himself before all his attendants, and he cried out, "Have everyone leave my presence!" So there was no one with Joseph when he made himself known to his brothers. And he wept so loudly that the Egyptians heard him, and Pharaoh's household heard about it.

Joseph said to his brothers, "I am Joseph! Is my father still living?" But his brothers were not able to answer him, because they were terrified at his presence.

Then Joseph said to his brothers, "Come close to me." When they had done so, he said, "I am your brother Joseph, the one you sold into Egypt!"

My wife and I had a discussion about the story of the patriarch Job. Linda had been teaching it to ninth-graders in her course "Introduction to Western Literature" and had asked the students to identify the "climax." Is the climax of Job at the end, when Job prays for his friends and is rewarded by God with twice as much wealth as he had before his sufferings? One can make a good case for that. Or is the climax of Job at the point of God's revelation of himself to Job in chapters 38–41?

My wife believes that the climax is in chapter 19, where Job stands by faith in regard to what he cannot see:

> I know that my Redeemer lives,
>   and that in the end he will stand upon the earth.
> And after my skin has been destroyed,
>   yet in my flesh I will see God;
> I myself will see him
>   with my own eyes—I, and not another.

Job 19:25–27

I asked whether the climax might not be as early as chapter 1, where we read:

Then he [Job] fell to the ground in worship and said:

> "Naked I came from my mother's womb,
>   and naked I will depart.
> The LORD gave and the LORD has taken away;
>   may the name of the LORD be praised."

In all this, Job did not sin by charging God with wrongdoing.

verses 20–22

Job is a complicated book, and it is understandable that people who study it may have different ideas as to what really constitutes its climax. But this is not the case with the wonderful but quite straightforward story of Joseph and his brothers told in Genesis 37–50. What is the climax of this story? Surely it is the text now before us, the moment in which Joseph reveals himself to his brothers for the first time. "I am Joseph!" In that declaration Joseph's emotions peak and the brothers' experience reaches a crescendo. There are few more dramatic moments than this in all history.

But the verses are climactic in another way also. As we have seen on other occasions, Joseph is an outstanding type of Jesus Christ. Consequently, his revelation of himself to his brothers aptly illustrates that great personal climax of a human life when Jesus reveals himself savingly to that person. I want you to see both of these as we turn to the story.

Knowledge before Knowledge

The parallel between Joseph and Jesus may be seen by four propositions. First, *Joseph knew his brothers before they knew him.* Joseph knew Benjamin when he first saw him. He knew Judah, Reuben, Simeon, Levi, and all the others. But on their part, the brothers thought him some mysterious Egyptian potentate about whom they knew virtually nothing. They did not perceive that he was Joseph until he revealed himself on this occasion. Genesis 42:8 says, "Although Joseph recognized his brothers, they did not recognize him."

Is it not strange that we should fail to know and recognize the God who has created us or the Lord Jesus Christ who is our Savior? The Bible says, "The ox knows his master, the donkey his owner's manger, but Israel does not know, my people do not understand" (Isa. 1:3). When Jesus, the Son of God, appeared on earth on that first Christmas, the same thing was true. John wrote, "He was in the world, and though the world was made through him, the world did not recognize him. He came to that which was his own, but his own did not receive him" (John 1:10–11). We did not know him; but he knows us, and he has known us from the beginning. David said that God knew him from the moment he formed him in his mother's womb (Ps. 139:15).

> O LORD, you have searched me
>   and you know me.
> You know when I sit and when I rise;
>   you perceive my thoughts from afar.
> You discern my going out and my lying down;
>   you are familiar with all my ways.
> Before a word is on my tongue
>   you know it completely, O LORD.
>
>   verses 1–4

David came to know God at a very early age. But David would have been the first to acknowledge that God knew him before he knew God.

Again, Jesus does not merely know you from the beginning—in the sense that he might simply know of your existence and have you within his general frame of reference. He knows you profoundly, deeply. He knows your "going out" and your "lying down." He knows the secrets, even the most guilty secrets, of your heart.

This was the case with Joseph and his brothers. The brothers had confessed their sin to each other, but never openly, and they supposed that there was not a creature in the universe who knew of it and was therefore capable of exposing their transgression. Yet Joseph knew. He had known all along, and he was now bringing what he knew to light. So also does the Lord Jesus Christ know you. He knows the sin you have tried to hide and have succeeded in hiding from all but himself. You think you have buried that sin forever. Jesus knows it and is exposing it so you may seek his forgiveness and find cleansing.

This is the explanation of how God so often uses sermons to expose hidden sin. I have often preached a sermon with my mind on the meaning and application of the text, and afterward someone has come up to me to ask, "Why were you preaching about me? Who told you about my past?" I did not even know the person, let alone anything about his or her past. But God had applied the message, and the sin was exposed.

Remember that although you may hide from other people and even from yourself, all things are open before the eyes of him with whom you have to do. And even if the sin is not exposed here, it is nevertheless known to God and will be exposed for his perfect judgment at the last day.

Love before Love

There is an additional parallel between Joseph and Jesus in the fact that *Joseph loved his brothers when they did not love him*. It is true, as the story shows, that the brothers came to love Joseph. But they did not love him yet. How could they? They hated him at first, so much that they sold him into slavery. Then they supposed that he had perished. As God worked on their consciences, they came to regret and then eventually to repent of their action, but they could hardly love a person whom they had only known more than twenty years before and whom they now supposed was dead. Yet Joseph loved them and was actually acting toward them in love, although they did not know it.

Moreover, Joseph loved them deeply. How deeply appears in this story as, overcome before Judah's poignant pleadings for Benjamin, Joseph breaks down and has to require his Egyptian attendants to leave him: "Then Joseph could no longer control himself before all his attendants, and he cried out, 'Have everyone leave my presence!' So there was no one with Joseph when he made himself known to his brothers" (Gen. 45:1). This is a moving story, but we must say that it is not at all remarkable. Joseph had been a lonely man for twenty years. He must have wondered whether he would ever see his family again; and then, when he did see his brothers, he kept his feelings bottled up while God worked through him to effect their conversion and test their new natures. It would have been a surprise if Joseph had not broken down at this point. True. But what are we to say of Jesus, whom we see weeping over Jerusalem? Was there ever a love like his? Joseph's love was great, but Jesus' love is greater. It is beyond all tracing out.

I notice too that Joseph loved his brothers in spite of any appearances to the contrary. And there had been some! He had spoken to them harshly when they had first come to Egypt. Later he had placed a heavy demand upon them: They were to bring their youngest brother with them when they again came to Egypt. Joseph had imprisoned Simeon. Then he had hidden his cup in Benjamin's sack in order to break their self-confidence. From the perspective of the brothers, these were hardly acts of love. Yet they were; they were the workings out of love. The truly loveless thing would have been for Joseph to have ignored his brothers and have allowed them to go on in their godless way and eventually perish in hell.

Are you an unsaved person, and is God buffeting you? If he is, it is for your benefit. It is because he loves you, not because he does not. Learn from Joseph that he is using these circumstances to drive you from sin and draw you to himself.

Saved yet Trembling

Again, not only did Joseph know his brothers before they knew him and not only did he love them when they did not love him, he also *saved them before they were aware of their salvation*. Everything that has happened in the story to this point has been an aspect of the salvation of these godless men, which God was effecting through Joseph. Yet they did not know it, and here—when they had actually repented of their sin and had given evidence of having become regenerated people—they were so unaware of what had happened that they were "terrified" and feared a harsh revenge at Joseph's hands (v. 3).

Review what God had done to awaken their consciences and bring them to spiritual life. First, he had subjected them to the pinch of physical want. They were starving and were forced to go down to Egypt to find food. Second, he had subjected them to the pain of harsh treatment, as I have just mentioned. These men were not used to such treatment; Joseph's words were a blow to their self-esteem and pride. Third, they had known the beneficial pressure of solitude as they had been forced to be still and think in Joseph's prison. Fourth, there had been the proof of God's presence through the inexplicable return of their money, which they had discovered on their first trip home. Fifth, there had been the pattern of an ordained necessity. In spite of their wishes, they were unable simply to return to "business as usual." Sixth, they were moved by the power of Joseph's affection, which they could not miss, though they also could not fully understand it. Finally, there was the purge of self-confidence through the discovery of Joseph's cup in the sack of young Benjamin. These were the means God used to turn them from sin and bring them to new life. Yet the brothers did not know it. It is only at this time that they discovered what God had been doing.

As a matter of fact, their condition was worse than one of mere ignorance. They not only did not know they were saved but actually feared the opposite. They were terrified because they believed they were lost.

Charles Haddon Spurgeon had a sermon on this passage in which he found the condition of the brothers when Joseph revealed himself to them to be the condition of every truly awakened sinner. In graphic terms Spurgeon portrayed their misery. They knew they were sinners who had no excuse for their sin. Earlier they had said, "Surely we are being punished because of our brother" (Gen. 42:21) and "What is this that God has done to us?" (Gen. 42:28). When the cup was uncovered in Benjamin's sack they saw it as an uncovering of their guilt: "How can we prove our innocence? God has uncovered your servants' guilt" (Gen. 44:16). These words are insights into what was happening in their hearts. Yet in this episode, when Joseph is revealed to them and the enormity of their guilt and its public disclosure is poured out on them, it is significant that they find themselves speechless. As those who will one day stand before the judgment seat of Christ, they found their mouths stopped and themselves accountable (Rom. 3:19).

Moreover, these brothers were not only overwhelmed with their guilt but conscious that they were in Joseph's absolute power. He was the monarch. He could do with them according to his good pleasure. Spurgeon took a cue from Jonathan Edwards at this point and wrote, "To the awakened sinner, this also is a part of his misery, that he is entirely in the hands of that very Christ whom he once despised; for that Christ who died has now become the judge of the quick and dead; he has power over all flesh that he may give eternal life to as many as his Father has given him. The Father judgeth no man; he has committed all judgment to the Son. Dost thou see this, sinner? He whom thou despised is thy Master. The moth beneath thy finger, which thou canst crush and that cannot escape from thee, may well fear; but thus art thou beneath the fingers of the crucified Son of God. Today he whom thou hast despised has thee absolutely at his will; he has but to will it and the breath is gone from thy nostrils and while yet in thy seat thou art a corpse. And more, at his will thou art in hell amidst its flames. Oh! what an awful thing it is to fall into the hands of the living God, for even our God is a consuming fire."[1]

Do you think you can escape the just judgment of God? If so, you are lost though you may think yourself safe. The brothers were never more lost than when they supposed their sin was forgotten and that in this life it would rise up to haunt them no more. If they had been right, theirs would have been a tragic story. It would have meant damnation for them all.

But they were wrong. They had put Joseph in a pit, but God took him out of the pit and placed him on a throne. They had embittered their father's life for twenty-two long years and cared not a wit for his anguish; but God caused them anguish instead and restored the lost son. In this moment—to their dread—the brothers saw that sin is futile, that it cannot be hidden, that its consequences cannot be escaped, that God must judge it fiercely.

Seeing this was their salvation. If you see it, though you justly fear judgment, you have actually been awakened by God and are in the process of being saved. For we must be aware of our sin before there can be repentance, and we must repent of our sin before we can trust in Christ for salvation.

Come to Jesus

The last parallel between Joseph and Jesus in this story is this: *Joseph called his brothers when they would have preferred to run from him,* and he called effectively. This is the way Joseph's announcement of his identity ends. He had told them who he was, and they were terrified. But he commanded them to "come close" to him; and although they must have feared that it was because he wished to harm them, to their surprise they discovered that it was not an angry master who so called, but a loving brother. Under different circumstances Joseph could have been angry; they could have been judged. But Joseph was not calling them in anger. He had turned them from sin; they were changed men.

Now he was calling them with the sweetness of a powerful and embracing love.

So also is Jesus calling you. If you hear his voice, it is because he has already made you one of his sheep. And though he could have judged you while you were yet in your sin, he has turned you from it—it is why you hear him—and now he wants you close to himself.

How does Jesus call? I notice that, like Joseph, who is a type of the Lord at this point also, Jesus usually calls in secret. It is when the attendants are put out and the Lord is alone with you in the quiet of your soul that you hear the still, small voice of God. This is why I distrust many "evangelistic" conversions. Oh, people may be saved—I am sure some are—among the noise and drama of some revival meetings. But I am also sure that people are saved far more often as God speaks to them quietly as they wait (sometimes tremblingly) before him. Are you quiet now? Are you listening? May your prayer be that of the invitation hymn.

> Speak, Lord, in the stillness,
> While I wait on thee,
> Hushed my heart to listen
>   in expectancy.

Second, I am sure that Joseph called his eleven brothers by name. Later on we are told that "he threw his arms around his brother Benjamin" and that "he kissed all his brothers and wept over them" (vv. 14–15). Can we imagine him to have done that without calling their names? He would have cried out, "Come here, Benjamin. Judah, don't be afraid; come. Come to me, Reuben. . . ." So on with all the brothers, one by one and name by name. Jesus calls you in the same manner. Do you hear him calling? He is not calling your neighbor. He is not calling the person seated next to you. He is not calling your husband or your wife or your children or your parents. He is calling you. Hear him. Respond to him.

Finally, he is calling you as your brother, just as Joseph called his brothers: "I am your brother Joseph, the one you sold into Egypt" (v. 4). You have done that and more to Jesus. But that is of no account now. Jesus is calling you as your brother, who loves you and is willing to provide for you both now and for eternity. It is not hard to win a brother's love. It is not hard to enjoy a brother's true affection. The Lord is here. He is calling. Can you not respond to his call and draw near to him as you have never done before? He is telling you of his love. All he has done in your life has been for love. Can you not tell him that you know that and love him too?

149

"God . . . God . . . God . . . God"

Genesis 45:5–9

"And now, do not be distressed and do not be angry with yourselves for selling me here, because it was to save lives that God sent me ahead of you. For two years now there has been famine in the land, and for the next five years there will not be plowing and reaping. But God sent me ahead of you to preserve for you a remnant on earth and to save your lives by a great deliverance.

"So then, it was not you who sent me here, but God. He made me father to Pharaoh, lord of his entire household and ruler of all Egypt. Now hurry back to my father and say to him, 'This is what your son Joseph says: God has made me lord of all Egypt. Come down to me; don't delay.'"

In studying the character of Joseph we have seen that its single most distinguishing feature was his ability to relate everything to God. God was in his thoughts constantly. There is hardly a sentence from his lips that does not have the name of God in it.

When Joseph was taken to Egypt and was tempted to commit fornication by the wife of Potiphar, the opinion of God was what Joseph chiefly cared about. "How then could I do such a wicked thing and sin against God?" Joseph asked the woman (Gen. 39:9).

When he was put in prison and was told that the chief cupbearer and the chief baker of Pharaoh had dreams that they were unable to interpret, Joseph responded, "Do not interpretations belong to God? Tell me your dreams" (Gen. 40:8).

Joseph said the same to Pharaoh: "I cannot do it, . . . but God will give Pharaoh the answer he desires" (Gen. 41:16). Later he said, "God has revealed to Pharaoh what he is about to do" (41:25; cf. vv. 28, 32).

Joseph named his first son Manasseh because, he said, "God has made me forget all my trouble and all my father's household" (Gen. 41:51). Manasseh means "forgetting." Joseph named his second son Ephraim because "God has made me fruitful in the land of my suffering" (v. 52). Ephraim means "twice fruitful."

At the very end of Genesis, Joseph tells his brothers, "You intended to harm me, but God intended it for good to accomplish what is now being done, the saving of many lives" (50:20). Again, "I am about to die. But God will surely come to your aid and take you up out of this land" (vv. 24–25).

Nothing is more characteristic of Joseph than his ability to relate everything that happened to him to God. But nowhere in the story is this more evident than in chapter 45 in the verses to which we come now. Here are five verses in which Joseph sought to allay his brothers' fears after he had revealed himself to them. In these verses the name of God occurs four times:

"It was to save lives that *God* sent me ahead of you."

"*God* sent me ahead of you to preserve for you a remnant on earth and to save your lives by a great deliverance."

"So then, it was not you who sent me here, but *God.*"

"*God* has made me lord of all Egypt" (Gen. 45:5–9, my emphasis).

By looking past secondary causes to God, who is the first cause, Joseph gained a stabilizing perspective on life and achieved a frame of mind out of which he was able to forgive and reassure his brothers. It is a perspective to be held by every Christian.

The Problem of Evil

This God-centered perspective is a profound insight. So it is not to be taken lightly as if it were merely Joseph's kind of wishful thinking. Nor is it as if Joseph had experienced only good in his life and was simply acknowledging that all good gifts come from God (cf. James 1:17). On the contrary, he had experienced much evil. He had been unreasonably hated, treacherously enslaved, falsely accused, and wrongly imprisoned. Again, it is not as if he were merely ignoring the evil or denying it. He was acutely aware of his brothers' evil and of their need to turn from it.

No, the unique importance of these statements lies in Joseph's attributing what was evil in its intent to God's providence. He was not saying that God is the author of evil. God is not. Rather, God is in charge even of the wicked designs and evil deeds of men, so that his purposes are accomplished, not theirs.

This means—since God is the author of Scripture and certainly sets his seal to what Joseph is declaring—that God assumes ultimate responsibility for the evil of men, and for evil events besides. A Boston rabbi, Harold S. Kushner, published a book entitled *When Bad Things Happen to Good People*. The book was an instant best-seller. It sold over half a million hardcover copies before going into paperback. The book was on the *New York Times* best-seller list for fifty-two weeks. Its thesis is that God is all-loving but not all-powerful, good but not sovereign. So when bad things happen to good people, it is because events are out of God's control. What are we to do? Kushner advises his readers to "learn to love [God] and forgive him despite his limitations."[1]

Kushner's thesis is an easy solution to the problem of evil. But it should be evident to any Bible student, particularly a rabbi, that a good but helpless God is not the God of Scripture. We may have trouble understanding how an all-powerful but good God can relate to the evil in this world. But one thing is certain: God does not beg off responsibility for what happens. He does not say, "Well, it's a big universe; you can't expect me to be everywhere at once." God *is* everywhere at once. He *is* in charge. He *is* all-powerful.

The proper relationship between the goodness and sovereignty of God on the one hand, and the prevalence of evil in the world on the other, is seen in the story of Job. Job suffered many things he did not deserve. Desert raiders carried away his oxen and donkeys. Lightning destroyed his sheep. Babylonian bandits stole his camels. Added to this, his seven sons and three daughters were killed suddenly by the collapse of the house in which they had been dining. Then Job had boils so painful that he bemoaned the day he was born. In all his suffering Job had not the slightest indication that any of this was for a meaningful purpose or that any good could come of it. Even after God appeared to him later and overwhelmed him with a reminder of his greatness and Job's impotence, there was still no explanation.

Yet the story begins with a scene in heaven—which Job could not see but that is provided for the benefit of the readers of the book—showing not only that God was in charge of what was happening and was limiting it, but that he actually initiated the test by calling Satan's attention to Job's godly character: "Have you considered my servant Job? There is no one on earth like him; he is blameless and upright, a man who fears God and shuns evil" (Job 1:8).

In the story we learn that God had a purpose in Job's suffering. He was demonstrating to Satan and his hosts that love for God really does exist apart from the benefits people get from the relationship. God showed that invisible things are greater than the visible, that love is greater than selfishness. Also, God was working even in Job's life to bring about a marked growth in faith and maturing of character.

The point is, *none of this was accidental*. God was in charge. Job could not see it; but God, who gives us the story, assumes full responsibility for every evil detail that occurs. God did not do the evil. Evil came from the malicious spirit of our great enemy, the devil. Yet God permitted evil and assumed responsibility for it. The reason bad things happen to good people is that God decrees it. Joseph saw this and declared it when he said, "It was not you who sent me here, but God" (45:8).

Good out of Evil

But Joseph was not merely saying that God was behind the evil that had happened to him, important as that preliminary statement is. By itself the statement means that tragedies are not accidents. It may even mean that God has some wise purpose in the tragedy, and that is helpful. It is always easier to bear something if you know there was a purpose to it. But Joseph was claiming more than that in his fourfold reference to God's hand in the details of his life. Besides saying that God was in charge of what happened, Joseph says that God was accomplishing a good purpose in it—so that the end was good despite the evil.

"It was *to save lives* that God sent me ahead of you. . . . God sent me ahead of you *to preserve for you a remnant* on earth and *to save your lives* by a great deliverance" (vv. 5, 7).

Here we can see how Joseph's statements regarding God's good purposes were true. The hatred of Joseph's brothers, which was evil, was the cause of their selling him into slavery, which got him to Egypt. The lust and lying of Potiphar's adulterous wife, which were evil, were the means of getting Joseph into prison, where he met the chief cupbearer and chief baker of Pharaoh. The forgetfulness of the cupbearer, whether unintentionally or intentionally cruel, meant that Joseph was still in prison to be brought out at the proper time two years later when Pharaoh had his dream. It is easy to see this in retrospect, as Joseph did. But this was twenty-two years after Joseph's initial captivity. During the early years it was not obvious how (or even if) God was going to bring good out of evil. Yet Joseph lived by faith in God during those years just as much as he did after the purposes of God began to be disclosed.

And so did Job! When God first permitted Satan to attack Job, causing the loss of his property and the death of his children, Job did not understand what was happening. He was so distressed that he tore his robe and shaved his head—two ancient symbols of deep mourning. Yet we read:

Then he fell to the ground in worship and said:

> "Naked I came from my mother's womb,
>   and naked I will depart.
> The LORD gave and the LORD has taken away;
>   may the name of the LORD be praised."

In all this, Job did not sin by charging God with wrongdoing.

Job 1:20–22

When God permitted Satan to inflict Job with boils all over his body, Job still had no idea what God's purpose was. Yet, although Job left his house and sat in ashes, scraping his sores, he did not curse God for his trouble. We read, "In all this, Job did not sin in what he said" (Job 2:10).

Job did not even have an explanation of what God was doing during that long and painful time when he was receiving "comfort" from his friends. He defended himself, arguing that he had done nothing to deserve the extraordinary measure of calamity that had been meted out to him. He did not understand it. Yet, like Joseph, Job was willing to believe that God was still in charge and that he would bring good out of his suffering.

There were three good things that Joseph claimed God accomplished by his suffering. First, God prospered Joseph, making him "lord of all Egypt" (v. 9). This was the highest position a person other than the pharaoh could enjoy in that day. But in Joseph's case it was reached by one in the lowest of all positions, an imprisoned slave.

There is a spiritual lesson here: namely, those whom God wishes greatly to honor he often greatly abases—no doubt because the humbling is necessary for the greatness. Moses was a man greatly used of God in the deliverance of the Jews from Egypt. He was Israel's first great leader. But before he was called by God and sent to Egypt with the command "Let my people go," he was driven from Egypt as a fugitive and spent forty years on the backside of the desert as a shepherd. David was greatly used of God. Yet David spent many years being harried from pillar to post by the jealous and vindictive King Saul. It was during these dog days that both Moses and David developed the necessary character for true greatness. So do not despair if life has not prospered you yet. God may be preparing you for great things to come. Whatever the future holds, you can know that God controls it and that the eventual outcome of any evil will be good for you personally.

Second, God saved the lives of the brothers through Joseph's fall and eventual rise to power. God was doing a number of things through Joseph's being sold into Egypt. This was his way of getting Jacob and the brothers to Egypt, where they would prosper and grow into a great nation, for instance. In order to get Jacob to Egypt God had to get Benjamin to Egypt. In order to get Benjamin to Egypt he had to get the brothers to Egypt. In order to get the brothers to Egypt he had to get Joseph to Egypt. All this was for the good of the brothers. But in addition to this and of even more immediate importance, Joseph's suffering was the means of saving their lives. This was a severe famine, and Joseph's family would have died if God had not sent Joseph ahead of the others "to preserve for you a remnant on earth and to save your lives by a great deliverance" (v. 7).

Remember this when you go through difficult times. Hard times may be God's means of saving you and others from an even greater disaster. David said, "Before I was afflicted I went astray, but now I obey your word" (Ps. 119:67).

Third, God saved other lives in the process of saving Jacob's household. As Joseph said, "It was to save lives that God sent me ahead of you" (v. 5). The world does not see this, of course. But the Scriptures teach that the wicked experience many special providences because of God's care for the righteous. God has spared many a nation because of an oppressed but faithful minority. Today he may even be preserving the Western world for this reason.

Forgiveness and Repetition

I come to my last two points. It should be clear that one of the benefits of Joseph's seeing everything that happened to him as having come from God is that he was able to forgive his brothers easily, as he would not have been if he had focused only on their responsibility for his suffering.

Donald Grey Barnhouse writes, "To see God in all things, both good and evil, enables us to forgive easily those who injure us. It does not incline us to condone their fault as if they were unconscious instruments impelled by him who made use of them, for they act as freely as if God had no part at all. But we can pity, forgive, and pray for them, as slaves to their own passions, enemies to their own welfare, and real, though unwitting, benefactors to our souls. This is strongly exemplified in Joseph, for he saw the hand of God over-ruling the designs of his brothers; and from that consideration, he not only readily forgave them but entreated them 'not to be grieved or angry with themselves,' since whatever had been their intentions, God had used their misdeeds to accomplish his own gracious purposes."[2]

Do you have trouble forgiving someone? Has someone deeply wronged you, and does your body tense up in anger whenever you think of him or her? Have you prayed about it and had little relief? If so, try thinking of the wrong as part of God's providence. See his hand in it. Think of the good he is accomplishing. If you gain that perspective, you will find your anger softening and discover at the last that you are actually able to forgive the one who has wronged you greatly.

Finally, I note the thing that has been obvious in this passage from the beginning, namely, the striking repetition of God's name. When God repeats something it is never for mere literary effect, but rather to help our little minds understand and finally grasp some great fact. When God wants us to grasp how sinful we are and how desperate our condition is apart from his great grace, he repeats three times over:

> There is no one righteous, not even one;
>   there is no one who understands,
>   no one who seeks God.

> All have turned away,
>> they have together become worthless;
> there is no one who does good,
>> not even one.

Romans 3:10–12; cf. Psalm 14:1–3; 53:1–3

This is something God wants us to know; we are ignorant of God, rebellious, dead in trespasses and sins. So also here. God wants us to know that he is in charge of the events of our lives. He is sovereign.

"*God* sent me ahead of you."

"*God* sent me ahead of you."

"It was not you who sent me here, but *God*."

"*God* has made me lord of all Egypt" (vv. 5–9, my emphasis).

Can you learn the lesson of these verses and benefit from it? The lesson is: "God . . . God . . . God . . . God."

150

"Come! Come!"

Genesis 45:4–13

Then Joseph said to his brothers, "Come close to me." When they had done so, he said, "I am your brother Joseph, the one you sold into Egypt! And now, do not be distressed and do not be angry with yourselves for selling me here, because it was to save lives that God sent me ahead of you. For two years now there has been famine in the land, and for the next five years there will not be plowing and reaping. But God sent me ahead of you to preserve for you a remnant on earth and to save your lives by a great deliverance.

"So then, it was not you who sent me here, but God. He made me father to Pharaoh, lord of his entire household and ruler of all Egypt. Now hurry back to my father and say to him, 'This is what your son Joseph says: God has made me lord of all Egypt. Come down to me; don't delay. You shall live in the region of Goshen and be near me—you, your children and grandchildren, your flocks and herds, and all you have. I will provide for you there, because five years of famine are still to come. Otherwise you and your house- hold and all who belong to you will become destitute.'

"You can see for yourselves, and so can my brother Benjamin, that it is really I who am speaking to you. Tell my father about all the honor accorded me in Egypt and about everything you have seen. And bring my father down here quickly."

The speech of Joseph in Genesis 45:4–13, in which he revealed himself to his brothers, is not very long—just eleven verses. Yet in them Joseph repeated the burdens of his announcement

1064

several times. We have already looked at one of these repetitions: the name "God." It occurs in verses 5, 7, 8, and 9. In this study I want to look at the word "come." It occurs three times in all, twice in a meaningful combination. In verse 4 Joseph said to his brothers, "*Come* close to me." In verse 9 he told them to tell his father, "*Come* down to me." Finally, in verse 11 he explained that this was because "five years of famine are still to *come*."

The two important "comes" are (1) the summoning of the brothers to Joseph, and (2) the invitation they were then able to pass on to their father in his name.

"Come unto Me"

It is hard to think of these invitations without thinking of the parallel invitations that the Lord Jesus Christ, our elder brother, gives us in spite of our treatment of him. This greater invitation is prefigured in Joseph's summoning of his brothers.

"Come" is a common word. It is not thought about often, but it is a powerful and wonderful word, particularly when spoken to sinful men and women by the Lord Jesus Christ. The wonders of this word can be seen in the following story. Some time ago the Reverend E. V. Hill, a great preacher from Los Angeles, was in Philadelphia speaking to an annual gathering of black Baptist churches. He was speaking on the expulsion of Adam and Eve from Eden. Dr. Hill is dramatic on any occasion, but he was especially so on this. Seated next to him on the platform was the leader of the Baptist Federation. When he got to the point of the story in which Adam and Eve were driven from Eden, Dr. Hill took off his long preaching robe and placed it on his distinguished colleague, using it to represent his sin. Then he ordered him out of the church! For many long minutes Hill kept telling him to leave—as his friend got up from his seat, walked down the steps from the platform, turned and made his way down the center aisle to the main door of the church, and stepped outside.

Then Dr. Hill posted two "angels" (who were deacons) at the door and insisted that they do their job and not permit the leader of the federation of churches to return.

There was a moment of silence after this outrageous demonstration. But then Hill began to preach grace. He explained how sin separates us from the presence of a holy God, but how Jesus died on the cross to remove this sin. He explained the gospel invitation. Before Christ's work, God's word to us was "Go!" Now his invitation is "Come!" At this point the preacher called to the "angel-deacons" who were still on duty in the back of the church and told them to throw the doors open. Then they were told to call the Baptist church leader to come back in, removing his black robe as they did so. At last the man was led back up the aisle to the platform, where he resumed his place at Hill's side.

"Come." A simple word! We use it every day. But it is a wonderful word when spoken in a gospel manner. Like Joseph's brothers, we have sinned greatly against our rightful Sovereign and Savior. We deserve to be driven from his presence. But he has died for us! He loves us! Now he reaches out with the gospel invitation to come to him.

"Come and See"

I think of another invitation to "come": the invitation of the angel to the women who wanted to anoint the body of Jesus at the tomb on Easter morning. This was an important "come," because it is prior even to the invitation to place one's faith in the Savior. You may not be ready to do that. You may not yet be convinced that Jesus is the Savior. If so, this "come" is for you—if you are not yet ready to believe but need to investigate the evidence.

The women had come to the tomb so early in the morning that some of the accounts describe it as being still dark. They were not expecting a resurrection; they were expecting to find a dead body. But suddenly they saw the angel and heard him say, "Do not be afraid, for I know that you are looking for Jesus, who was crucified. He is not here; he has risen, just as he said. Come and see the place where he lay. Then go quickly and tell his disciples: 'He has risen from the dead'" (Matt. 28:5–7).

I can think of many things that might have hindered the women at this point. The place itself might have hindered them. It was a graveyard, after all, clearly not the most attractive place to be. They could have said to each other, "Let's go home; we'll come back again when it's lighter." Or the edict of Rome might have hindered them. The tomb had been sealed by Pilate's orders. Soldiers had been stationed to guard it, though they were gone now. Something unexplained had happened. The great covering stone had been removed. The seal had been broken. Rome had been disobeyed. The women might have said, "We can't go closer. Rome forbids it. We can't look in." Again, their sin might have hindered their coming. Here was something holy, miraculous. They might have said, "We are unclean; we cannot come." If they had said any of those things, we would have understood them, for we recognize that fear, secular authority, and sin often keep a person from the Savior.

Yet the women were not hindered by these things. Here was an invitation to come forward, the same kind of invitation the Lord himself had given on many occasions. The women recognized the authentic voice of God in the word of the angel, and obeyed it.

Why were the women to come forward? The angel explained. It was to "see the place where the Lord lay." Think for a minute about why we should see the grave and how we may profit by it.

First, we come to the grave to see the *humility of the Lord Jesus Christ*. Jesus is not just a man for whom death would be natural. Jesus is the Lord! He is Jehovah! Jesus was with God in eternity—equal to God, equal in power and glory. Yet he laid aside that glory to take upon himself the form of a man to die to save us. Oh, the condescension of one who would come from the glories of heaven to this earth and then die and lie in such a tomb! When we look at the grave we see the humility of our Lord.

We see something else too. We see *the horror of sin* that placed him there. Jesus did not die for his own sin; he was sinless. He died in our place: "He was pierced for our transgressions, he was crushed for our iniquities; the punishment that brought us peace was upon him, and by his wounds we are healed" (Isa. 53:5). When we see the place where the Lord lay and say, "It is my sin that brought him to this end," we begin to develop a proper awareness of sin and hatred of it.

The third reason why we should come to the tomb is to be reminded of *where we also will lie,* unless the Lord comes for us beforehand. We too must die. There is a time when we will be separated from all we know. We will leave friends and loved ones behind. We will leave our material possessions. When we come to the tomb we learn of our mortality. We learn that there is a life beyond this life for which we must prepare.

Fourth, and most important, we come to the tomb not just to see the humility of our Lord, not just to see the horror of our sin, not just to be reminded that we too must die; but we come to the tomb to see that *Jesus is not in it now.* He is risen! He has conquered death! The empty tomb is one great evidence for the resurrection.

There are other evidences too, of course. There is the change in the character of the disciples. Before the resurrection they were anxious, afraid, scattering. After Easter they went through the whole Roman world proclaiming the gospel. Moreover, they were not afraid to die for their convictions. There is the change of the day of Christian worship from the sabbath, the Jewish "seventh day" of the week, to Sunday, the first day of the week. Virtually all the early Christians were Jews. Why would they change the day of worship from Saturday, which Jews had observed for centuries, to Sunday, if it were not for the fact that Jesus rose from the dead on that day and that they were celebrating his resurrection? Besides these things there is the evidence of the grave clothes. They were still in the tomb and were undisturbed.

Greater than all these, however, is the evidence of the empty tomb. Most of those who have written seriously about the events of these early weeks notice—if they are honest—that in all the reports we have of the resurrection, whether those of the New Testament or those preserved indirectly in secular writers such as Josephus or in the Jewish Talmud, there is not one instance of any attempt to deny that the grave was empty. Sometimes there is the argument—which is also reported in the New Testament—that the disciples came and stole the body. But not one writer, either secular or religious, denies that the tomb was empty and the body gone. What accounts for it? Not theft by the enemies of Christ; if they had the body, they would have produced it later when claims of a resurrection were made by the disciples. Not theft by the disciples either; if they had stolen the body, they would not have been willing to die (as many of them did later) for what they knew to be a fabrication.

While we are looking at the tomb we notice a fifth lesson. It is not only that *Jesus* rose from the dead, but that *we also shall rise* if we are united to him. Jesus did not come to this earth to teach, die, and rise again in order that at the last he might lose those for whom he died. He came, as the Scriptures say, to save to the uttermost those who believe on him. We are saved, not just in spirit in order that we might have fellowship with God now; not just in soul in order that we might be transformed during the days of our earthly life. We are saved in body also. The salvation that Jesus brings is complete. When we come to the empty tomb we see that one day we too shall rise and be with him.

Have you done that? Have you heard the voice of the angel and accepted the invitation to come forward and investigate Christ's claims? You need to do that. But after you have investigated them, you will need to respond to Christ's own invitation to come to him in simple faith. Jesus says, "Come to me, all you who are weary and burdened, and I will give you rest. Take my yoke upon you and learn from me, for I am gentle and humble in heart, and you will find rest for your souls" (Matt. 11:28–29).

"Everybody Come"

The second important "come" in the story of Joseph's revelation of himself to his brothers is the invitation they are to pass on to their father Jacob in Joseph's name. First, the brothers were to come to Joseph, assuring themselves of his love for them and his forgiveness of their sin against him. Then they were to carry his invitation to Jacob: "Now hurry back to my father and say to him, 'This is what your son Joseph says: God has made me lord of all Egypt. Come down to me: don't delay'" (v. 9). We have a similar commission. If we have heard and answered the invitation of the Lord Jesus Christ, it is now our responsibility to take that same invitation to others.

I give you three other biblical examples. First, there is the remainder of the angel's invitation to the women to come and investigate the Lord's tomb. Their response to the first command was important, but it did not represent the whole of what they were to do. Having seen the empty tomb and thus having been confronted with the reality of the resurrection, they were then to "go quickly and tell his disciples: 'He has risen from the dead'" (Matt. 28:7). The fact that Jesus was risen was good news, and good news must be passed on. If the women did not tell it, it would be proof that they did not recognize the good news for what it is.

Second, I mention the disciples who had followed Jesus as the result of John the Baptist's witness: "Look, the Lamb of God, who takes away the sin of the world!" (John 1:29; cf. v. 36). They had started out after Jesus when they had heard that, and we are told that when Jesus saw them he turned about and asked, "What do you want?"

They said, "Rabbi, where are you staying?" It was a polite way of asking if they could go with him and get to know him.

Jesus answered, "Come, and you will see."

The disciples did come. They accepted Jesus' invitation to come and see (just as the women had accepted the angel's invitation). They spent a day and a night in his company. Apparently on that same day one of these two disciples, Andrew, found his brother Simon Peter and brought him to Jesus. Then on the next day, Jesus found Philip, who in turn found Nathanael. Philip told Nathanael, "We have found the one Moses wrote about in the Law, and about whom the prophets also wrote—Jesus of Nazareth, the son of Joseph."

Nathanael was skeptical. "Nazareth!" he exclaimed. "Can anything good come from there?"

Philip said, "Come and see" (John 1:46; cf. vv. 29–51).

Where did Philip learn to invite others to Jesus Christ in that fashion? He learned it where he had learned everything else: from Jesus. Jesus had told John's two disciples: "Come, and you will see." They had come and had invited others to come. Now Philip does the same. He has been called by Jesus. Now he calls others. After they had spent time with him they were constrained to go out and call others to come also.

The third example is the witness of the woman of Samaria. Her meeting with Jesus is what we would call an accident—though nothing is accidental with God. The woman had simply come out of the city of Sychar to draw water at Jacob's well, as she did every day, and she had found Jesus sitting by it. He struck up a conversation in the course of which he stimulated her interest in spiritual things and quickened her awareness of sin. He raised the matter of her husbands, saying, "Go, call your husband and come back" (John 4:16). She did not like that topic of conversation and tried to change the subject. But although, as she later discovered, Jesus knew all things and was able to tell her "everything" she ever did, what struck her most about this part of their conversation was the word "come." Jesus was not driving her away because of her sin but rather had come to save her from it. Therefore, when she later made her way into the city to call her neighbors to Jesus, this word formed the core of her testimony: "Come, see a man who told me everything I ever did. Could this be the Christ?" (v. 29).

Hers was a very effective testimony, for many came at her invitation and ended by saying, "We no longer believe just because of what you said; now we have heard for ourselves, and we know that this man really is the Savior of the world" (v. 42).

I do not know of a more wonderful word in all the Christian vocabulary when it is fully understood. "Come" is the great word of the gospel. It has been heard by millions and has brought peace to countless restless hearts and satisfaction to countless empty souls.

Think of the great verses that contain it. It was God's word to Abraham: "*Come* into a land which I shall show thee" (Acts 7:3 KJV). It was God's word to Moses when he was called to be the means of Israel's deliverance from Egypt: "*Come,* I will send you back to Egypt" (Acts 7:34). David wrote, "*Come* and see the works of the LORD, the desolations he has brought on the earth" (Ps. 46:8). Isaiah conveyed God's great invitation:

> "*Come* now, let us reason together,"
>   says the LORD.
> "Though your sins are like scarlet,
>   they shall be as white as snow;
> though they are red as crimson,
>   they shall be like wool."
>
> Isaiah 1:18

The angels at the tomb spoke the word: "*Come* and see the place where he lay" (Matt. 28:6). Philip said, *"Come"* (John 1:46). The woman of Samaria said, *"Come"* (John 4:29). "Come" was the Lord's own invitation: "*Come,* follow me" (Mark 10:21). "*Come* to me, all you who are weary and burdened, and I will give you rest" (Matt. 11:28).

"Come" is the song of the angels as they invite the redeemed to the marriage supper of the Lamb: "*Come,* gather together for the great supper of God" (Rev. 19:17); and of Jesus, as he says to his own: "*Come,* you who are blessed by my Father; take your inheritance, the kingdom prepared for you since the creation of the world" (Matt. 25:34).

If you have never responded to that great invitation, respond right now. Now is the time to come. "Come!" If you have responded, it is your privilege to pass that word on. The Lord himself will call others through you.

151

A Day to Remember

Genesis 45:14–15

Then he threw his arms around his brother Benjamin and wept, and Benjamin embraced him, weeping. And he kissed all his brothers and wept over them. Afterward his brothers talked with him.

I do not know if there was one word above others that the Egyptians of Joseph's day used to describe their national character. But if there was one, I suspect it was the Egyptian equivalent of "inscrutable." The *Oxford English Dictionary* defines inscrutable as "impenetrable, unfathomable to investigation, entirely mysterious." It quotes Hallam in his *History of Literature* as applying the word to the Christian doctrine of the Trinity. Hallam referred to the Trinity as something "theologians agree to call inscrutable, but which they do not fail to define and analyse with the most confident dogmatism."

This word seems especially suited to the Egyptian character. Stand before the colossal carving of Rameses II at the great temple of Abu Simbel, now raised more than two hundred feet above its original site to escape the rising waters of the Nile. Look into that massive stone face and ask, "What is Rameses thinking? What is he feeling?" There is no answer, no clue. Even more inscrutable is the majestic Sphinx, stretched out more than a football field in length not far from the modern city of Cairo. The meaning of that face has puzzled visitors to Egypt for centuries.

When you live in a place long enough you tend to become like that place or like the people among whom you live. Joseph must have had that experience. When we read the account of his many years in Egypt, particularly his dealings with his brothers on the occasions of their visits to Egypt to buy food, we sense that he was acting as "impenetrable, unfathomable to investigation, entirely mysterious" as the Egyptians. Twenty-two long years in Egypt had taught Joseph to hide his feelings. So when his brothers came to Egypt there was not the slightest clue that he was actually their long-lost brother. Even the Egyptians, who knew something of Joseph's background as a former slave, did not suspect it. Joseph's face revealed nothing.

Ah, but deep inside, Joseph was no Egyptian. He was a Hebrew like his fathers Abraham, Isaac, and Jacob before him, and it was not the way of the Hebrews to be stoics. Hebrews had feelings. They expressed them. They let their emotions be known. Consequently we are not surprised to find a place in the story (the place to which we have now come) in which Joseph at last broke down and wept so loudly and profusely that the Egyptians heard him and reported his unusual behavior to Pharaoh. When Joseph was about to make himself known to his brothers he sent his attendants away. But they no doubt lingered outside the door, as servants will, and heard the commotion.

The text says, "[Joseph] wept so loudly that the Egyptians heard him, and Pharaoh's household heard about it" (Gen. 45:2). Later we read, "Then he threw his arms around his brother Benjamin and wept, and Benjamin embraced him, weeping. And he kissed all his brothers and wept over them. Afterward his brothers talked with him" (vv. 14–15).

What a remarkable day! It has been called "a day to remember."[1] And it was remembered! It was remembered in the oral traditions and then in the written records of Israel as the most memorable moment of all the many memorable moments in Joseph's distinguished life. This incident marked the release of Joseph's long-bottled-up emotions, the salvation of the brothers, and the first bonding of the fathers of the tribes of Israel.

An Aching Heart

I am impressed with what verses 14 and 15 tell us about Joseph. They tell us how desperately isolated and lonely he must have been during the long years of separation from his father and family—even, we must note, after he had come to a position of great prestige in Egypt.

We do not have difficulty imagining how frightened he must have been as a boy of seventeen when he was seized by his brothers and sold into Egypt as a slave. Joseph was young, defenseless. He was being taken to a country where he would not even be able to speak the language. We can imagine how forgotten he must have felt during the two long years he spent in the prison of the captain of the guard. He had hoped at one point that the chief cup-bearer of Pharaoh, whom he had encouraged by a favorable interpretation of his dreams, might remember him and speak favorably to Pharaoh on his behalf. But he was forgotten and may well have expected to remain in Potiphar's prison indefinitely. So we can understand that loneliness.

But we remember that Joseph was then brought out of the prison and promoted to the second highest position in Egypt. We expect his loneliness to have been removed at this point, and we remember that when his sons were born he gave them uplifting, positive names, signifying "forgotten" and "doubly fruitful" because, as he said, "God has made me forget all my trouble and all my father's household" and "God has made me fruitful in the land of my suffering" (Gen. 41:51–52).

What a different picture we have in this latter scene in which we see Joseph weeping on the necks of Benjamin and his other brothers. Now we see that although Joseph had certainly borne his afflictions well and had been blessed to the degree that he could claim forgetfulness of his trouble and of his father's house, his loneliness had nevertheless only been bottled up inside. He was as desperately lonely now as ever, and it took only a moment for the anguish and isolation of twenty years to come forth in a torrent.

Remember this when you look at someone who seems to be at the pinnacle of success. We see his or her outward circumstances and say, "Certainly a person like that has everything. If anyone on earth was ever happy, it is that person." But we do not see the heart, and the very one who seems so favored may be the one who hides the greatest measure of despair or loneliness and most needs the love of God and others.

I think of Edwin Arlington Robinson's poem "Richard Cory." Robinson describes Cory as "a gentleman from soul to crown, clean-favored, and imperially slim." He was rich and so distinguished that "he glittered when he walked." But the last stanza of the poem says,

> So on we worked, and waited for the light,
>   And went without the meat, and cursed the bread;
> And Richard Cory, one calm summer night,
>   Went home and put a bullet through his head.

"Richard Cory" is a poem of despair, but many people are like that person. Even many believers suffer deep tragedy. From Joseph we learn to be attuned to suffering and not to envy anyone.

"Behold, How He Loves"

This memorable picture of Joseph weeping with his brothers shows us something else about him, something even more commendable than the tender loneliness of his heart. It shows us love. It is not so self-evident that Joseph should have loved his brothers, even Benjamin, who was the child of his mother as well as of his father. Joseph had been absent from home for more than twenty years, and his absence was the result of the hatred of his brothers. There would be some in Joseph's position who would have allowed the injustice of this treatment to rankle within them, petrifying their emotions and freezing their souls. Over the years people like this become increasingly unable to like or love anyone. They turn inward in anger. When at last they might meet brothers such as these, it would not be love that would erupt from within them, but the most virulent hatred. They would plot to destroy the architects of their misery. Or if not that, they certainly would remind them that they were the cause of the persons' own great sufferings—and never allow them to forget it.

Not Joseph! Joseph had endured twenty-two years of loneliness, but he had mastered his heart during those long decades and had not allowed misfortune to sour him. How? He had drawn close to God, as we have seen repeatedly. If he had allowed suffering to pull him away from God, his feelings would have hardened. As it was, he allowed suffering to bring him close to God, and he found the love of God sufficient to enrich his soul.

Forgiveness

The third remarkable thing about Joseph was his ability to forgive, seen here in the same incident. When we read of Joseph throwing his arms around his full brother, Benjamin, and weeping over him, we understand it to be an act of pure love. Benjamin was not with the others when they fell upon Joseph and sold him into slavery, nor would he have been. There was a deep and wonderful bond between these two brothers. Joseph reasonably loved Benjamin. But the next verse says that not only did Joseph weep over Benjamin, he kissed and wept over Simeon, Levi, Reuben, and the others too.

This was love, of course. Joseph truly loved them. But it was more than love, since these were they who had wronged him so many years before. This is love fused to grace. It is forgiveness.

Martin Luther spent a great deal of time on this point in his careful treatment of these last chapters of Genesis, making two interesting comparisons. First, he compared the actions of Joseph in this story with the prophecy of his father Jacob concerning all the brothers in chapter 49. Genesis 49:5–7 contains an analysis of the character of Simeon and Levi, whom Luther believed largely responsible for Joseph's suffering, and concludes with a curse on their anger. The text reads:

> Simeon and Levi are brothers—
>   their swords are weapons of violence.
> Let me not enter their council,
>   let me not join their assembly,
> for they have killed men in their anger
>   and hamstrung oxen as they pleased.

> Cursed be their anger, so fierce,
> and their fury, so cruel!
> I will scatter them in Jacob
> and disperse them in Israel.

Luther noted how Jacob could not altogether forgive and forget their crimes, but how Joseph did forgive them.

The second comparison is between Joseph and Moses. The reference here is to Deuteronomy 33, in which Moses is pronouncing a blessing upon the various tribes of Israel. But, as Luther noted, Simeon is omitted. There is no blessing—not even a mention—of Simeon.

Luther concludes: "You see, then, that in the forgiving of sins Joseph excels his own father and Moses, since he does not mention the selling. But his father will curse Reuben, Simeon, and Levi; and Moses passes over Simeon in silence. Joseph alone addresses them in a loving manner and deals very tenderly with them. 'Ah, my dear brothers Simeon and Levi, I pardon you from my whole heart and forgive you!' At that time they were in his power, and according to the laws, he could have avenged the injury he had received at their hands; but his outstanding compassion and kindness of heart does not permit this. He thinks of nothing else than forgiveness, well-doing, and comforting. For their conscience has been gravely wounded, and they are afflicted by very bitter pains, which cannot be soothed or easily removed."[2]

This scene of Joseph embracing and kissing even those brothers who had wronged him is unsurpassed in the Bible, except for the descriptions of our Lord loving and even kissing those who wronged him. Judas had lived with and learned from the Lord for three years. In spite of this Judas betrayed him. Yet Jesus did not withdraw from Judas's company. He ate the Last Supper with Judas, even passing the piece of dipped bread to him as a sign of special favor. When Judas came to him later in the garden to identify the Lord with a kiss, we do not read that Jesus turned away his cheek.

This is the Jesus who reaches out to you. You too have betrayed him, but he loves you and died in order that you might have forgiveness of sins. If you have not responded to his love, see him standing before you as he stood before Jerusalem, weeping and crying out, "If you . . . had only known on this day what would bring you peace . . ." (Luke 19:41). Or again, "O Jerusalem, Jerusalem, . . . how often I have longed to gather your children together, as a hen gathers her chicks under her wings, but you were not willing" (Matt. 23:37).

Allow that love to melt your heart, and come to him.

A Wise Counselor

The last sentence of this short passage suggests still another characteristic of Joseph. The sentence tells us, "Afterward his brothers talked with him" (v. 15). We know from the verses preceding this and from the account following that Joseph was anxious to see his father and that he was urging his brothers to go to him and bring him down to Egypt quickly. The verses contain three expressions of Joseph's understandable haste: "Hurry back to my father" (v. 9); "Say to him, . . . 'Come down to me; don't delay'" (v. 9); and "Bring my father down here quickly" (v. 13). Yet in spite of his understandable impatience to see his father, the verse beginning "Afterward . . ." indicates that Joseph took considerable time to be with his brothers, talk to them, and reassure them of his love and forgiveness.

Obviously he did this because he knew their need for reassurance. It was a shock to him to see them. But it was a far greater shock to them to discover that the brother they thought they had killed was alive and was in fact standing before them. They had to get to know him again. They had to overcome their anxiety and be assured of his favor. This was so difficult for them that even years later, after they had brought Jacob down to Egypt, where he eventually died, they were still afraid that Joseph might exact vengeance on them, and Joseph had to reassure them again (cf. Gen. 50:15–21). Joseph knew this and showed unusual wisdom in spending time with these men.

This characteristic of Joseph also has a parallel in the actions of Jesus with his disciples following his death and resurrection. Jesus did not return to heaven immediately, but rather spent forty days with his own, reassuring them and teaching them about what he had come to do and suffer. They might have felt guilty. They probably did, since they had all deserted him (and Peter had denied him). Jesus reassured them, saying, "How foolish you are, and how slow of heart to believe all that the prophets have spoken! Did not the Christ have to suffer these things and then enter his glory?" (Luke 24:25–26).

In Peter's case, the Lord took special pains to reassure him. Peter had denied Jesus three times. So Jesus asked three times, "Peter, do you truly love me?" When Peter replied that he did, the Lord repeated the commission: "Feed my sheep" (see John 21:15–17). Jesus could have derided Peter for his sad failure, but he did not. Instead, he wisely spent time with him, healing his wounds.

Homes for Healing

I said earlier that Martin Luther makes much of this incident, and I turn to Luther now. For Luther concluded by noting that, like Joseph's household, the churches today are places where those who are guilty, lost, and terrified find healing. Luther wrote, "The churches are nothing else than lodging places of this kind in which the people who feel sin, death, and the terrors and vexations of an afflicted and wounded conscience are healed."[3]

But that raises the question: Are our churches really such healing places and are we people who show affection and forgiveness, as Joseph did?

Joseph showed four things in this incident. He showed genuine *humanity*, for he was not aloof from the common emotions of humankind. He too was lonely; he too was subject to tears. He was not afraid to show this. Second, he demonstrated great *love,* just as Jesus showed love in giving himself for his brethren. Third, Joseph modeled true *forgiveness.* He had been wronged, but he did not hold the wrong against his brothers. Rather, he reached out to them to forgive the wrong and allay their fears. Fourth, he acted in profound *wisdom,* for he knew enough to take time to reestablish a good relationship with these men and let them know that his love for them and his forgiveness of them were both real and permanent.

Is that not what we are to do in the church in Christ's name? The only difference between Joseph and us is that he was innocent. He had been wronged, but he had done no wrong himself. We, on the other hand, have been as lost, guilty, and terrified as those we seek to comfort. We stand with them in our need in God's grace. If we have found it, it is on the basis of our discovery that we now have the privilege of calling them to the Lord.

152

Favor in Pharaoh's Eyes

Genesis 45:16-23

When the news reached Pharaoh's palace that Joseph's brothers had come, Pharaoh and all his officials were pleased. Pharaoh said to Joseph, "Tell your brothers, 'Do this: Load your animals and return to the land of Canaan, and bring your father and your families back to me. I will give you the best of the land of Egypt and you can enjoy the fat of the land.'

"You are also directed to tell them, 'Do this: Take some carts from Egypt for your children and your wives, and get your father and come. Never mind about your belongings, because the best of all Egypt will be yours.'"

So the sons of Israel did this. Joseph gave them carts, as Pharaoh had commanded, and he also gave them provisions for their journey. To each of them he gave new clothing, but to Benjamin he gave three hundred shekels of silver and five sets of clothes. And this is what he sent to his father: ten donkeys loaded with the best things of Egypt, and ten female donkeys loaded with grain and bread and other provisions for his journey.

I t is difficult to say anything about the Egyptian pharaoh under whom Joseph served as prime minister. We do not know who this king was, but even if we did, we would have problems. This is a period of history for which our historical facts are quite scanty.

A few things can be said, however. Though we do not know the exact dates of Joseph's entry into Egypt (or even the date of the Exodus), it is generally

1078

assumed today that Joseph and his family were received into Egypt and grew in wealth and prominence during the reign of more than a century of the Hyksos or "shepherd" kings. This period is known as the Second Intermediate Period. It began with the Hyksos invasion about 1700 B.C. and ended with the expulsion of the Hyksos from Egypt by Ahmosis I in 1567 B.C. The Hyksos came from the area that is now Turkey, and they were able to occupy the northern portions of Egypt. They were Semites, which would explain why it was possible for Joseph to rise to power under their rule. They had their capital at Tanis in the Delta region, which would explain why Joseph's family was settled in Goshen. It is probably the change of rule at the end of this period that is referred to as the rise of "a new king, who did not know about Joseph" in Exodus 1:8.

If Joseph entered Egypt toward the beginning of the Hyksos period, the 430 years during which the Jews lived in Egypt would bring the time of the Exodus to the reign of the austere Rameses II, who would be the pharaoh of the Exodus.

This is significant background to the account of Joseph's finding favor in Pharaoh's eyes. For although it is possible that a man of Joseph's character might have found favor in the eyes of any monarch, it is easier to understand how he might have found favor in the eyes of one who was of the same ethnic stock as he was—and why it might suit Pharaoh's strategy to settle increasing numbers of Semites in Goshen. Genesis 43:32 tells us that the Egyptians—perhaps ethnic Egyptians—could not eat with Hebrews, counting that "detestable." Yet this Egyptian—probably Hyksos—ruler favored Joseph's family.

A Solemn Promise

In the Book of Esther there is a scene in which King Xerxes of Persia asks Haman, the villain, "What should be done for the man the king delights to honor?" (Esther 6:6). Haman thinks the king is talking about him, when he is actually talking about Mordecai, whom Haman hates. Haman answers extravagantly:

> For the man the king delights to honor, have them bring a royal robe the king has worn and a horse the king has ridden, one with a royal crest placed on its head. Then let the robe and horse be entrusted to one of the king's most noble princes. Let them robe the man the king delights to honor, and lead him on the horse through the city streets, proclaiming before him, "This is what is done for the man the king delights to honor!"
>
> verses 7–9

Haman is aghast when this is done for Mordecai and he is required to be the attending nobleman.

If someone had asked the pharaoh of Joseph's day what should be done for the man the king delights to honor, Pharaoh could hardly have replied in a more extravagant way than he did when word came that Joseph's brothers had arrived in Egypt.

He might have been offended, of course. He could hardly have failed to know (if the story had been reported accurately) that these were the very men who had sold Joseph into slavery years before. Such an unnatural crime deserved stern punishment. Again, Pharaoh might have seen these men as an unwelcome challenge to the time and loyalty of Joseph, whose attention until now he had had entirely to himself. But this pharaoh was apparently a great man. He was not deterred by petty jealousies, and he did not allow officious attention to judicial matters to mar the joy of Joseph's long-awaited reunion. No doubt it was his love for Joseph that predominated. Joseph was happy; Pharaoh was happy with him. Joseph wanted his father and brothers, their wives and their children to come to Egypt; Pharaoh also wanted this for Joseph's sake.

The first way in which Pharaoh showed favor to Joseph was by a solemn promise for his brothers: "Tell your brothers, 'Do this: Load your animals and return to the land of Canaan, and bring your father and your families back to me. I will give you the best of the land of Egypt and you can enjoy the fat of the land'" (vv. 17–18). This was an honest promise. The region of Goshen, in which the family later settled, was the best land of Egypt. More than that, it was some of the best land anywhere. For centuries the Nile had been depositing rich topsoil in the delta region, where, even today, a rich profusion of grain, fruits, vegetables, and other edibles flourishes. It may have been a time of famine. But here, if anywhere, a family as large as Joseph's could survive. After the drought it would become a paradise.

A Visible Pledge

The second way Pharaoh showed favor to Joseph was similar to King Xerxes' provision of the robe and horse for Mordecai. That is, there was a visible outward pledge of Pharaoh's favor. In this case it concerned the carts from Egypt. Pharaoh said, "You are also directed to tell them, 'Do this: Take some carts from Egypt for your children and your wives'" (v. 19).

We cannot understand the significance of this without using our imagination. What do you think of when you hear the word "cart"? I think of a rickety, unpainted wood container riding on two irregular rustic wheels, pulled by a donkey. As a symbol, "cart" suggests primitive, poor, struggling, peasant, disadvantaged. The opposite is a Rolls Royce. We need to expunge this thinking if we are to understand Pharaoh's sending Egyptian carts to Canaan. No one else in the world at this time had carts, least of all Joseph's nomadic family or their neighbors. Theirs was a world of beasts of burden—and walking. The brothers had probably come to Egypt on foot leading their donkeys, which would return loaded with purchased grain. To return to Canaan with "carts from Egypt" was the cultural equivalent of landing a jumbo jet among a tribe of isolated savages. It would have been the stuff legends are made of.

Moreover, these were not just rude carts. I think of that classic story involving archaeologist Howard Carter and his discovery of the tomb of King Tutankhamen in the Valley of the Kings at Western Thebes in 1922. The site had been excavated for years and was thought by many to have been exhausted. Nevertheless, three days into the work, Carter's workmen discovered steps leading downward to a sealed doorway. Carter summoned his sponsor, Lord Carnavon, from England, and when he arrived a small hole was opened into what proved to be a thirty-three hundred-year-old tomb.

Carter described what happened: "As my eyes grew accustomed to the light, details of the room within emerged slowly from the mist, strange animals, statues, and gold—everywhere the glint of gold." The room was packed to the ceiling with treasure: furniture, jars, statues, chariots, walking sticks, bows and arrows, scarabs, bouquets, clothing. Carter wrote, "I was struck dumb with amazement, and when Lord Carnavon, unable to stand the suspense any longer, inquired anxiously, 'Can you see anything?' it was all I could do to get out the words, 'Yes, wonderful things.'"[1]

To be sure, Tutankhamen lived three hundred years after Joseph, and his funeral appointments are the richest ever found. Still, even discounting the growth of the country during those three hundred years, we have a suggestion of the splendor of things normally associated with the pharaohs. Joseph's pharaoh was giving as a king when he dispatched his meticulously fashioned and richly ornamented carts with Joseph's brothers.

Why did Pharaoh go to such elaborate lengths to help Joseph? No doubt his chief motivation was affection for Joseph; this is what Pharaoh does to "the man the king delights to honor." It was also an expedient way of getting a family of seventy persons, their livestock, and some of their considerable possessions to Egypt.

I wonder, however, if Joseph might not have been speaking to Pharaoh and have indicated how difficult it would be for his father Jacob to believe the report the brothers were bringing back from Egypt. In the next verses we read that at first Jacob did *not* believe them. When he had last seen his sons, they had not been very honest men; he had reason to distrust them. In view of this problem (no doubt foreseen by Joseph), the carts may have been proof of Pharaoh's favor and a pledge of more favor to come. They would have been similar to the gift of gold and silver jewelry and articles of clothing to Rebekah's family, when the servant of Abraham had sought her as a bride for his master's son several centuries earlier.

An Earnest Plea

The third means Pharaoh showed Joseph favor was an interesting plea through Joseph to the brothers: "Never mind about your belongings" (v. 20). It is interesting because it is the Old Testament equivalent of Philippians

3:13–14. In those verses Paul writes of his deepest aspirations: "Brothers, I do not consider myself yet to have taken hold. . . . But one thing I do: Forgetting what is behind and straining toward what is ahead, I press on toward the goal to win the prize for which God has called me heavenward in Christ Jesus."

Pharaoh was telling Joseph's family to leave their baggage behind, taking along only what would be needed for their journey—just as, to use the same image, we are to "travel light" in Christ's service. It is interesting that the Latin word for "baggage" is *impedimenta,* which has come down to us as the English word "impediment," meaning "hindrance" or "obstruction." It occurs in the marriage service in the Anglican Book of Common Prayer: "I require and charge you both . . . that if either of you know any impediment, why ye may not be lawfully joined together in Matrimony, ye do now confess it."

What a large amount of baggage we often cling to on the road to glory! What an impediment to progress in the Christian life!

Does this mean that a Christian should not own a house? No, only that the house must not own him. Does it mean that you cannot have money in the bank or life insurance policies or stocks? No, only that you must not be possessed by these possessions. Your true deposits must be in the bank of heaven "where moth and rust do not destroy, and where thieves do not break in and steal" (Matt. 6:20), and you must look to God to guard your deposits (2 Tim. 1:12).

Full Provision

The fourth part of Pharaoh's favor to Joseph was his provision of whatever the family might need on its way to Egypt. The text says that Joseph gave his brothers carts "as Pharaoh had commanded." Presumably he also gave provisions at Pharaoh's command as well. "To each of them he gave new clothing, but to Benjamin he gave three hundred shekels of silver and five sets of clothes. And this is what he sent to his father: ten donkeys loaded with the best things of Egypt, and ten female donkeys loaded with grain and bread and other provisions for his journey" (vv. 22–23).

Earlier, when the brothers had first been invited to eat with Joseph on the occasion of their second journey to Egypt, Joseph gave Benjamin five times as much food as anyone else (cf. Gen. 43:34). At another time and place the brothers might have been jealous of the favor shown to Benjamin. But they were not jealous then, nor are they now when Benjamin receives five sets of clothes to their one and is given three hundred shekels of silver too. Their acceptance of this is one evidence that the brothers had been truly born again. Benjamin received an abundance. Jacob received a special gift of donkeys and all good things the donkeys could carry. But that did not matter. The ten brothers themselves had clothes to wear and food to eat. Besides, they had been reconciled to Joseph and had been forgiven of their sin, which was the important thing.

This is the position in which we too are found in God's service. Some have more than we do, some less. But we have what we need and fully enjoy the one essential thing: forgiveness of sins and fellowship with God. Paul said, "My God will meet all your needs according to his glorious riches in Christ Jesus" (Phil. 4:19). A more contemporary Christian said, "God's work done in God's way will never lack God's supply."

Favor in Jesus' Eyes

This brings us to my final point, which is: However wonderful it may have been that Joseph found favor in the eyes of Egypt's great pharaoh, it is far more wonderful that we have found favor in the eyes of heaven's king, the Lord Jesus Christ, our Savior. For we are saved by grace, and that is what "favor" is: grace. It is God's favor to the utterly undeserving.

Jesus' grace is so great that no amount of exposition can exhaust it. Still, something of the scope of that grace can be seen in comparison with Pharaoh. Pharaoh gave a solemn promise, dispatched a visible pledge, voiced an earnest plea, and made a full provision. So also does Jesus. Jesus has given us a solemn promise of a goodly land to come. Pharaoh said, "I will give you the best of the land of Egypt and you can enjoy the fat of the land" (v. 18). Jesus said, "I am going . . . to prepare a place for you. And if I go and prepare a place for you, I will come back and take you to be with me that you also may be where I am" (John 14:2–3). In that land we are to enjoy the fat of God's favor.

In the meantime, Jacob, the eleven brothers, their wives, and their children were in Canaan or would be en route to Egypt. For that interval Pharaoh gave a pledge of his favor and a proof of good to come—by means of the carts. Jesus has also given us a pledge of heaven in the person of the Holy Spirit, who comes to live in and be with every believer. Jesus said, "I am going to him who sent me. . . . But . . . I will send [the Holy Spirit] to you. When he comes, he will convict the world of guilt in regard to sin and righteousness and judgment. . . . He will guide you into all truth. . . . He will bring glory to me by taking from what is mine and making it known to you" (John 16:5, 7–8, 13–14). Paul called the Holy Spirit a "seal" and a "deposit guaranteeing our inheritance" (Eph. 1:13–14).

Pharaoh told Joseph's family to forget their possessions and come quickly to Egypt (v. 20). Jesus said, "If anyone would come after me, he must deny himself and take up his cross daily and follow me" (Luke 9:23).

Finally, there is a parallel in the matter of our daily provisions. Pharaoh sent Jacob whatever was necessary for the trip from Canaan to Egypt. Jesus likewise provides for our needs. He told us to ask God for "our daily bread," being confident that God would supply it (Matt. 6:11; cf. vv. 25–34). He said, "Ask and it will be given to you; seek and you will find; knock and the door will be opened to you. For everyone who asks receives; he who seeks finds; and to him who knocks, the door will be opened" (Matt. 7:7–8). Paul wrote,

"My God will meet all your needs according to his glorious riches in Christ Jesus" (Phil. 4:19).

Are you one to whom God will be gracious? Do you have a claim on his favor? Pharaoh was kind to Joseph's brothers, as we have seen. But it was not because of who they were or because of any great service to Egypt that they had done. The contrary was actually the case. If these men deserved anything from Pharaoh, it was death because of their crime against Joseph. Why was Pharaoh favorable? Obviously, it was for Joseph's sake. Joseph had the closest possible relationship to Pharaoh, and Pharaoh was favorable to these men solely because they were his brothers.

The same principle can be applied spiritually. We have no natural claim on God. But he is favorable if we are sisters and brothers of his Son, Jesus.

Charles Haddon Spurgeon knew of a wretched soldier who returned from battles to the home of an English family who also had a son in the service. "Does So-and-so live here?" he said, asking for the son's father.

"Yes."

"Can I see him?"

"Yes."

When the father came to the door the soldier said, "I have a letter from your son, whom I left in the army. He was my closest friend."

The soldier looked disreputable. He was pale and undernourished. His uniform was torn. He was evidently destitute. But he produced the letter and handed it to the father who read, "Father, this is a choice companion of mine, and I want you, when he reaches home, to treat him kindly for my sake. Tell Mother that anything she does for him shall be the same as if she had done it to her own boy."[2] Naturally, he was received for the son's sake.

This is how we are presented to God the Father by Jesus Christ. He who always found favor in the eyes of his Father—"This is my Son, whom I love; with him I am well pleased" (Matt. 3:17)—enables us also to find favor.

153

No Quarreling

Genesis 45:24

Then he sent his brothers away, and as they were leaving he said to them, "Don't quarrel on the way!"

I do not think Joseph intended to be funny when he told his brothers, who were leaving for Canaan, "Don't quarrel on the way!" But his warning strikes me as humorous anyway. Whenever I read it, I think of the lyrics of a popular song of many years ago:

> That'sa right, don'ta fight;
> Everything gonna be all right—
> Have a piece of fruit.

It is amusing to hear Joseph admonishing his brothers—almost like admonishing bad children—to behave themselves and not to get into trouble on their way to Canaan.

This warning was one of several important things Joseph had for them. First, he had a great message. They were to tell their father that Joseph was not dead but was living and was the ruler of all Egypt. Second, they were commanded to hurry. Theirs was good news; they were not to dally on their way: "Hurry back to my father and say to him, 'This is what your son Joseph says: God has made me lord of all Egypt. Come down to me; don't delay'" (Gen. 45:9). Third, the brothers were given ample provisions; they were to take clothes, grain, bread, and other necessities. It is only at the last, after these more obvious matters were attended to, that Joseph called out, "And don't forget: no fighting; I don't want to hear that you've been misbehaving on the way home."

I think of this as Joseph's personal version of the new commandment: "A new commandment I give you: Love one another. As I have loved you, so you must love one another" (John 13:34).

Conflict among Brothers

Joseph was a shrewd judge of character. If he had not been, he would not have been a successful manager of Potiphar's affairs or a successful prime minister of Egypt. So we understand that though Joseph was profoundly moved and even overcome by his reunion with his brothers, he had not lost his senses and still knew that in many respects Judah, Simeon, Levi, Reuben, and the others were much like they had been. They were converted men—I am convinced the story teaches this—but they were still sinners, and it was possible that the old bickering that had undoubtedly characterized their past days in Jacob's household might break out again once they were out of Joseph's hearing.

Joseph must have realized that things would be different when they were away from Egypt. In Egypt there was the magnificence of the court and the air of absolute authority that surrounded everything associated with the pharaoh. In Egypt the brothers stood understandably in awe of Joseph. His word was law. They were even terrified of him. What would happen once they had escaped the country? Would their regeneration prove false or their repentance shallow once they were beyond his influence?

There was also the looming necessity of appearing before their father Jacob and of confessing the whole sordid story to him. Theirs would be good news; Joseph was alive. But they could not tell this without explaining how they had once plotted to kill Joseph, had sold him into slavery, and had perpetrated a cruel hoax on their father. They had slaughtered a goat and had dipped Joseph's richly ornamented robe in its blood. "We found this," they said. "Examine it to see whether it is your son's robe" (Gen. 37:32). When Jacob concluded that a wild animal had killed his son and had torn him to pieces, the brothers had allowed him to persist in this sad delusion. How would they explain what they had done? Who would explain it? How would the guilt for their actions be apportioned?

Joseph probably imagined the self-serving statements and eventual arguments that could follow. Reuben might have protested, "When we get back to Canaan and have to tell Father what happened, remember that I tried to save Joseph. I told you not to kill him. I said, 'Throw him into this cistern,' because I wanted to come back later and pull him out and take him back home where he would be safe."

"Well, don't look at me!" Judah might have added. "You were going to kill him, all of you. I'm the one who really saved his life, because I said, 'Let's sell him to the Ishmaelites.' I remember saying that he was our own flesh and blood and that we shouldn't kill him for that reason."

"I didn't do it all by myself," Simeon might have objected. "You were all part of it."

"Not as much as you," the others might have protested. "You took the lead."

"Well, at least I didn't have anything to do with it," Benjamin might have said. "I wasn't even there. I was back with Father at Hebron."

"Look who's the goody-goody now!"

"You're as bad as Joseph was."

"You're just lucky it was Joseph instead of you."

There is nothing in the story to indicate that this is what happened, of course. On the contrary, there is reason to believe that the brothers were thoroughly changed men and that the self-sacrificing and humble spirit Judah showed in pleading for Benjamin, as recorded in chapter 44, was actually true of them all. They deeply sensed their guilt and were not at all inclined to excuse themselves either now or later. They had labored under a burden of guilt for decades. They were not about to come under its baleful influence again willingly.

Still, this is how sin works, and Joseph was right to protest against it. "Don't quarrel on the way!" he said. It was a way of telling the brothers to live like saved people and not to allow sin to have a victory in their lives.

Cause of Quarrels

We have a New Testament equivalent of Joseph's warning in James. This very practical book says:

> What causes fights and quarrels among you? Don't they come from your desires that battle within you? You want something but don't get it. You kill and covet, but you cannot have what you want. You quarrel and fight. You do not have, because you do not ask God. When you ask, you do not receive, because you ask with wrong motives, that you may spend what you get on your pleasures.
>
> You adulterous people, don't you know that friendship with the world is hatred toward God? Anyone who chooses to be a friend of the world becomes an enemy of God. Or do you think Scripture says without reason that the spirit he caused to live in us tends toward envy, but he gives us more grace? That is why Scripture says:
>
> > "God opposes the proud
> > but gives grace to the humble."

Submit yourselves, then, to God. Resist the devil, and he will flee from you. Come near to God and he will come near to you. Wash your hands, you sinners, and purify your hearts, you double-minded. Grieve, mourn and wail. Change your laughter to mourning and your joy to gloom. Humble yourselves before the Lord, and he will lift you up.

James 4:1–10

These words are not only an equivalent of Joseph's warning to his brothers, recorded in Genesis 45:24, but also a biblical commentary upon them. They analyze the cause of quarreling and prescribe a cure.

Many years ago a former chancellor of the University of Chicago said that war begins in the minds of men. But James's analysis goes deeper than this. He says that quarrels arise from our inward and unruly desires. We want things but cannot have them. So our spirits are a tossing sea of emotions. It is out of this emotional turmoil that fights, quarrels, and conflicts come.

One commentator writes, "James is saying that war begins within men's emotions. Its genesis is not merely on the intellectual level; it goes down into the vast emotional reservoir of life and conduct that underlies the intellectual. It is in this emotional center of man, called by Scripture 'the heart,' that James says war begins, when the lusts within a man strive together."[1]

Cure for Fighting

Nothing in the Genesis account indicates that Joseph analyzed the causes of quarrels among brothers in this way, as James later did. But he might have, and if he had, the brothers might have asked how the fighting that had characterized their relationships for years could be avoided. If they were really changed men, they might have asked, "Joseph, tell us how we can avoid these unseemly fights and bickering. We have been quarreling for twenty-two years, and some of us for much longer than that. How can we live as if we have really met God and know the blessing of having sins forgiven?"

Again, we do not know what Joseph might have said under such conditions and in response to such questions. But we can imagine him answering like James.

First, James told the Christians of his day to *"submit . . . to God"* (v. 7, my emphasis). I can hear Joseph giving this advice, for it is precisely the thing that most characterized his own outstanding life. When Joseph was carried away into slavery as a result of his brothers' intense hatred of him, he might have chaffed under the injustice and have blamed God for it. "God, how could you let this happen to me?" he might have protested. "All I was doing was carrying out my father's wishes. I was genuinely interested in my brothers' well-being. But they fell on me and sold me into slavery. How could you let that happen? How can there be such evil in a world run by a good and powerful God?"

Again, Joseph might have rebelled against God when he was falsely accused by Potiphar's wife and was imprisoned. He might have said, "God, I was only trying to do what was right. I was trying to live a moral life. You should have rewarded me for that, not have allowed me to be slandered and then imprisoned. Why should I follow you after that? Why shouldn't I conclude that it is better to go with the tide, better to run with the ungodly?" As I say, Joseph might have argued along these lines. But he did not! On the contrary, he submitted himself to God and was content to live the life God gave him.

This is why his speech was so often filled with the name of God. "How then could I do such a wicked thing and sin against *God?*" (Gen. 39:9, my emphasis).

"Do not interpretations belong to *God?*" (Gen. 40:8, my emphasis).

"*God* will give Pharaoh the answer he desires. . . . *God* has revealed to Pharaoh what he is about to do" (Gen. 41:16, 25, my emphasis).

"*God* has made me forget all my trouble and all my father's household" (Gen. 41:51, my emphasis).

"*God* has made me fruitful in the land of my suffering" (Gen. 41:52, my emphasis).

"It was to save lives that *God* sent me ahead of you" (Gen. 45:5, my emphasis).

"You intended to harm me, but *God* intended it for good to accomplish what is now being done, the saving of many lives" (Gen. 50:20, my emphasis).

"I am about to die. But *God* will surely come to your aid and take you up out of this land" (Gen. 50:24, my emphasis).

When we considered these verses before, I pointed out that they show something of Joseph's theocentric worldview. He recognized that God was in perfect control of everything. But there is more. Joseph recognized what we call the sovereignty of God. It is possible to recognize this and still struggle against it. But Joseph did not. Thus, to his conviction of the presence and power of God in all things, Joseph added submission. He could say, as did the great seventeenth-century hymnwriter Samuel Rodigast:

> Whate'er my God ordains is right:
>   Holy his will abideth;
> I will be still whate'er he doth,
>   And follow where he guideth:
>   He is my God;
>   Though dark my road,
> He holds me that I shall not fall:
> Wherefore to him I leave it all.
>
> Whate'er my God ordains is right:
>   He never will deceive me;
> He leads me by the proper path;
>   I know he will not leave me:
>   I take, content,
>   What he hath sent;

His hand can turn my griefs away,
And patiently I wait his day.

Whate'er my God ordains is right:
    Though now this cup, in drinking,
May bitter seem to my faint heart,
    I take it, all unshrinking:
        My God is true;
        Each morn anew
Sweet comfort yet shall fill my heart,
And pain and sorrow shall depart.

Whate'er my God ordains is right:
    Here shall my stand be taken;
Though sorrow, need, or death be mine,
    Yet am I not forsaken;
        My Father's care
        Is round me there;
He holds me that I shall not fall:
And so to him I leave it all.

A person who has submitted to God is not likely to be quarreling with his brothers along the way.

The second thing James tells Christians, which Joseph might also have told his brothers, is that it is necessary to *"resist the devil,"* who at times attacks even God's most submitted servants. This is another way of saying that, in spite of our intentions to submit to God, temptations nevertheless do come and we must be prepared to fight them.

Joseph could have spoken of this personally. He was submitted to God during his early days in Egypt and had been blessed in Potiphar's eyes. But that did not stop temptation from coming in the person of Potiphar's wife. Joseph had to be ready for it. In the same way, the brothers would have to be ready to resist their natural bent to quarreling. Whenever it reared its head, they would have to stamp it out. They would have to say, "I shouldn't say that." Or "Forgive me, I don't want to give offense." We remember that Jesus himself resisted the devil when Satan worked through Peter to suggest that Jesus might avoid having to go to the cross: "Get behind me, Satan! You are a stumbling block to me; you do not have in mind the things of God, but the things of men" (Matt. 16:23).

But remember the order: first, submit yourself to God; then, resist the devil. If you do it the other way around—that is, if you try to resist the devil in your own strength—the result will not be as James says: "and he will flee from you" (James 4:7). On the contrary, the devil will attack you. It is only when you submit to God and put on the whole armor of God that you can take your stand against the devil's schemes (Eph. 6:11).

Third, James tells us to "come near to God," which means *pray*. Why do we need to pray? Obviously, because by praying we turn our minds to God, seek his way, submit to his will, and draw on his strength to resist Satan's temptations. Prayer was clearly a concern of James, as evidenced by encouragements to pray throughout the epistle. In chapter 1 James encourages us to pray for wisdom if we lack it, for "God . . . gives generously to all without finding fault" (James 1:5). In chapter 4 we are warned against failing to pray, which is why we do not always have what we need, and against praying with wrong motives, which is one reason why God does not always honor our requests (vv. 2–3). In his last chapter James commends prayerful perseverance, using the prophet Elijah as an example: "Elijah was a man just like us. He prayed earnestly that it would not rain, and it did not rain on the land for three and a half years" (James 5:17). His conclusion is that "the prayer of a righteous man is powerful and effective" (v. 16).

How does prayer relate to quarreling? Simply that if we are looking to God for our needs and are seeing him answer and supply them, we will not be lashing out at others for failing to do what we want or provide what we desire.

Hearing and Healing

James's last point, which again might well have been spoken by Joseph, is that believers are to *turn from sin* and *humble themselves* before God. James says, "Wash your hands, you sinners, and purify your hearts, you double-minded. Grieve, mourn and wail. Change your laughter to mourning and your joy to gloom. Humble yourselves before the Lord, and he will lift you up" (James 4:8–10). James's language is strong at this point, because he does not want the need for repentance to be taken lightly. If we are to draw near to God, it must be with clean hands and a pure heart. Beyond any doubt, James is thinking of Psalm 24:3–4 as he says this:

> Who may ascend the hill of the LORD?
> Who may stand in his holy place?
> He who has clean hands and a pure heart,
> who does not lift up his soul to an idol
> or swear by what is false.

This is what is required of submissive, resisting, prayerful men and women of God. And it is important! The people who have washed thier hands of sin, purified their hearts, and humbled their spirits are not likely to be quarreling.

154

What Can I Believe?

Genesis 45:25–28

So they went up out of Egypt and came to their father Jacob in the land of Canaan. They told him, "Joseph is still alive! In fact, he is ruler of all Egypt." Jacob was stunned; he did not believe them. But when they told him everything Joseph had said to them, and when he saw the carts Joseph had sent to carry him back, the spirit of their father Jacob revived. And Israel said, "I'm convinced! My son Joseph is still alive. I will go and see him before I die."

The English don and Christian apologist C. S. Lewis gave a series of talks for the British Broadcasting Corporation during World War II in which he discussed some of the basic ideas of Christianity. Two of those talks, later published in *Mere Christianity,* were on faith. Lewis's point was that faith, which should be natural to us because of its being based on reason, is actually a problem, because our emotions, deeply affected by sin, fight against it.

Lewis imagines a situation in which he has a sound rational faith in his doctor, the operation to be performed, and the anesthesia that is to make him unconscious during the operation. "But," he says, "that does not alter the fact that when they have me down to the table and clap their horrible mask over my face, a mere childish panic begins inside me. I start thinking I am going to choke, and I am afraid they will start cutting me up before I am properly under. In other words, I lose my faith in anaesthetics. It is not reason that is taking away my faith: on the contrary, my faith is based on reason. It is my imagination and emotions. The battle is between faith and reason on one side and emotion and imagination on the other."[1]

On the basis of this analysis, Lewis advises us to recognize that our moods change and to fight against them by the Christian disciplines of daily prayer, Bible reading, and churchgoing if we would grow in our belief.

The ancients knew this too, although they saw it for the most part secularly. Ovid said, "We are slow to believe that which if believed would hurt our feelings." Demosthenes voiced the counterpart of Ovid's statement: "Nothing is so easy as to deceive one's self; for what we wish, that we readily believe."[2]

Faith in Bad Tidings

Emotions are not the only things that influence our faith, often keeping us from what our reason tells us is true, particularly in spiritual matters. But they are one factor, and they were certainly a factor in Jacob's strange turmoil when told that Joseph was alive and ruler of all Egypt. At first Jacob refused to believe it (v. 26). But after he had heard the full story and had looked at the Egyptian carts sent by Pharaoh, his spirits revived, and he said, "I'm convinced! My son Joseph is still alive. I will go down and see him before I die" (v. 28).

This episode is worth examining for what it tells us about Jacob. But since it deals with faith and since faith is a matter of concern to believers in all ages, it is also worth examining for what it tells us about ourselves. We are often like Jacob!

There are some ways in which any true believer is like Abraham, who was a giant in faith, and Joseph, whose life was one long demonstration of faith. But when we consider ourselves carefully we have to confess that usually these giants show us to be spiritual pygmies, and we sense that we do not have a lot in common with them. Our faith is not great. Our Christian lives are not marked by a constant and growing trust in God's sovereignty.

How different in the case of Jacob! He was a believer, at least after God had mastered him in the wrestling match at Jabbok. But he was always up and down. At times he was strong in faith, giving glory to God. At other times he was weak and self-pitying, as when he complained, "Everything is against me!" (Gen. 42:36). It is a dull Christian who cannot see his or her own vacillating faith in Jacob's inconsistencies.

One point in which we often resemble Jacob is his readiness to believe bad tidings. Demosthenes said that we readily believe what we want to believe. But in his early days Jacob seemed more inclined to believe bad news than good. Thus, when his sons came to him with Joseph's bloodstained coat he replied, "It is my son's robe! Some ferocious animal has devoured him. Joseph has surely been torn to pieces" (Gen. 37:33). Jacob could have held off accepting this. He could have sent someone to see if Joseph might merely have been wounded or at least to find the body. But Jacob did not. He immediately assumed the worst and grew despondent.

We can find excuses for Jacob. We can point out that Jacob had undoubtedly had a rough life (though much of it was caused by his own failures). His father had preferred his twin brother, Esau, to him and was determined to give Esau the inheritance. After he had cheated Esau, Jacob was forced to flee from home and take refuge with his Uncle Laban in Haran. There Laban had taken advantage of him. He was cheated in his first marriage. His wages were changed ten times, always to the advantage of Laban rather than himself. He said of those days, "This was my situation: The heat consumed me in the daytime and the cold at night, and sleep fled from my eyes. It was like this for the twenty years I was in [Laban's] household" (Gen. 31:40–41).

On the way home Laban pursued him, and for a while Jacob felt that his life was in danger. An angel (or the Lord himself) wrestled with him, and his hip was dislocated. His sons killed the Shechemites, and he was then in danger of reprisal by the Canaanites. His beloved wife, Rachel, died while giving birth to Benjamin. Then, at last, he suffered what he believed to be the death of his favorite son, Joseph. Yes, Jacob had indeed suffered a lot. But notice: He had not suffered as greatly as Joseph had, nor as innocently. Yet Joseph was not complaining. Joseph did not fail to have faith in God; he did not allow his battered emotions to cause him to believe bad news and reject the good.

What is the problem with Jacob? It is exactly what C. S. Lewis referred to: his emotions. The clue to his frame of mind is seen just two chapters after this, in Genesis 47:9, where Jacob tells Pharaoh, "My years have been few and difficult." Difficult? Possibly. But not few. Jacob was 130 years old at this time. What the comment really shows is that Jacob was again feeling sorry for himself and was trying to get sympathy. Consequently he was not strong in faith and giving glory to God, as Joseph and his fathers Abraham and Isaac before him had been.

Doubt of God's Goodness

Jacob was unreasonably willing to believe bad news. It is part of this same picture that he was also unreasonably reluctant to believe what was good. The brothers came with the report: "Joseph is still alive! In fact, he is ruler of all Egypt" (v. 26). But "Jacob was stunned; he did not believe them" (v. 26). Earlier Jacob had believed the bad report that Joseph was dead, although in fact that report was not true. Now he refused to believe the good report that Joseph was alive, although by contrast this report was accurate.

How like people today when they first hear the gospel! The gospel is good news: God loves you, Jesus Christ has died for your sins, Jesus has gone to prepare a place for you and will return to receive you to himself forever. But to the unsaved these things sound like mere fantasies. I think of the Emmaus disciples, Cleopas and probably his wife, Mary. They had been in Jerusalem during the crucifixion and had no trouble believing that Jesus was dead and buried. Bad news was quite believable.

But when news came to them by way of the women who had been at the tomb that Jesus' body was no longer there and that angels had appeared to say that he was risen as he had said, they did not believe the women. In fact, they did not even go to the tomb to investigate the reports. They continued collecting their belongings and then started out for home. This was the best news the world has ever heard. But the Emmaus disciples would not believe it, because they had allowed their downward-crashing emotions to blot out everything Jesus had told them about his coming victory over death.

Is that you? Are you so wrapped up in yourself, so disheartened by circumstances, that you cannot believe the good news? If so, you must turn to the Scriptures. You must pray that Jesus will himself expound them to you and reveal himself to you as he walks with you along the way.

Sunrise of Faith

Jacob was gloom personified. But even though he inclined naturally to bad news, the gospel is nevertheless good news and what is true has an inevitable way of pushing itself forward and demanding belief. The good news that Joseph was alive pressed on Jacob in three ways.

First, Jacob was confronted by the personal testimony of those who knew what they were talking about. There was much the brothers did not know. In the short time they had spent with Joseph in Egypt after he had revealed himself to them, they would have been unable to learn very much about his past history. They would have known little about his family, little about his relationship to the pharaoh, little about his work in the administration of Egypt. And on the spiritual side, they would have known next to nothing about the way God had ordered world events to preserve Joseph and place him at the pinnacle of power in Egypt. If Jacob had asked them how it had happened, they would have had to reply simply, "We do not know." Yes, but they knew the important thing! They had met Joseph, and they knew he was alive. Consequently they returned to their father with convincing testimonies.

Is it not exactly the same today in respect to those who witness to the resurrection of Jesus Christ and his present rule over this great universe? Perhaps you are one who can hardly believe such good news. "Too good to be true," you say. But look! Look at the great company who testify that they have felt his power and experienced his rule. Is theirs false testimony? Is theirs a witness you can disregard easily?

Second, Jacob was given an account of everything that had happened. The text says "everything Joseph had said to them," but I cannot imagine that they were able to tell this without at the same time confessing their own sad part in selling Joseph into Egypt. Part of the report must have been a confession of their sin and their subsequent lies to cover up that sin.

There is something convincing about the confession of sin—for the simple reason that it is so unusual. Men and women do not naturally confess their sin. On the contrary, they deny it and make excuses for their conduct. Since this is undoubtedly true, does it not follow that the disciples of Christ, who acknowledge themselves to be sinners, have had something extraordinary happen? Is it not reasonable to believe that they have actually had an encounter with the true and living Christ, as they say?

I do not want to pass over the fact that the text actually says the brothers reported "everything *Joseph* had said to them." Charles Haddon Spurgeon comments on this in one of his sermons: "Those words of Joseph were remarkable words, for he traced God's providence in all that had happened. He said to his brethren, 'God sent me before you to preserve you a posterity in the earth, and to save your lives by a great deliverance. So now it was not you that sent me hither, but God, and he hath made me a father to Pharaoh, and lord of all his house, and a ruler throughout all the land of Egypt.' Jacob knew that those words were after the manner of Joseph, for Joseph always lived in the fear and love of God. . . . Joseph also spoke somewhat about his own position and power. 'Tell my father,' he said, 'thus saith thy son Joseph, God hath made me lord of all Egypt.' . . . Joseph had also spoken to them very tenderly and kindly about their father. He would do everything for his father and his brethren, giving them the best of the land."[3] Would not Jacob say to himself, "There is something convincing about this. Those words are very much like Joseph. They sound true"?

If you are not yet a full believer in Jesus Christ, you may have noticed that the followers of Christ are often quoting his words. And if you have listened at all closely, you may have noticed that those words have a fair ring about them. Have you never asked yourself whether words like that are not likely to be true? I put it to you that they are. I suggest that if you read those words yourself as they are found in the New Testament, you will find yourself concluding—as the well-known English scholar and Bible translator J. B. Phillips concluded after he had translated the four Gospels—that the words of Jesus are "alive with power" and bear within them "the ring of truth."[4]

The third factor that moved Jacob from his gloomy unbelief to final joyful acceptance of Joseph's being alive was the evidence of the carts that had been brought from Egypt. The text says, "But when they told him everything Joseph had said to them, and *when he saw the carts* Joseph had sent to carry him back, the spirit of . . . Jacob revived" (v. 27, my emphasis).

Are there spiritual parallels to these carts from Egypt? I think there are. Spurgeon, whom I quoted earlier, saw the Sabbath as just such a token. He said, "As I came here this evening, I thought to myself, 'Why has God appointed a Sabbath day if he does not mean it to give rest to men?' . . . The very institution of the Sabbath seems to me to be a 'wagon' in which to bring you to Christ."[5]

According to this gifted expositor and preacher, God's calling of ministers to preach his gospel is another such token. He argued, "Surely, God did not send us to speak in his name, and move us to an agony about your souls, if he did not mean to bless you."[6]

Neither of these exhausts the many tokens God sends to assure you of his love and of Christ's work on your behalf. The Bible tells us that "every good and perfect gift" is from God (James 1:17). Your very life is from him. It is a cart from heaven. So is health and friendship and love and everything else you value. God has given these precisely so that your eyes may be opened and you might be brought to full faith in Jesus Christ.

Jacob or Israel?

My final point is the obvious one: These forces for good eventually had their way with Jacob, and he responded with positive action that can only be called the fruit of true faith. "Israel said, 'I'm convinced! My son Joseph is still alive. I will go and see him before I die'" (v. 28).

It is significant that the Bible refers to Jacob by his covenant name of Israel at this point. Up to now the name has been Jacob. In fact, "Jacob" has been used three times in this passage: "So they went up out of Egypt and came to their father *Jacob* in the land of Canaan. . . . *Jacob* was stunned. . . . When he saw the carts Joseph had sent to carry him back, the spirit of their father *Jacob* revived" (my emphasis). Jacob . . . Jacob . . . Jacob. But now suddenly "Israel!"

"And *Israel* said, 'I'm convinced. My son Joseph is still alive. I will go and see him before I die.'" This takes us back to the story in which Jacob wrestled with the angel (who was probably the Lord himself), was overcome by him, and as a result received the name "Israel," which (as I suggested when we studied that earlier story) means "God rules," "God commands," or "God overcomes." When Jacob is in charge we get Jacob, a whining, self-pitying, complaining type of man. When God overcomes, we get Israel, a true child of God. It is as Israel that this man draws himself together, rises to his full height, collects his numerous family, and sets out for Egypt to see his son Joseph before he dies.

When you are racked by doubt and are feeling sorry for yourself, you think that one reason why you must not commit yourself to God is that you will be changed, and you want to keep your identity. There is truth in that. No one has ever surrendered himself or herself to God who has not been changed as a result. But what a change! What "Israels" such captured ones become! Why not be changed? Why not believe? How can you be harmed, even though changed, by him who has always held your own best interests in his heart?

155

"Jacob! Jacob!"

Genesis 46:1–7

So Israel set out with all that was his, and when he reached Beersheba, he offered sacrifices to the God of his father Isaac.

And God spoke to Israel in a vision at night and said, "Jacob! Jacob!"

"Here I am," he replied.

"I am God, the God of your father," he said. "Do not be afraid to go down to Egypt, for I will make you into a great nation there. I will go down to Egypt with you, and I will surely bring you back again. And Joseph's own hand will close your eyes."

Then Jacob left Beersheba, and Israel's sons took their father Jacob and their children and their wives in the carts that Pharaoh had sent to transport him. They also took with them their livestock and the possessions they had acquired in Canaan, and Jacob and all his offspring went to Egypt. He took with him to Egypt his sons and grandsons and his daughters and granddaughters—all his offspring.

I do not know of a large number of places in the Bible where God suddenly called out to a servant of his by name, but there are a few of them. I think of God's call to Samuel when he was just a lad. The Lord said, "Samuel! Samuel!" (1 Sam. 3:10). When the boy understood at last that it was God calling and not Eli the priest, he responded, "Speak, for your servant is listening." A second example is Paul, called Saul before he was converted. God stopped him when he was on the road to Damascus to murder Christians, saying, "Saul, Saul, why do you persecute me?" (Acts 9:4). God called Abraham in the matter of the sacrifice of his son: "Abraham! Abraham" (Gen. 22:1, 11).

In our text there is a similar call of Jacob. Jacob had started down to Egypt to see Joseph, but he had paused at Beersheba, being fearful of what might lie ahead. The Lord reassured him.

"Jacob! Jacob!"

"Here I am," he replied.

The Lord continued, "I am God, the God of your father. Do not be afraid to go down to Egypt, for I will make you into a great nation there. I will go down to Egypt with you, and I will surely bring you back again. And Joseph's own hand will close your eyes" (Gen. 46:2–4). This revelation was all Jacob needed. The next verses picture him going on his way confidently, and we do not read of his being fearful again.

In each of these instances there was a major crisis in a believer's life. But there was also a word from God, and that made all the difference. Samuel became a distinguished leader in Israel, a transition figure between the judges and the kings. Paul became a great missionary. Abraham grew to be a giant in faith. In this study we want to see what happened to Jacob.

Fear and Trembling

The clue to understanding Jacob's experience is to recognize that he was fearful—justifiably so. He was fearful of many things. Jacob had come to Beersheba, the place that marked the southernmost boundary of the land God had given to his grandfather Abraham and to Abraham's descendants. Each of the patriarchs had lived at Beersheba for at least one period of their lives: Abraham (Gen. 21:31), Isaac (Gen. 26:23), and Jacob (Gen. 28:10). There was an altar there at which Abraham and Isaac had worshiped. In later years the phrase "from Dan to Beersheba" was used to designate all the territory of Israel (Judg. 20:1; 1 Sam. 3:20). While Jacob remained in Beersheba he was on what we would call "his own turf." But beyond Beersheba was desert, and beyond that was Egypt. Jacob had never been beyond Beersheba. What would he find if he started south? Would he be safe in that country? Would a move at this stage in his life really be beneficial to his large family?

Charles H. Spurgeon once preached a very effective sermon on this passage in which he noted four possible causes for Jacob's alarm.

First, *Jacob was an old man,* and apart from any other considerations, a change of this magnitude at this stage of his life was difficult. Old people do not like changes. It is different with youth. Young men and women can move easily from place to place; it does not bother them. On the contrary, a move in youth is adventure. It seethes with excitement. In old age a person tends to settle down, grow accustomed to the living environment, and fear changes. Jacob was about 130 years old at this time (cf. Gen. 47:9). He had lived in Canaan for many years. It was as difficult for him to pull up stakes as it is for many older people today to break with their past and follow the Lord's leading to a new field of service.

Second, *Egypt was a very pagan country.* Jacob may not have known much about Egypt, but he would certainly have known its two most significant characteristics. First, it was noted for its age, prosperity, and technology. Egypt had been around as long as humanity could remember, and during the long centuries of its history it had developed a superb understanding of mathematics, architecture, astronomy, agriculture, and medicine. It was the most highly developed and most civilized nation on earth at this time.

Yes, but it was also pagan, its other noteworthy characteristic. It had a pantheon of gods: Osiris, Hapimon, and Tauret, who were gods of the Nile; Nu, the god of life in the river; Geb, god of the land. There were Nephri, the grain god; Anubis, guardian of the fields; Min, deity of the harvest and crops. There were gods in the form of animals: Apis, the bull god; Hathor, the cow goddess; Sekhmet, the lion; Khnum, the ram; Sobek, the crocodile; Thoth, the ibis; Horus and Month, the bird gods. Nut was the sky; Shu, the atmosphere. Greatest of all was Ra, the sun god, thought to be embodied in the reigning pharaoh.

Egypt was the perfect example of Paul's portrait of degenerate religion in Romans 1:21–23: "For although they knew God, they neither glorified him as God nor gave thanks to him, but their thinking became futile and their foolish hearts were darkened. Although they claimed to be wise, they became fools and exchanged the glory of the immortal God for images made to look like mortal man and birds and animals and reptiles."

Even though Jacob may not have known all the details of this debased paganism, he must have known enough about it to fear it. Besides, he would have remembered the effect on his family of the far less sophisticated sins of Canaan. Jacob had had a difficult enough time keeping his family close to God there. What would happen to them in the far more dangerous environment of Egypt? Would they not end up going the way of the ungodly entirely?

Third, *Egypt had bad past memories for Jacob.* The patriarchs remembered what had happened to their fathers and grandfathers, and Jacob would have been aware of Abraham's fall when he went down to Egypt. Abraham was a giant in faith, a model for his posterity. Yet, in spite of his stature there was a time when Abraham had gone to Egypt and there had lied about his wife, saying she was his sister for fear that the men of Egypt would kill him in order to take her. In fact, the pharaoh did take Sarah into his palace. The story tells how God protected Sarah—and even Abraham. But Abraham was rebuked by Pharaoh: "What have you done to me? Why didn't you tell me she was your wife? . . . Now then, here is your wife. Take her and go!" (Gen.

12:10–20). This was the lowest point in Abraham's long life, and it was associated with Egypt. Jacob would know this. So he would have seen how easy it would be (since even Abraham had fallen) for his family to be carried down as well.

Fourth, *Jacob had been warned of future evils*. Back in the early history of this people God had appeared to Abraham to say that his descendants would be "strangers in a country not their own" and that they would be "enslaved and mistreated four hundred years" (Gen. 15:13). Spurgeon wrote that in his opinion, "The old man, with prescient eye, began to suspect that this was to be the land which caused Abraham the horror of great darkness, which was set forth before him as the fiery furnace and the smoking land; and so he was afraid to go down into Egypt."[1]

This is not unlike things that make many of us fearful, especially as we grow older. It is true, we do not have a specific prophecy of specific suffering to come. But we know enough of life to see that "man is born to trouble as surely as sparks fly upward" (Job 5:7). Such knowledge causes us to tremble before change.

Time to Pray

Jacob had trembled before, of course. He had trembled for fear of Esau when he had cheated him of the birthright and had been forced to run away. He had trembled again on the banks of the Jabbok when he was about to meet Esau again after twenty years. Jacob was trembling now. But he had learned something from those two earlier occasions, and it stood him in good stead. On each of those former occasions God had appeared to him: once at Bethel in the vision of the great ladder reaching from heaven to earth, and once at Jabbok when the heavenly messenger appeared to wrestle him to personal submission. Jacob had never been the same after that. So now, instead of waiting for God to manifest himself to him in some new or startling way, Jacob actually sought God. The story tells us that he worshiped by offering "sacrifices to the God of his father Isaac" (Gen. 46:1). We must suppose that he worshiped by acknowledging God's past blessings and faithfulness and by praying for guidance.

Spurgeon suggests that Jacob would have offered sacrifices for three reasons at least. First, *to purge his household* of any sin that might lie upon it. He did this earlier at Bethel, so we are probably not wrong in thinking that he did something similar again now (cf. Gen. 35:1–7). Second, *to give thanks*. He was going to Egypt because Joseph, his beloved son, was alive and was there. Joseph had bid him come, and this was a cause of thanksgiving. Third—and I am sure this was the main reason—Jacob worshiped *to seek the mind of God* in his moving.

At Bethel, when Jacob was setting out for Haran for fear of Esau, God said that he would be with him wherever he would go (Gen. 28:12–15). But God had also been firm in telling the patriarchs that they were to live in Canaan and seek spiritual blessing there. God seemed to be acting providentially in sending Joseph before him to Egypt to preserve many people, including his own family. But how could Jacob be sure? It was a propitious time to seek the will of God—and Jacob did.

Many Christians get into trouble at this point. They are confronted with change. They suspect that God may be leading. But they never pause to ask him whether he is or not, and as a result they often go off in wrong directions and waste precious years of their lives.

A group of Christians was talking about a problem in their community, and one of them suggested quite reasonably that something tangible should be done. They formed a committee and launched an organization. They raised money and worked and did many other things besides. But they neglected to pray and so made a great mistake. The project seemed reasonable enough, but God was not in it. Years later, after much wasted effort and frustration, one of the participants sadly admitted, "You know, nothing ever came of that. The time was wasted."

Earlier in his life Jacob had himself wasted more than twenty years because he had thought that he could help God out by cheating his father. But he had learned! Now he worshiped the Lord and sought his guidance before going forward.

"Do Not Be Afraid"

When we are fearful or in great perplexity we often wonder if God will hear us when we pray to him. God is always more eager to answer than we are to ask, more eager to guide than we are to follow. This was the case here. Jacob worshiped, and it was immediately after this, perhaps that very night, that God told him he was on the right track, that God would bless him even in the distant and dangerous land of Egypt.

God's words fall into several parts. First, *God called him by name*—"Jacob! Jacob!" (v. 2)—thereby showing that he knew him and was still his own personal God, every bit as much as he was the God of his fathers Isaac and Abraham before him. It is wonderful to come from a believing family, so you can say, "My God is the God of my father and mother and of their fathers and mothers before them." The benefits of a pious upbringing are not to be despised. Still, wonderful as this is, the important thing is whether God is your God and whether you are known by him personally. Is God your God? Has he ever called you personally?

If God has never called your name, thereby leading you out of previous allegiances into his own flock of believing people, I warn you not to take another step until this personal relationship is settled. God must be your shepherd. Jesus must be your Savior before anything else can be settled.

Second, *God reaffirmed his covenant with Jacob* by the words, "I am God, the God of your father" (v. 3). This was not an idle statement. If the God who was speaking to Jacob was the God of Abraham, he was therefore also the God of

Isaac, both of whom he had led with utter faithfulness. God had led Abraham out of Ur of the Chaldeans, brought him to a new land, and there preserved him in the midst of natural disasters and external threats from enemies. He had kept and protected Isaac. Jacob could point to God's faithfulness.

What a God he is, this God of the covenant! He is Abraham's God; he was faithful to Abraham throughout his long life. He is Isaac's God, Jacob's God, Moses' God, David's God. He is your God and mine. This very continuity should strengthen us for whatever lies ahead.

Third, *God had a promise for Jacob.* He told him not to fear going down to Egypt, "for I will make you into a great nation there" (v. 3). I do not know what special promise God may have for you in a similar crisis in your life. But if there is no other specific promise, there is at least a promise analogous to Jacob's—that God will work in us and others to build a people to the praise of the glory of his grace. We have a picture of this people in Revelation, where countless millions surround the throne of God and cry out to Jesus:

> "You are worthy to take the scroll
>   and to open its seals,
> because you were slain,
>   and with your blood you purchased men for God
>   from every tribe and language and people and nation.
> You have made them to be a kingdom and priests to serve our God,
>   and they will reign on the earth."
>
> Revelation 5:9–10

Often we have a small view of what God is doing. But it will calm our fears if we can see our work as a part of his large plan and know that one day we will be part of that great company.

God's final word for Jacob was the most important of all. *He promised to go with him* as he went to Egypt, to be with him even in death, and eventually to bring his body back to Canaan, the land of promise. "I will go down to Egypt with you, and I will surely bring you back again. And Joseph's own hand will close your eyes" (v. 4).

Was not Egypt still a frightening place to have before him? Yes, it was! Was there not a genuine danger of spiritual decay and even physical enslavement? Yes, that too! But what a difference when the God of the covenant says that he will go with us, bless us, and bring us back again! If God were not with me, I should fear to take even a single step. But because God is with me, I can walk through anything, even hell, and come forth again unscathed.

Apparently Jacob understood and believed this, for he responded positively in spite of the danger and his old age. The text says:

> Then Jacob left Beersheba, and Israel's sons took their father Jacob and their children and their wives in the carts that Pharaoh had sent to transport him. They also took with them their livestock and the possessions they had acquired

in Canaan, and Jacob and all his offspring went to Egypt. He took with him to Egypt his sons and grandsons and his daughters and granddaughters—all his offspring.

verses 5–7

The reiteration is meant to show Jacob's total obedience. He left, leaving not a person or possession behind.

Strong to the End

This truth has applications to others in similar situations. You may be on the verge of a major change, and you may be uncertain about it—even fearful. If so, do not take a step until you seek God's face. Ask him to show you the direction you should go. If God is silent, remain where you are. If he speaks, go forth boldly and fear nothing. He will be with you not only in Egypt but to the uttermost parts of the earth.

Others may be old, some even on the point of dying. If that is the case and you sense that the days of your earthly wandering may be drawing to a close, know that the God who has been with you throughout life will also be with you in death. He will close your eyes, and you will not lose your inheritance or reward. Death is an enemy, but death is not necessarily or inevitably gloomy. It is possible to sing and even shout joyously in death. God's people do not die as the heathen. They die in Christ, and the way they die gives proof of the gospel we preach as well as evidence of the divine strength that sustains us to the end.

156

Seventy in All

Genesis 46:8–27

These are the names of the sons of Israel (Jacob and his descendants) who went to Egypt:

Reuben the firstborn of Jacob.

The sons of Reuben:

> *Hanoch, Pallu, Hezron and Carmi.*

The sons of Simeon:

> *Jemuel, Jamin, Ohad, Jakin, Zohar and Shaul the son of a Canaanite woman.*

The sons of Levi:

> *Gershon, Kohath and Merari.*

The sons of Judah:

> *Er, Onan, Shelah, Perez and Zerah (but Er and Onan had died in the land of Canaan).*

The sons of Perez:

> *Hezron and Hamul.*

The sons of Issachar:

> *Tola, Puah, Jashub and Shimron.*

The sons of Zebulun:

> *Sered, Elon and Jahleel.*

These were the sons Leah bore to Jacob in Paddan Aram, besides his daughter Dinah. These sons and daughters of his were thirty-three in all.

The sons of Gad:

Zephon, Haggi, Shuni, Ezbon, Eri, Arodi and Areli.

The sons of Asher:

Imnah, Ishvah, Ishvi and Beriah.

Their sister was Serah.

The sons of Beriah:

Heber and Malkiel.

These were the children born to Jacob by Zilpah, whom Laban had given to his daughter Leah—sixteen in all.

The sons of Jacob's wife Rachel:

Joseph and Benjamin. In Egypt, Manasseh and Ephraim were born to Joseph by Asenath daughter of Potiphera, priest of On.

The sons of Benjamin:

Bela, Beker, Ashbel, Gera, Naaman, Ehi, Rosh, Muppim, Huppim and Ard.

These were the sons of Rachel who were born to Jacob—fourteen in all.

The son of Dan:

Hushim.

The sons of Naphtali:

Jahziel, Guni, Jezer and Shillem.

These were the sons born to Jacob by Bilhah, whom Laban had given to his daughter Rachel—seven in all.

All those who went to Egypt with Jacob—those who were his direct descendants, not counting his sons' wives—numbered sixty-six persons. With the two sons who had been born to Joseph in Egypt, the members of Jacob's family, which went to Egypt, were seventy in all.

Genesis 46 lists Jacob's children and grandchildren who went with him to Egypt. It is not the first time a list like this appears in the Bible. Genesis 4 lists eight descendants of Cain. Genesis 5 contains a "written account of Adam's line," which traces his godly descendants from father to son through ten generations to the time of Noah. Genesis 10 lists the people who descended from Noah's sons, Shem, Ham, and Japheth: these spread out over the earth to repopulate it after the great flood. Chapter 11 lists Shem's descendants through his son Arphaxad, leading to the birth of Abraham. Somewhat later, in the middle portion of Genesis, there is a listing of the sons, rulers, and other chief descendants of Isaac's son Esau (Genesis 36).

These five chapters together list approximately two hundred names, and now in chapter 46 we have seventy more. Could anything be less interesting than nearly three hundred very ancient names? Some would say this. Yet they are obviously not uninteresting to God. We may find names boring, but to God they represent individuals whose lives and personal histories are significant.

Paul Tournier, the Swiss psychologist, notes this interest in names. "God says to Moses: 'I know thee by name' (Ex. 33:17). He says to Cyrus: 'I am the Lord, which call thee by thy name' (Isa. 45:3). These texts express the essence of the personalism of the Bible. One is struck, on reading the Bible, by the importance in it of proper names. Whole chapters are devoted to long genealogies. When I was young I used to think that they could well have been dropped from the biblical canon. But I have since realized that these series of proper names bear witness to the fact that, in the biblical perspective, man is neither a thing nor an abstraction, neither a species nor an idea, that he is not a fraction of the mass, as the Marxists see him, but that he is a person."[1] We need to keep this in mind as we study the listing of Jacob's descendants in this chapter.

Seventy or Seventy-five?

Genesis 46 contains several problems that we do well to deal with. One of these arises when we compare Genesis 46 with the two parallel name lists in Numbers 26 and 1 Chronicles 2–8. Here spellings of names vary, and there are occasional omissions or additions. For example, Numbers 26:12 and 1 Chronicles 4:24 do not list Ohad as a son of Simeon, though his name occurs in Genesis 46:10. Again, the names of the descendants of Benjamin vary widely. Genesis 46:21 lists ten "sons" of Benjamin. But Numbers 26:38–40 lists only five, two of whom are different, and 1 Chronicles 7:6 has three. However, in these later lists other descendants are given who may be the equivalent of the additional five or seven names in Genesis. We are encouraged to think along these lines by the fact that in Numbers 26:40 two of the "sons" in Genesis are said actually to have been grandsons.

A comparison of these lists unearths a number of problems, but most have reasonable explanations. There is no cause to think that they express real contradictions.

The second problem with Genesis 46 is more puzzling. In that chapter the number of Jacob's descendants who are said to have gone down to Egypt with him is seventy. There are seventy people listed in verses 8–25, minus Er and Onan (who died while the family was still in Canaan) and Manasseh and Ephraim (who, being sons of Joseph, were born in Egypt). That reduces the number to sixty-six persons, but to it we add Jacob and a wife (whichever one was living at this time) and Manasseh and Ephraim. This makes "seventy" again (Gen. 46:27). However, in Stephen's telling of this story as recorded in Acts 7, seventy-five people are said to have been involved: "After this, Joseph sent for his father and his whole family, seventy-five in all" (v. 14). This seems a clear contradiction. Liberal scholars note that the Septuagint translation of Exodus 1:5 has the figure seventy-five, which is where Stephen is supposed to have found his "error."

Various solutions have been suggested. Some have suggested that Stephen did indeed make an error, but they add that this does not mean that the Bible is an errant book, since Acts does not say that seventy-five people went down to Egypt but only that Stephen said that there were seventy-five people. The error would be Stephen's. The accuracy would lie in the Bible's reporting of what Stephen said.

A second attempt to resolve this problem has been by appeal to the Bible's use of round numbers. Robert Candlish takes this position. "Probably the number seventy or seventy-five—for evidently it was not held to be material which of the two was preferred—was technical and artificial, if we may so speak—not intended to be an exact historical enumeration, but a kind of convenient, shorthand summary—representing clearly enough to the successive generations of Israelites the state of the household at the time of the settlement in Egypt—and capable of easy application to the more complete and regular arrangement of the tribes, whether on their coming out of Egypt, or in the wilderness, or in Canaan."[2]

I do not have difficulty with either of these explanations personally, since there are other examples both of the Bible's quotation of an erring person's error and of the Bible's use of round numbers. But in this case I think there is a better explanation.

It is true that the Septuagint translation of Exodus 1:5 gives the number of Jacob's descendants who entered Egypt as seventy-five. But if those who suppose this to be an error would also read the Septuagint translation of Genesis 46:26–27, they would see how the translators arrived at this total. The Septuagint of Genesis 46 says, "And all the souls who came with Jacob into Egypt, who issued from his loins, apart from the wives of the sons of Jacob, were sixty-six persons. And the sons of Joseph who were born in Egypt were nine persons. All the souls of the house of Jacob who entered Egypt were seventy-five." In other words, the total of seventy-five arrived at by the Septuagint includes nine descendants of Joseph, rather than just two. These could have been younger sons of Joseph but were probably sons of Manasseh and Ephraim, that is, Joseph's grandsons, who would not have been born at the time of Jacob's migration to Egypt but would have been by the time of Jacob's death there seventeen years later.

The Hebrew texts of Genesis 46 and Exodus 1 get the figure seventy by including twelve sons of Jacob, fifty-two grandsons of Jacob, four great-grandsons of Jacob born in Canaan (for a total of sixty-six), plus Manasseh, Ephraim, Jacob, and Jacob's wife. The Septuagint gets the figure seventy-five by omitting Jacob and his wife but counting Joseph's seven additional descendants.[3]

A Slow Beginning

There are several lessons that we should learn from these names. First, it is difficult to read this chapter—even with what seems to be many names—without sensing that it was a very small number in relation to what the descendants of Jacob were to become. Indeed, that had been the case from the very beginning.

In Genesis 12:2, in the midst of the account of his calling Abraham out of Ur of the Chaldeans to go to Canaan, God had said, "I will make you into a great nation." Three chapters after this, God had taken Abraham outside his tent on a clear, starry night and had told him to look at the heavens and count the stars if he could count them. Then he said, "So shall your offspring be" (Gen. 15:5). In Genesis 17 Abraham was told that he would become the father of "many" nations (v. 4). In Genesis 22 the promise was expanded even further: "I will surely bless you and make your descendants as numerous as the stars in the sky and as the sand on the seashore. Your descendants will take possession of the cities of their enemies, and through your offspring all nations on earth will be blessed" (vv. 17–18). Yet hundreds of years went by with very marginal fulfillment of these promises.

Abraham was eighty-six years old before his first son, Ishmael, was born. He was even older—one hundred years old—when Isaac, the promised son, was born. Isaac was sixty years old before his twin sons, Esau and Jacob, were born. Jacob was getting along in years before he had any children. Even though with Jacob the stream of descendants began to widen somewhat so that at one point he boasted that he had become "two groups" (Gen. 32:10), here there were still just seventy true descendants to go down to Egypt. This is 215 years after God had first appeared to Abraham to say that he would become a great nation!

Yet Israel did become a great nation. Thus, 430 years after these events, at the time of the exodus, 600,000 Israelite men left Egypt for Canaan. Together with their wives, children, and hangers-on, the number could not have been less than two million.

We have to remember how God works when we begin some spiritual enterprise. We live in a time of hurry, when success is measured by speed of accomplishment rather than permanence. If we do not see immediate results, we get discouraged. Young people particularly are prone to think like this. This is not God's way. God can act quickly and with large numbers. It is remarkable how quickly the Jewish people multiplied once they got to Egypt. They grew from one to seventy (or seventy-five) in 215 years, but in the next 430 years (just twice that time) they grew to two million. God can bring large numerical results. But he starts slowly. He is careful to lay sound groundwork.

I would say to anyone who is young and planning a career in Christian service, "Start slowly. Think of a career in God's service as a parabola with a very flat curve at the beginning but with a steeper curve at the end. Do not cut basics. Above all, learn all you can about the Bible, make changes slowly, and invest in people. Remember that Jesus focused a lifetime of ministry in just twelve disciples."

God's Company

The second thing I notice about this company of seventy persons who went down with Jacob to Egypt is their unity. There were times when they had not been unified. They were quarrelsome. They sold Joseph into slavery and were probably each scattering to his own separate way before the famine. Yet here they are all apparently of one mind. They *all* go to Egypt. It is significant that Jacob did not see fit to leave a garrison, as it were—a string tied to the land of God's promise. Jacob was not abandoning his faith in that promise, but his faith was in God who gave it. God was sending the little band to Egypt. Therefore, despite the dangers, Jacob was going to trust God to preserve them in Egypt and lead them out of it in his own proper time. To this they were committed.

It would be a great thing if God's people were thus unified today. I do not mean that God's people must always be in the same place doing the same thing. God gives a variety of gifts and calls to a variety of ministries. But I do mean that there should be unity. We should know that we are part of one company, moving to one destination, answering to one master: Jesus Christ.

How are we to discover and express this practically? There are many answers to that question, but a large part of the answer lies in our knowing that we are as much a part of one large spiritual family as ever Jacob's children were a part of his family. That makes a difference. If the church is essentially an organization—or worse yet, a number of organizations—then one can join or not, as he or she wishes. Or one can switch from organization to organization just as one might switch clubs.

It is quite different if the church is a family. No one has a choice of what family he or she will belong to. So if the church is essentially a family, we do not have a choice whether or not we will be identified with it. These are our people. That fellow Christian is our mother. That other believer is our father or sister or brother. We must stand with them and work with them now, for it is certain that we shall stand with them before God's throne in the final day.

What Mark on Canaan?

My last thought on this list of names concerns Canaan, the place the patriarch and his children were leaving. The descendants of Abraham had been in Canaan for two centuries. With the exception of a brief visit at the time of the burial of Jacob (Genesis 50), it would be 430 years before they would set foot in it again. I wonder what impact they had left on Canaan? Canaan was now being abandoned to sin until her iniquities should be full and judgment would come in the form of the invading Hebrew armies.

If you are a Christian, you are in the world and it is worth asking what influence you are having on the place you occupy. What will those you leave behind think when you have gone on? Will they remember you as a savor of life unto life, as one who was a blessing to their neighborhood? Or will they regard you as one whose presence was harmful and whose departure was cheered?

Robert Candlish asked that question of Israel.

What traces, what memories, what influences have the Israel of God bequeathed, now that the time of their sojourn is for the present over? Alas! how much there is to humble and sadden them, if they will but pause and think, as they cast their last look on the plains and on the people they are leaving behind them! Crimes and sins of heinous dye—instances of unbelief in God and conformity to an ungodly world, unbrotherly dissensions, unneighbourly revenges, scandals, stumbling-blocks, which their evil lusts and passions have put in the way of those whom a consistent walk and holy example and pure and warm charity might have won—such recollections may well overwhelm them with bitter shame and sorrow, as they bid a final adieu to the scenes of their long sojourn in the land of their pilgrimage.

Some recollections of piety and love will doubtless linger, when they are gone, among the people who have been the witnesses of their walk. But ah! how dimly has their light been shining! How uncertain a sound has their trumpet been giving! It would have been good for them, during the years of their witness-bearing for God among ungodly men, had they been anticipating the day when that witness-bearing must cease, and had they asked themselves beforehand how then, at its close, they would be able to stand the retrospect![4]

So too for all who profess to know and serve God! If you are a believer, you must live for and testify to Christ now—while you have the opportunity—for the day is coming when the place where you are living will know you no more.

157

Reunion

Genesis 46:28–34

Now Jacob sent Judah ahead of him to Joseph to get directions to Goshen. When they arrived in the region of Goshen, Joseph had his chariot made ready and went to Goshen to meet his father Israel. As soon as Joseph appeared before him, he threw his arms around his father and wept for a long time.

Israel said to Joseph, "Now I am ready to die, since I have seen for myself that you are still alive."

Then Joseph said to his brothers and to his father's household, "I will go up and speak to Pharaoh and will say to him, 'My brothers and my father's household, who were living in the land of Canaan, have come to me. The men are shepherds; they tend livestock, and they have brought along their flocks and herds and everything they own.' When Pharaoh calls you in and asks, 'What is your occupation?' you should answer, 'Your servants have tended livestock from our boyhood on, just as our fathers did.' Then you will be allowed to settle in the region of Goshen, for all shepherds are detestable to the Egyptians."

From time to time the student of Scripture comes to a chapter division that seems awkward. Such is the case here. Genesis 46 tells of Jacob's departure for Egypt from Beersheba after having been reassured by God, followed by a listing of those who went down with him into Egypt (and perhaps some additional persons who were born there, as in the case of Benjamin's sons or grandsons). The third part of this chapter then tells of his arrival in Egypt and his reception there by Joseph. Unfortunately, this latter portion really belongs with the first part of chapter 47. For the verses in Genesis 46 and 47 are linked together and really tell of a twofold reception of the patriarch: first by Joseph, then by Pharaoh himself. After this, chapter 47 goes on to describe Joseph's management of Egypt during the years of famine.

The interesting thing about these two linked receptions of Jacob in Egypt is that they might well have been different. It had been many years since Joseph had seen his father, and he had risen to a position of great prominence in the meantime. Joseph was second in command in Egypt. Jacob was only a wandering shepherd. How many stories are there in the long history of the world in which a son or daughter, suddenly become prominent, thereafter had no use for the father or mother who gave him or her a start? How many children are there who have been ashamed of a less sophisticated father or a less educated mother? There are many such cases.

Joseph could have been one of these parent-dishonoring, forgetful children. Yet he was not, as the story shows. Instead of a vain, distant approach to his aged father, Joseph actually displayed the most tender affection. The story says that he "appeared before him, threw his arms around his father and wept for a long time" (v. 29).

The other reception, which we will look at in the next chapter, might also have been different. We do not know the reason for this fact, but the story says that "all shepherds [were] detestable to the Egyptians" (v. 34). Since that was so, we can imagine Pharaoh refusing to see Joseph's father and brothers. After all, he was the pharaoh. He had a reputation to sustain and standards to keep up. He could have treated Joseph's relatives badly, as another pharaoh did sometime later. This is not what happened. Pharaoh received Jacob kindly, made polite inquiries about him, and then permitted him and his household to settle in the best portion of Egypt.

How did this happen? How is it that the aged patriarch was received so honorably in Egypt? Joseph is the key. Joseph honored his father, as the law later instructed children to do. And it was for his sake that Pharaoh also acted kindly.

A Great Yearning

The reunion of Joseph and Jacob after twenty-two years is an emotional scene, as it should be. It is one we can understand only if we enter into the emotional experience and yearnings of these men.

When we were studying Joseph's naming of his two sons, Manasseh and Ephraim, I showed how lonely Joseph must have been during his long years in Egypt. Joseph went to Egypt as a slave, and he undoubtedly experienced much hardship and deprivation at the beginning. He was falsely accused and imprisoned. Then, although he rose to prominence as a result of his interpretation of Pharaoh's dream, he still knew himself to be a foreigner in an alien country and must have felt his estrangement there deeply.

How many times, as he lay on his couch at night, would his mind go back to those distant, pleasant days in Canaan? How often, as he went about his work, would a face in the crowd suddenly catch his eye and remind him of Benjamin or the others he used to sport with during his childhood? When Pharaoh gave him Asenath, the daughter of Potiphera, priest of On, as a wife, and when he began to have children—Manasseh, whose name means "forgetting," and Ephraim, "doubly fruitful"—Joseph's life improved. He now had a home of his own and children to warm his heart. But, of course, he had not really "forgotten" his father and brothers. Although God had made him "fruitful," he could not but remember the lost fruit of those earlier days.

Joseph was a lonely man. He missed everyone—his eleven brothers, their children, servants, even the hangers-on! But chiefly he missed his father. We know this because he kept asking about him. In Genesis 43, after the brothers returned to Egypt for the second time, Joseph met with them and made formal inquiry of their well-being. Then he asked, "How is your aged father you told me about? Is he still living?" (v. 27).

Chapter 45 is even more revealing. This is the part of the story in which Joseph revealed himself to the brothers, and the words are these: "I am Joseph! Is my father still living?" (v. 3). Apparently it was his father who was chiefly on his mind. Later in the same chapter he gave instructions designed to bring his father down to Egypt quickly: "Now hurry back to my father and say to him, 'This is what your son Joseph says: God has made me lord of all Egypt. Come down to me; don't delay'" (v. 9). Again, "Tell my father about all the honor accorded me in Egypt and about everything you have seen. And bring my father down here quickly" (v. 13).

There is another detail that opens a window for us into the tender yearning of Joseph's great heart. I refer to his tears. Earlier in his life Joseph had undoubtedly wept on occasion, probably when he was initially sold into slavery, perhaps also during the early years of his mistreatment. But we are not told of Joseph's tears at that time, and it is certainly the case that he mastered his emotions. Instead of feeling sorry for himself he learned to trust God and rejoice in circumstances.

How difficult it was when his family appeared again after two decades! When Joseph put his brothers in prison, God used solitude to soften their hearts and they had confessed, "Surely we are being punished because of our brother. . . . Now we must give an accounting for his blood." We are told that Joseph turned away from them and began to weep (Gen. 42:24). Later, when he saw Benjamin for the first time, Joseph was "deeply moved at the sight of his brother" and "hurried out and looked for a place to weep" (Gen. 43:30). The same thing was true when he finally revealed himself to them: "Then he threw his arms around his brother Benjamin and wept, and Benjamin embraced him, weeping. And he kissed all his brothers and wept over them" (Gen. 45:14–15).

Here is a tender man, whom circumstances had not hardened. We are not surprised when he finally met his father and, as the text says, "threw his arms around his father and wept for a long time" (Gen. 46:29).

I wonder if this might not be a proper encouragement to us to show our emotions when the situation demands it. Most of us are afraid to show emotion. We are afraid to show tears. We should notice that this was not true of the Bible's characters. The men and women of Scripture are not stoics, not emotional cripples. They are persons of great passions. They weep in agony when bad events come. (David wept for days when the child that had been born to him and Bathsheba was dying.) They also weep for joy in blessed circumstances. We would surely be richer if we were able to release our true, proper emotions, as they did.

Jacob's Joy in Joseph

The reunion of Genesis 46:28–34 does not involve just Joseph, however. A reunion requires more than one person. In this case it involved Joseph's father Jacob too. It is worth entering into his experience.

In the second part of this story, when Jacob appears before Pharaoh, Jacob describes the years of his life as having been "few and difficult." Earlier I suggested that this was another example of Jacob's distasteful habit of feeling sorry for himself, since, whatever else may be said of his statement, it was certainly not true that Jacob's years had been few. He was 130 years old at the time, and he was going to live for 17 more years.

Jacob is self-pitying. Nevertheless, although the years had not really been few, they had been difficult. Much of the difficulty he had brought on himself. He had cheated his brother Esau and had found it necessary to run away from home as a result. This led to his living in Haran with his unscrupulous Uncle Laban for twenty years. There, as we know, he was cheated in the matter of his wife and in his wages. Jacob himself said to Laban, "If the God of my father, the God of Abraham and the Fear of Isaac, had not been with me, you would surely have sent me away empty-handed" (Gen. 31:42).

Sometime during those twenty years his mother died; Jacob never saw her again, once he had started out for Haran. Then, most tragic and painful of all, Jacob's beloved wife Rachel died while giving birth to Benjamin. Jacob never recovered from that, because years later in the midst of blessing Joseph's two sons, Manasseh and Ephraim, Jacob's mind wandered back to that event—as the minds of old men will—and he interrupted himself to tell Joseph: "As I was returning from Paddan, to my sorrow Rachel died in the land of Canaan while we were still on the way, a little distance from Ephrath. So I buried her there beside the road to Ephrath" (Gen. 48:7).

In reality, that was the last of Jacob's great losses. But he did not know this, and for a time events appeared quite different. First, Joseph was lost. The brothers intimated that he had been torn to pieces by a wild beast. Then Simeon was retained in Egypt. Finally, Benjamin was taken on the return trip, and Jacob must have trembled violently as he saw all his children, including Benjamin, go off to that distant pagan country. He could not be sure he would ever see them again.

This is the necessary background to Jacob's meeting with Joseph again after all these years. For whatever his sad past experiences may have been, at this point at least everything seemed perfectly and divinely right. Rachel was gone, but Jacob now had her two children, Joseph and Benjamin. And Joseph was even the prime minister of Egypt! What overwhelming joy! No wonder Jacob wept with Joseph and exclaimed at last, "Now I am ready to die, since I have seen for myself that you are still alive!" (v. 30). Jacob meant, "I am content to die. Though I should live longer than Methuselah, my joy can never be greater than it is at this moment."

I make two applications. First, nothing makes a good parent's joy greater than the success, particularly the spiritual success, of a son or daughter. And conversely, nothing makes a parent's heart break more irreparably than the spiritual shipwreck of a willful child. You who are children, be careful to honor your parents by your moral choices. If you have any compassion for them—any love for a mother, any love for a father—do not disgrace them by disgraceful conduct. Do your very best for Christ. Use the talents he has given you—in part through your genetic inheritance from your parents. And then, when you have achieved everything you can achieve, honor them at the same time you place your crowns of achievement at the feet of Jesus.

You may not understand this until you are a parent, but I tell all children this story. A certain Greek at one of the original Olympic games had the joy of seeing three of his sons victorious in three events. His joy was intensified when, following their victories, the sons came and placed on his head the laurel crowns they had earned as the reward of their triumphs. The spectators were overwhelmed at this show of honor for a parent, and they cried out, "Die now; die at once. You can never die in a happier time than this moment."[1] The story says that the father was so overcome that he expired on the spot.

Second, I have this application for parents. If the success of a son or daughter is the greatest of all earthly joys, strive to be good parents. Yearn to be a good mother. Take time to be a good father. What can it profit you to be president of the company or organizer of the most successful charity in town if your son or daughter is not walking with God but is instead going to the devil in high gear? A parent who wins that kind of recognition but who loses his children is an imbecile.

A Last Reunion

But I acknowledge this: Children have a mind of their own, and it is not always possible for a parent, even with the greatest measure of faithfulness or the most selfless outpouring of time, to keep his or her offspring godly. Children will rebel. But since that is the case, do not cease to pray for them. From your perspective the situation may seem hopeless. But remember, it is not hopeless to God. With God all things are possible.

Jacob himself is an encouragement. He raised a large family, but except for Joseph (and probably Benjamin), they were not a godly family. His sons were hard, ruthless men. After the massacre of the Shechemites, Jacob complained to Simeon and Levi that they had made him a stench to the Canaanites and Perizzites (Gen. 34:30). Judah married a Canaanite woman. Reuben dishonored his father by sleeping with his father's concubine Bilhah. Together the sons sold Joseph into Egypt. An ungodly bunch! What cause for grief on Jacob's part! Nothing seemed to change this downward spiraling pattern of sin for nearly forty years.

But then God intervened. God brought the sin of the sale of Joseph to light and achieved a conversion in these brothers. God saved them, and Jacob's joy at his reunion with Joseph was intensified by this additional great blessing. In one sense the brothers were also part of this reunion, for they too had been lost and were found. They had been dead and were resurrected spiritually.

Leslie Flynn tells this story in his study of Joseph's life. One New Year's Eve several men were in a bar, and one of them was Samuel, the son of the local minister. He had been living sinfully for many years and was a disgrace and grief to his father. The town skeptic entered. "I just walked by the church," he said. "They're having a watchnight service over there. Let's have one here." He took a drink and turned to the group. "Brother Jones, will you please lead in prayer?" He was imitating a preacher's tone, and Brother Jones quickly picked it up. He dropped to his knees and gave a mock invocation.

"Now let's sing a hymn," the skeptic went on. Everyone joined in. He turned to Sam. "Sam, your father is the town preacher. Why don't you preach us a sermon for our spiritual good?" Sam did not want to do it, but the others insisted. "Preach on the text: 'The spirit is willing, but the flesh is weak.'" At last Sam agreed to say a few words.

He began by mumbling that in spite of their good intentions—for they all thought themselves good fellows—they would eventually find that the flesh was indeed weak and that, unless they made a break with their old sinful past, they would end in destruction. By this time the sermon sounded so strong that the skeptic jeered, "Why, I think the fool's serious!"

Sam went on. He remembered parts of his father's sermons, words of his long-dead mother, verses he had been taught in Bible school. His audience, who were surprised and then resentful at first, began to sober up and listen in silence. Finally Sam's preaching got through even to himself. He said, "If these things are true, I ought to get down on my knees and pray to God for mercy right now." So he did—right there in the middle of the barroom.

Two others became Christians that night. The skeptic did not, but he was never again heard to mock Christianity. As for Sam, he went to find his father, making his way home from the watchnight service, and told him what had happened. The man's joy was inexpressible. He wept with his son. Then he spent the rest of the night on his knees thanking God for his son's deliverance.[2]

There are parents who have died without seeing the conversion of their erring offspring. But remember that the end is not death. The conclusion is still to be told, and it will be told in the day of that final grand reunion of all the people of God in heaven. In that day, the years of our lives will seem to have been few and difficult, but the best will lie ahead. In that day all tears will have been wiped away, and we will be filled with joy, being from that moment on forever with one another and forever with the Lord.

158

Jacob Blessing Pharaoh

Genesis 47:1–12

Joseph went and told Pharaoh, "My father and brothers, with their flocks and herds and everything they own, have come from the land of Canaan and are now in Goshen." He chose five of his brothers and presented them before Pharaoh.

Pharaoh asked the brothers, "What is your occupation?"

"Your servants are shepherds," they replied to Pharaoh, "just as our fathers were." They also said to him, "We have come to live here awhile, because the famine is severe in Canaan and your servants' flocks have no pasture. So now, please let your servants settle in Goshen."

Pharaoh said to Joseph, "Your father and your brothers have come to you, and the land of Egypt is before you; settle your father and your brothers in the best part of the land. Let them live in Goshen. And if you know of any among them with special ability, put them in charge of my own livestock."

Then Joseph brought his father Jacob in and presented him before Pharaoh. After Jacob blessed Pharaoh, Pharaoh asked him, "How old are you?"

And Jacob said to Pharaoh, "The years of my pilgrimage are a hundred and thirty. My years have been few and difficult, and they do not equal the years of the pilgrimage of my fathers." Then Jacob blessed Pharaoh and went out from his presence.

So Joseph settled his father and his brothers in Egypt and gave them property in the best part of the land, the district of Rameses, as Pharaoh directed. Joseph also provided his father and his brothers and all his father's household with food, according to the number of their children.

I t may be as difficult for a man to be godly *and* a politician as it is for a camel to go through the eye of a needle, but it is not impossible. If you think so, consider Joseph. Joseph was godly. He was a model of consistently upright behavior in a place and time when much lower standards were normative. Yet he was also a successful politician. In fact, he was probably one of the wisest and most successful politicians who has ever lived.

We see his ability strikingly in Genesis 46:28–47:12, where we are told of a twofold reception of Jacob and his family into Egypt: first by Joseph himself, then by the Pharaoh. The latter reception involved some delicacy. To begin with, Joseph's relatives were shepherds and, as he acknowledged, "all shepherds are detestable to the Egyptians" (Gen. 46:34). Moreover, it was Joseph's desire to settle his family in one of the best regions of the land: in Goshen, located in the delta region of the Nile toward the desert. He had already said that he would settle them there. But could he? Did he have the right to dispose thus of Egyptian territory? To make good on his promise it was necessary for Joseph to present his family to Pharaoh and have Pharaoh officially decree the arrangements.

How carefully he went about it! First, Joseph primed his brothers, telling them of his plans to present them to Pharaoh and what they should answer when Pharaoh addressed them. Second, he went to Pharaoh himself, announcing that his father and brothers had come to Egypt and that they were staying (at least temporarily) in Goshen. Third, he presented a delegation of his brothers, five of them. They made a formal request for settlement. Finally, Joseph presented his father to Pharaoh. Thus, "Joseph settled his father and his brothers in Egypt and gave them property in the best part of the land, the district of Rameses, *as Pharaoh directed*" (Gen. 47:11).

In arranging this settlement Joseph showed himself to be completely at ease both with his own people and with the Egyptians. And he was ashamed of neither! This was because he knew that God had chosen him for his task and had given him the spiritual and political wisdom to fulfill it.

A Double Blessing

The climax of these arrangements is the meeting of the aged Hebrew patriarch Jacob and the powerful Egyptian ruler Pharaoh. It is this meeting that should primarily command our attention. The text says:

Then Joseph brought his father Jacob in and presented him before Pharaoh. After Jacob blessed Pharaoh, Pharaoh asked him, "How old are you?" And Jacob said to Pharaoh, "The years of my pilgrimage are a hundred and thirty. My years have been few and difficult, and they do not equal the years of the pilgrimage of my fathers." Then Jacob blessed Pharaoh and went out from his presence.

verses 7–10

The first thing we notice is that Jacob blessed Pharaoh—not only once, but twice! Coming in he blessed Pharaoh, and going out he blessed Pharaoh. The text says, "After Jacob blessed Pharaoh, Pharaoh asked him, . . ." Then, "Jacob blessed Pharaoh and went out from his presence."

Some of the more critical scholars treat these blessings lightly, as if they were no more than a greeting. But that only shows how lightly these scholars regard a spiritual blessing. Their opinion contains no insight at all. To understand this story we need to remember the importance the Hebrews put on words, especially words spoken on formal occasions. A word was not a light thing, as we think it is. A word spoken was a deed done. Words spoken on formal occasions could be expected to have consequences. We cannot imagine that Jacob would have blessed Pharaoh with any lesser thought than that he was conveying on him the favor of almighty God, the God of his fathers Abraham and Isaac. Jacob was giving testimony to the name and nature of the only true God, whom he worshiped, and he was expecting that true God to bless Pharaoh.

But there was more to Jacob's blessing than this. Think of the contrast between this aged Jewish wanderer—a shepherd, like those the Egyptians despised—and the illustrious, glittering Pharaoh. We do not know exactly who this pharaoh was, as I have observed before. But we have paintings and artifacts from the tombs of these pharaohs that give some idea of the splendor in which they lived. The pharaohs were surrounded by servants. One pharaoh boasted of carrying off 232 Asian princes, 323 princesses, and 270 court women in just one campaign. They enjoyed the world's trade. Ships built in Egypt traveled as far as Crete and Phoenicia and up the Nile, bringing back incense, myrrh, gum, and ivory. Cups were made of alabaster. Chairs were made of gold. In fact, gold was everywhere. What splendor there was on Pharaoh's side of this encounter! Jacob blessed Pharaoh. The wealth of the monarch did not intimidate him.

There is this important factor too: According to Egyptian theology, the reigning pharaoh was no mere mortal. Pharaoh was a god, the earthly embodiment of the great sun god Ra. In this unbalanced encounter it would seem that the blessing should have been given by Pharaoh to Jacob. Instead, it was the other way around.

Hebrews 7:7 tells what was happening. This verse is written of Abraham's encounter with Melchizedek in which Melchizedek blessed Abraham. The author of Hebrews wanted to show how great a man this little-known king of Salem was. So, having described the blessing, he wrote, "Without doubt the lesser person is blessed by the greater." That is, Melchizedek, who blessed, is greater than Abraham, who received the blessing.

That is true. But if we are to apply that principle to the story of Jacob's blessing Pharaoh, as we have every right to do, we must say that in spite of worldly appearances, the fact that Jacob blessed Pharaoh showed him to be the greater of the two individuals. Jacob had a blessing to give, and Pharaoh apparently accepted that blessing without protest. It may even be that he acknowledged Jacob's right to bless him by his question concerning Jacob's age, which followed immediately after the blessing. Though probably not then a believer in Jacob's God, Pharaoh may nevertheless have acknowledged a blessing from one who was his senior.

The outlook of Jacob here is something all Christians should have. We tend to be dazzled by the world, particularly its wealth. In the presence of those the world thinks important we stand mute. We need to learn, as Jacob learned, that we as Christians have more to offer the world than the world, for all its wealth and "importance," has to offer us.

What do we have to offer? We have the "treasure" of the gospel (2 Cor. 4:7). We have knowledge of the true God (2 Cor. 4:6), which is salvation (John 17:3). We are the "fragrance of life" to those who respond to our testimony (2 Cor. 2:16). No greater wealth exists. There is no greater good to be done for anyone than to offer him or her the gospel of salvation through Jesus Christ, in whom alone sinners can escape the wrath of God to come.

Jacob had a few great moments in his life, as when he stood up against his Uncle Laban and let the anger and frustration of twenty long years pour out. He has a greater moment later on as he blesses Joseph's two sons, a blessing noted in the Book of Hebrews. But there is no grander scene than the one in this chapter. Instead of bowing abjectly before Pharaoh, as many courtiers would, Jacob drew himself to his full height and gave a blessing. Candlish says, "Lifting up his hands, at the full height of his stature, without one preliminary word of salutation or gesture of compliment to the king, the old man pours out his soul in prayer—asking God's blessing on the royal head—and in God's name, pronouncing the customary blessing of Abraham's house and seed."[1]

What of Pharaoh? We are not told what happened to him, but he had been exposed to two great witnesses to the true God: Joseph, his favorite, and Jacob, Joseph's father. Some generations later Egypt turned from her traditional polytheism to the worship of one God. Akhenaton, husband of Nefertiti, embraced this "heresy." Is it not possible that earlier in the line of these pharaohs was one who, blessed by Jacob, came to know and worship the true God of Israel secretly?

This World, Not Our Home

In the New International Version of his speech, Jacob's words to Pharaoh number just thirty. In Hebrew there are only twenty-one words. Yet these words contain a great deal of godly witness. The first thing we notice—the second chief point of this encounter—is that Jacob refers to life as a "pilgrimage." In fact, he manages to do it twice, just as he managed to bless Pharaoh in the name of the God of his fathers twice. He calls his own life a pilgrimage ("The years of my pilgrimage are a hundred and thirty"), and he calls the lives of his ancestors a pilgrimage ("They do not equal the years of the pilgrimages of my fathers").

A pilgrim is a traveler, a person with no present abode. There is a sense in which this was literally true of Jacob. Most of his life had been involved in some kind of wandering—first from home to Haran, then as a shepherd working for Laban, still later as a wanderer in his own country, moving from Shechem to Bethel to Bethlehem. At last he had come to Egypt.

Still, it is hard to read this statement without suspecting that there is more in it than a mere reference to wanderings. For one thing, Jacob refers to the pilgrimage of his father, Isaac, and Isaac had not really wandered much. It is not mere physical movement that Jacob has in mind but rather the spiritual truth that for God's people this world, however much we may settle into it, is not our true home. We are pilgrims here until we come at last to that heavenly home God has prepared for us.

This is what the author of Hebrews says was in the mind of the patriarchs. He says this in the middle of a discussion of Abraham, but he undoubtedly refers both to Abraham's ancestors and to those who followed Abraham in faith, which includes Jacob. These verses, Hebrews 11:13–16, say:

> All these people were still living by faith when they died. They did not receive the things promised; they only saw them and welcomed them from a distance. And they admitted that they were aliens and strangers on earth. People who say such things show that they are looking for a country of their own. If they had been thinking of the country they had left, they would have had opportunity to return. Instead, they were longing for a better country—a heavenly one. Therefore God is not ashamed to be called their God, for he has prepared a city for them.

Like Abraham, Jacob was "looking forward to the city with foundations, whose architect and builder is God" (v. 10).

Since this was Jacob's true hope, according to Hebrews, it is probably what he had in mind in his one great opportunity to testify before Pharaoh. He was telling the earthly monarch, living in such luxury as the world has seldom known either before or since, that this life is not the end and that there is an eternity to prepare for. He was telling him that life is to be lived as a pilgrimage in which our eyes are set upon God's distant city.

Few things make such an impression on the world as this conviction. The world only has what it can see—cars, homes, bank accounts, nice clothes—and it can hardly think of disposing of these for the sake of something to come. Yet this alone makes a difference. I think of the testimony of Aleksandr Solzhenitsyn, the Russian writer who was confined in the Soviet Union's notorious prison system for eleven years and lived to tell about it in *The Gulag Archipelago*.

Solzhenitsyn saw the dehumanizing practice of the Soviet guards and the equally dehumanizing practices of some of the prisoners. He saw some break and others grow strong. He asked, "So what is the answer? How can you stand your ground when you are weak and sensitive to pain, when people you love are still alive, when you are unprepared? What do you need to make you stronger than the interrogator and the whole trap?"

He answered, "From the moment you go to prison you must put your cozy past firmly behind you. At the very threshold, you must say to yourself: 'My life is over, a little early to be sure, but there's nothing to be done about it. I shall never return to freedom. I am condemned to die—now or a little later. But later on, in truth, it will be even harder, and so the sooner the better. I no longer have any property whatsoever. For me those I love have died, and for them I have died. From today on, my body is useless and alien to me. Only my spirit and my conscience remain precious to me.'

"Confronted by such a prisoner, the interrogator will tremble.

"Only the man who has renounced everything can win that victory."[2]

Shortness of Years

One other point in Jacob's testimony deserves special notice: his reference to his years being short. He calls them "few and difficult." When I referred to this earlier, I suggested that it was another case of Jacob's feeling sorry for himself, since he had already lived 130 years and would live 17 years more. In fact, he could not know how long he might live. He could have lived longer even than Abraham's 175 years or Isaac's 180.

I still believe this. Jacob seems always to be feeling just a bit sorry for himself. Nevertheless, whatever his mood or intention was, his words about years convey a truth Pharaoh needed—and that we also need to hear. Life *is* short. Our days *are* difficult. One of the psalms of Moses says clearly, "The length of our days is seventy years—or eighty, if we have the strength; yet their span is but trouble and sorrow, for they quickly pass, and we fly away" (Ps. 90:10). But the psalm adds the proper application: "Teach us to number our days aright, that we may gain a heart of wisdom" (v. 12). Wisdom is "the fear of the Lord" (Ps. 111:10). Therefore the very shortness of our years should turn us from our own ways to Christ that we may find salvation.

A Better Testimony

Thus far in our study of Jacob's blessing I have applied the text in two ways. First, I applied it to Pharaoh and those like him who need to hear a true Christian testimony. If you are one, learn that (1) true blessing comes from the Bible's God, (2) life is a pilgrimage, and (3) time is short. Prepare to meet God.

My second application was to Christians whom I have challenged to give a testimony as faithful and effective as Jacob's. He gave his testimony in spite of Pharaoh's worldly eminence.

I want to close on this additional note. Jacob's words in Genesis 47:9 are a faithful testimony, as I have indicated. But although they are faithful, they are not as good a testimony as he could have given had he been walking closer to the Lord and feeling less sorry for himself. I say this because some years later Jacob does give a stronger testimony and it is so much stronger that we almost wonder if it is a testimony by the same man. It is in the moment of Jacob's blessing the two sons of Joseph. Jacob says,

> "May the God before whom my fathers
> Abraham and Isaac walked,
> the God who has been my shepherd
> all my life to this day,
> the Angel who has delivered me from all harm
> —may he bless these boys"

Genesis 48:15–16

Think of the contrast between these texts. In the first Jacob says, "My years have been few and difficult." In the second, "God . . . has been my shepherd all my life to this day" and "the Angel . . . delivered me from all harm."

Remember that God had promised to be with Jacob and watch over him wherever he went (Gen. 28:15). Remember that the Angel was Jesus, whom Jacob here explicitly identifies with God, and that he had delivered Jacob even from himself when he wrestled with him in the night beside the Jabbok. Is this second not a better testimony? Is this not a better pattern for our own? True, there is a sense in which Jacob's days had been "few and difficult," as ours often are also. But God, the Good Shepherd, had been with him through them all. There had been much evil, much harm. But Jesus had delivered him. And here at the end is Jacob, testifying to these facts.

Do not wait until you are 130 or 140 to give that testimony. It is unlikely that you will live that long. Give it now. Tell everyone, "God has been my shepherd all my life to this day." And be sure to say, "Jesus has delivered me from harm."

159

Joseph and the Famine

Genesis 47:13–26

There was no food, however, in the whole region because the famine was severe; both Egypt and Canaan wasted away because of the famine. Joseph collected all the money that was to be found in Egypt and Canaan in payment for the grain they were buying, and he brought it to Pharaoh's palace. When the money of the people of Egypt and Canaan was gone, all Egypt came to Joseph and said, "Give us food. Why should we die before your eyes? Our money is used up."

"Then bring your livestock," said Joseph. "I will sell you food in exchange for your livestock, since your money is gone." So they brought their livestock to Joseph, and he gave them food in exchange for their horses, their sheep and goats, their cattle and donkeys. And he brought them through that year with food in exchange for all their livestock.

When that year was over, they came to him the following year and said, "We cannot hide from our lord the fact that since our money is gone and our livestock belongs to you, there is nothing left for our lord except our bodies and our land. Why should we perish before your eyes—we and our land as well? Buy us and our land in exchange for food, and we with our land will be in bondage to Pharaoh. Give us seed so that we may live and not die, and that the land may not become desolate."

So Joseph bought all the land in Egypt for Pharaoh. The Egyptians, one and all, sold their fields, because the famine was too severe for them. The land became Pharaoh's, and Joseph reduced the people to servitude, from one end of Egypt to the other. However, he did not buy the land of the priests, because they received a regular allotment from Pharaoh and had food enough from the allotment Pharaoh gave them. That is why they did not sell their land.

Joseph said to the people, "Now that I have bought you and your land today for Pharaoh, here is seed for you so you can plant the ground. But when the crop comes in, give a fifth of it to Pharaoh. The other four-fifths you may keep as seed for the fields and as food for yourselves and your households and your children."

"You have saved our lives," they said. "May we find favor in the eyes of our lord; we will be in bondage to Pharaoh."

So Joseph established it as a law concerning land in Egypt—still in force today—that a fifth of the produce belongs to Pharaoh. It was only the land of the priests that did not become Pharaoh's.

For many chapters of the story of Joseph's rise to power in Egypt we have had smooth sailing. The narrative has been straightforward, the teaching clear, the applications evident. At this point we run into a problem. It is not that the story is unclear. On the contrary, the account of Joseph's handling of the crisis caused by the seven years of world famine is quite lucid. It tells how Joseph sold the grain he had previously collected and how, after the Egyptians' money had run out, he exchanged grain first for their livestock and then for their lands and even their own persons. In the end the people were in "bondage," held their lands in fief, and were required to give a fifth of what they produced to Pharaoh every year thereafter.

It is not the story that creates the problem. It is rather that Joseph's conduct at this point does not seem compatible with what we expect of a wise and benevolent ruler. By our categories he seems to be a tyrant.

There is this factor too. There is no reason in itself why Joseph may not in fact have become a tyrant. Lord Acton was speaking truth when he said, "All power corrupts, and absolute power corrupts absolutely." It is conceivable that Joseph may have been corrupted by the power he attained and that the Bible is merely reporting this accurately when it records how he conducted himself during the famine years.

But this is not the way these events are related. In a note on "Joseph the Administrator," the *Interpreter's Bible* says this text "is obviously a panegyric upon Joseph. Here is recounted his foresight, his acumen, his clearly calculated and unswerving purpose."[1] The tone of the text is praise for Joseph. Yet, as we read the story, images of Hitler and Stalin (so the *Interpreter's Bible*), not to mention Machiavelli (so Robert Candlish), come to mind.

A Managed National Economy

Thirty years ago the Mid-Continent Publishing Company of Topeka, Kansas, released a small but classic statement of this position by a well-known free enterpriser of the time named John T. Brink. It was entitled *Joseph of*

Egypt and His Managed National Economy. Brink presented three arguments to support his thesis.

First, he remarked at how little attention was paid to this section of Genesis in the Sunday school literature of his day. Apparently the lessons he saw all skipped the section. A widely distributed volume entitled *The Bible, Designed to Be Read as Living Literature* did the same, beginning chapter 47 of Genesis with verse 27. If Brink were writing today, he would note that the popular *Reader's Digest Condensed Bible* also does this. Brink maintained that the chapter was apparently "too hot" for Christians (and Jews) and implied that there was even something of a conspiracy to protect the reputation of one of the Bible's great characters.

Second, Brink interpreted Joseph's initial appearance before Pharaoh as a "nimble-witted" and opportunistic grab for power. He argued that Joseph must have known of the pharaoh's dream beforehand and have been ready with his interpretation as well as his self-serving suggestion that Pharaoh search out a man equal to the task of managing Egypt in the emergency to come. He called it "the age-old pattern of dictatorship: first, establish the misleading and erroneous idea that you alone know all the answers; second, declare that a national emergency is imminent—then see to it, also, that it is created!—and third, without at all seeming to, have yourself set up as the only one that can cope with it successfully."[2]

Most serious of these accusations was the charge that Joseph created the famine by his managed economy. Since no one could "lift hand or foot in all Egypt" without his permission (Gen. 41:44), the gross national product naturally declined, he argued.

Third, Brink castigated Joseph for the "confiscatory terms" he used with the desperate Egyptians in the emergency. He called it "a great wickedness and sin against God to impoverish, dispossess and enslave them."[3] He even suggested that there is a connection (perhaps divine retribution) between the slavery of the Egyptians by Joseph, a Hebrew, and the later enslavement of the Hebrews by the Egyptians.

What should we say to these charges? We may begin by ameliorating some of them. One charge advanced by Brink (and the article on "Joseph the Administrator") is unfounded. Brink argued that Joseph consolidated his rule by displacing large segments of the Egyptian population—on the basis of the King James translation of Genesis 47:21 ("And as for the people, he removed them to cities from one end of the borders of Egypt even to the other end thereof"). The uprooting of people is a trick of dictators who thereby break traditions and family ties and leave the populace open to what we would call "reprogramming." Actually, Joseph did not do this. Newer, more accurate translations say that Joseph "reduced the people to servitude" or "set them to work as slaves" from one end of the kingdom to the other (New International Version, New English Bible, Jerusalem Bible). That may be judged bad enough, but at least it is not the "utterly inhuman act" Brink refers to.

Again, the outcome of the story (at least as the Bible tells it) was praise for Joseph rather than blame. The people are reported as saying, "You have saved our lives. . . . May we find favor in the eyes of our lord; we will be in bondage to Pharaoh" (v. 25).

We must remember that these were exceedingly desperate times. Most of us have never known serious hunger, let alone real famine. We are well nourished. At most we are sometimes troubled by an unavoidable postponement of a meal. This has not been true throughout history, and it is not even true for all people throughout the world today. If we want an idea of what the famine in Joseph's time meant, we might read reports of the famine conditions in North Africa in this decade and study pictures of those ravished by a continuing lack of nutrition. We must see emaciated human forms and pencil-thin children with bloated bellies making their way across dry, barren fields in search of food, or picking their way through deposits of the dead and dying. In such conditions there is little thought for the political system under which one is eventually to live. The concern is just to survive. A person who can help others achieve this is worthy of gratitude.

Finally, the conditions that emerged were not nearly as terrible as they may sound. True, they were not those of free enterprise or a democracy. But there was little of the former and virtually none of the latter in ancient times anyway. The Greeks are probably the first people on earth who can be said to have lived under a democracy, and even that did not last long. What emerged from Joseph's famine policy was something like the feudal system of the Middle Ages. The land was held by the crown or local ruler. The people were serfs. They worked the land and in exchange were cared for and protected by the authority. We would not like this. We prefer our own system with its illusions of government being "of the people, by the people, and for the people." But feudalism was a stable system that often brought prosperity and, in any case, lasted longer than many modern democracies, perhaps even longer than the ultimate life span of our own.

Nor was the 20 percent taxation rate bad. Government gives the impression that taxes are being kept low, particularly for those who can least afford them. But our system is so riddled with hidden taxes that most of us cannot even tell how much tax we are paying. There are a federal income tax, state income tax, city wage taxes, sales taxes, taxes on property—and those are only the taxes we ourselves pay. Hidden in the price of items are taxes levied on the manufacturer, the middleman, and the sales outlets. There may be excise taxes and other taxes as well. Edgar K. Browning and William R. Johnson, in *The Distribution of the Tax Burden*, point out that in American society the tax rate for the bottom third begins at more than 60 percent, averages more than 40 percent for the middle group, and moves up again toward 50 percent for the top fifth of all wage earners. And that does not include the substantial tax increases (including social security tax increases) enacted since 1976.[4]

At the considerably lower taxation rate enacted by Joseph, the country prospered. In later days the pharaohs even became powerful enough to drive out the foreign Hyksos rulers, consolidate their power, and settle many generations of true Egyptian rulers on the throne.

Serving the Lord

Yet it is true that power corrupts and that a people delegate power to those who govern them at their peril. We may defend Joseph. We should defend him, for the Bible praises him and it is unquestionably true that under God he was the means of saving countless thousands if not millions of people during this crisis. Yet we do not live in Joseph's time, and we look back on that history with minds and hopes quite different from those of his contemporaries. While not condemning him, we nevertheless learn three important lessons.

1. *We learn to be on our guard against tyranny.* Joseph did not necessarily tyrannize the Egyptians. On the contrary, the exercise of his authority seems to have been benign. But although Joseph may not have been cruel, others have been, and the course of history suggests that this is most often the case where government is without checks and balances. We may go further than this and argue for a minimum of governmental power—enough only to get the necessary minimum jobs done.

We Americans are particularly vulnerable at this point, because we think of government as being the answer to most human woes. We want government to take care of the poor, when that is clearly a responsibility the Bible puts upon those to whom God has given means. We want government to take care of the elderly, when that is a responsibility the Bible puts upon children. Even businessmen want government to give them special tax benefits, protective tariffs, or subsidies, not recognizing that in this way government takes control even of the way they do business. They protest "big government" but seek to profit from it at the same time.

We should listen to the French writer Jacques Ellul, who writes in rebellion against the stagnant political structures of his own country. He tells us to demythologize the state, arguing, "It is important above all never to permit oneself to ask the state to help us. This means that we must try to create positions in which we reject and struggle with the state, *not* in order to modify some element of the regime or force it to make some decision, but, much more fundamentally, in order to permit the emergence of social, political, intellectual, or artistic bodies, associations, interest groups, or economic or Christian groups totally independent of the state, yet capable of opposing it, able to reject its pressures as well as its controls, and even its gifts."[5]

Sometimes, as in Joseph's day, people fall under the power of an authoritarian state due to unavoidable circumstances. But they should not do so willingly. We must oppose increasing governmental power and intrusion. We must be on guard against tyranny.

2. From Joseph's story we *learn to value the right of private property*. This is a biblical right implied in the eighth of the Ten Commandments: "You shall not steal" (Exod. 20:15). That command is a warning to me that I must not take what belongs to another. But it is also a command for those others that they must not take what is mine. Some have objected to this right of private property on Christian grounds, pointing to the action of the early church, which, according to the Book of Acts, held "everything in common" (2:44) or to God's judgment on Ananias and Sapphira, who were punished for lying about the sale of their property and the gift of part of the proceeds to the Christian assembly (5:1–11). But in the first case the action of the church at Jerusalem was voluntary. No law of God compelled the distribution of private goods. And in the second case the sin of Ananias and Sapphira was in lying about the gift of their property, not in failing to give all of it. In fact, the story actually affirms their right to private property, for in the midst of the incident Peter told Ananias, "Didn't it belong to you before it was sold? And after it was sold, wasn't the money at your disposal?" (v. 4).

Private property is an important biblical right and a great blessing both for the individual and for society. But this has been lost for many, just as it was lost by the Egyptians in Joseph's time. Will it be lost for us one day? It could be. We must value the right of property and defend that right for others if we would retain it ourselves.

3. *We can learn from Joseph's faithful and diligent spirit* during the years of his administration. F. B. Meyer writes of this, noting that like Paul's admonition in Romans 12:11, Joseph was "diligent in business, fervent in spirit, serving the Lord." He wrote:

> Some men do their lifework as if every joint were stiff with rheumatism, or as if they were exuding some adhesive viscus, making their snail progress as painful as it is slow. Others are somnambulists, looking for something and forgetting what they seek; not able to find their tools; always late, taking their passage when the ship has sailed; insuring their furniture when the house is in flames; locking the door when the horse is gone. Beware of imitating any of these. First choose a pursuit, however humble, into which you can rightly throw your energy, and then put into it all your forces without stint. . . .
>
> Make the most of your time. . . . Be methodical. . . . Be prompt. . . . Be energetic. . . .
>
> There are a good many unfaithful servants about in the world; and if you rebuke them, you receive an answer, "My wages are so poor"; "My mistress takes no interest in me"; "I am treated as a slave"; "I shall leave as soon as I can." Stop! Who put you where you are? Had Christ anything to do with it? If not, how came you there without asking his leave? If he had, how dare you leave unless you are sure he calls you away? And as for service—why do you serve? For money, or thanks, or habit? No, *for Christ*. Then do your best for him. Every room you enter is a room in his temple. Every vessel you touch is as holy as the vessels of

the Last Supper. Every act is as closely noticed by him as the breaking of the alabaster box. On every fragment of your life you may write, "Sacred to the memory of Jesus Christ." . . . Those who are called as free are slaves to him; and those who are slaves to men are free in him. And all life reaches its true unity and ideal just in so far as he is its Head and Lord (1 Cor. 7:22).[6]

160

Prospering in Egypt

Genesis 47:27

Now the Israelites settled in Egypt in the region of Goshen. They acquired property there and were fruitful and increased greatly in number.

Afer reporting Joseph's administra-
tion of Egypt during the famine years, the narrative returns to the history
of Israel, saying that "the Israelites settled in Egypt in the region of Goshen.
They acquired property . . . and increased greatly in number." On the surface
these sentences seem like throwaways—"the descendants of Jacob settled
down and did well"—and a transition to the rest of Jacob's story. They are
more than that. They are thought provoking.

For one thing, since they follow the account of Joseph's treatment of the
Egyptians during the famine crisis, they suggest a contrast between the two
peoples. On the one hand, the Egyptians ended the famine years in bondage;
the Israelites ended the same period as free persons. Again, the Egyptians
had lost their lands to the pharaoh; our text says the Hebrews "acquired property." Finally, the text emphasizes that the Israelites "increased greatly in number." This means that the Egyptian years were ones of unprecedented growth

for God's people; the same was not true for those in whose land they were living. In fact, in later years the extraordinary growth of the Hebrews became a matter of concern for the pharaoh, and he decided to reduce their numbers by harsh treatment and eventually by the murder of their male children (cf. Exodus 1).

How quickly did they grow? Henry Morris calculates that the initial group of five (Jacob and his four wives) had grown to a clan of perhaps one hundred (the seventy mentioned in Genesis 46:27 plus the wives of the sons and the grandchildren, who are not mentioned) in fifty years. That works out to a growth rate of just over 6 percent per year. At that rate there would be several million descendants by the time of the exodus 430 years later—and we know from Exodus that there were that many. When Jacob died, seventeen years after the entry into Egypt, the people would have numbered about 270 by the same calculations.

One lesson of this verse is the reality of God's care for his people in a hostile environment. We too are kept free, fruitful, and multiplying in spite of many secular pressures to the contrary.

"Be Fruitful and Multiply"

Other lessons lie in the words "were fruitful and increased greatly in number" because this or a similar phrase occurs twelve times in Genesis.

In Genesis 1:22, after creating the birds, fish, and animals, God blessed his creatures, saying, "Be fruitful and increase in number." Similarly, in Genesis 1:28, after creating man and woman, God said, "Be fruitful and increase in number; fill the earth and subdue it. Rule over the fish of the sea and the birds of the air and over every living creature that moves on the ground."

This was a creation ordinance. The animals were to increase in number, and so were the people. They were to increase in numbers sufficient to fill the earth and exercise their God-ordained rule over the animal world. This mandate was not removed by the fall. We know this because after the flood God repeated the same command in reference both to the animal world and to the flood's human survivors. In Genesis 8:17 God told Noah, "Bring out every kind of living creature that is with you—the birds, the animals, and all the creatures that move along the ground—so they can multiply on the earth and be fruitful and increase in number upon it." To Noah and his family God said, "Be fruitful and increase in number and fill the earth" (Gen. 9:1) and "As for you, be fruitful and increase in number; multiply on the earth and increase upon it" (Gen. 9:7).

A strange thing happened then. Sin entered, and a proper fulfillment of this mandate was thwarted. It was thwarted in three ways.

First, the race as a whole did increase in number, but the culture that resulted was godless. We find this expanding culture diagnosed in Genesis 4. It was a culture of great sophistication, featuring industry and the arts (cf. vv. 21–22). It was focused in great cities (v. 17; cf. Gen. 10:10–12; 11:1–9).

But it was a godless, vicious culture. It is summarized in Genesis 4 by the song of Lamech, in which he boasts of killing a man for merely wounding him.

> "Adah and Zillah, listen to me;
>   wives of Lamech, hear my words.
> I have killed a man for wounding me,
>   a young man for injuring me.
> If Cain is avenged seven times,
>   then Lamech seventy-seven times."
>
> verses 23–24

The antediluvians obeyed the mandate to "be fruitful and multiply," but they did it in such a way that it would have been better had the command been disobeyed. The earth would have been better with fewer rather than more of these people, a judgment God himself made by sending the flood to drown them.

Second, the command to "be fruitful and increase in number" was thwarted in the relationship of the human race to creation. As originally intended, the command subjected creation to the benign rule of those created in God's image. But in their fallen state human beings do either of two wrong things. Either they abuse creation—raping rather than ruling it—or they worship things rather than the God who made them (cf. Rom. 1:25). Again, a decrease rather than an increase of idolaters would best fulfill God's mandate.

The third way in which this creation ordinance to "be fruitful and increase in number" was thwarted is the most interesting. To judge from the early chapters of Genesis, it was not at all difficult for the ungodly race of Cain and his descendants to increase and fill the earth. Indeed, even though the flood destroyed this first godless race, after the flood people were at it again. The interesting thing is that this did not seem to be happening to the godly race, the descendants of Adam through his godly son Seth. In stark contrast to the race of Cain, these seemed barely to keep their line alive, and at the time of the flood there were only eight godly persons: Noah and his wife, his three sons, and their wives. Judging from this history, any reasonable observer would conclude that Satan was winning the struggle for world dominion and that the people of God were soon to perish from the earth.

"I Will Make You Fruitful"

The next stage in the history of this divine mandate began with God's call of Abraham, the first of the Hebrew patriarchs. It is present in God's first words to Abraham, although in other terms: God said that he would make him into "a great nation." In Genesis 17:2, 6, the exact terms of God's original command occur, only now as a promise. God tells Abraham, "I will . . . greatly increase your numbers. . . . I will make you very fruitful; I will make nations of you, and kings will come from you." Later in the same chapter this is said of Ishmael, Abraham's son by Hagar: "And as for Ishmael, I have heard you: I will surely bless him; I will make him fruitful and will greatly increase his numbers. He will be the father of twelve rulers, and I will make him into a great nation" (v. 20).

Being a promise, this was a word to be received by faith. And Abraham did have faith; he believed God, although he did not see the fulfillment of the promise in his lifetime. We know the story. In its original form Abraham's name meant "father of many," but for many years he actually had no children at all. When he was eighty-six he had his son Ishmael by Hagar, because he and Sarah thought that this might be a means of getting God out of a fix and helping to fulfill God's promise.

This was not God's plan. God had promised a son to Abraham and Sarah, and Abraham was later strong in believing this when God spoke to him again, although he was ninety-nine years old by that time. On that occasion God changed his name from Abram, meaning "father of many," to Abraham, "father of a great multitude of peoples." Abraham stuck by that name even though, after the birth of Isaac, he still had only one son in the line of promise.

How the early chapters of Genesis were repeating themselves! In those early chapters the line of the godly was a thin line: Adam gave birth to Seth, who gave birth to Enosh, who gave birth to Kenan, and so on. Later Abraham gave birth to Isaac, and Isaac gave birth to Jacob. The race was still small.

Yet God continued to reiterate the promise. He told Isaac, "I will make your descendants as numerous as the stars in the sky and will give them all these lands" (Gen. 26:4). Isaac later observed, "Now the LORD has given us room and we will flourish in the land" (v. 22). But they did not, at least not numerically. The command to "fill the earth and subdue it" remained only a promise.

Isaac, are you going to believe a promise like that? God promised Abraham that he would increase in number so that his children would be like the stars of heaven and like the sand on the seashore. He told you that your descendants would also be as many as the stars. Look what has happened! Abraham had one son; you are that son. Look at yourself! You have had two children, twin boys. One of them is godless; the other is a cheat. I doubt if anything will come of either of them. Do you still believe God? Do you really believe that you are going to have numerous offspring?

Isaac answers, "Yes, I do." Thus we find him bidding farewell to Jacob, who was being forced to go to Haran because of Esau's threat to kill him, saying, "May God Almighty bless you and make you fruitful and increase your numbers" (Gen. 28:3).

A very few hours after this, Jacob is resting at Bethel on the first stage of his flight. God appears to him and reiterates the promise: "Your descendants will be like the dust of the earth, and you will spread out to the west and to the east, to the north and to the south. All peoples on earth will be blessed through you and your offspring" (Gen. 28:14). After Jacob's return to Bethel twenty years later, God said, "I am God Almighty; be fruitful and increase in number" (Gen. 35:11). In Egypt Jacob referred to this revelation, saying, "God Almighty appeared to me at Luz in the land of Canaan, and there he blessed me and said to me, 'I am going to make you fruitful and will increase your numbers. I will make you a community of peoples'" (Gen. 48:3–4).

But, Jacob, surely you are not going to believe an old promise like that at this point in history! Look how long it has been: three generations! Abraham had one son of promise. Isaac had two. It is true that you have had twelve sons by four wives. But really! Even if you count all the people who went down to Egypt with you—seventy in all (Gen. 46:27)—that is still just a handful of the world population. You mean to tell me you are trusting God's promise after all these years?

"Yes, I am," Jacob answers. "God said that he would make me into a great nation, and I believe him."

In Genesis 47:27 we have the first historical fulfillment of that promise. We have the growth of a people who, while they are in Egypt, become numerous enough later to conquer and possess the Promised Land.

"They Increased in Number There"

Genesis 47:27 is a lesson in God's ability to keep and prosper his people even when others are not flourishing. It is a lesson to be strong in faith in those times—there are many of them—when the fulfillment of the promise is delayed. Those lessons are important in themselves. But there is another significant lesson for believers in our day. It concerns the conditions under which God made the people prosper.

If you were entrusted with arranging the circumstances under which the people of God could best be "fruitful and increase in number," what circumstances would you provide? You would not choose Babylon or Ur; they were wicked, oppressive places. You certainly would not choose Egypt; it was the most pagan, spiritually debased area of the ancient world. Probably you would choose Canaan—a land of some depravity, to be sure, but still a land with a few righteous men, like Melchizedek. Most important, it provided room to grow. Canaan was sparsely settled. There was room for wandering shepherds like Abraham and his descendants. There, if anywhere, people could grow to be a nation.

If you thought that way, you would be wrong. For 215 years the patriarchs lived in Canaan,[1] and during that time the Hebrew clan grew to only about a hundred persons. Under ideal (or nearly ideal) conditions the growth was quite slow. But in Egypt, particularly in the time of persecution, the growth was rapid. In Egypt the people increased to more than two million.

This is God's way, and it is seen not only in numerical growth but in spiritual growth as well. I think here of the condition of the church in China. In a recent article on "The Place of Suffering in the Christian Life" by Jonathan

Chao, director of the Chinese Church Research Center in Hong Kong, there is an interesting comparison between the growth of the church during the relatively peaceful years of the nineteenth and early twentieth centuries and the years since 1950 when the Communists took over. By the end of the early "missionary" period, there were approximately 840,000 Christians. Today, less than four decades later, after the most intense persecutions and great suffering, the church numbers about fifty million, according to Chao's calculations. Chao writes, "In my opinion, the church in China is growing by leaps and bounds because it has suffered for Christ's sake and has learned that suffering is central to Christian maturity and church growth."[2]

Let's apply this to the American church. We have a false sense of well-being in the United States, because we have inherited the legacy of an older, more godly generation. We have great buildings, successful programs, television-type personalities. But the church is stagnant. Growth, where it exists, is often artificial, and Christianity has little impact on our decaying culture.

What is the trouble? There are probably multiple causes, but one great cause is that we are clearly too materialistic. God said that we are to be in the world but not of it. Instead, we are very much of the world and not even in it to a meaningful degree.

What will happen? I suggest that God will allow hard times to come upon the American church. We will be attacked and harassed—as we already are in some matters. We will be forced out of the mainstream of society. We will be made to pay a price for our faith so that it becomes costly rather than beneficial to follow Jesus. That is not bad. Like the church in China, it will be in such circumstances that the strength of true Christian commitment will be seen and the church will begin to be fruitful and increase in numbers again.

I also apply this to individuals who are suffering, whether by personal attacks or by such impersonal blows as sickness, loss of a job, or accidents. Events like these are not outside the sovereign will of God but are sent by him—lovingly and for our own spiritual growth and fruitfulness. Jesus referred to his disciples as branches and himself as the vine, saying, "Every branch that does bear fruit he prunes so that it will be even more fruitful" (John 15:2).

Jonathan Chao reports that an American student came to the Research Center in Hong Kong. Before he left America, a Christian friend had asked him, "If God loves the Chinese church so much, why did he allow so much suffering to come upon it?" The young man had no answers to the question. But then he traveled to China and had personal fellowship with Christians who had gone through suffering and were still zealously doing the work of evangelism. This completely changed his life. "I now have the answer to my friend's question," he told Mr. Chao. "I am going back to America and ask him this question: If God loves the American churches so much, why hasn't he allowed us to suffer as he did the church in China so that our faith might be strengthened, our lives purged and our relationship with Christ deepened to serve him wholeheartedly?"[3]

Christianity is not something that requires ideal conditions to survive. It thrives best in hardships. In our hardships God's strength is made perfect in weakness, and godliness springs like a root from dry ground.

161

Jacob's Last Days

Genesis 47:28–31

Jacob lived in Egypt seventeen years, and the years of his life were a hundred and forty-seven. When the time drew near for Israel to die, he called for his son Joseph and said to him, "If I have found favor in your eyes, put your hand under my thigh and promise that you will show me kindness and faithfulness. Do not bury me in Egypt, but when I rest with my fathers, carry me out of Egypt and bury me where they are buried."

"I will do as you say," he said.

"Swear to me," he said. Then Joseph swore to him, and Israel worshiped as he leaned on the top of his staff.

The Bible is a book of life, and it follows that rarely does it deal at length with deathbed scenes. The death of Abraham is described in just a few verses, the chief verse saying, "Then Abraham breathed his last and died at a good old age, an old man and full of years; and he was gathered to his people" (Gen. 25:8). Isaac's death is told briefly. So is the death of Joseph. In the New Testament the deaths of most chief characters, including that of the great apostle Paul, are not even recorded.

1140

In light of this understandable treatment it is somewhat surprising to find that the death of Jacob, the last of the great patriarchs of Genesis, is reported extensively. The account of Jacob's death begins near the end of Genesis 47, but he does not actually die until the final verse of chapter 49. Even then the story is not over: the first half of chapter 50 tells of Jacob's burial. Altogether, parts of four chapters are given to this account—a total of seventy-three verses. There are three deathbed scenes. First, Jacob meets with Joseph, his favored son, and exacts a promise that he will bury him in Canaan rather than in Egypt. Second, Jacob meets with Joseph and Joseph's sons, Manasseh and Ephraim, and blesses them. Finally, Jacob calls all his sons to him, including Joseph, and utters a prophecy about the future of the tribes that were to descend from them.

One commentator remarks on how natural this series of encounters is.[1] It has the ring of truth about it and is one of the most delightful human stories in the Bible. I think it illustrates that beautiful fourth stanza of the hymn "How Firm a Foundation."

> E'en down to old age all my people shall prove
> My sovereign, eternal, unchangeable love;
> And when hoary hairs shall their temples adorn,
> Like lambs they shall still in my bosom be borne.

Israel Must Die

Yet it is a deathbed scene! There were moments earlier in the story when Jacob thought about dying. When he was presented to Pharaoh by Joseph after he had come to Egypt, Jacob undoubtedly thought that he was then at the end of his life's journey: "The years of my pilgrimage are a hundred and thirty. My years have been few and difficult, and they do not equal the years of the pilgrimage of my fathers" (Gen. 47:9). But Jacob lived seventeen years after that, no doubt to his own surprise. What sustained him? Perhaps the climate of Egypt or even the relative ease of his new life in Goshen. No doubt also the presence of his beloved son Joseph. In Canaan the thought that he had lost Joseph was inclining his head to the grave. But in Egypt he had Joseph again and life was full. These were beautiful years in the life of a man whose days had indeed been difficult.

Yet Jacob had to die, as do all. The Bible says, "Man is destined to die once, and after that to face judgment" (Heb. 9:27). In Genesis the King James Version suggests the same truth when it translates the clause "when the time came near for Israel to die" by saying, "Israel *must* die."

Death is inevitable. Every day our death approaches nearer. George Lawson wrote on this passage, "Today we are twenty-four hours nearer to our latter end than yesterday, and three hundred and sixty-five days nearer to it than we were a year ago. At all times they are inexcusable who are warned by the decay of their strength that death is approaching, if they banish it from their thoughts, when they ought to be hastening their preparations to meet it with firmness."[2] Jacob was not banishing thoughts of death. Instead of rejecting the inevitable, he embraced it as a believer in God and prepared to testify to his faith to the end.

A Future in the Land

Jacob's chief concern in these verses is that he not be buried in Egypt, but that his body be returned to Canaan for burial in the tomb of his fathers at Machpelah. This was not a superstitious wish or even merely the common desire of a dying person to be returned to one's own country. In Jacob's case, the desire to be buried in Canaan concerned God's promises to him about the land. God had promised great things to Abraham, Isaac, and Jacob. He had promised to bless them, making them into a great nation, the members of which would be like the stars of heaven or the sand of the seashore. He had promised to send a deliverer through that nation, the Messiah. Finally, he had promised to give them a land that would be a possession for themselves and their seed forever.

These promises were almost always given together. So when Jacob required Joseph to bury his body in the Promised Land, it was like saying that he continued to stand on God's promises. He wanted his body to lie in the land where God would again one day bring the Jewish people and where the Messiah would eventually be born and perform the work of redemption.

This remarkable thing amounts to a Christian or biblical view of world history—the idea that God is at work in history and that, because of God's working, our own place in history is meaningful, even to the point of what we do with our bodies.

The world has three basic views of history. The modern view is that of *inevitable historical progress,* symbolized by that Time-Life newsreel series of half a generation ago entitled "The March of Time." Those who lived through that era and saw those newsreels recall the stirring martial music, the voice of an enthusiastic announcer, the fast-moving sequence of scenes from around the world. The title seemed to say it all. Time did seem to be marching along, perhaps even racing. No one doubted that—undergirded by the philosophy of Darwinian evolution and buttressed by the apparent gains in science, medicine, and technology—the march was forward and the race was to the strong. They would have argued that history was progress and progress was inevitable. They would have said the Golden Age was just around the corner.

Unfortunately, that vision of the Golden Age tarnished. World War II and the many smaller but no less horrible wars since have all but dispelled the notion. But so has a declining faith in Darwinism and science as saviors. Thomas Bethell, in an article for *Harper's Magazine,* described evolution as being fatally flawed and in the process of being discarded by scientists. He wrote, "It is beginning to look as though what he [Darwin] really discovered was nothing more than the Victorian propensity to believe in progress."[3] As for science, although its benefits are not to be denied, it is increasingly difficult to speak of inevitable progress when we have developed the frightening ability to blow ourselves off the face of the planet.

The second view of history was that of the Greeks and some other ancient peoples. It viewed time as *a circle that constantly turned on itself.* The Greeks knew that there was change in history, but it was change that always returned to its starting point just as the planets or seasons do. Individuals would rise to prominence. Nations would become powerful. But neither individuals nor nations would get anywhere by their rise, nor would others advance by their fall. Epicurus said, "Nothing new happens in the universe, if you consider the infinite time past" (*Fragments,* 55). Marcus Aurelius wrote, "Those who come after us will see nothing new, nor have those before us seen more; but in a manner, he who is forty years old, if he has any understanding at all, has seen by virtue of the uniformity that prevails all things that have been and all that will be" (*Meditations,* xi, 1).

The Greek view of history can be symbolized by the carnival barker's description of his ferris wheel or the gambler's description of his spinning wheel of chance: "'Round and 'round and 'round she goes, and where she stops nobody knows!'"

The modern view of history is flawed because "natural" selection does not explain evolution and because its corresponding faith in man is misplaced. The Greek view is inadequate because it denies meaningful change and thus real meaning. The only hope for the individual is to escape from history. But notice, this is not the way Jacob thought, nor was it the outlook of any of the biblical characters. These men operated in the framework of a universe created and spoken to by God. This God interacted with his people and made promises to them. This God was in history and was also over history, so that the meaning of a person's life is seen not merely in what happens to him at one particular moment or even in all the moments that make up his earthly existence but rather in the total flow of history of which each individual is a part. Jacob testified to this outlook when he gave instructions to Joseph to carry him out of Egypt and bury him in Canaan.

I wish more Christian people could have this faith. I wish more would declare to the world that we do not gain our worth by what we accomplish or even by what the whole race can do through its technology. Our worth is in our being made by God, in his image, and in being placed by him within the framework of what he is doing in history. One way we can do this is by identifying with God's people and with the places God is working.

At Rest with the Fathers

The verses we are studying are only a small section of the account of Jacob's final days, and the verses in which he speaks are just three. In the New International Version Jacob's speech requires only fifty-two words. Yet in these few words Jacob gives another great testimony to his faith by saying that his death will mean being at "rest with [his] fathers" (v. 30).

Some scholars have argued that this means only that Jacob would die, that references to being with or going to one's fathers only mean being buried in the same plot of ground as one's ancestors. But that is patently not the case here. In some accounts the ideas of burial and "going to the fathers" might be construed as synonyms. But here there is a clear distinction. Jacob speaks of his death as resting with his fathers, but he adds that besides this he wants his body to be taken back to Canaan and to be buried where the bodies of his ancestors lie interred. The second of these references is to burial. But the first obviously is an expression of Jacob's faith in a life to come. This has been the faith of the people of God through all the many ages of God's faithful dealings with them.

When Abraham died, we read, he was "gathered to his people" (Gen. 25:8). That is, he was taken to paradise, where he enjoyed the presence of God and fellowship with those who had died in faith before him: Adam, Abel, Seth, Enosh, and others. When Isaac died, he was "gathered to his people" (Gen. 35:29)—that is, united with his father, Abraham, and the others.

When David's son by his wife Bathsheba died and his servants were afraid to tell him of the death, thinking that his sorrow would now know no bounds, David rose up and worshiped God, explaining, "While the child was still alive, I fasted and wept. I thought, 'Who knows? The LORD may be gracious to me and let the child live.' But now that he is dead, why should I fast? Can I bring him back again? I will go to him, but he will not return to me" (2 Sam. 12:22–23).

The writer of Psalm 49:10–15 points out that all persons die, the wise and the foolish. But he distinguishes between the two classes. Those who trust in themselves are "like sheep . . . destined for the grave; . . . death will feed on them." The godly have hope. The psalmist says, "But God will redeem my life from the grave; he will surely take me to himself" (v. 15). Psalm 73 contains a great testimony:

> Yet I am always with you;
>   you hold me by my right hand.
> You guide me with your counsel,
>   and afterward you will take me into glory.
> Whom have I in heaven but you?
>   And earth has nothing I desire besides you.
> My flesh and my heart may fail,
>   but God is the strength of my heart
>   and my portion forever.

verses 23–26

Job wrote

> I know that my Redeemer lives,
>   and that in the end he will stand upon the earth.
> And after my skin has been destroyed,
>   yet in my flesh I will see God;
> I myself will see him
>   with my own eyes—I, and not another.
>
>   Job 19:25–27

There are differences between this imperfect, groping faith of Old Testament believers and the completed, settled faith of Christians founded on the bodily resurrection of Jesus and his specific teaching. There is progression from hope to more hope, from dim perception to the full light of a later revelation. But it is the same hope because it is in the same God!

This is what Jacob had. He had lived with the Lord throughout a long and difficult life, and he had learned through those years that the God of his fathers could be trusted. God had made promises and he had kept them. So whether it was the promise of his continuing presence—"I am with you and will watch over you wherever you go, and I will bring you back to this land. I will not leave you" (Gen. 28:15)—or the promise of life beyond the grave, Jacob rested in that promise and, when he died, testified to his faith in the God who gave it.

Israel Worshiped

These verses tell of one more thing Jacob did. We are told that after Joseph had sworn to him that he would fulfill his request and bury him in Canaan, "Israel worshiped as he leaned on the top of his staff" (v. 31).[4] Israel worshiped! That is, Jacob praised God as he was dying. Interestingly, this is what Jacob is praised for in the Book of Hebrews. From the many events of Jacob's long life the author of Hebrews picks these final moments and says of him, "By faith Jacob, when he was dying, blessed each of Joseph's sons, and worshiped as he leaned on the top of his staff" (Heb. 11:21).

Testimony to the grace and faithfulness of God is valuable at any period of life and in any circumstances. But it is especially meaningful at the end of life as death threatens. To stand at that point and look back over a long life in which God has neither left you nor forsaken you and praise him for it—that is a great testimony. It is one of the chief opportunities of old age.

I saw this recently. I participated in the funeral service of an elderly member of Tenth Presbyterian Church, and although there were sad moments—closing the casket and thus saying good-bye for a time to one who has long been loved—there was nevertheless a strong testimony as those who remained spoke of the faith of the one departed and witnessed of God's grace to relatives and friends alike. I was particularly struck by the closing moments later on at the grave site. At the request of the closest relatives we all sang a hymn to God's faithfulness:

> My hope is built on nothing less
> Than Jesus' blood and righteousness;
> When all around my soul gives way,
> He then is all my hope and stay.
> On Christ, the solid Rock, I stand;
> All other ground is sinking sand.

That is the victory that overcomes the world, the victory of faith.

162

The Living Church

Genesis 48:1–11

Some time later Joseph was told, "Your father is ill." So he took his two sons Manasseh and Ephraim along with him. When Jacob was told, "Your son Joseph has come to you," Israel rallied his strength and sat up on the bed.

Jacob said to Joseph, "God Almighty appeared to me at Luz in the land of Canaan, and there he blessed me and said to me, 'I am going to make you fruitful and will increase your numbers. I will make you a community of peoples, and I will give this land as an everlasting possession to your descendants after you.'

"Now then, your two sons born to you in Egypt before I came to you here will be reckoned as mine; Ephraim and Manasseh will be mine, just as Reuben and Simeon are mine. Any children born to you after them will be yours; in the territory they inherit they will be reckoned under the names of their brothers. As I was returning from Paddan, to my sorrow Rachel died in the land of Canaan while we were still on the way, a little distance from Ephrath. So I buried her there beside the road to Ephrath" (that is, Bethlehem).

When Israel saw the sons of Joseph, he asked, "Who are these?"

"They are the sons God has given me here," Joseph said to his father.

Then Israel said, "Bring them to me so I may bless them."

Now Israel's eyes were failing because of old age, and he could hardly see. So Joseph brought his sons close to him, and his father kissed them and embraced them.

1147

Israel said to Joseph, "I never expected to see your face again, and now God has allowed me to see your children too."

Some years ago I was in Chicago for a taping of the *Chicago Sunday Evening Club*, the most widely viewed Christian television program in that area. I was to give the sermon this particular day. But before I began, the format called for a briefer, testimony-type segment called "Living Philosophy." I was struck by this name. So some years later, when we decided to incorporate a testimony time into our morning services at Tenth Presbyterian Church in Philadelphia, I picked up on that title and called our segment "The Living Church." For a while that testimony time became one of the most appreciated portions of our services.

We have something like a "living church" testimony in the words of Jacob in Genesis 48. The patriarch had been declining for some time. When he first sensed that the time of his death was approaching he called Joseph and extracted the promise concerning his burial recorded at the end of chapter 47. But Jacob did not die immediately, and Joseph, being a busy man, was unable to wait in Goshen indefinitely. Apparently Joseph returned to his duties, leaving instructions to call him if Jacob grew worse.

One day word came: "Your father is ill" (Gen. 48:1). So Joseph returned to his father, this time taking along his two sons, Manasseh and Ephraim. What follows is the high point of Jacob's long life. Hearing that Joseph was coming, Jacob collected his little remaining strength, sat up boldly in bed, and took charge of his death.

We can almost hear the protests of Jacob's attending family members: "Oh, don't do that, Father! You're too weak to sit up. Here, I'll help you lie down." But Jacob was not to be dissuaded. He was dying, but he was still alive. And while he was alive he would act the patriarch and testify to the greatness of God and bestow blessings. One commentator writes, "What he [Jacob] did on his deathbed was the magnificent triumph of his life. Like a runner who had been outdistanced by others, he now got his second wind and swept by them all, taking the prize."[1] This is the perseverance of a true child of God to the very end.

Strikingly, this scene is picked up by the author of the Book of Hebrews as additional evidence of Jacob's genuine faith: "By faith Jacob, when he was dying, blessed each of Joseph's sons, and worshiped as he leaned on the top of his staff" (Heb. 11:21).

First, Last, and Always

This portion of Jacob's final testimony deserves analysis, and the first thing we notice as we look at it carefully is that it begins and ends with God. Jacob began his testimony with God's appearance to him at Bethel, where his spiritual life started: "*God Almighty* appeared to me at Luz in the land of Canaan, and there he blessed me . . ." (v. 3, my emphasis). He ended it by referring to God's goodness in allowing him to see not only Joseph but Joseph's children: "I never expected to see your face again, and now *God* has allowed me to see your children too" (v. 11, my emphasis).

Happy is the life that begins and ends with God! Blessed is the testimony that sees all life from that perspective!

This was not always the case with Jacob. Earlier in his life Jacob had been more noted for his neglect of God than for his attention to him. In fact, the first time the name of God was found on his lips he was lying. He had been pushed by his mother to impersonate his older brother Esau to gain Isaac's blessing. So he dressed in Esau's clothes, covered his arms and the smooth part of his neck with goatskins, and then came to his blind father bearing the kind of tasty food Isaac liked and which he had sent Esau to prepare. His father was suspicious about his quick return. "How did you find it so quickly, my son?" Isaac asked.

"The LORD your God gave me success," Jacob replied (Gen. 27:20).

The next time Jacob mentioned the name of God was at Bethel, where God gave him the vision of a great stairway reaching from earth to heaven. Jacob was frightened on this occasion. He said, "Surely the LORD is in this place, and I was not aware of it. How awesome is this place! This is none other than the house of God; this is the gate of heaven" (Gen. 28:16–17). Two chapters later Rachel is chiding Jacob because she did not have children, and Jacob was angry. He said, "Am I in the place of God, who has kept you from having children?" (Gen. 30:2). In all these chapters Jacob shows a nodding acquaintance with God and a dependence on the promises of God received at Bethel. But we cannot feel that he was really close to God. He seems never to pray. He is always trusting in his own cleverness rather than waiting on God's sovereign direction of his life.

At the end this had changed. Jacob had not always been close to God, but God had been close to Jacob. He had called him at Bethel, and he had directed his paths and fulfilled his promises to him for all the many long years in which he raised his family and eventually settled them in Canaan. Jacob recognized that now and wanted to give testimony to it. So he began his testimony with God: "God appeared to me at Luz," and he ended it in a similar manner: "Now God has allowed me to see your children too."

This is what Jacob wanted to pass on to his children. He was right to want this. Is it not sad that so many people try to pass on almost everything else and neglect this one thing that alone is of eternal importance? We try to leave our children well situated in life, with good educations, useful friends and contacts, and sometimes good bank accounts or other assets. But these can perish overnight. It is the knowledge of God and faith in God that alone remain.

The commentator I mentioned earlier wrote of Jacob: "[He] wished his sons to have, as their last memory of him, the scene in which he gave God all the credit, all the glory. This would enable them to stand firm in the days of slavery and in the furnace of judgment. The greatest legacy any man can leave to his children is unswerving faith in God and the memory of a testimony that gave God all the glory and witnessed to his unchanging faithfulness. God says that he is not ashamed to be called the God of Jacob because in this scene the spirit triumphed over the flesh and God was acknowledged as all in all. When our earthly inheritance is gone, when lands are eroded, stocks depreciated and money spent, the legacy of unwavering faith in God will be the most that we can pass on to our children."[2]

My parents did exactly this on the occasion of their fiftieth wedding anniversary. The children and grandchildren had collected from various corners of the country: the Northeast, Alabama, California. All were there—the children, their husbands and wives, and the grandchildren. We had a dinner. My sisters gave remembrances. I gave a tribute. Then my parents spoke and testified to the faithfulness of God throughout the long years of their lives together. My mother in particular shared three passages of Scripture:

Psalm 91:14–16: "'Because he loves me,' says the LORD, 'I will rescue him; I will protect him, for he acknowledges my name. He will call upon me, and I will answer him; I will be with him in trouble, I will deliver him and honor him. With long life will I satisfy him and show him my salvation.'"

Psalm 121:7–8: "The LORD will keep you from all harm—he will watch over your life; the LORD will watch over your coming and going both now and forevermore."

Proverbs 3:5–6: "Trust in the LORD with all your heart and lean not on your own understanding; in all your ways acknowledge him, and he will make your paths straight."

My mother concluded by saying, "I want you children especially to remember that your grandparents were Christians and that we tried to serve the Lord Jesus Christ together faithfully for fifty years. We found him to be faithful. He has never failed us." Can you think of any legacy greater than that? There is nothing so honoring to God as faithful testimony.

Thanksgiving for Blessings

When life's portrait is framed by the great reality of God, there are effects in other areas. These too are seen in an examination of Jacob's testimony. The first is Jacob's thankfulness to God for past blessings.

This is an important thing, because without it people who are entering old age fall into one of two destructive errors. Either they think themselves chiefly responsible for their own blessings and are therefore always bragging about them; or they feel sorry for themselves, for the blessings they have missed, and are therefore bitter at the memory of those who have (or are thought to have) wronged them. We hear old persons say, "Remember when

I worked out that deal? They thought I couldn't do it, but I did. I sure showed them." Or they boast of how smart they were: "I was the smartest person in my class at the University of Pennsylvania. I was better than anyone else in my first job." A little testimony goes a long way. So does complaining: "I would have gotten that job if it hadn't been for Joe Smith. You don't know how hard my life has been."

There was nothing of this at this stage in Jacob's life. So his old age is pleasant and beautiful instead of being a horror. Jacob is thankful for all that God has done for him in his long life. He begins by remembering God's gracious promises to him at Bethel. He claims those promises. Then he ends by thanking God for the blessing of seeing Joseph and even Joseph's two sons.

Consolation for Sorrows

The second effect of a God-oriented outlook on life is that it gives strong consolation for life's sorrows. Jacob had much to thank God for, but there had been hard times too. If he had possessed a secular outlook, these might have made him bitter. Instead he saw these as being in the hand of God and was therefore consoled. Sorrow was there, but there was no anger.

This portion of Jacob's testimony is the most touching of all his recorded utterances, and it is one of the most touching scenes in all Scripture. Rachel had been Jacob's true love. Although he had married two women (the sisters Rachel and Leah) and had also had children by two others (their handmaidens, Bilhah and Zilpah), Rachel was nevertheless the one he had loved intensely from the very first moment he saw her at Haran. She was little more than a child then. But he promised her father Laban that he would work for her for seven years, and when he was cheated by being given Leah instead of Rachel, he was willing to work seven more years for her. The Scripture says that he counted this long period as but a moment, so great was his love for her.

Well, Jacob had not set out to say anything about Rachel. He was telling of God's appearance to him at Bethel and of his desire to adopt Joseph's sons as his own, thus bringing them into the covenanted blessings that had been promised to him. But as he spoke he was looking into the face of Joseph, his beloved first son by Rachel, and no doubt something of her beauty in Joseph's face suddenly brought a vision of Rachel back to his mind, and he digressed from his point, as old persons will, and began to talk about her. "'As I was returning from Paddan, to my sorrow Rachel died in the land of Canaan while we were still on the way, a little distance from Ephrath. So I buried her there beside the road to Ephrath' (that is Bethlehem)."

I find that immensely touching. As he looks at Joseph, Jacob's mind goes back to that distant day when Joseph himself was just a boy. He sees the road to Ephrath and remembers how Rachel went into labor, how the caravan was stopped, and how a tent was pitched for her in which to give birth. He relives the birth of Benjamin, followed quickly by the death of Rachel. He remembers the burial, which left a void in his heart that nothing in the years since had filled. Yet Jacob is not bitter. His loss was great, but the consolation of the Lord was equal to his loss.

I feel sorry for those who go through life without God, particularly as they experience the natural human allotment of life's sorrow. What a blessing to see God's hand even in the sorrows and be turned from bitterness to blessing!

Strength for Present Tasks

The third effect of Jacob's viewing life as bounded by God is that he was strengthened to do what he needed to do in the present circumstances. Physically he was not strong. It would seem from this story that he was already too enfeebled to stand; he merely drew himself up in bed at news of Joseph's coming. His eyesight was failing. Although the sons of Joseph were standing before him and although he had been talking about them, he nevertheless had to ask Joseph who the two boys were. Because of his wandering train of thought, we are probably to think that his mind was also somewhat less sharp than it had been.

Failing? Yes, but not utterly, and not beyond ability to do what God required of him. He knew the truth of Moses' prophetic words, spoken later on: "As thy days, so shall thy strength be" (Deut. 33:25 KJV).

Jacob had strength for two tasks. First, he had strength to show the sons of Joseph affection. It is a touching scene. Manasseh and Ephraim had been standing by as Jacob launched into his final testimony. But when Jacob noticed them and called them forward to bless them, they must have fallen at the old man's knees. For his part he must have thrown his feeble arms around them in an embrace. Sometimes the young draw back from such tender moments, fearing emotion. But affection is a beautiful thing, and moments like this should be cherished, not shunned. Here was a good man and a good family, showing love as the children of God always should show love in their relationships with one another.

Second, Jacob had strength to admonish and bless the two boys. I do not know what was in his mind as he pronounced this blessing, but I suspect that Jacob may have been thinking of the particular temptations in Egypt to which these boys were subjected. Joseph had been born in Canaan and had spent his early years in the patriarch's tents. Moreover, he had risen to power in Egypt through much personal abuse and suffering, which tend to stabilize a person.

Not so with Manasseh and Ephraim. They had never known Canaan. They were born in Egypt and lived amid the glories of the court. Moreover, they were sons of Joseph, Pharaoh's favorite, and Asenath, the daughter of a priest. Joseph, writes one commentator, "had it in his power to procure the most elevated stations for his sons. Asenath, the daughter of one of the noblest families in Egypt, might think it a hard matter to have her children placed in the same manner with the abhorred shepherds of Palestine. What if Manasseh and

Ephraim should be tempted to think that it was better to enjoy the dignities of Egypt than to suffer the reproach of the God of Abraham!"[3]

Jacob was determined to avert such a development. He collected his strength, adopted Manasseh and Ephraim as his own sons, and blessed them, saying: "May they be called by my name and the names of my fathers Abraham and Isaac, and may they increase greatly upon the earth" (Gen. 48:16).

Earlier in life Jacob had been given the name "Israel," which signified the change in Jacob once he had been brought to submit fully to God as the result of the angel's wrestling with him at Jabbok. There were many times after that when Jacob was nevertheless still called Jacob, no doubt with deep meaning. Although God's child, Jacob still often operated as an immature believer. He lived in the flesh rather than in the power of the Spirit.

But I notice that at the end, in these verses that describe Jacob's last acts and final testimony, the name Israel is prominent and the name Jacob hardly occurs. "*Israel* rallied his strength and sat up on the bed" (v. 2, my emphasis). "When *Israel* saw the sons of Joseph, he asked, 'Who are these?'" (v. 8, my emphasis). "Then *Israel* said, 'Bring them to me so I may bless them'" (v. 9, my emphasis). "*Israel's* eyes were failing because of old age. . . . So Joseph brought his sons close to him, and his father kissed them and embraced them" (v. 10, my emphasis). "*Israel* said to Joseph, 'I never expected to see your face again, and now God has allowed me to see your children too'" (v. 11, my emphasis).

Israel had been conquered by God, and that is why he saw life from God's perspective. That is why he had strength to rally himself even in old age and point the new generation in a right direction. We need such men and women today. Will you be one? We need you for the gospel's sake and for the sake of our children.

163

A Faithful Blessing

Genesis 48:12–20

Then Joseph removed them from Israel's knees and bowed down with his face to the ground. And Joseph took both of them, Ephraim on his right toward Israel's left hand and Manasseh on his left toward Israel's right hand, and brought them close to him. But Israel reached out his right hand and put it on Ephraim's head, though he was the younger, and crossing his arms, he put his left hand on Manasseh's head, even though Manasseh was the firstborn.

Then he blessed Joseph and said,

> *"May the God before whom my fathers*
>   *Abraham and Isaac walked,*
> *the God who has been my shepherd*
>   *all my life to this day,*
> *the Angel who has delivered me from all harm*
>   *—may he bless these boys.*
> *May they be called by my name*
>   *and the names of my fathers Abraham and Isaac,*
> *and may they increase greatly*
>   *upon the earth."*

When Joseph saw his father placing his right hand on Ephraim's head he was dis-
pleased; so he took hold of his father's hand to move it from Ephraim's head to Manasseh's
head. Joseph said to him, "No, my father, this one is the firstborn; put your right hand
on his head."

But his father refused and said, "I know, my son, I know. He too will become a people,
and he too will become great. Nevertheless, his younger brother will be greater than he,
and his descendants will become a group of nations." He blessed them that day and said,

> *"In your name will Israel pronounce this blessing:*
> *'May God make you like Ephraim and Manasseh.'"*

So he put Ephraim ahead of Manasseh.

One of the great characters of Greek literature is Tiresias of Thebes, the blind prophet whom Odysseus consults in the course of his return to Ithaca from Troy. Tiresias lacks physical sight. But his blindness to things about him is compensated by his gift of seeing things to come.

There is something like this in the final chapters of Genesis. Jacob is coming to the end of his life and is about to die at the age of 147 years. He has been failing for some time. When his beloved son Joseph comes to see him, bringing his two sons, Manasseh and Ephraim, Jacob can only pull himself up on the bed to bless them. Moreover, Jacob's eyes were failing. The text says, "Now Israel's eyes were failing because of old age, and he could hardly see" (Gen. 48:10). Failing? Yes. But although his sight was almost gone, Jacob saw clearly what others with good eyes could not see. He saw the future, like Tiresias of Thebes, and testified to it. It is chiefly on this note of prophecy that Genesis ends.

The Blessing on Joseph's Sons

Jacob's prophecies fall into two parts in these chapters. The longer and more obvious part is the oracle recorded in chapter 49. It gives a word for each of Jacob's twelve sons: Reuben (vv. 3–4), Simeon and Levi (vv. 5–7), Judah (vv. 8–12), Zebulun (v. 13), Issachar (vv. 14–15), Dan (vv. 16–17), Gad (v. 19), Asher (v. 20), Naphtali (v. 21), Joseph (vv. 22–26), and Benjamin (v. 27). But there is an important though less obvious part in chapter 48. In this section Jacob blesses Joseph's sons, Manasseh and Ephraim, who are thereby adopted as Jacob's own children and become fathers of two of the Hebrew tribes.

So how many tribes of Israel were there? That is a tricky question. The normal answer is twelve, the twelve I have suggested by listing Jacob's twelve sons. But to be precise, there were actually thirteen tribes. Each of the eleven sons of Jacob, excepting Joseph, became father of a tribe. But instead of there being a tribe named Joseph, Joseph's sons became tribal patriarchs. In this way, although Joseph himself was not the father of a tribe, he received a double portion of honor because of the two tribes descended from his two sons. And yet, although there were thirteen tribes, only twelve had a land inheritance. Ephraim, Manasseh, and ten of the others possessed portions of the land. But Levi was the tribe of priests and possessed no land inheritance. Levi's portion was the Lord.

The blessing of Manasseh and Ephraim is significant, for it is nothing less than the passing on of the messianic blessing to these lads. It has three parts. First, there is a *prayer* that the God of Abraham and Isaac, who is also the God of Jacob, might bless Manasseh and Ephraim. This is a powerful recitation of God's faithfulness to these three patriarchs.

Second, there is the *formal adoption,* in which Jacob says, "May they [that is, Manasseh and Ephraim] be called by my name and the names of my fathers Abraham and Isaac" (v. 16). This is Jacob's performance of what he had promised Joseph earlier. He had said, "Now then, your two sons born to you in Egypt before I came to you here will be reckoned as mine; Ephraim and Manasseh will be mine, just as Reuben and Simeon are mine. Any children born to you after them will be yours; in the territory they inherit they will be reckoned under the names of their brothers" (vv. 5–6). It is because of this adoption that Ephraim and Manasseh became the fathers of two of Israel's tribes and were given tribal territory.

Third, there is the *blessing of great posterity:* "and may they increase greatly upon the earth" (v. 16). This was part of the original blessing to Abraham in which God promised to make him into a great nation (Gen. 12:2; 15:5; 17:2; 22:17). It was repeated to Isaac after Abraham's death (Gen. 26:4) and to Jacob himself when God appeared to him at Bethel (Gen. 28:14).

These blessings on Joseph's sons may mean that Jacob here transferred the rights of the firstborn to Joseph and his descendants, removing them from Reuben, who had forfeited his rights by dishonoring his father. Strictly speaking, the text does not say that Joseph was to receive these rights. But Jacob's blessing of Joseph's son is comparable to Isaac's blessing Jacob rather than Esau, as narrated in Genesis 27. Besides, in 1 Chronicles 5:1–2, there is a statement that this is what happened, though it is not explicitly traced to the scene in Genesis 48: "Reuben . . . was the firstborn, but when he defiled his father's marriage bed, his rights as firstborn were given to the sons of Joseph son of Israel; so he could not be listed in the genealogical record in accordance with his birthright, and though Judah was the strongest of his brothers and a ruler came from him, the rights of the firstborn belonged to Joseph."

Ephraim before Manasseh

The rights of the firstborn bring us to the most interesting part of Jacob's blessing. For it is not only in the case of Joseph that the right of the firstborn was switched from one who was the oldest (Reuben) to one who was not

(Joseph). We can understand why that happened; it was, as 1 Chronicles says, because "he defiled his father's marriage bed" (cf. Gen. 35:22). Rather, it is the case that also in the blessing of Manasseh and Ephraim the rights of Manasseh, who was the oldest, were given to Ephraim, who was younger. The interesting point is that there is not even the slightest indication of why that might have been necessary.

It is an interesting story. When Joseph brought his sons forward to receive Jacob's blessing, he brought them in what he thought was the proper and desirable manner. The chief blessing was given with the right hand. So Joseph took Manasseh, the firstborn, in his left hand in order to bring him to Jacob's right; and he took Ephraim, his second son, in his right hand in order to bring him to Jacob's left. Presumably the sons bowed before Jacob, as Joseph himself had done, and then waited to receive their blessing. Then something very unusual happened. Instead of stretching his right hand directly forward to place it on Manasseh's head and his left hand forward to place it on Ephraim's head, Jacob crossed his arms in order to give the greater blessing to Ephraim, although he was the younger. It was in that posture that he pronounced the blessing we have just analyzed.

This displeased Joseph, the story tells us. Perhaps he thought it a quirk of his father's old age, perhaps just a simple mistake. Whatever the case, he tried to intervene. He took hold of his father's hand to move it from Ephraim's head to Manasseh's.

Jacob was unmoved: "I know, my son, I know. He too will become a people, and he too will become great. Nevertheless, his younger brother will be greater than he, and his descendants will become a group of nations" (v. 19). Then he continued his blessing, saying, "In your name will Israel pronounce this blessing: 'May God make you like Ephraim and Manasseh'" (v. 20). Thus he put Ephraim ahead of Manasseh and transferred the rights of the firstborn to him.

What is going on here? Is this merely an arbitrary decision on Jacob's part or, worse yet, the stubborn perversity of an old man who for some reason was attracted to the younger rather than the older son? Surely no one who reads this story carefully can believe this was the case. These are solemn moments, not times for arbitrary actions. Besides, Jacob is speaking under the inspiration of the Holy Spirit and is therefore telling, not what he wants, but what shall be: "He too *will* become a people, and he too *will* become great. Nevertheless, his younger brother *will be* greater . . ." (my emphasis). This is the precise opposite of Jacob indulging his desires. He is putting his own will aside and is blessing Ephraim first in obedience to the leading of God.

I am sure that as he did this, Jacob must have been thinking back to his own blessing by Isaac before his flight to Haran. Isaac had been stubborn. In that case, God had announced that "the older will serve the younger" (Gen. 25:23), but this did not suit Isaac. Isaac loved Esau because of Esau's manly nature, and he was determined to bless him. Moreover, because his wife favored Jacob, Isaac schemed to bless Esau privately—on the sly, as it were. We know the story. Rebekah overheard Isaac's explanation of his plan to Esau and, while Esau was gone, sent Jacob to her husband to impersonate his older brother. Isaac was suspicious. But the smell of Esau's clothes, which Jacob was wearing, and the goatskin on his arms eventually convinced him that the imposter was Esau, and he blessed him, saying,

> "May nations serve you
>   and peoples bow down to you.
> Be lord over your brothers
>   and may the sons of your mother bow down to you."

Genesis 27:29

Later, when Esau returned and the ruse was discovered, Isaac trembled violently. He had tried to fight against God and had failed. But he had learned his lesson and so stuck by his blessing (v. 33).

As I say, Jacob must have remembered this incident—how could he forget it?—and was determined not to repeat his willful father's error. God had spoken; he had chosen Ephraim, and Jacob was not going to argue with God or disobey him. This is the reason why this incident is singled out by the author of Hebrews as the chief evidence of Jacob's faith: "By faith Jacob, when he was dying, blessed each of Joseph's sons, and worshiped as he leaned on the top of his staff" (Heb. 11:21).

The Sovereign God

This blessing is an expression of God's sovereignty. Every blessing flows from sovereignty, of course, for no one deserves God's favor. Yet in a choice like this, sovereignty is especially seen. It is good it is so, for by it God exalts himself and human plans are humbled.

Robert Candlish writes:

Israel is acting in this matter for God, announcing, not a wish of his own or a determination of his own will, but an oracle of God. And one proof of its being so is the sovereignty which it asserts and vindicates as belonging to God. It is a sovereignty which it is his prerogative to exercise, without giving account to any. And it is his pleasure to exercise it—especially in the sacred family and in connection with the covenant-promise of redemption by the angel, of which that family is the depository—in a way that reverses human notions and makes it plain that all is of God. "For the purpose of God, according to election, must stand, not of works, but of him that calleth. It is not of him that willeth, nor of him that runneth, but of God that showeth mercy."

So it had ever been in God's dealings with the patriarchs in time past; so it was to be still. So it was, and is, in the time of the complete fulfillment of the promise, when the Angel of the Covenant actually accomplishes the redemption from all evil of which Jacob speaks. The law or rule under whose operation the economy of grace ordinarily proceeds is always the same, humbling to human wisdom, glorifying to the divine sovereignty. The last are often first, and the first last. "He came unto his own, and his own received him not. But as many as received him, to them gave he power to become the sons of God, even to them that believe on his name: which were born, not of blood, nor of the will of the flesh, nor of the will of man, but of God" (John 1:11–13).[1]

Hope for Younger Sons

This blessing is also a ground of hope for younger sons. It is often—perhaps usually—the case that older sons are favored and sons that come later are given second place. If you are a younger son (or even a younger daughter), do not be discouraged by this, but rather look to God, who exalts the lowly and blesses those who fear him.

The Bible is full of hope for younger sons. Isaac was a younger son; Abraham's first son was Ishmael, whom he had by Hagar. Ishmael mocked Isaac (see Gen. 21:9). But God set his favor on Isaac, and even though Ishmael was also blessed by God, it was in Isaac that the promises were established and through him that the Messiah came.

Jacob was a younger son. We have studied his history. He thought he had to cheat his brother and deceive his father, which he did not have to do. But even though he trusted in his own cunning rather than in God, God blessed him and was faithful to him so that he could say, as he does in this blessing, "God . . . has been my Shepherd all my life to this day" (Gen. 48:15).

Joseph was a younger son. He was despised by his brothers and was sold into slavery by them. But God exalted Joseph to be the chief power in Egypt and even to inherit Reuben's birthright.

Ephraim was a younger son.

So was Moses.

So was Gideon.

So was David.

F. B. Meyer writes, "It is not an unmitigated blessing to be born into the world with a great name and estate and traditions; it is better to trust in one's own right arm and in the blessing of the Almighty. God is no respecter of persons, and he will lift the youngest into the front rank if only he sees the qualities which warrant it; whilst he will put back the foremost into the lower ranks if they are deficient in noble attributes."[2]

Hope for All

Our hope is even stronger than that. It is true that God is no respecter of persons and that he will exalt those of character and diligence regardless of their background. That was the case with Joseph and David. But think of Ephraim: He had done nothing to stand before Manasseh in the judgment either of men or of God. Jacob was less attractive than Esau as a person. Moses was slow of speech. Gideon was timorous. Yet God took them and blessed them. He seems often to choose "the foolish things of the world to shame the wise; . . . the weak things of the world to shame the strong . . . the lowly things of this world and the despised things—and the things that are not—to nullify the things that are, so that no one may boast before him" (1 Cor. 1:27–29).

It is not pleasant to be placed among the foolish, weak, lowly, and despised of this world. But that is often where we find ourselves. We need to say it. And yet, it is often through such people—who have nevertheless been made great in the power of God—that God does the truly important things and brings honor to his name.

164

The Lord Is My Shepherd

Genesis 48:15–16

Then he blessed Joseph and said,
> *"May the God before whom my fathers*
> *Abraham and Isaac walked,*
> *the God who has been my shepherd*
> *all my life to this day,*
> *the Angel who has delivered me from all harm*
> *—may he bless these boys."*

We have already studied in Genesis 48 the blessing of Jacob on Joseph and his two sons twice, once for Jacob's personal testimony and a second time for the blessing itself. Now I return to these verses once more because of their importance.

Sometimes in examining a text I will refer to the Authorized or King James text for a particularly beautiful rendering, but this is a case where the modern translations are better in bringing out the true meaning. In the King James

1161

Version, Genesis 48:15 reads, "God, before whom my fathers Abraham and Isaac did walk, the God which fed me all my life long unto this day." That is not a wrong rendering. But the phrase "God which fed me" actually refers to a shepherd's work and reads somewhat better as the New International Version has it: "the God *who has been my Shepherd* all my life to this day" (my emphasis).

Shepherding is the root idea. And this is important, not only because it is a strong and provocative image (as we know it to be), but also because it is the first appearance of this image in the Bible.

We can think of other occurrences. Best known is the beautiful Twenty-third Psalm, written by King David: "The Lord is my shepherd; I shall not be in want" (v. 1). The image appears in Psalm 80: "Hear us, O Shepherd of Israel, you who lead Joseph like a flock" (v. 1), and in the great fortieth chapter of Isaiah: "He tends his flock like a shepherd: he gathers the lambs in his arms and carries them close to his heart; he gently leads those who have young" (v. 11).

Jesus developed this image in his discourse on the Good Shepherd recorded in John 10: "I am the good shepherd; I know my sheep and my sheep know me—just as the Father knows me and I know the Father—and I lay down my life for the sheep. I have other sheep that are not of this sheep pen. I must bring them also" (vv. 14–16). After this the image appears in 1 Peter, where Jesus is called "the Shepherd and Overseer" of our souls (2:25), and in the great blessing that ends the Book of Hebrews: "May the God of peace, who through the blood of the eternal covenant brought back from the dead our Lord Jesus, that great Shepherd of the sheep, equip you with everything good for doing his will, and may he work in us what is pleasing to him, through Jesus Christ, to whom be glory for ever and ever. Amen" (13:20–21).

Each of these verses is so important that it might well be explored by itself. Yet Genesis 48:15 is the seedbed of them all. It was Jacob, not David, who first called God his Shepherd.

Two Shepherds

It is not surprising that this is so, of course. Like David, Jacob was himself a shepherd and thus naturally thought of God's care as shepherding. Jacob knew two things about shepherding.

First, Jacob knew how difficult shepherding is—how difficult it is, even in human terms, to find a good shepherd. He knew this by experience. In his moving confrontation with Laban, after Laban had pursued him on his flight from Haran back to his homeland and Jacob had burst forth in what seems to have been the longest and most impassioned speech of his career, Jacob articulated the difficulty of the shepherd's life. He said:

> I have been with you for twenty years now. Your sheep and goats have not mis-carried, nor have I eaten rams from your flocks. I did not bring you animals

torn by wild beasts; I bore the loss myself. And you demanded payment from
me for whatever was stolen by day or night. This was my situation: The heat
consumed me in the daytime and the cold at night, and sleep fled from my
eyes. It was like this for the twenty years I was in your household. . . . If the God
of my father, the God of Abraham and the Fear of Isaac, had not been with
me, you would surely have sent me away empty-handed. But God has seen my
hardship and the toil of my hands, and last night he rebuked you.

Genesis 31:38–42

That is a powerful statement. But if the truth be told, it is an understatement. Philip Keller, in his best-selling book *A Shepherd Looks at Psalm 23*, shows
how "sheep do not 'just take care of themselves' as some might suppose."
But rather, "they require, more than any other class of livestock, endless attention and meticulous care."[1] Sheep are timid and easily panicked. Even a stray
rabbit suddenly jumping from behind a rock can stampede a flock and do
damage. Sheep are cruel and competitive. The larger and stronger will take
the best grazing spots and drive others from it. Sheep are prone to parasites
and insects and have no defense mechanisms against them. Worst of all, sheep
will graze land to death, eating grass to the soil and then even pulling up
and consuming the roots. If sheep are not systematically moved from pasture
to pasture and the lands are not cared for, the flock will languish, and dry,
sunburned wastelands will result.

Keller tells how, when he was a shepherd, he was on duty every hour of
the day and night and how he was constantly battling one enemy or another
to ensure the sheep's welfare. Jacob knew this kind of experience. So when
he called God his Shepherd, he was not "speaking through his hat," as we
say. He knew how difficult the job was and how perfect a shepherd God had
been to him.

Jacob had learned a second thing also. He had learned how great a failure
he was when he had been trying to shepherd himself. This is an image, of
course. "Self-shepherding" means trying to run your own life. But that is precisely what Jacob had been trying to do all the long years that led up to his
confrontation with God at Jabbok. He was like many Christians. He acknowledged God. He would have described himself as a believer. But he had taken
the opposite course from that wise and godly path described in Proverbs
3:5–6: "Trust in the LORD with all your heart and lean not on your own understanding; in all your ways acknowledge him, and he will make your paths
straight." In his early days Jacob's paths were not straight. They went in many
devious ways. But even though he was not aware of it then, Jacob had possessed a Good Shepherd: the Lord Jehovah. And the Lord eventually straight-
ened him out and prospered him.

Here at the end, having learned that he could not be his own shepherd
but that he needed God to keep, protect, and guide him, Jacob pointed to
that God and commended his shepherding to Joseph's sons.

True to His Promises

It is a wonderful thing to look back on a long life and be able to say God has been true to his promises. Jacob had received the promises of God at Bethel. There God had appeared to him in connection with the vision of a great stairway stretching from earth to heaven, saying:

> "I am the LORD, the God of your father Abraham and the God of Isaac. I will give you and your descendants the land on which you are lying. Your descendants will be like the dust of the earth, and you will spread out to the west and to the east, to the north and to the south. All peoples on earth will be blessed through you and your offspring. I am with you and will watch over you wherever you go, and I will bring you back to this land. I will not leave you until I have done what I have promised you."
>
> Genesis 28:13–15

Some parts of that promise were future: the promise of blessing through Jacob's offspring, which was Christ. Some were in the process of fulfillment: the multiplication of his seed, so that his descendants might spread out over the earth like dust. The present part, the part that pertained to Jacob himself, was fulfilled to the letter. God *had* kept him. God *had* watched over him and brought him back to his own land. Even in Egypt God had not left him, but was doing the things of which he had told him.

If you are a follower of Jesus Christ and know him to be your Good Shepherd, you should be able to give a testimony similar to Jacob's. You should be able to point to God's promises and declare that God has kept them:

"Come to me, all you who are weary and burdened, and I will give you rest" (Matt. 11:28).

"I am the vine; you are the branches. If a man remains in me and I in him, he will bear much fruit" (John 15:5).

"Ask and you will receive" (John 16:24).

"Never will I leave you; never will I forsake you" (Heb. 13:5; cf. Deut. 31:6).

"Surely I am with you always, to the very end of the age" (Matt. 28:20).

These and hundreds of other promises found throughout Scripture are for us. They are promises we can look back on and see that they have been fulfilled. It is a great thing to point to the faithfulness of our Good Shepherd, as Jacob did.

Under-Shepherds

There is another great truth in these verses. We should not only look to our Great Shepherd God and praise him for being a good shepherd, but we should learn from him too—so that we take on some of his characteristics in our similar responsibilities for guiding others.

It is instructive for us to know that three times in the New Testament Jesus is represented as a shepherd, and in each case the word "shepherd" is preceded by a different adjective. In John 10 Jesus is called the *good* shepherd—"I am the good shepherd. The good shepherd lays down his life for the sheep" (John 10:11). Here the emphasis is on the voluntary and vicarious death of the Shepherd. In Hebrews 13:20–21 Jesus is called the *great* shepherd—"May the God of peace, who through the blood of the eternal covenant brought back from the dead our Lord Jesus, that great Shepherd of the sheep, equip you with everything good for doing his will. . . ." In these verses the emphasis is on Christ's resurrection and therefore also on his ability to work through and accomplish his purposes in his sheep. The third passage speaks of Jesus as the *chief* shepherd and stresses his second coming to reward those who have served him as under-shepherds. It is 1 Peter 5:4: "And when the Chief Shepherd appears, you will receive the crown of glory that will never fade away."

These passages highlight the focal points of Christ's ministry. As the Good Shepherd, Christ dies for the sheep. As the Great Shepherd, Christ rises from the dead so that he might serve the sheep. As the Chief Shepherd, Christ returns to reward those who have been faithful in the responsibilities to which they have been assigned as under-shepherds. It is the last of these that communicates the point I am making.

When Jesus described himself as the Shepherd he revealed important aspects of what he is to us, just as Jacob revealed aspects of what Jehovah was to him when he called God his Shepherd. But at the same time these references also reveal what we should be to others, for we are all shepherds (to a greater or lesser extent) in terms of our responsibility.

In what ways should we be like the Good Shepherd?

1. The first and most obvious characteristic of the Good Shepherd is that he is *faithful*—faithful not only when the skies are sunny and the countryside is peaceful but also when times are hard and danger threatens. God was faithful to Jacob in easy times as well as hard times. Jesus made the same point when he drew a contrast between himself and the hired hand who, "when he sees the wolf coming . . . abandons the sheep and runs away" (John 10:12).

There is much in the Word of God about faithfulness. Jesus spoke of stewards who proved they were faithful by the way they handled their master's goods (Matt. 24:45–46; 25:14–30; Luke 12:42–43; 19:11–27). Paul wrote, "It is required that those who have been given a trust must prove faithful" (1 Cor. 4:2). He told Timothy, "The things you have heard me say in the presence of many witnesses entrust to reliable men who will also be qualified to teach others" (2 Tim. 2:2). Faithfulness is a primary need in those who have responsibility. So whatever other good characteristics we may have, they will be of very little value unless we possess this great quality.

2. We must be *hardworking*, as God is. The Twenty-third Psalm teaches that the one who has God for his shepherd does not lack rest, guidance, safety,

provision, or a heavenly home. Why? The answer obviously is that the Shepherd provides these things through his diligent care of the flock and hard work. It is the same in the church. Most of the needs of God's people are met by God through the instrumentality of under-shepherds. So if God's people do not receive good spiritual food, it is usually because some minister is not working hard enough to provide it. If children lack love and security, it is usually because parents are not working hard enough to provide these things in the home. If the widows are not cared for, it is because the deacons are slothful. The list could be carried on indefinitely.

3. The Shepherd is *patient.* God was patient with Jacob and the other biblical figures; he is patient with us. We need to learn that characteristic also. Sheep are different from one another. Some go too fast; we need to be patient with them. Some sheep go too slowly; we need to be patient with those. Some are belligerent. Some are exceedingly wayward. Most are just plain stupid. In each case the under-shepherd needs to be patient, as the Chief Shepherd is with all.

4. The Shepherd of Israel is also *a good example.* This is what Peter is primarily talking about in the verses in which Jesus is called "the Chief Shepherd." Peter is writing to elders in these verses, though his words also apply more widely. He says:

> To the elders among you, I appeal as a fellow elder, a witness of Christ's sufferings and one who also will share in the glory to be revealed: Be shepherds of God's flock that is under your care, serving as overseers—not because you must, but because you are willing, as God wants you to be; not greedy for money, but eager to serve; not lording it over those entrusted to you, but being examples to the flock. And when the Chief Shepherd appears, you will receive the crown of glory that will never fade away.
>
> 1 Peter 5:1–4

Are we like that? Are we examples of mature Christian understanding, faithfulness amid persecution, morality, love, joy, peace, long-suffering, gentleness, goodness, faith, meekness, self-control, and all other virtues? The point of these words is that we should be such examples and that we should also be examples in our careful feeding of the sheep.

5. A shepherd must be *self-sacrificing.* This is what most characterizes the Good Shepherd in Jesus' description in John 10. Above all, he gives his life for the sheep. We will never be able to give our lives as Jesus gave his life for us; he died for us as our sin-bearer. Nevertheless, there are other ways we can give ourselves for others. We can give time to help them. We can sacrifice things we would rather do or have in order to serve and give to others.

Simply put, we must put others ahead of ourselves. The world says, "Me first, others second, God last." The proper order is: "God first, others second, myself last." This order does not sound attractive to the natural mind, but this is the right way to a full and joyful life. It takes self-sacrifice if a parent is to raise a child properly, if a pastor is to guide and teach his people effectively, if a manager is to develop his employees or if an employee is to do good work.

Looking to Him

I make my last point with emphasis. The only place we will learn to be good, faithful, hardworking, exemplary, self-sacrificing under-shepherds of God's people is from him who is the Chief Shepherd. It is by looking to God, who has been faithful in shepherding us all our lives long. Is this not where the biblical people learned about spiritual shepherding? Let us ask them.

Jacob was not a particularly praiseworthy character, as we have seen. He was willful, weak. At times he was dishonest. Yet in one respect he was praiseworthy: He was a good shepherd. Nobody ever faulted him for failures in this regard. "Jacob, where did you learn to be a good shepherd? Where did you learn faithfully to care for sheep?"

Jacob replies, "It is true that I cared for the sheep; but I did not learn it of myself. It was not that I was faithful. I learned it rather from the Good Shepherd, the Shepherd of Bethel, who revealed himself to me and who cared for me during my years of exile."

Next we turn to Joseph and say to him, "Joseph, you too were a shepherd in your youth. It is said of you that you were faithful in tending the sheep (Gen. 37:2). Moreover, you were later used by God to feed many people, for as ruler in Egypt you were used to store up grain to preserve many millions during the great famine. Where did you learn that? Where did you learn that kind of faithfulness?"

Joseph answers, "From the God of my fathers, who kept and fed me during the years of my slavery and imprisonment."

"Moses, even you were a shepherd. You were raised in Egypt in the court of Pharaoh, but you spent the next forty years in the deserts of Midian caring for the flock of Reuel. It is said that you *watered and guided* the sheep (Exod. 2:16–17; 3:1), just as under God you later watered, protected, and guided the people of Israel during the forty years of their desert wandering. Where did you learn to do that? Where did you learn to give such care?"

Moses tells us that it was not from himself that he learned it, but rather from God's protection and guidance of him as he fled from Egypt.

Finally, we see David. "David, you are preeminently the great shepherd king. As a boy you cared for sheep; for you were the youngest in the family, and it was the job of the youngest to care for them. During those years you showed prowess in *defending* the sheep, for we read that you killed both a lion and a bear in rescuing your sheep (1 Sam. 17:34–36). Later you showed similar prowess in defending Israel against even greater enemies. Where did you learn such courage?"

David answers that he learned it from the Great Shepherd about whom he had written.

Who is adequate for these things? No one, certainly! We are not faithful or hardworking or patient or self-sacrificing in ourselves. But we can learn to be faithful if we keep close to God our Good Shepherd and imitate him.[2]

165

God with Us

Genesis 48:21–22

Then Israel said to Joseph, "I am about to die, but God will be with you and take you back to the land of your fathers. And to you, as one who is over your brothers, I give the ridge of land I took from the Amorites with my sword and my bow."

The last words of Jacob to Joseph prior to the prophecy of Genesis 49 concern the gift of a ridge of land he said he took from the Amorites of Canaan. It is hard to know what to make of this gift. But it is not hard to know what to make of the statement that comes immediately before it. In that utterance Jacob says, "I am about to die, but God will be with you and take you back to the land of your fathers." That utterance is a great testimony based on a great experience of God's presence.

It is also a climax. Charles Haddon Spurgeon once preached a sermon in which he linked this text to three other references to God's presence in Jacob's story. In Genesis 28, after Jacob had been forced to leave home because of Esau, God appeared to him at Bethel and said, *"I am with you"* (v. 15, my emphasis). In chapter 31, where God appeared to Jacob to send him back to his own land from Haran, God said, *"I will be with you"* (v. 3, my emphasis). Two verses later, where Jacob was reflecting back over his experiences of God's blessing at Haran, he says, *"God . . . has been with me"* (v. 5, my emphasis); he says the same thing in chapter 35: *"God . . . has been with me* wherever I have gone" (v. 3, my emphasis).

The last reference is the one in our text, spoken on Jacob's deathbed. Having been told that God was with him and would be with him, and having seen the fulfillment of that promise, Jacob applied those truths to his descendants, saying, *"God will be with you"* (Gen. 48:21, my emphasis). His was a full life, and this is a full scope of testimony.

"I am with you" (Gen. 28:15).

"I will be with you" (Gen. 31:3).

"God . . . has been with me" (Gen. 31:5; 35:3).

"God will be with you" (Gen. 48:21).

At the end of life each of us should be able to look back on years of walking with God and say that God has indeed been with us, as he promised to be. And we should be able to share that hope with others.

"I Am with You"

When God made the first of these promises to Jacob it was in a context that undoubtedly enhanced their impact for him. Jacob was alone. He had been raised in a stable home by a doting mother. As the son of his father, the patriarch of the clan, he had experienced special privileges. But suddenly he had been forced to flee from home and was now alone on a mountainside with an unknown and questionable destiny before him. Jacob was like many people who are alone today: widows, widowers, single people, people torn from their environment by a change of jobs, people who are sick, rejected. Jacob felt alone in the world, and he was frightened by it.

What a wonderful thing it must have been for Jacob to have been given a revelation of God and to have been told that God was with him! Spurgeon writes:

> How precious it must have seemed as it came to Jacob in that den of a place, where he lay with the hedges for his curtains, the heavens for his canopy, the earth for his bed, stones for his pillows and God for his companion. "I am with thee." Tomorrow when thou shalt open thine eyes thou wilt look back to the west and say, "I have left my father's house and my mother, Rebecca, behind me"; and the tears will be in thy eyes; and thou wilt look to the east and say, "I am going to the house of my mother's kindred, and I know them not, save that I have heard concerning Uncle Laban that he is hard and grasping; and I know not how he will receive me."
>
> But is not that a precious thing to start upon a journey with—"I am with thee"—I, the ever blessed? Though thy mother is not with thee, "I am with thee." Is any young friend here who is leaving home? Are you going away for the first time, and do you feel sad? Or are you about to go to a far country, and does your heart feel heavy? Do not go at all till you can get a hold of this. "I am with

thee." Say unto the Lord, "If thy Spirit go not with me, carry me not up hence." Wait till he gives the answer, "My Spirit shall go with thee, and I will give thee rest." This ought to be the blessing of your opening life, "I am with thee."

Is God with you tonight? Can God be with you? Some come to service after having quarreled with their wives and families; God is not with them. People who are following ill trades, and living ill lives, and rejecting the gospel, God cannot be with them. "Can two walk together except they be agreed?" If you are a believer in Christ, and the Spirit of God has produced in you the true fruits of the Spirit, then you may say, "He is with me," but not else.[1]

Everyone should be able at least to start at this point of Jacob's testimony. If you are Christ's and are serious about following him as your Lord, then know that he is with you, regardless of what your other circumstances may be. If you are not Christ's, then come to him. Embrace him as your Savior.

"I Will Be with You"

The second statement is so like the first that it might properly be thought to be a part of it: "I will be with you." This is because the God who makes the first promise—"I am with you"—is an immutable God who does not vary in his purposes. The calling of God is without repentance. Consequently, if he is once with us in a saving way, we can be sure that he will be with us to the end.

Yet there is something additional in this promise, if only because from our perspective it refers to things that lie ahead. This was the case with Jacob. Jacob was in a difficult situation when these words were first spoken. He had served his uncle for twenty years. During that time God had richly blessed him. He had worked fourteen years for his wives, Leah and Rachel. Then he had worked six more years for a share of Laban's flocks. In this last period God had increased Jacob's flocks until Laban became jealous and his sons also complained that "Jacob has taken everything our father owned and has gained all this wealth from what belonged to our father" (Gen. 31:1). Certainly God had been with Jacob. But Jacob was now having to leave Laban and return to his own land, and he knew Laban was not likely to take this move kindly. Jacob would set out for Canaan. But Laban would pursue him, and who knew where that might end? Laban might even kill him, take back his daughters, and seize the flocks.

Besides, the only place Jacob had to go was to Canaan, where Esau was living—Esau who had vowed to kill him because Jacob had cheated him of his father's blessing. If Jacob obeyed the Lord, he was going to find himself between what we call "a rock and a hard place." To the west would be Esau, coming to meet him with four hundred armed men. To the east, pursuing him from that direction, would be Laban with his angry sons and servants. In between Jacob would be crushed like an insignificant worm.

"I will be with you."

God would be with Jacob when Laban fell upon him suddenly in the Galilean hills, boasting that he had power to harm him if he so chose. God would warn Laban not to harm Jacob, not even to speak bad words.

God would be with Jacob when Esau marched toward him with his army. Jacob would be terrified, trembling on the banks of the Jabbok. But God would change his brother's heart and effect a reconciliation.

God would protect Jacob from the Canaanites when his older sons invited retaliation by murdering the people of Shechem.

God would be with him when Rachel died.

God would be with him when reports came of the death of his beloved son Joseph.

God would be with him when famine swept down like a lion on the Near Eastern world.

God's promise to Jacob was exactly like Jesus' great promise to us, found at the end of Matthew's Gospel. Before this, Jesus had spoken of the disasters that will befall this world: false Christs (Matt. 24:5), wars (vv. 6–7), famines and earthquakes (v. 7), persecutions (v. 9), apostasy (v. 10). He spoke of days so terrible that, unless they were cut short, no one would survive (vv. 15–28). He spoke of terrors in the heavens:

> "The sun will be darkened,
>   and the moon will not give its light;
> the stars will fall from the sky,
>   and the heavenly bodies will be shaken."
>
>   verse 29

But shortly after this, having died and been raised again, Jesus commissioned his followers to the task of world evangelism, concluding, "Surely I am with you always, to the very end of the age" (Matt. 28:20). Nothing will ever come into our lives that Jesus Christ has not foreseen. Nothing will ever happen to us that he does not control.

"God Has Been with Me"

The third statement is the heart of Jacob's testimony. For having been told that God was with him and would be with him always, and having lived in that hope for many years, Jacob was able to review his life and say that this was precisely what God did. In fact, he said it twice. He said it once when he was explaining to his wives Leah and Rachel why he had decided to return to Canaan from Haran: "I see that your father's attitude toward me is not what it was before, but the God of my father has been with me" (Gen. 31:5). This refers to his years of hardship in Haran. Jacob said it a second time when rededicating himself and his family to God at Bethel after his return to Canaan: "Let us go up to Bethel, where I will build an altar to God, who answered me in the day of my distress and who has been with me wherever I have gone" (Gen. 35:3). This refers to God's protection of him when he was pursued by Laban and opposed by Esau.

I hope you are able to give a testimony like that. You may have lived with the Lord only for a little while, but you should be able to say, "He has been with me even for this short time." You may have been a believer for long years. These should stretch out your testimony so that you can say, "God has been with me for all these many years in many circumstances."

Notice that God was with Jacob in spite of his faults and failures. Jacob was fearful, the very opposite of being strong in faith. Even after God had told him to return to Canaan and assured him that he would be with him, we find Jacob trembling at the approach of Esau's army. He divided his live-stock so that if Esau attacked one part, the other part would escape. He sent presents to Esau. Even then, he was so afraid he could not sleep. Is this the great man of God, the father of Israel? Yes, it is. It is Jacob fearful and trem-bling. But although Jacob did not have his eyes on God and so was frightened, God had his eyes on Jacob and protected him. Thus, years later, in spite of his fear at the time, Jacob was able to look back and say, "God . . . has been with me wherever I have gone."

Look at Peter walking toward Jesus on the water. Is Jesus with him? Of course; if not, he could not have walked on the water. But notice: he looks at the waves; his faith fails; he begins to sink into the deep. Is Jesus still with him? Yes, then too. In fact, Jesus was never closer to him than when he was sinking. For suddenly the Lord was at his side, drawing him up and quickly bringing the boat to land.

I think Peter must often have referred to that sinking, for it is usually the case that in looking back over our lives we find that we can best testify to the comforting presence of Christ in what most terrified us. This is what Spurgeon said:

> If you trust in God, this shall be your verdict at the close of life. When you come to die you shall look back upon a life which has not been without its trials and its difficulties, but you shall bless God for it all: and if there is any one thing in life for which you will have to praise God more than for another, it will prob-ably be that very event which seems darkest to you.
>
> Did God ever do a better thing for Jacob than when he took Joseph away and sent him to Egypt to preserve the whole family alive? It was the severest trial of the poor old man's career, and yet the brightest blessing after all. . . . Inside that hard-shelled nut there is the sweetest kernel that you have tasted. Rest assured of that. Your father's rumbling wagons have woke you out of sleep, and you are frightened at them; but they are loaded with ingots of gold. You never have been so rich as you will be after your great trouble shall have passed away.[2]

"God Will Be with You"

The last of these four statements is the perfect place to end, for it takes the promise to the one who has come to the end of his race and passes it on to the generation soon to pick up the torch. Jacob is dying. His testimony is that God has been with him all his days. That is a great thing. But as he dies he looks on Joseph, Ephraim, and Manasseh, who would also soon have their hard times, and says that God will be with them as he had been with him.

I address three classes of people. First, there may be some like Jacob who are nearing the end of life. You can testify that God has been faithful to you. But as you look at what you are leaving behind, you see children and grand-children as yet unconverted. You see problems for your sons and daughters. I ask, will God be less faithful to them than he has been to you? You have trusted God with your life. Can you not also trust him with the lives of your children? Will he not also bring your grandchildren to faith?

Second, I speak to those who are children and who are witnessing the passing of a parent or older relative. You are thankful to God for that life, but you are wondering if you can live as that father, that mother, that grandparent, or uncle or aunt lived. "God was adequate for them and their problems," you say, "but can he be adequate for me?" You know the answer: God is almighty, and he is unchanged. He will be with you, just as he was with the saints of old.

Finally, I speak to those who think of this in terms of contemporary leaders and their passing. Jacob was the last of the three great patriarchs. We witness his departure, and we wonder if God will have another to replace him. We see the passing of a Donald Grey Barnhouse, a C. S. Lewis, or a Francis A. Schaeffer, and we wonder if God will raise up others in their place. What will happen to that work when the minister is taken? What will happen when a person who has been greatly used in my life no longer has the strength or ability to carry on?

The answer is, God will be with you. Spurgeon wrote, "If Abraham dies, there is Isaac; and if Isaac dies, there is Jacob; and if Jacob dies, there is Joseph; and if Joseph dies, Ephraim and Manasseh survive. The Lord shall never lack a champion to bear his standard high among the sons of men. Only let us pray God to raise up more faithful ministers. That ought to be our prayer day and night. We have plenty of a sort, but, oh, for more that will weigh out sixteen ounces to the pound of gospel in such a way that people will receive it. We have too much of fine language, too much of florid eloquence, and too little full and plain gospel preaching; but God will keep up the apostolic succession, never fear of that. When Stephen is dying, Paul is not far off. When Elijah is taken up, he leaves his mantle behind him."[3]

The time is coming when each of us must pass to glory. But God is faithful. Jesus has promised to be with his church until the end of the age. His name is Emmanuel—"God with us." He will never leave us until he has accomplished all that he has spoken.

166

Reuben: The First Shall Be Last

Genesis 49:1–4

Then Jacob called for his sons and said: "Gather around so I can tell you what will happen to you in days to come.

> *"Assemble and listen, sons of Jacob;*
> *listen to your father Israel.*
> *"Reuben, you are my firstborn,*
> *my might, the first sign of my strength,*
> *excelling in honor, excelling in power.*
> *Turbulent as the waters, you will no longer excel,*
> *for you went up onto your father's bed,*
> *onto my couch and defiled it."*

N ot all saints have opportunity to speak for God on their deathbeds. Not even all the biblical saints did so. George Whitefield, the great nineteenth-century evangelist, spoke no final words, a friend having said to him, "Mr. Whitefield, you have borne so many living testimonies to so many thousands that your master wants no dying testimony of you."[1]

But some believers do speak dying words of testimony, and when they do it is an encouraging and glorious thing. When Matthew Henry was dying, that great biblical commentator and scholar said, "A life spent in the service of God and in communion with him is the most pleasant life that any one can live in the world."[2]

Thomas Halyburton, a great Scottish preacher of the eighteenth century, said when he was dying, "You may believe a man venturing on eternity. I have weighed eternity this last night—I have looked on death as stripped of all things pleasant to nature—and under the view of all these I have found *that* in the way of God that gave satisfaction, a rational satisfaction, that makes me rejoice." At the very end he said to one standing by, "When I fall so low that I cannot speak, I'll show you a sign of triumph if I am able." And so, when he could no longer speak, he lifted up clasped hands in a token of victory and so passed to glory.[3]

A Dying Prophecy

I said that not even all biblical saints have had a chance to give this kind of testimony. But that is an understatement. Actually few biblical characters are recorded as having done so. So it is remarkable and of great importance that we have extensive dying words from Jacob. So far in Genesis we have had no dying words from anyone. Adam spoke no such words. Noah is silent. No final admonitions flow from the lips of Abraham or from his son Isaac. But now suddenly Jacob dies, and we have extensive testimony and profound revelation.

All in all, we have three deathbed scenes. In the first (Gen. 47:28–31), Jacob meets with his favored son Joseph and extracts a promise from him that he will not be buried in Egypt, but will be taken back to Canaan to be buried there. In the second (Gen. 48:1–22), Jacob meets with Joseph and his two sons, Manasseh and Ephraim, and blesses this particular branch of his family. The blessing is unusual because of the reversal of Manasseh and Ephraim's roles. In the third scene (Gen. 49:1–33), Jacob calls all his sons to him and pronounces a blessing that is at the same time a prophecy of the future history of those tribes that were to descend from them.

And that, too, is unusual! For this is not only the first deathbed testimony in Genesis, it is also the first literal prophecy spoken by any human being. There is a prophecy of the seed of the woman who should crush the head of Satan in Genesis 3:15, but it is spoken to Satan by God. Genesis 15 contains another great prophecy of the coming bondage and eventual deliverance of the Jews in Egypt; but these also are God's words. True, some small words of blessing that have overtones of prophecy occur in Isaac's blessing Jacob and Esau. But with this possible exception, the first predictive prophecy by any man in all the Word of God is the prophecy of the history of the tribes of Israel recorded in Genesis 49.

It is a great prophecy. We shall see how it was aptly suited to each of Jacob's sons and accurately foretold the history of their descendants.

Advantages of Birth

Jacob begins with the sons born to him by Leah—Reuben, Simeon, Levi, Judah, Zebulun, and Issachar, his first sons (Gen. 29:31–35; 30:17–20)—and of these he rightly begins with Reuben, who was the firstborn. In fact, he calls attention to this in the prophecy: "Reuben, you are my firstborn, my might, the first sign of my strength, excelling in honor, excelling in power" (v. 3). According to the practice of those days, the firstborn in any household was entitled to twice the inheritance received by the other sons and he was honored above those others. Like Jacob himself, or Isaac before that, Reuben was born to be the head of his brothers and to fill a place of unparalleled honor among them.

This leads to the observation that there are often genuine advantages flowing from one's birth or status in life and that these should not be despised. Some people are uneasy with this, thinking perhaps that inequalities in life should not exist. But whatever we may think about them, such advantages (and disadvantages) do exist. We see it in material things. Some children are born to wealth and influence and profit from the advantages their backgrounds bring. We see it in physical things. Some children inherit keen minds, attractive personalities, valuable talents, or beautiful faces from their parents, and these undoubtedly give them an edge in our rough-and-tumble, dog-eat-dog world.

Far more important than material or physical advantages, however, are spiritual advantages. Wise is the person who employs these to the full. The apostle Paul did so. He was distressed in his day by the fact that the gospel was being well received among the Gentiles and that the Jews for the most part were rejecting it. He was a Jew, so that was a distressful thing personally. But the situation also involved the right of being spiritually firstborn, which Israel was. The Jews were God's special people. Yet most were rejecting the gospel. How could that be? asked Paul. Could it be the case that there are then no advantages at all in being a member of the ancient chosen people? "What advantage, then, is there in being a Jew, or what value is there in circumcision?" (Rom. 3:1).

Paul answered, "Much in every way! First of all, they have been entrusted with the very words of God" (v. 2). Later on in Romans he develops this thought further: "Theirs is the adoption as sons; theirs the divine glory, the covenants, the receiving of the law, the temple worship and the promises. Theirs are the patriarchs, and from them is traced the human ancestry of Christ" (Rom. 9:4–5). These are important passages, because they tell us that

Israel continued to possess great spiritual advantages, even though at this period of history the majority of Jews were living in unbelief.

So also today! Now as then, it is of supreme significance to have the law of God, spiritual worship, knowledge of the promises concerning Christ, and other things. It is a great blessing to be a Jew. It is a blessing to be a child of Christian parents. It is a significant blessing to be enabled to attend a Christian church, learn in a Christian school, converse with Christian friends, and read Christian books. Compared with these blessings, the advantages of wealth, family, or power are paltry treasures.

But these spiritual advantages alone do not guarantee salvation. It is possible to be a Jew and go to hell. It is possible to have all the advantages of a Christian upbringing, yet perish utterly. Even in less drastic terms, it is possible to have great spiritual treasures, yet squander them, to live a mediocre life instead of a life that bears spiritual fruit and gives God glory.

Loss of Advantages

This is what Reuben did! On the basis of Jacob's prophecy we have no reason to argue that Reuben lost his salvation through sin. On the contrary, the full story of Joseph's brothers leads us to think that all were converted from sin to faith in God and thus became saved men. Reuben gives evidence of a true conversion. Yet Reuben sinned against his father and so lost the advantages of being born first.

Reuben's sin was committing adultery with his father's concubine Bilhah, which is noted briefly in Genesis 35:22. The brevity is perhaps important, for it was certainly a passing incident—a moment's sinful pleasure. Yes, but with what long-lasting consequences! It was long-lasting for Reuben; as long as he lived, he would know he had lost first place among his brothers and that his place was given over to his much younger half-brother Joseph (cf. 1 Chron. 5:1–2). It was also long-lasting for his descendants, because his displacement affected them forever.

If you learn nothing else from this prophecy, at least learn this lesson: *Sin has consequences.* Unconfessed sin has eternal consequences. It can take you to hell, where the worm never dies and the fire is not quenched. But even confessed sin has consequences. Presumably Reuben's sin was confessed. He was forgiven. He was a saved man. Still, what he did lived on in human memory, and the just effects of that sin affected many.

This is worth emphasizing. Sin has consequences, and some of the consequences are for others. This was the case with the very first occurrence of sin in human history. Adam and Eve may have said—perhaps they did say—"What we do is our own business; it will affect no one but ourselves." But if this justification for disobedience was in their minds, it was patently erroneous. Adam and Eve's sin did affect others. In fact, it affected all who have ever lived, and that in the most radical ways. God had told Adam that in the day in which he disobeyed by eating of the forbidden tree, he would "surely die" (Gen. 2:17). And he did die! But not only Adam! Not only Eve! By Adam's disobedience, death, which is the consequence of sin, passed upon the entire human race.

The same principle is stated in a less radical manner in the Ten Commandments: "I, the LORD your God, am a jealous God, punishing the children for the sin of the fathers to the third and fourth generation of those who hate me, but showing love to a thousand generations of those who love me and keep my commandments" (Exod. 20:5–6).

Let us establish that clearly. If you live for Christ and are godly, your children will benefit. But if, on the contrary, you live for yourself and are ungodly, your children—and probably others—will pay the consequences. You cannot escape this law. Sin is not private. Sin is far-reaching. This fact alone should restrain sin and lead to godliness.

When Jacob spoke his prophetic words of judgment on Reuben he said, "Turbulent as the waters, you will no longer excel" (v. 4). The first half of this judgment is descriptive; it tells us that Reuben was "unstable" (KJV), "uncontrolled" (NASB), or undisciplined. He showed this by his sin. The second half of the judgment is prophetic; because of his sin, neither Reuben nor his descendants would excel in Israel.

This is precisely what happened. I have a valuable chart called the "Adam and Eve Family Tree" prepared by a former Sunday school teacher named Mary Lou Farris. It traces the biblical descendants of Adam down to the Lord Jesus Christ, listing in particular the mentioned descendants of all the tribes of Israel. On this chart Judah occupies the largest space. There are scores of kings like David, Solomon, and Josiah. There are distinguished men like Boaz, Jesse, and Caleb. The tribe of Joseph is large. Levi is large, and so are others.

But Reuben? Listed under the tribe of Reuben are only a few names, virtually all of them unknown. They are men like Hanoch, Pallu, Hezron, and Carmi. In all I count only twenty-eight names. One commentator says, "We never find that any one of the tribe of Reuben was distinguished by peculiar honours; neither the priesthood nor the royalty was given to the tribe of the firstborn of Jacob. None of the ancient heroes, whose names are yet famous, belonged to this tribe. There were kings of different tribes, but none, as far as we know, of the tribe of Reuben. There were doubtless many of the sons of Reuben who found favour with God (1 Chron. 5). But none of them ever obtained such glory in this world as many of the other tribes obtained."[4]

Nearly 450 years after this, Moses pronounced a similar prophecy on the tribes of Israel. But although it is a long prophecy containing many words about many of the Jewish tribes, only one sentence is spoken about Reuben. The text says, "Let Reuben live and not die, nor his men be few" (Deut. 33:6).

Apparently this was in danger of happening. At the first numbering of the tribes, recorded in Numbers 1, the men of Reuben were counted as 46,500 (v. 21). At the next numbering the total had decreased to 43,730 (Num. 26:7). When it came time for the people of Israel to settle the Promised Land, Reuben was one of the tribes (together with Gad and the half-tribe of Manasseh) who remained east of the Jordan. The land to the east was less valuable than that of the major part of Palestine. Moreover, to Reuben was apportioned the south-ernmost and smallest of these areas. Here they apparently declined even fur-ther, for at a later date, when David was organizing the administration of his united kingdom, he placed capable men of Hebron over Reuben. "Jerijah had twenty-seven hundred relatives, who were able men and heads of families, and King David put them in charge of the Reubenites, the Gadites and the half-tribe of Manasseh for every matter pertaining to God and for the affairs of the king" (1 Chron. 26:32).

Still later, as God began to pour out his judgments upon the ungodly states of Israel and Judah, Reuben was one of the first tribal areas to be overcome. We have two records of this destruction. In 2 Kings 10:32–33, we read: "In those days the LORD began to reduce the size of Israel. Hazael overpowered the Israelites throughout their territory east of the Jordan in all the land of Gilead (the region of Gad, Reuben and Manasseh), from Aroer by the Arnon Gorge through Gilead to Bashan."

The other evidence is the so-called Moabite Stone, containing a record of the military victories of King Mesha of Moab, discovered in 1868. It tells of victories over the cities of Medeba, Baal-meon, Qaryaten, and Dibon—all cities in the ancient tribal area of Reuben.[5] This happened in the late ninth century B.C., about one hundred years before the fall of the northern king-dom of Israel to the Assyrians.

The Last Will Be First

The prophecy concerning Reuben is a study of sin's sad consequences. It shows the sins of the father being visited upon the children, not merely to third and fourth generations but throughout the entire earthly history of the tribe. It reveals how the first become last when they fall away from righ-teousness and indulge in sin.

As far as Reuben is concerned, this is the whole of his history. There is nothing to add. But on the basis of the entire Word of God we can add that in some cases there is another story. It is true that the first often do become last—through sin. But it is also the case that the last often become first—through Christ and faith in him. Earlier I wrote of Paul's sense of the value of a spiritual inheritance. It is appropriate that I turn to Paul a second time for the other side of that matter. Paul says it is good to have spiritual advantages. But he also says it is not hopeless not to have them. In fact, it is often the case that those without such advantages prosper spiritually.

Paul wrote along these lines to the Corinthians. They had been bothered by some in their fellowship who thought themselves to be very wise by worldly standards and who were probably throwing their weight around, as people who think themselves smarter than others are inclined to do. Paul rebukes that show of wisdom, reminding the believers at Corinth that it is not God's normal way to choose the wise, the mighty, or the noble to accomplish his purposes, but rather those the world calls foolish, weak, and ignoble—in order that boasting might be erased and glory given to God. The apostle said:

> Brothers, think of what you were when you were called. Not many of you were wise by human standards; not many were influential; not many were of noble birth. But God chose the foolish things of the world to shame the wise; God chose the weak things of the world to shame the strong. He chose the lowly things of this world and the despised things—and the things that are not—to nullify the things that are, so that no one may boast before him.
>
> 1 Corinthians 1:26–29

This is our hope. We should value every spiritual advantage. But we should know that our salvation is not in the advantages—certainly not in our being the firstborn or in being prominent in any other way—but in Jesus, the first-born of God, and in his gospel, which makes the foolish wise, the despised noble, and the weak of this world strong.

167

Simeon and Levi: Brothers in Wickedness

Genesis 49:5-7

"Simeon and Levi are brothers—
their swords are weapons of violence.
Let me not enter their council,
let me not join their assembly,
for they have killed men in their anger
and hamstrung oxen as they pleased.
Cursed be their anger, so fierce,
and their fury, so cruel!
I will scatter them in Jacob
and disperse them in Israel."

There are some things in life about which a person cannot speak with experience, and for me having a brother is one of those things. I grew up with three sisters, which was an experience in itself—especially since they were all younger. But I had no brothers. Therefore, I can only refer to others when I say that, according to them, the relationship between brothers is one of the closest relationships on earth. A brother is the person you stick by at all times regardless of the cost. A brother is a person you defend even when he is wrong. In some cases he is one you give your life for.

This special relationship is reflected in the use of the words for "brother" in various languages. The English word derives from the German word *Bruder*. It appears in terms like "brotherhood" or "blood brother" and in the names of various religious organizations like the Brothers of the Common Life, Brothers of the Poor, Brethren in Christ, and Plymouth Brethren. In 1787 the British and Foreign Anti-Slavery Society approved a seal of the society that showed a slave in chains, kneeling and uttering the words, "Am I not a man and a brother?" It was reproduced on china by the Wedgewood company and became a widespread slogan of the anti-slavery movement. The Latin word for brother is *frater,* which has given us "fraternal," "fraternity," "fraternize," and "fratricide." A Latin synonym for brother, *germanus,* may have given us the proper name "Germany," referring to a nation of specially bonded brothers.

Although I have not experienced this special "brother" relationship, I know that like other relationships it can be either good or bad. Brothers can help each other, encourage each other, and stick by each other in trouble. Or they can drag one another *down and further behavior more wicked than either* would attain alone.

Violence and Treachery

This seems to have been the case with Simeon and Levi, the next sons about whom Jacob speaks a word of prophecy. These were the second and third of Jacob's twelve sons and, like Reuben, were born of Leah. Instead of standing by one another for good, as would have been right, they seem to have stood by one another in wickedness and thus encouraged a violent and treacherous streak in each other. Jacob called them fierce and cruel.

As in the case of Reuben, who preceded Simeon and Levi in this prophecy, there is a historical incident in view. In the former case it was the sin of Reuben's sleeping with his father's concubine Bilhah. In the case of Simeon and Levi it was the violence practiced on the unsuspecting people of Shechem shortly after Jacob and his sons returned to Canaan from Haran.

The story began with an offense against Jacob and his family by Shechem, the son of the ruler of Shechem. He raped Dinah, Jacob's daughter. That was a great evil, of course, although there was probably sin on both sides. But it was not so great an evil as it could have been. Years later, when Amnon, David's son, forced Tamar, we are told that afterward "he hated her more than he had loved her" (2 Sam. 13:15). He rejected her harshly. Not so with Shechem! Shechem really loved Dinah. So although he seemed insensitive to the wrong done, he nevertheless wanted to do what he thought was right and marry the girl. He came to Jacob with his father Hamor and proposed marriage. Together they offered a dowry, friendship, and a proposal for an intermingling of the two peoples.

It is here that the sin of Jacob's sons appears even worse than that of the Canaanites. Their pride was offended, chiefly because Dinah was their sister; they felt the violation to be against them personally. They plotted revenge.

What is worse, they drew on their religious traditions to do it. They told the Shechemites:

> We can't do such a thing; we can't give our sister to a man who is not circumcised. That would be a disgrace to us. We will give our consent to you on one condition only: that you become like us by circumcising all your males. Then we will give you our daughters and take your daughters for ourselves. We'll settle among you and become one people with you. But if you will not agree to be circumcised, we'll take our sister and go.
>
> Genesis 34:14–17

This was treachery, for Simeon and Levi had no intention of giving Dinah to Shechem and settling down among the native people. They were plotting to kill them. Later they defended their murder by claiming in an exaggerated fashion that Shechem and Hamor had treated their sister like a prostitute (v. 31). They were prostituting the sign of the covenant in their designs.

Three days after the circumcisions, when the men of Shechem were in the greatest pain, Simeon and Levi "took their swords and attacked the unsuspecting city, killing every male. They put Hamor and his son Shechem to the sword and took Dinah from Shechem's house and left" (vv. 25–26). Then the other sons came and looted the city. "They seized their flocks and herds and donkeys and everything else of theirs in the city and out in the fields. They carried off all their wealth and all their women and children, taking as plunder everything in the houses" (vv. 28–29). Jacob felt that Simeon and Levi had made him "a stench" to the people of the land.

Years later Jacob was recalling this incident when he spoke his prophecy about the two brothers. When the event happened, he had no strong words of rebuke. He seemed rather to be concerned for his own safety. But by the time of this prophecy, Jacob had grown considerably. Here he calls evil evil and says that he wants no part of it himself: "Let me not enter their council"—their council was false; a man could be murdered there. "Let me not join their assembly"—the brothers had assembled for war in a bad cause; no righteous man could be a part of it.

This statement of Jacob is worth remembering, for by it he distances himself from his sons even though they are his sons. We often do otherwise. Because our children are *our* children, we defend their shortcomings and excuse their sins. This is an offense against God. It is harmful to them. George Lawson writes, "Parents, beware of bringing the guilt and dishonor of your children's faults upon yourselves. Will you plead for sin? Will you say that a conduct evidently wicked is either justifiable or excusable, because your children are charged with it? Your children ought to be dear to you, but the law of God ought to be far dearer. If they are dear to you, endeavor to make them sensible of all the evil of their conduct, that they may confess before God the sinfulness of their ways. If they confess their sins, and implore the mercy of God in Christ, God is faithful and just to forgive their sins. But you are unfaithful to their souls if by frivolous excuses you make them believe that they stand in little need of forgiveness."[1]

Scattered in Israel

Jacob's prophecy concerning Simeon and Levi has three parts: a denunciation of Simeon and Levi's sin, which flowed from their character; a disengagement from it by Jacob, who wanted no part in such treachery; and a judgment upon them, which contains a curse on their anger and a prophecy that they would possess no land of their own but would rather be scattered throughout Israel. We have looked at the first two parts. We come to the last part now.

The curse on Simeon and Levi's anger is an explanation of the judgment concerning their being scattered in the land. It is because of their cruelty that they were to lose their proper share of the tribal territory in Canaan. On most Bible maps, where the tribal areas are indicated, the territory of Simeon is located to the south and southwest of Judah, which occupied the area around Jerusalem.

This seems to be a true tribal area, but actually it was not. In Joshua 19:1–9 the distribution of the land to the tribe of Simeon is described—along with distributions to the other tribes—but the text makes it clear that Simeon's territory was actually a part of Judah:

> The second lot came out for the tribe of Simeon, clan by clan. Their inheritance lay *within the territory of Judah*. It included: Beersheba (or Sheba), Moladah, Hazar Shual, Balah, Ezem, Eltolad, Bethul, Hormah, Ziklag, Beth Marcaboth, Hazar Susah, Beth Lebaoth, and Sharuhen—thirteen towns and their villages; Ain, Rimmon, Ether and Ashan—four towns and their villages—and all the villages around these towns as far as Baalath Beer (Ramah in the Negev).
>
> This was the inheritance of the tribe of the Simeonites, clan by clan. The inheritance of the Simeonites was taken *from the share of Judah*, because Judah's portion was more than they needed. So the Simeonites received their inheritance *within the territory of Judah*.

Apparently some other scatterings followed. In a section of 1 Chronicles 1–11, where the descendants of the sons of Jacob are listed by clan and territory, the cities listed for Simeon in Joshua 19 are named again (4:28–33). But the text adds that two further expansions and settlements followed the earlier division. Some of the Simeonites went "to the outskirts of Gedor to the east" (v. 39). Others under the leadership of Pelatiah, Neariah, Rephaiah, and Uzziel, the sons of Ishi, invaded "the hill country of Seir" and settled there (v. 42). It was a fulfillment of Jacob's brief prophecy.

The tribe of Levi experienced a similar scattering, though in a quite different way. In the conquest of Canaan the Levites became the priests and thus, instead of being given tribal territory, were scattered throughout the land. The Levites were based in forty-eight Levitical cities in order to teach the Lord's statutes to the other tribes. In David's day there were further divisions and refinements. David counted 38,000 Levites above thirty years of age. Of these, 24,000 were assigned to service in the temple, 6,000 were officials and judges, 4,000 were gatekeepers, and 4,000 more were appointed to praise the Lord with musical instruments (see 1 Chron. 23:2–5).

The Curse Changed to Blessing

We notice something wonderful at this point. In the context of Jacob's prophecy in Genesis 49 the determination of God to scatter the descendants of Simeon and Levi in Israel is a judgment. It is a way of saying that Simeon and Levi were not to possess their own land. This was a judgment undoubtedly felt keenly by these brothers. Yet God is a gracious God, and in this case (as in so many other cases, even in our own lives) what *was* a judgment was changed in the flow of events into what must eventually be seen as a blessing.

Levi is the most obvious example. The descendants of Levi were scattered in Israel as priests; their homes were in the forty-eight Levitical cities. In addition, they traveled back and forth to perform their share of the duties connected with the temple worship. But although the descendants of Levi had no land of their own, it was nevertheless no small honor for them to have been made priests. And it was said of them that they had "no portion" in the land because "their portion was the Lord" himself. Moreover, they produced great leaders among the people. With the exception of the tribe of Judah, which produced most of the kings, the tribe of Levi contributed more distinguished men and leaders to Israel than any other.

Moses was a Levite. Moses was born in Egypt at the period of the greatest oppression of the Jewish people. He had godly parents, *Amram* and *Jochebed,* both of whom were of the Levitical tribe. Moses was more highly educated than anyone else of his day. He held a position of great privilege and power in Egypt. It is possible that he could have become a future pharaoh. But Moses did not side with the Egyptians. He sided with his own people. Hebrews tells us:

> By faith Moses, when he had grown up, refused to be known as the son of Pharaoh's daughter. He chose to be mistreated along with the people of God rather than to enjoy the pleasures of sin for a short time. He regarded disgrace for the sake of Christ as of greater value than the treasures of Egypt, because he was looking ahead to his reward. By faith he left Egypt, not fearing the king's

anger; he persevered because he saw him who is invisible. By faith he kept the Passover and the sprinkling of blood, so that the destroyer of the firstborn would not touch the firstborn of Israel.

Hebrews 11:24–28

Aaron was a Levite. He was Moses' brother and was given special duties as the high priest of Israel. The First Book of Chronicles says, "Aaron was set apart, he and his descendants forever, to consecrate the most holy things, to offer sacrifices before the LORD, to minister before him and to pronounce blessings in his name forever" (23:13).

Phinehas was a special leader in the tribe of Levi. He was the third high priest, and he served faithfully in that role for nineteen years. He is chiefly known for an incident recorded in Numbers 25. The people had fallen into sexual immorality with the women of Moab, who had invited them to the sacrifices to their gods. As a result the judgment of God in the form of a plague had fallen on the people. Phinehas was offended by this wickedness. So when he saw Zimri, a member of the tribe of Simeon, take a Moabite woman into his tent, he snatched up a spear and followed them and then drove the spear through Zimri into the woman's body. Because of this the plague was stopped and God praised Phinehas for his zeal. God said, "I am making my covenant of peace with him. He and his descendants will have a covenant of a lasting priesthood, because he was zealous for the honor of his God and made atonement for the Israelites" (Num. 25:12–13).

Eli was a Levite. Eli lived to be ninety-eight years old and was a priest in Shiloh. He served as a judge in Israel for forty years (1 Sam. 4:12–18).

Ezra was a Levite. Ezra was a distinguished scribe who served with Nehemiah at the time of the return of the people of Israel from Babylon. He wrote the Book of Ezra, the first of the post-captivity writings.

John the Baptist was a Levite. He was the son of *Zacharias,* who was a priest in the division of *Abijah,* and *Elizabeth,* who was in the line of descent from *Aaron* (Luke 1:5). God called John to be a forerunner of Christ in fulfillment of the last words of the Old Testament: "See, I will send you the prophet Elijah before that great and dreadful day of the LORD comes. He will turn the hearts of the fathers to their children, and the hearts of the children to their fathers" (Mal. 4:5–6). Jesus praised John extravagantly, saying, "I tell you the truth: Among those born of women there has not risen anyone greater than John the Baptist" (Matt. 11:11).

Thus we see that the tribe of Levi is an outstanding example of how God often transmutes that which began as a judgment into great blessing.

But we must not forget Simeon, because the same thing happened to this tribe, although in a very different way. Simeon was absorbed into Judah's territory, as I indicated. But this meant that in the bad days of Jeroboam and his successors, Simeon together with Judah (and the adjoining tribe of Benjamin) was kept from the general apostasy and so was given grace to survive and prosper for some years. The judgment of God fell on the northern kingdom of Israel in 721 B.C., but it did not come to the southern kingdom of Judah until 586 B.C., 135 years later.

Mercy with the Lord

Each of us should be encouraged by these prophecies. Here we see God's righteous judgment on sin, but as we trace the prophecies we see these judgments turned to blessing. Sin has consequences. But if you are suffering from what others have done—perhaps from the sin of a parent, like the descendants of Simeon and Levi—do not think that you are therefore excluded from God's favor or that it is impossible for you to gain God's favor again by godly living. God punishes children for the sin of the fathers "to the third and fourth generation of those who hate me" (Exod. 20:5), but he also "repents" of evil and brings blessing where he sees repentance (Exod. 32:14; Jer. 18:8; 26:3, 13; Joel 2:13).

Do not despair even if you are suffering for your own sins. On my desk is a card containing a spiritual quotation from Washington Irving, the American writer. Irving said, "It lightens the stroke to draw near to him who handles the rod." That is true. If you are suffering from sin, draw near to God and find that he is far more ready to forgive and transmute the punishment than you are to come to him.

We serve a merciful God. Just? Yes, but merciful too, and it is his mercy that draws us rather than drives us from him. We sing in a hymn:

> Come, ev'ry soul by sin oppressed,
>   There's mercy with the Lord,
> And He will surely give you rest
>   By trusting in His Word.
>
> Only trust Him, only trust Him,
>   Only trust Him now;
> He will save you, He will save you,
>   He will save you now.

Will you not draw near to him and trust him? It is wonderful to serve a merciful God.

168

Judah: Pride of Lions

Genesis 49:8–12

"Judah, your brothers will praise you;
your hand will be on the neck of your enemies;
your father's sons will bow down to you.
You are a lion's cub, O Judah;
you return from the prey, my son.
Like a lion he crouches and lies down,
like a lioness—who dares to rouse him?
The scepter will not depart from Judah,
nor the ruler's staff from between his feet,
until he comes to whom it belongs
and the obedience of the nations is his.
He will tether his donkey to a vine,
his colt to the choicest branch;
he will wash his garments in wine,
his robes in the blood of grapes.
His eyes will be darker than wine,
his teeth whiter than milk."

Some years ago a book appeared in American stores on the proper collective terms for animals. It is hard to think of a book on that subject being popular. But it did sell widely, and for a time

1189

the proper use of these words became a trivia pursuit for some people. I heard television personalities Ed McMahon and Johnny Carson debate what one properly calls a group of geese. The correct word is *gaggle*—a *gaggle* of geese. How about fish? That one is easy: a *school* of fish. We are also familiar with a *swarm* of bees, a *pack* of wolves, and a *litter* of pigs. A *bed* of clams does not surprise us.

But how about a *bevy* of quail?

A *clutch* of chicks?

A *cry* of hounds?

A *gam* of whales?

A *leap* of leopards?

A *mob* of kangaroos?

A *muster* of peacocks?

A *troop* of monkeys?

Or a *watch* of nightingales?

The proper term for the king of the beasts is *pride*—a *pride* of lions. That word is used in the title of this chapter in that sense. The caption "Judah: Pride of Lions" does not refer to any supposed heightening of the first deadly sin in Judah and his descendants, but rather to the numerous, distinguished leaders that were to come from this family. The text says, "You are a lion's cub, O Judah. . . . Like a lion he crouches and lies down, like a lioness—who dares to rouse him?" (v. 9). The chief verse says, "The scepter will not depart from Judah, nor the ruler's staff from between his feet, until he comes to whom it belongs and the obedience of the nations is his" (v. 10).

"Praise the Lord"

Judah would not have been expecting this blessing. Judah was the fourth of Jacob's twelve sons, and he had already heard the stern denunciations against the first three. Reuben was the firstborn, but Jacob told Reuben that he would "no longer excel" because he had dishonored his father by sleeping with his father's concubine Bilhah (v. 4). Simeon and Levi were likewise denounced for their violence. Jacob spoke as God for them, saying, "I will scatter them in Jacob and disperse them in Israel" (v. 7).

Judah must have trembled as he heard these harsh words. If he was a saved man—as he apparently was—he would have known something of the sin in his own heart and would have been aware that he was also guilty of offenses. If nothing else, Judah had slept with his daughter-in-law Tamar when she was disguised as a prostitute. It had been he who had suggested selling Joseph into Egypt: "What will we gain if we kill our brother and cover up his blood? Come, let's sell him to the Ishmaelites and not lay our hands on him; after all, he is our brother, our own flesh and blood" (Gen. 37:26–27).

As Judah thought of these things he must have expected a judgment similar to that pronounced on his three older brothers. But remarkably, a judgment does not follow. Instead of punishment, Jacob speaks of praise, preeminence, and prosperity.

Judah's name sounds like and may be derived from the Hebrew word for "praise." When he was born, his mother Leah said, "This time I will praise the LORD." The text adds, "So she named him Judah" (Gen. 29:35). When Leah named her son Judah she was expressing her gratitude to God for having given her a fourth son. That is, she was praising God. But here, in Judah's prophecy, a word that originally referred to praise to God is turned about to denote the praise Judah would himself receive from his brothers: "Judah, your brothers will praise you; your hand will be on the neck of your enemies; your father's sons will bow down to you" (Gen. 49:8). According to Jacob, Judah would be praised for supremacy in Israel. From Judah would come the natural military leaders and eventually the kings of the nation.

At first glance this change of meaning, from praise to God to praise of Judah, seems wrong to us. And of course, it could be. It *is* wrong to take glory due God and give it to mere men. Yet this is not the case here. Although it is possible to praise men *rather than God* and thus rob God of his glory, it is nevertheless also possible to praise God *through* our praise of men. That is, we can recognize what human beings have accomplished, praise them in every proper way, and at the same time acknowledge that these blessings have been given to us by God and thank him for them.

The Bible does this. Do you remember that wonderful scene in the Book of Revelation in which the twenty-four elders, who represent the church, lay their crowns before God and cry out:

> "You are worthy, our Lord and God,
>   to receive glory and honor and power,
> for you created all things,
>   and by your will they were created
>   and have their being."

> Revelation 4:11

Where did these crowns come from? The text does not say explicitly. But in the chapters immediately before this, there is a recurring phrase: "to him [or he] who overcomes." It is found seven times—once in each of the letters to the seven churches—and it is accompanied each time by promises of blessing, authority, and rule. Clearly, these crowns have been given to the saints by God in recognition of their spiritual victories. The saints are praised. But immediately after appearing before God with the crowns of praise that he gave, the saints lay them at God's feet and thus acknowledge him as the one who alone is worthy to receive all honor.

Something like this is present in Judah's case and should be present in the achievements of us all. Do we do a good job in our calling? Are we praised for it? That is good. There is nothing wrong with that. But if we do well and if we are praised, let us make certain that the praise is then given back to God. We should know that we have nothing but what we have first received from him (1 Cor. 4:7) and that in his sight we are at best still unprofitable servants (Luke 17:10).

King of Beasts

The second thing Jacob speaks about is preeminence. This is a strange thing, because in some respects preeminence, which was a right of the first-born, had already been given to Joseph, who took Reuben's place. The first-born normally had two rights. First, he became the leader of the family, the new patriarch. Second, he was entitled to a double share of the inheritance, receiving twice as much as any of the other brothers. This last benefit was apparently conveyed to Joseph when Jacob adopted Joseph's two sons. Each would receive a portion, thus doubling the share to Joseph's family. The chief text in support of Joseph's having taken Reuben's place (1 Chron. 5:1–2) speaks of the rights of the firstborn being given "to the *sons* of Joseph," not Joseph himself. Of course, Joseph was already ruling in Egypt, and a number of leaders, particularly judges, came from him.

Because of Joseph's prominence and because of his receiving a double portion of the inheritance, we might think that the right of rule was also his. But in a strange way this passes to Judah and not Joseph. When Joseph received his dreams of the sheaves of wheat and the moon and stars, it was prophesied that his father and brothers would bow to him. And so they did! But in the long view it was to the descendants of Judah that the others would bow. Judah would be father of the kings of Israel until the Messiah came.

What a list of kings they are! The first king of Israel was Saul, who was of the tribe of Benjamin. But the first great king—in fact, the greatest of all the kings—was *David,* a man described as being "after God's own heart." He was from Judah. David was the youngest son of Jesse, who was the son of Obed, the son of Boaz and Ruth. But he was first in character and a great leader. He ruled for forty years.

James Hastings wrote in *The Greater Men and Women of the Bible:* "The David of Israel is not simply the greatest of her kings; he is the man great in everything. He monopolizes all her institutions. He is her shepherd boy—the representative of her toiling classes. He is her musician—the successor of Jubal and Miriam and Deborah. He is her soldier—the conqueror of all the Goliaths that would steal her peace. He is her king—numbering her armies and regulating her polity. He is her priest—substituting a broken and a contrite spirit for the blood of bulls and rams. He is her prophet—presaging with his latest breath the everlastingness of his kingdom. And he is her poet—all her psalms are called by his name."[1]

The descendants of Judah never received greater praise than in the person of King David. Judah's sons were never more preeminent than in him.

Solomon was another great king. He was not as great a person as David his father, but Solomon was nevertheless a great man. It was during his reign that Israel rose to the pinnacle of her outward glory. Solomon built the majestic temple in Jerusalem. He wrote or at least was responsible for three of the Bible's books of poetry: Proverbs, Ecclesiastes, and the Song of Songs. Solomon was known for his wisdom. The Bible says of him: "God gave Solomon wisdom and very great insight, and a breadth of understanding as measureless as the sand on the seashore. Solomon's wisdom was greater than the wisdom of all the men of the East, and greater than all the wisdom of Egypt. He was wiser than any other man" (1 Kings 4:29–31).

After David and Solomon there were kings of lesser stature and some who were quite evil, although generally the kings of Judah were more righteous than the kings of the northern kingdom during this period. There were kings like Asa, Jehoshaphat, Uzziah, Jotham, and Hezekiah, each of whom is described as having done "right" in evil times (1 Kings 15:11; 22:43; 2 Kings 15:34; 18:3).

Josiah is outstanding in this period. He came to the throne when he was only eight years old, and he reigned for thirty-one years. When he was eighteen the priests discovered the Book of the Law, which had long been forgotten, and this was read to the king. Josiah recognized how much the people had departed from God's commandments and led the entire nation in a public confession of sin and a renewal of the covenant. For his part, Josiah purified the temple, destroyed the high places where false gods were worshiped, banished the mediums and spiritists, and reinstituted the Passover.

The Bible says of Josiah: "He did what was right in the eyes of the LORD and walked in all the ways of his father David, not turning aside to the right or to the left. . . . Neither before nor after Josiah was there a king like him who turned to the LORD as he did—with all his heart and with all his soul and with all his strength, in accordance with all the Law of Moses" (2 Kings 22:2; 23:25).

Even after the exile the line of Judah was intact and produced great leaders. One of these was *Zerubbabel,* the governor who led a group of returning Jews from Babylon to Jerusalem. He is mentioned in the Books of Ezra and Nehemiah. The minor prophet Haggai closes with a special word of encouragement for this man.

After Zerubbabel came *Abiud,* then *Eliakim, Azor, Zadok, Anim, Eliud, Eleazar, Matthan, Jacob,* and finally *Joseph,* who was the adoptive father of the Lord Jesus Christ.

A more illustrious line never existed in the annals of human history. No human family has ever become so prominent.

Prosperity

The third blessing spoken over Judah in Jacob's prophecy is prosperity. This is what is meant by the figurative language of verses 11 and 12: "He will tether his donkey to a vine, his colt to the choicest branch; he will wash his garments in wine, his robes in the blood of grapes. His eyes will be darker than wine, his teeth whiter than milk."

These verses may have a fuller application than I am about to give now; they may refer to the Messiah. But whatever additional meanings they may have, these words refer at least to a period of great prosperity in Judah as the result of God's blessing. We remember that four hundred years after this, when the Hebrews were led out of Egypt, God gave them "a good land—a land with streams and pools of water, with springs flowing in the valleys and hills; a land with wheat and barley, vines and fig trees, pomegranates, olive oil and honey, a land where bread will not be scarce and [they would] lack nothing" (Deut. 8:7–9). This is the imagery of Jacob's prophecy. The land of Judah was to be so prosperous that every man would have his own donkey and his own vine, and the fruit of the vine would be so plentiful that he could wash his clothes in it, figuratively speaking. In such a place and with such prosperity a man's eyes would become dark and flashing and his teeth as white as milk.

Prosperity is God's doing, as was the case with Judah's prospering. Are you prospering? If you are, do you acknowledge God as the source of such blessings? Judah did not deserve these things. Neither do we. But for that very reason we should be zealous in our thanksgiving. We should "praise God from whom all blessings flow."

King of Kings

I said a moment ago that there are parts of this prophecy that may have greater and higher meaning than I have developed in this study. But even here it is impossible to overlook the fact that each of these items—praise, preeminence, and prosperity—is fulfilled supremely in the Lord Jesus Christ, who was born of Judah's line and is portrayed in Revelation as "*the* Lion of the tribe of Judah" (Rev. 5:5). Jacob referred to him explicitly when he declared that "the scepter will not depart from Judah, nor the ruler's staff from between his feet, until he comes to whom it belongs and the obedience of the nations is his" (v. 10).

Jacob told Judah that he would be the object of his brothers' *praise*. But is this not true of Jesus in the most exalted sense? Jesus has been given "the name that is above every name" (Phil. 2:9). To him "every knee" shall bow (v. 10). Jesus Christ is the ultimate fulfillment of even Joseph's dreams, for the sun and moon and eleven stars bow to him and to no mere mortal. Charles Haddon Spurgeon wrote that on earth to praise him is "our sweetest employment," and in heaven it will be "our highest delight."[2]

We see that Jacob prophesied preeminence for Judah. But whatever *preeminence* Judah rightly had has been eclipsed by Jesus. Jacob thought of his fourth son as a lion, tearing his enemies apart and dominating his kingdom. Jesus has done this preeminently. In the spiritual sense there are two lions in this world. There is the Lion of the tribe of Judah, who is Jesus, and there is the devil, that "roaring lion" who prowls about seeking whom he may devour (1 Peter 5:8).

Jesus has defeated that old lion, wresting his kingdom from him and freeing all those who throughout their lives were subject to his bondage. That struggle took Jesus to the depths of the pit. But from the pit he has risen up to assume the highest place. Today Jesus is King of kings and Lord of lords. He is our King and our Lord. He is preeminent in the universe and must be preeminent in our lives.

Finally, Jacob spoke of *prosperity* to come through Judah. Even that physical prosperity came through Jesus, for Jesus is God and "every good and perfect gift" comes from him (James 1:17). But more important even than physical prosperity is that spiritual blessing Christ brings. Jesus brings life out of death, love out of hate, joy out of sorrow, peace out of lifelong alienation. Thus, the one who has Jesus has everything, though he loses the whole world. And the one who does not have him, though he gains the whole world, perishes.

169

Shiloh

Genesis 49:10

"The scepter will not depart from Judah,
nor the ruler's staff from between his feet,
until he comes to whom it belongs
and the obedience of the nations is his."

Many believers have a favorite title for the Lord Jesus Christ, and Jacob, the ancient patriarch of Israel, was no exception. His favorite name was "Shiloh." "Shiloh" does not appear in many modern Bibles (including the New International Version), which choose to render the Hebrew in some other way. But the Hebrew text says "Shiloh," and a literal rendering of this verse is close to the King James translation: "The sceptre shall not depart from Judah, nor a lawgiver from between his feet, until Shiloh come; and unto him shall the gathering of the people be."

This is a great passage, as most commentators on Genesis recognize—the last of three great prophecies of the Messiah found in Genesis. The first is Genesis 3:15, in which the prophecy of a deliverer was given to Adam and Eve in Eden. God is speaking to the serpent, pronouncing judgment: "I will put enmity between you and the woman, and between your offspring and hers; he will crush your head, and you will strike his heel." Adam and Eve believed that promise and were saved by it.

The second prophecy is Genesis 22:18, the climax of God's many revelations to Abraham. Early in the story God promised Abraham a land, a son, and posterity as numerous as the stars in heaven. But in the context of his testing of Abraham, recorded in Genesis 22, God surpassed these earlier revelations with the words "and through your offspring all nations on earth will be blessed" (Gen. 22:18). This prophecy could have referred merely to a blessing of others through the chosen nation of Israel. But it is actually a reference to the Messiah, as Paul points out in Galatians 3:16. It was to be a singular descendant of Abraham (Jesus) through whom Gentiles as well as Jews would be saved. Abraham believed this promise just as Adam and Eve had believed the promise given to them in Eden.

The third prophecy is Genesis 49:10.

In the first prophecy it is said that the Messiah would destroy the devil and his works. In the second it is said that he would redeem his people, thus bringing salvation to both Jew and Gentile. In the third prophecy it is said that all rule is his and that all peoples of earth will eventually bow before him.

A Puzzling Name

In spite of the importance of this prophecy, which nearly all commentators recognize, the name Shiloh itself is puzzling. It is a name for the Messiah. But it is not merely a name. It means something, and that meaning is elusive. Here are the possibilities:

1. "Shiloh" might mean "sent," like that similar word that occurs in the New Testament in the story of the healing of the blind man: "'Go,' he told him, 'wash in the pool of Siloam' (this word means Sent)" (John 9:7). I remember puzzling over this interpretation of Genesis 49:10 during graduate study in Switzerland, before I had made the connection with the New Testament passage. I pondered whether "Shiloh" might not be derived from the common Hebrew verb *shalach*, which means "send." In this case "Shiloh" would mean "the sent one" or "the one whom God will send."

This is a good meaning. It fits the text, which is a prophecy of the sending of the Messiah. Moreover, it fits with many other statements in Scripture, such as Isaiah 61:1–2, which Jesus quoted in Nazareth at the start of his public ministry: "The Spirit of the Sovereign LORD is on me, because the LORD has anointed me to preach good news to the poor. He has *sent* me to bind up the brokenhearted, to proclaim freedom for the captives and release from darkness for the prisoners, to proclaim the year of the LORD's favor." Jerome was attracted to this interpretation of Genesis 49:10, because the Latin Vulgate, which he produced, contains the words *qui mittendus est* ("who must be sent").

The problem is that this involves a textual emendation. The Hebrew word for "send" contains the consonants *sheen, lahmed,* and *chait.* But the word "Shiloh" contains the consonants *sheen, lahmed* and *hay.* To be sure, the difference is slight.

In print *chait* looks something like the scientific symbol *pi*. *Hay* is similar, except that one of the two legs does not quite reach the top bar. Nevertheless, *hay* is not *chait*, and there is no textual justification for the change.

2. An old interpretation of "Shiloh," going back to Jewish commentators, is that the word means "son." This is based on the resemblance of the name to the Hebrew root *shiljah*, which is taken to mean "son." This would be a wonderful meaning, since Jesus is certainly *the* son in all important senses. He is the Son of God, the Son of Man, the Son of Judah, the Son of David. Isaiah 9:6 would fit in well here: "To us a child is born, to us a son is given, and the government will be on his shoulders. And he will be called Wonderful Counselor, Mighty God, Everlasting Father, Prince of Peace." So would Matthew 3:17: "This is my Son, whom I love; with him I am well pleased."

Unfortunately, although this was the preferred interpretation of "Shiloh" by both Martin Luther and John Calvin, it is based on a mistranslation of *shiljah*. *Shiljah* means not "son," but "afterbirth." So to derive Jacob's name for Jesus from this word seems mistaken.

3. During the last centuries the most popular interpretation of "Shiloh" has been to derive it from the same root word as *Salem* or *shalom*, which means "peace." In this view "Shiloh" would mean "peace-giver" or "the one who brings peace." I said earlier that "Shiloh" probably does not mean "the sent one," because the final consonant is *hay* rather than *chait*. However, if *hay* is retained, then the word is the verb "to be quiet" or "to be at ease," which is what peace involves.

Jesus is the Peace-giver. He is the one who made reconciliation between man and God by his death for sin on the cross. Robert Candlish liked this interpretation of the name.[1] So did George Lawson. He wrote, "The peaceful one, or he that is the giver of tranquility, appears to be the true meaning."[2]

Charles Haddon Spurgeon applied this meaning of the name eloquently: "Have you ever said to yourself, 'There is nothing I desire—nothing that I wish for; I am satisfied—perfectly content; I am without a fear, without a dread'? 'No,' say you, 'I never reached that elysium.' You may be worth millions of money without ever coming to that pass. All the gold in the world will never fill a man's heart; and you may have broad acres across which a swift horse could hardly rush in a day, but you will not have enough. All the land in the world cannot fill a heart. You may have all the beauty, rank, honor and fame that ever can come to a human being, and yet say, 'Ah me! I am wretched still.' But full many who have found Jesus have been able to say, 'It is enough: I need no more.' Believing in Jesus, and learning to yield up everything to his will, living to his glory, and loving him supremely, we do enjoy peace with God—a 'peace that passeth all understanding,' which 'keeps our heart and mind' by Jesus Christ."[3]

We could do worse than adopt the translation of "Shiloh" that sees it as "he who gives rest." We do badly indeed if we do not find true rest in him, regardless of the meaning of the word.

4. There is still a fourth possibility, and in the judgment of most modern translators it is to be preferred over the others. It derives "Shiloh" from the Hebrew particle of relationship, *sher* (or *'asher*), here rendered "whose" or "whom," and *l*, which means "to." The meaning would be "he to whom," and the verse would read like the New International Version: "until he comes to whom it belongs." This is the way the Septuagint, the Greek translation of the Old Testament, reads, using a phrase that literally means "until the things laid up in store come into his possession." It would have an exact parallel in Ezekiel 21:27, which says, "It will not be restored until he comes *to whom it rightfully belongs; to him I will give it.*"

This is probably the right translation, in which case "Shiloh" refers to Jesus' rightful rule and authority. It looks forward to the day when these will be his and the nations properly will bow before him (cf. Phil. 2:9–11).

Only One Shiloh

Thus far I have been assuming that "Shiloh," whatever its meaning, refers to Jesus, who fulfills that meaning. But this is worth spelling out in detail. The point of this prophecy is that an eternal ruler should come in Judah's line, that Jesus came in that line and fulfills the prophecy, and that if he has not fulfilled it, there will at least never be another person who can do so. The proof lies in Jesus' genealogies.

In the previous study, as I spoke of the rulers who had descended from Judah in the line of David, I mentioned Abiud, Eliakim, Azor, Zadok, Eliud, Eleazar, Matthan, and Jacob, who were the links between Zerubbabel and Joseph, the adoptive father of Jesus Christ. Jacob was Joseph's father, and Abiud was the son of Zerubbabel (cf. Matt. 1:13–16). This puts Jesus in the line of David, through David's son Solomon.

There is a problem here, however, because one king in this line, Jehoiakim, received a curse from God saying that no descendant of his would ever sit upon the throne of David. "Record this man as if childless, a man who will not prosper in his lifetime, for none of his offspring will prosper, none will sit on the throne of David or rule anymore in Judah" (Jer. 22:30). If Jesus had been a natural descendant of Jehoiakim (also called Jeconiah and Jechonias), the curse would have applied to him and he would not have been eligible to fulfill Jacob's prophecy.

But there is another line through which Jesus' descent from David is also reckoned: the line of Mary, Jesus' mother. Mary was a descendant of King David through Nathan, Solomon's older brother. In the chart called "The Adam and Eve Family Tree," which I have mentioned before, Mary's ancestors are printed alongside the ancestors of Joseph leading back to Solomon. Mary's line contains forty-one names, counting Joseph, who is listed as a son-in-law of Heli, Mary's father (cf. Luke 3:23). Joseph's line contains twenty-nine names, omitting Joseph.

But notice this problem. Before the birth of Christ to Mary and his adoption by Joseph, there were two lines of descent, each of which had a claim to the Davidic throne but each of which would have been challenged by the other. Joseph's ancestors had ruled, but they were under a curse. No children of Jehoiakim ever did rule in Jerusalem, nor did any of their sons rule. Jehoiakim died in Babylon. Mary's line had no curse, but no one in that line had ruled. Any ancestor of Mary would have been challenged by those who had descended from Solomon.

How could this be resolved? In one line there is a lack of reigning royalty. In the other there is a curse. Humanly speaking, the problem is unsolvable. But when God the Father caused the Lord Jesus Christ to be born of the Virgin Mary without benefit of a human father, the child that was born became the seed of David according to the flesh. And when Joseph married Mary at God's command and thus took the unborn child under his adoptive and protective care, the Holy One to be born became his heir also and thus took to himself the title that had come down to Joseph through his illustrious ancestor Solomon.

In this way Jesus exhausted both lines; he was the oldest son of both Joseph and Mary and he himself had no children. By this divinely simple means Jesus became the true Messiah, the royal Messiah, the uncursed Messiah, the only possible Messiah. So I repeat, if Jesus is not the fulfillment of Jacob's prophecy, there will at least never be another to fulfill it. Anyone who should ever come into the world purporting to be the Messiah will actually be a false Messiah, a liar, and the Antichrist.[4]

Lord of Lords

Yet we have not considered the central content of this prophecy. We have examined the possible meanings of the word Shiloh. We have seen that Jesus is that Shiloh, indeed the only Shiloh there can ever be. But the heart of the prophecy is that the nations of the world will be gathered to this one, will obey him, and will be prospered in so doing.

It is a wonderful thing that this prophecy of Jacob to his son Judah about the Messiah included the gentile nations, for most Christians today are Gentiles and are therefore included in this blessing. Thus far in Genesis the work of God seems to have moved in the opposite direction. We began with one world, indeed one race spreading out to take possession of that world. But the race became increasingly corrupt. So instead of a universal salvation, we have seen God stooping to call and bless one unique people. God called Abraham, then Isaac, then Jacob, then Jacob's twelve sons. It is a narrowing thing, and the book is to close with a focus on this small group of chosen people.

How wonderful is this last prophecy, for it opens our eyes to the other nations again! It tells us that although God is going to work through this one people for a time, the day will come when he will open the door of salvation to all people. Those from *all* nations will bow before Jesus.

And it is happening! Look at China, where the gospel of Shiloh has been ruthlessly suppressed for decades. When missionaries left China in the face of the Communist onslaught, there were less than one million professing Christians in that vast land. Today by some estimates there are more than fifty million who have professed obedience to Christ. The gathering of the people of China is to him.

I correspond with a woman who attended Tenth Presbyterian Church while in the United States to prepare for a ministry in her own country, the Philippines. I last saw her in India. She was on her way home to present Jesus to her family and village. She has written since that her father has become a Christian and has joined in her work. She has several weekly Bible studies and is active in a local church. Scores are now bowing the knee to Christ through her witness. The gathering of the people of the Philippines is to him.

On the same trip on which I saw this woman I visited Nepal. For years Nepal was closed to the gospel, and the best that Christians could do for that country was to camp on the border, pray for, and witness to those few Nepalese who crossed it in search of jobs or trade. In my lifetime Nepal has opened to the gospel, and missionaries have entered that land. It is illegal for a person to convert from one faith to another in Nepal. So even when Christians were allowed into the country, they were not to convert anybody, and Nepalese who left their faith for Christianity were imprisoned. Scores of native believers have suffered that punishment. They were imprisoned for bowing the knee to Christ. Yet they did bow before him. The rulers of Nepal set their faces against the Lord's anointed. But still he rules, and to him shall the obedience of the Nepalese be.

There is a member of Tenth Presbyterian Church who has worked in Nepal for years. She is fluent in Nepalese. But suddenly another formerly closed country opened: Bhutan. So she went there to be a vehicle by which the people of that nation will learn the gospel and obey Christ's call.

This is the flow of history. According to the prophecies of the coming of the Messiah in Genesis, Jesus was to defeat Satan, redeem his people, and gather the nations. The first two of these have been done. Jesus defeated Satan on the cross; he also made full and perfect atonement for his people's sins. Today it is the last of these alone that is unfolding. This is the day of Christ's gathering. It is the reaping time. It will continue until all Christ's saints are gathered together around his throne, singing:

> "Worthy is the Lamb, who was slain,
> to receive power and wealth and wisdom and strength
> and honor and glory and praise."

> Revelation 5:12

Do not miss that gathering. Do not shun that call. Fall before him. Praise him as your Shiloh.

170

Zebulun and Issachar:
At Ease in Zion

Genesis 49:13–15

*"Zebulun will live by the seashore
and become a haven for ships;
his border will extend toward Sidon.*

*Issachar is a rawboned donkey
lying down between two saddlebags.
When he sees how good is his resting place
and how pleasant is his land,
he will bend his shoulder to the burden
and submit to forced labor."*

Genesis 49 does not describe the positioning of the sons of Jacob as they stood by their father to receive his dying words. But we are probably not far off the mark if we imagine them grouped together according to their mothers. Reuben, the firstborn, would

1202

have been closest to his father. Next to him would have been the other sons of Leah: Simeon and Levi, Judah, Zebulun and Issachar.

This may explain why Jacob utters his prophecy regarding Zebulun and Issachar after that of Judah. They were not his fifth and sixth children. After the first four sons had been born of Leah, Jacob had sons of the two concubines, Bilhah and Zilpah. Zebulun and Issachar were actually Jacob's ninth and tenth sons, though, to be accurate, we must note that Issachar was the ninth and Zebulun was the tenth. The only way we can explain the order of the prophecies is to assume that these six were standing together and that Jacob simply focused on each of them as he proceeded deliberately around the circle.

Neither of the tribes that descended from Zebulun and Issachar was particularly prominent. At least they produced almost no remembered leaders. Zebulun produced one judge, Elon, who is mentioned in Judges 12:11. Issachar produced another judge, Tola, who is mentioned in Judges 10:1–2. But aside from that there is hardly any person of distinction. Between the two tribes only twenty-eight people are mentioned in all the Old Testament.

A Place Appointed

Yet Jacob's prophecies concerning Zebulun and Issachar contain important lessons. Zebulun's prophecy deals with the areas of Canaan this tribe was eventually to occupy. It is the only one of the prophecies that describes specific territory. But since the territory of the tribes was later determined by lot, it is a reminder, as Paul later told the Athenians, that God "made every nation of men, that they should inhabit the whole earth; and he determined the times set for them and the exact places where they should live" (Acts 17:26).

In Zebulun's case there is difficulty determining exactly how Jacob's words were fulfilled. Jacob said that Zebulun would "live by the seashore and become a haven for ships" (v. 13). But in the division of the land of Canaan, as most students see it, the tribe of Asher actually occupied the seacoast, and Zebulun, although toward the coast in the northwest portion of the land, actually was somewhat inland. The tribe of Zebulun lived on the Plain of Esdraelon between the Sea of Galilee and the Mediterranean.

How is this to be explained? Some interpreters, like Martin Luther, plead ignorance of the true location of Zebulun, suggesting that the people may at one time have extended their territory as far as the port at the base of Mount Carmel. But it is more likely that our translations just do not catch the sense of the original Hebrew. It seems significant to me that the Hebrew does not say that Zebulun will live "by" or "on" the seashore but rather "to" or "toward" it, in the same way that his northern border was to extend toward Sidon. In my judgment, the text should read somewhat as H. C. Leupold has it in his commentary: "Zebulun shall dwell toward the seashore; yea, he shall be toward the shore where ships come, and his flank shall be toward Sidon."[1]

The meaning is not that Zebulun should become a seafaring people, for the tribe did not. Rather it is that it should be in a position well situated for trade. One border would be toward the sea, another toward the great trading center of Sidon. From there Zebulun would be able to move commerce east toward Galilee and northeast toward Damascus.

You, like Zebulun, may have been placed in a highly advantageous position. It may be financial. Because of where you live or work, because of the specific nature of your business, because of your unique positioning in the marketplace, you have unusual opportunities to make money. If this is so, recognize that God is the source of this good fortune and thank him for it. In addition, regard your wealth as something given to you by God and be responsible to him for how you use it.

Or you may have a different kind of advantage. You may be in a position of influence. Because you are prominent or well known, other people look up to you and even copy you. Be careful how you use that influence. Be careful to be like the Lord Jesus Christ so that, in copying you, others actually begin to learn what it means to copy him.

Other people are in a position to get things done. I consider myself to have this kind of opportunity. I am able to guide organizations, launch new projects, and attract others to needy areas. This too is from God. So if you find yourself in this kind of a position, be sure to make your opportunities to get things done count. Do not waste your advantages, but use them so that at the last you will hear the Lord say, "Well done, good and faithful servant! You have been faithful with a few things; I will put you in charge of many things. Come and share your master's happiness" (Matt. 25:21, 23).

There is a warning in Jacob's prophecy concerning Zebulun. Jacob said that Zebulun's border would extend toward Sidon, but Sidon, we remember, was a wicked city that frequently proved a snare to Israel. Jezebel, the wicked wife of King Ahab, was a princess of that country, and when she came to Israel she brought her idols with her. They were a cause of destruction not only to her husband's house and family but to many thousands of others in the northern kingdom.

It is a significant blessing to be in a position of great opportunity. But remember, prominence also brings danger with it. It is hard to be godly *and* famous. It is hard to live for Christ and *at the same time* be sought after by the world. Every believer should remain close to Jesus at all times, but those in high positions especially should do so. There is no advantage to gaining the world if the price of the conquest is one's soul.

Strong but Satisfied

The sixth son of Leah was Issachar, whom Jacob characterizes as a "rawboned donkey" (v. 14). To call Issachar an "ass" or "donkey" did not have the pejorative meaning in ancient times that either of those terms has for us today. To us a donkey is an ignoble, stupid animal. But in those times a donkey was a valuable beast. People of rank frequently rode upon them (Judg. 10:4; 12:14). Ziba, the steward of Mephibosheth, when he was seeking a favor of King David, presented him with a string of donkeys, which, he said, were for the king's household to ride on (2 Sam. 16:1–2). We should not think of comparing Issachar to a donkey as unfavorable any more than we should think so later on in the chapter when Dan is compared to a serpent, Naphtali to a doe, or Benjamin to a wolf.

On the contrary, the comparison is to the chief virtue of these animals, and in Issachar's case this refers to the donkey's uncommon patience and great strength. This seems to have been characteristic of Issachar's descendants. At the time of the judges, the tribe of Issachar (together with Zebulun) was courageous in rallying to Deborah and Barak in their struggle against the Canaanites (cf. Judg. 5:15, 18). Some of the other tribes were inactive.

In Numbers 26, where the numbering of the men of each tribe able to go to war is recorded, we find that only Judah and Dan produced more able-bodied men than Issachar, and Dan's number exceeded Issachar's by only one hundred. Later Issachar's numbers became even stronger. In Numbers 26:25 the warriors of the tribe of Issachar are listed as 64,300. But we read in 1 Chronicles 7:5, in the time of the kings, "The relatives who were fighting men belonging to all the clans of Issachar, as listed in their genealogy, were 87,000 in all." This is not a great deal of material to build on, but as far as it goes it shows the men of Issachar actually to have been strong and trustworthy in the nation's battles.

Yet there was a weak side too, as the prophecy of Jacob also indicates. Issachar was strong, but the tribe of Issachar was also complacent and without ambition. There is a problem here in knowing what the word translated "saddlebags" refers to. The Hebrew is *mishpethayim*, which my dictionary defines as a "doubtful word." Some commentators have identified it as two "sheepfolds" (RSV, ASV, JB) or "cattle pens" (NEB), which led Donald Grey Barnhouse to comment: "Between the sheepfolds was where the manure was flung. The strong ass bedded down on the dung heap because of its warmth. Thus Jacob described the son who was willing to wallow in filth for his own comfort."[2] The King James Version translates that word as "burdens," which is similar to "saddlebags," preferred by the New International Version. Other commentators think the word means "borders," among them Lawson, who wrote, "Issachar is like a strong-boned ass lying down between the two borders or extremities of his inheritance."[3]

Probably we just do not know enough to make a choice between these three or four possibilities. But whatever the proper choice is, the idea seems to be much the same. It is a picture of contentment in which the descendants of this tribe fail to exert themselves to vigorous activity. As a result, says Jacob, the time will come when Issachar "will bend his shoulder to the burden and submit to forced labor" (v. 15).

We do not know exactly how this prophecy was fulfilled either. But we do know that the fertile, desirable land of Issachar was frequently invaded, and we may suppose that the people were often forced into servitude. Of course, when Tiglath-Pileser annexed this territory to the Assyrian empire in 732 B.C., Issachar lost all rights of self-government. And in 721 B.C. this tribe, along with all the others of the northern kingdom, was carried into exile.

Always Press On

Jacob does not draw a moral from his prophecy concerning Issachar, his words ending with a description of what was to come. But a moral is implied. The moral is that diligent effort and hard work never stop for God's people. Rather than lying down in Zion, as Issachar did, we ought to press on in God's service throughout the whole of life.

I think here of the example of the apostle Paul as he wrote of his aspirations to the Philippians:

> Not that I have already obtained all this, or have already been made perfect, but I press on to take hold of that for which Christ Jesus took hold of me. Brothers, I do not consider myself yet to have taken hold of it. But one thing I do: Forgetting what is behind and straining toward what is ahead, I press on toward the goal to win the prize for which God has called me heavenward in Christ Jesus.

> Philippians 3:12–14

To know Jesus *is* his goal. But it is not a goal that enables him to rest on past successes or even wallow in past failures. On the contrary, precisely because he wants to know Jesus in the power of his resurrection and the fellowship of his sufferings (v. 10), he keeps pressing on to achieve everything God has for him.

Paul's conduct at this very moment is an example. He was in prison in Rome near the end of a long and very fruitful career as a missionary. In the course of that career he had received the standard thirty-nine lashes of punishment five times, had been beaten with rods an additional three times, was stoned once, and suffered shipwreck three times; he was constantly in danger—"in danger from rivers, in danger from bandits, in danger from [his] own countrymen, in danger from Gentiles; in danger in the city, in danger in the country, in danger at sea; and in danger from false brothers." He was hungry, thirsty, cold, and naked. Besides this, he faced "daily the pressure of [his] concern for all the churches" (see 2 Cor. 11:24–28). Then he had to come to Rome in chains, had been incarcerated in Caesar's prisons, and was largely forgotten by the Christian population. We know this because at this time a Christian by the name of Onesiphorus came to Rome to find Paul, and did find him at last, but only after diligent searching (2 Tim. 1:16–17). No one seemed able to tell Onesiphorus where Paul was.

If anyone in all the history of the church had an excuse to sit back and do nothing, it was surely Paul during the time of his Roman imprisonment. He had been faithful in his missionary assignment. He had been persecuted and then abused. He could have retired in those days. If he had said, "I have paid my dues; I have put in my time; I have run my race," there is nobody on earth—certainly not ourselves—who could have faulted him.

But Paul did not retire. He did not cash in his chips. Instead he pressed on, knowing that he was not free to take his ease until he rested in that heavenly Zion the Lord has prepared for all his faithful servants.

And he did press on, even in prison. Early in Philippians the apostle tells how "it has become clear throughout the whole palace guard and to everyone else that I am in chains for Christ" (1:13). How was it that the gospel was spread throughout "the whole palace guard"? It was not by those Christians who were on the outside, making trouble for Paul, as we know they were. It was by Paul himself as he testified, first to one soldier who was chained to him to guard him, and then to another. I suppose the guards were posted in four- or eight-hour shifts. That means that Paul would see either three or six guards per day. When he was with them he did not spend his time talking about the weather or complaining about the unjust treatment he had received. He talked about Jesus. He testified about him, laying down the basics of the Christian gospel. And when the guard was changed, Paul would begin with the next soldier. When a previous soldier returned, Paul would pick up where he had left off. In that manner, in time, I suppose Paul worked his way through a large percentage of the emperor's choice troops. Thus the gospel spread throughout the palace and among the highest personages of the Roman Empire.

It was because Paul did not take his ease in Zion. It was because he pressed on to the very end, until God called him home to heaven.

Galilee of the Gentiles

There is one more point regarding Zebulun and Issachar that brings these prophecies even closer to us. The territory occupied by these tribes was what later came to be called "Galilee of the Gentiles," and it is significant that it was from this area that all Jesus' disciples came, with the exception of Judas. By Jesus' day this area had been overrun by invaders and then resettled. But Galilee, unlike Samaria, was strongly—even zealously—Jewish, and it is not impossible that a large percentage of the descendants of Zebulun and Issachar were among the apostolic band.

Issachar had been complacent in the possession of its territory. As a result it had fallen into forced labor. This tribe had lost its freedom. But when Jesus came, those who had lost their freedom in an even greater sense—they had become slaves to sin—were released from bondage and were given vigorous work to do for him.

As for Zebulun—well, Zebulun had been given a specific territory. The tribe was to dwell between the Sea of Galilee and the Mediterranean. It was a privileged area, though limited. But when Jesus came, those from this very area (and others also) were given the world for their territory, since their commission from Jesus was to "go and make disciples of all nations, baptizing them in the name of the Father and of the Son and of the Holy Spirit," teaching them "to obey everything" Christ has commanded and, while they were doing this, to know that he would be with them "always, to the very end of the age" (Matt. 28:19–20).

This is our commission. We are not to desist from doing it until we die or Christ returns in glory.

171

Dan, Gad, Asher, Naphtali

Genesis 49:16–21

"Dan will provide justice for his people
as one of the tribes of Israel.
Dan will be a serpent by the roadside,
a viper along the path,
that bites the horse's heels
so that its rider tumbles backward.

*"I look for your deliverance, O L*ORD.

"Gad will be attacked by a band of raiders,
but he will attack them at their heels.

"Asher's food will be rich;
he will provide delicacies fit for a king.

"Naphtali is a doe set free
that bears beautiful fawns."

I was talking to a young woman who had a good job working for a U.S. senator, but she felt unimportant and inferior. She thought that other people were better educated, possessed greater influence, or were more effective in their work.

Many people in our society feel this way about themselves. They feel insignificant for a variety of reasons. Some lack education and so stand in awe of those who have better educational backgrounds than they do. Some are shy; they tremble before the bold. Most problematic are those who grieve over the circumstances of their birth. Some come from broken homes, some from homes racked by mental illness or alcoholism. Some live under the cloud of being illegitimate.

Four of the sons of Jacob could have been thinking this way as he spoke his prophecy and pronounced his blessings on the six sons of his first wife, Leah. There was no doubt that these six sons would be blessed and that one presumably would be given the right of the firstborn. But what about themselves? Dan and Naphtali had been born of Rachel's servant, Bilhah, who had been given to Jacob as a concubine. Gad and Asher had been born of Leah's servant, Zilpah.

In those days it was permissible for a woman to give her servant to her husband to see if he could raise up children by her. The children of the concubine were considered the children of the wife for legal purposes. This is what Sarah did in presenting Hagar to Abraham. Still, to be born of a concubine was not the same thing as being born of a wife; so Dan, Gad, Asher, and Naphtali may have been wondering if they would be included in this blessing.

I imagine that this is the reason why they were standing together, as I suppose they were because of the order in which Jacob addresses them. Strictly speaking, they were not even grouped by their mothers. If this were the case, Dan would have been with Naphtali, and the other two would have been standing separately. I suppose the four of them recognized instinctively that they were in the same position and were therefore merely waiting together to see if they counted.

In view of this situation, it is worth noting that the prophecies Jacob utters over them are not very long. Compared with the words about Judah they are actually quite short. On the other hand, these are all positive predictions. Jacob knew that among his descendants no distinction was to be made between the children of the free women and the sons of the concubines. Each was to have his divinely appointed place.

It is the same for spiritual Israel, the church. In Christ there is neither Jew nor Greek, bond nor free, male nor female (Gal. 3:28). We are all one in Christ Jesus. So there should be no feelings of inferiority. We are all in Christ and are equipped for the place in which he has appointed us to serve.

Justice in Israel

This point is explicit in Jacob's words about Dan, which are no doubt meant to cover the next three sons as well. Dan "will provide justice for his people *as one of the tribes of Israel*" (v. 16, my emphasis). To speak of the tribes of Israel is itself significant, for it shows that Jacob was looking ahead to God's fulfillment of his promises to Abraham, according to which he was to become the father of a great people. Jacob saw this by faith and predicted that the sons would indeed become fathers of tribes. But what is striking here is that he speaks of being "one of the tribes of Israel" to Dan, who might have thought that he would be excluded. As one commentator says of these sons, "Their judgment and their dignity [were] to proceed as much from themselves as if they had sprung from Rachel or Leah."[1]

Jacob speaks of Dan's providing justice and describes his method of fighting as that of a "serpent by the roadside, a viper along the path, that bites the horse's heels so that its rider tumbles backward" (v. 17). We tend to think of a snake in negative terms. But we should not do so here any more than we should think negatively when Issachar is compared to a "rawboned donkey" (v. 14). In Jacob's day these animals were thought of for their virtues. The serpent is linked to Dan chiefly for the subtle and effective way it strikes from hiding.

Both of these characteristics—providing justice and striking like a serpent—are embodied in the best known of the descendants of this tribe, the judge Samson. His story is told in Judges 13–16. Samson was a ruler of Israel for twenty years. But he was an unusual judge, being distinguished more for his strength than for his wisdom. No Hebrew was ever bolder than he was. He was so strong he once attacked a lion and tore it apart with his bare hands. He was also subtle in warfare. On one occasion he fell upon his enemies suddenly and killed a thousand of them.

Samson was most magnificent in his death. He had been blinded by the Philistines after having revealed the secret of his great strength. His strength was in his hair, which they shaved off. In captivity his hair began to grow again, and with it his strength returned. Thus, when he was brought into the temple of Dagon to be mocked for the Philistines' entertainment, he suddenly dislodged the main supporting pillars, destroyed the temple, and killed many thousands of his enemies. The text says, "Thus he killed many more when he died than while he lived" (Judg. 16:30).

There is one puzzling feature of the Bible's references to Dan, which does not grow out of this passage but from others, chiefly the listing of the twelve tribes of Israel in 1 Chronicles 1–7 and Revelation 7:5–8. It is hard to find an answer for it. The problem is that Dan is not mentioned in these genealogies. In 1 Chronicles the list includes Ephraim and Manasseh, Joseph's two sons, but not Joseph—making twelve tribes. In Revelation the list includes Manasseh, who takes the place of Dan, plus Joseph, but not Ephraim—also making twelve tribes. There is no explanation of why Dan is excluded.

Some commentators, like Arthur W. Pink, make a great deal of this fact, arguing that God blotted out the tribe of Dan because of its apostasy.[2] Dan was the first of the tribes to set up false idols and worship them (Judg. 18:30). In Amos 8:14 the phrase "your god, . . . O Dan" refers to an idol. On the basis of these facts other commentators have supposed that the Antichrist of the end times will emerge from this tribe. That is mere speculation, and even the view that God destroyed the tribe of Dan because of its apostasy is an assumption based on the apostasy itself and not on the explicit teaching of Scripture. We remember that, although first, Dan was not the only tribe to go after false gods, and although Dan is omitted from the lists of tribes in 1 Chronicles 2–7 and Revelation 7, the tribe nevertheless appears in the sixteen or so other listings in Scripture.

Here is a case in which we ought not to assume too much. But at the same time we ought to be warned by Dan's sin. We must be warned not to make false idols of anything—even success or another person. Instead we must remain faithful followers of our Savior throughout our lives.

Looking to Jesus

Genesis 49:18 is a digression from Jacob's prophecy, but it may be related to what he had just spoken concerning Dan. I have said that the comparison between Dan and a serpent was not pejorative, the image intending only to highlight Dan's military tactics. But it is possible that, although Jacob did not refer to the serpent for this reason, mention of the serpent carried his mind back to that early appearance of the serpent in the oldest stories of Israel—the occasion of the devil's use of the serpent in the Garden of Eden—and the mere thought of that serpent brought forth an exclamation of hope through the one who was yet to come: "I look for your deliverance, O Lord" (v. 18). That means, "In spite of what I am prophesying, I want to say again that my hope of deliverance is in the Messiah and his future work."

The text does not necessarily imply faith in a specific deliverer to come. The word is "deliverance" or "salvation," and it is used of many kinds of deliverances of the people by God. It can refer to a military victory, to deliverance from a plague or other natural calamity, and to other things.

But there is this to be said. Eight verses before this, Jacob had spoken of the "Shiloh," declaring, "The scepter will not depart from Judah, nor the ruler's staff from between his feet, until he comes to whom it belongs and the obedience of the nations is his" (v. 10). A prophecy so weighty would probably still be in his mind. Moreover, when Jacob spoke of "deliverance" or "salvation," the word he used was actually the Hebrew name for "Jesus"—*Yeshuah*, which in turn means "Jehovah saves." This is the first use of the word "salvation" in the Bible! It is probably too much to suggest that Jacob was anticipating the birth of Jesus by name. But it is not unreasonable to think that he was expecting a personal deliverer who would come in God's own time.

He was waiting for this one, just as all the Old Testament saints waited—from Adam right up to the aged Simeon who, by the grace of God, at last held the Christ child in his arms.

Today we look back to Christ much as the Old Testament figures looked forward. We know who Christ was. We know him by name. However, we also look forward to his second coming, so that Jacob's cry of personal faith continues to be ours. We look for God's final deliverance when we cry, "Come, Lord Jesus" (Rev. 22:20).

Three More Prophecies

The briefest prophecies in this long chapter concern Gad, Asher, and Naphtali. In the New International Version they receive only two lines apiece.

Jacob tells *Gad* that he "will be attacked by a band of raiders, but he will attack them at their heels" (v. 19). This is a meaningful statement in view of this tribe's settling to the east of the Jordan River in an area exposed to raids by some of the deadliest enemies of Israel: Ammon and Moab. We read of attacks on the territory of Gad several times in the Old Testament. In spite of their vulnerability and the attacks frequently made on them, the prophecy says that Gad would be able to retaliate in kind. In 1 Chronicles 12:8 there are special words of praise for these men from the time of David: "Some Gadites defected to David at this stronghold in the desert. They were brave warriors, ready for battle and able to handle the shield and spear. Their faces were the faces of lions, and they were as swift as gazelles in the mountains."

The Hebrew text is fascinating at this point. It has a play on the word "Gad" due to the fact that "Gad"—"band of raiders (a troop)"—and "attack (or press)" build on the same root word. The repetition of this word has the sound of galloping horses. This was to be Gad's history, but the tribe would be able to give as well as take.

The people of Gad chose the dangerous land east of the Jordan for themselves at the time of the Israelite conquest (v. 32). No doubt it seemed good to them at the time since it was largely pastureland and they had large herds. The territory was called Gilead, which has become a term for all that is pleasant: "There is a balm in Gilead to soothe the sin-sick soul." But this land had dangers they did not know about, and it brought frequent warfare. Beware of trusting your own judgment as to where you should live and what you should do with your inheritance. It is hard to choose wisely. It is wiser to allow the Lord to choose for you.

Jacob's prophecy about *Asher* is that his "food will be rich; he will provide delicacies fit for a king" (v. 20). It might better have been said of Asher than of Zebulun that this tribe would "live by the seashore and become a haven for ships," but the words given are appropriate enough. Zebulun enjoyed the advantages of the seaport trade, as I pointed out in the previous chapter. Yet Asher was actually on the seacoast and profited not only from that trade but from the extraordinary fertility of the coastal soil and the abundant rainfall on the west slope of the coastal mountains.

"Asher" means "happy" or "fortunate," and indeed he was. In material things the inheritance of this tribe was more abundant than that of any of the others. Yet there is danger in abundance, and in the days of the judges this tribe wallowed in its coastal luxuries while the people of Zebulun and Naphtali were fighting Israel's enemies (Judg. 5:17–18).

Yet even in Asher there remained a remnant of those who feared the Lord and were waiting for his salvation. One of these was Anna, a prophetess, the daughter of Phanuel, who identified the infant Jesus as the redeemer of his people when he was brought to Jerusalem by his parents for circumcision.

Naphtali was described by Jacob as "a doe set free that bears beautiful fawns" (v. 21). This text has been a puzzle to many, because the best Hebrew text says, "Naphtali is a hind (or doe) set free; he utters beautiful words" (cf. KJV). In the view of some the first part of this verse does not seem to match the second. So they suggest various textual emendations. In the past, slight changes have been made in the Hebrew word for "doe" to get the word "terebinth," or "oak," a tree. But a tree does not utter beautiful words either. So the second part of the verse is altered (by a change of vowel points) to give the reading "producing goodly shoots." In this view Naphtali is compared to a tree producing fine branches.

The New International Version takes a different approach. It retains the original word "doe," but alters the second word by doubling the middle consonant. Thus *"emrey"* ("words") becomes *"emmerey"* ("fawns"), with the reading: "Naphtali is a doe set free that bears beautiful fawns." (In Hebrew some middle consonants are doubled simply by placing a dot in the middle. So the emendation leading to this reading is slight.)

In my judgment the New International Version alteration is reasonable and may well be correct. But I am not sure that I see the necessity for the change. The image is not as neat if a doe is said to speak beautiful words. But it is not impossible to use the image of a doe in the first part of the sentence to indicate the unfettered spirit of the people of Naphtali and then follow it in the second part of the sentence with a statement that these same people would be noted for poetic speech.

They may have been! We read of few descendants of Naphtali. Barak, who fought with Deborah against Jabin, a king of Canaan, is the only prominent Naphtalite we know of. Yet Barak, a heroic general, is joined with Deborah as author of the great "Song of Deborah" in Judges 5. These are surely "beautiful words."

Beautiful Words

The greatest fulfillment of this prophecy lies probably not in Barak but in the Lord Jesus Christ, who, although not a descendant of Naphtali, nevertheless spent much of his public ministry in that area. It was in Naphtali that the Lord first preached:

> When Jesus heard that John had been put in prison, he returned to Galilee. Leaving Nazareth, he went and lived in Capernaum, which was by the lake in the area of Zebulun and Naphtali—to fulfill what was said through the prophet Isaiah:

"Land of Zebulun and land of Naphtali,
　　the way to the sea, along the Jordan,
　　Galilee of the Gentiles—
the people living in darkness
　　have seen a great light;
on those living in the land of the shadow of death
　　a light has dawned."

Matthew 4:12–16

The words of Jesus preached in Naphtali and throughout the entire land of Canaan were great words, beautiful words, true words. Indeed, as the soldiers who were sent to arrest him on one occasion said, "No one ever spoke the way this man does" (John 7:46). No one ever did. No one ever will.

It is wise to hear Jesus and learn to follow him as the one the patriarchs, priests, prophets, and kings before us have both heard and followed. He is life. In his service there is joy forevermore.

172

Joseph: A Fruitful Vine

Genesis 49:22–26

"Joseph is a fruitful vine,
a fruitful vine near a spring,
whose branches climb over a wall.
With bitterness archers attacked him;
they shot at him with hostility.
But his bow remained steady,
his strong arms stayed limber,
because of the hand of the Mighty One of Jacob,
because of the Shepherd, the Rock of Israel,
because of your father's God, who helps you,
because of the Almighty, who blesses you
with blessings of the heavens above,
blessings of the deep that lies below,
blessing of the breast and womb.
Your father's blessings are greater
than the blessings of the ancient mountains,
than the bounty of the age-old hills.
Let all these rest on the head of Joseph,
on the brow of the prince among his brothers."

Jacob spoke by inspiration of the Holy Spirit in the prophecies about his twelve sons. But inspiration does not eliminate the human element, and the character and emotions of Jacob are evident in these utterances. We see this especially in his words about Joseph. Jacob's words so far have been somewhat restrained, and his last prophecies have been brief. Issachar and Dan received but six lines of prophecy apiece; Gad, Asher, and Naphtali received only two. But now Jacob comes to Joseph, and his eyes suddenly seem to light up and his tongue is loosened.

Joseph was the favorite son and the most godly character in his family. He was also the first son of Jacob's beloved wife, Rachel. Spurgeon says, "The blessing which Jacob pronounced upon Joseph was infinite in extent; he seemed to ransack heaven and earth in order to express the desire of his soul, and what he knew as a prophet to be the purpose of God."[1]

Each son had his own characteristics, of course, and the characteristic given to Joseph's tribe was fruitfulness. This had been his own outstanding feature. Although he had been unjustly and maliciously attacked, Joseph had stood his ground and had prospered. He was the most fruitful of his brethren. So also for a time were his descendants. The Bible speaks of "the ten thousands of Ephraim" and "the thousands of Manasseh" (Deut. 33:17).

All this was because Joseph depended on God. I have pointed out many times that the chief characteristic of his speech was his constant referral of every circumstance of his life to God. Almost every sentence Joseph speaks has the name of God in it. And that is what we also find in his father's prophecy about him. The prophecy is in three parts. Part 1 speaks of Joseph's fruitfulness. Part 2 explains the secret of that fruitfulness as Joseph's dependence on God, giving a stirring list of names expressing God's attributes. Part 3 concludes that the blessings of this God are greater than anything possibly found on earth. The theme of this prophecy is the same as John 15:1–17, of which it is the Old Testament equivalent. In that passage Jesus described himself as the "true vine" and showed that the secret of spiritual fruitfulness is union with him.

The Vine and Its Branches

The prophecy begins with two images to portray Joseph's character: (1) a vine planted near a spring, and (2) an archer steady under attack.

> "Joseph is a *fruitful vine*,
>   a fruitful vine near a spring,
>   whose branches climb over a wall.
> With bitterness archers attacked him;
>   they shot at him with hostility.
> But *his bow remained steady*,
>   his strong arms stayed limber."
>
>   verses 22–24, my emphasis

These images aptly describe Joseph so far as we have been told about him. He was a man who had been attacked on many fronts. His brothers were in the first rank of those bitter and hostile archers who shot at him; they conspired against him, threw him into a cistern, and eventually sold him into slavery. The wife of Potiphar was another who took aim against him; she wanted to draw him aside into sin. Potiphar himself was an archer; he had Joseph imprisoned without benefit of trial. Indeed, for the first thirty years of his life Joseph could be said to have been under attack by countless armed enemies. Yet through it all he remained steady and undaunted, as Jacob indicates in his prophecy.

Joseph was fruitful too. Later in the Old Testament the image of a vine is used widely of Israel, whom God brought up out of Egypt and planted in a new land (Ps. 80:8–16; Isa. 5:1–7; Jer. 2:21; Ezek. 15:1–8; 19:10–14; Hosea 10:1). But the image is always used in a bad sense. Israel was a choice vine that did not bear good fruit. This is not said of Joseph. Joseph was a vine that not only produced fruit for his own household, the Hebrews, but for other peoples as well. His branches climbed over the wall and blessed even the Egyptians.

What is said of Joseph is also a prediction of the fruitfulness of those who would descend from him, particularly the tribe of Ephraim. Ephraim produced five of the fifteen judges of Israel: Gideon (the fifth judge), Abimelech (sixth), Jair (eighth), Jephthah (ninth), and finally Samuel (fifteenth), who was also a transition figure between the judges and the kings. This tribe produced Joshua, Moses' successor, who led the people in their conquest of Canaan.

The Mighty One of Jacob

But as important as the prophecy concerning Joseph's fruitfulness may be, we cannot feel that it is really the heart of Jacob's utterance. It is clear that he wished to give Joseph the greatest possible blessing, and he did. But the blessing is because of God, and for that reason it is Jacob's words about God particularly that command attention. In the second part of the prophecy he presents a succession of great names for God, which express God's attributes:

> ". . . because of the hand of *the Mighty One of Jacob*,
>   because of *the Shepherd, the Rock of Israel*,
> because of *your father's God*, who helps you,
>   because of *the Almighty*, who blesses you
> with blessings of the heavens above,
>   blessings of the deep that lies below,
>   blessings of the breast and womb."

> verses 24–25, my emphasis

This was the secret of Joseph's fruitfulness and victory, of course. If Joseph had tried to stand against the archers in his own strength, as some do, he would have been overpowered rapidly. He would have proved precisely what Jesus said when he told his disciples, "Apart from me you can do nothing" (John 15:5). Joseph did not do that. On the contrary, in the words of Jesus' parable of the vine and branches, he "remained" [or "abode," KJV] in God and was therefore able to produce "fruit," "much fruit," and "fruit that [would] last" (vv. 4–5, 8, 16). Genesis 49 teaches this by the image of God placing his strong hands upon the hands of Joseph as he draws his bow, much as a father might steady and guide his son in archery lessons: "his bow remained steady, his strong arms stayed limber, because of the hand of the Mighty One of Jacob" (v. 24).

Jacob mentions five titles: (1) the Mighty One of Jacob, (2) the Shepherd, (3) the Rock of Israel, (4) your father's God, and (5) the Almighty. It is worth looking closely at each one.

1. *The Mighty One of Jacob.* If Jacob had been stronger in himself, he might not have been so impressed with God as his Mighty One. But Jacob was not strong, and he was not impressed with himself. So when he looked back over his life and his experiences of God's strength in times of trouble, this is what he chiefly thought of.

We can sense Jacob's reverie as we read these words. He would have been thinking of that terrifying day he set out from his father's home in Beersheba to go to Haran. He had the death threats of his brother Esau behind him and an uncertain future filled with danger before. But God appeared to him at Bethel to bless him and promise protection. In Haran he had been at his Uncle Laban's mercy, and he must have thought of that equally terrifying time when he left Haran and again set his face toward Canaan. Laban had pursued him uttering threats, but God had appeared to Laban and had warned him not to harm Jacob. Jacob had also been afraid of Esau, but God softened Esau's heart and so protected Jacob from that menace.

Jacob was not mighty. He was weak, timorous, and vulnerable. God was the Mighty One. But it was a joy to Jacob, as he lay dying, that he could point to that God and declare that he had shown himself to be the Mighty One in his life.

I like the way Jacob puts it, calling God "the Mighty One *of Jacob.*" It is so personal. He could have called God "the Mighty One of Abraham" or "the Mighty One of Isaac," his forefathers. Earlier in his life he would probably have done this. But here he wants to give personal testimony of God's faithfulness. He wishes to say that God was mighty to *him* and that he kept *him* in every circumstance.

A philosopher friend and I were speaking about some of the rational arguments for God. He explained that he is most impressed, not merely with those who give rational arguments but by those who are content to put God to the test in respect to their own ministries and God's provision for them in those ministries. He mentioned Francis Schaeffer as one who never asked for money for his work, but rather prayed (along with others of the L'Abri family) that

God would supply it. To him this was a great demonstration of Christianity. It showed God to be real, powerful, and involved in the cares of his particular people.

This is what Jacob was saying. Alexander Maclaren wrote, "The God of Jacob is to the patriarch also the God of Abraham, and of Isaac, and of Jacob. But that comes second, and this comes first. Each man for himself must put forth the hand of his own faith, and grasp that great hand for his own guide. '*My* Lord and *my* God' is the true form of the confession."[2]

Jacob's confession of faith in God rings so true that later generations referred back to it to encourage themselves in times of difficulty. David referred to himself as "the man anointed by the God of Jacob" (2 Sam. 23:1); the designation "God of Jacob" occurs many times throughout the Psalms and Prophets. Psalm 132:2 and 5 refer to "the Mighty One of Jacob." Psalm 46:7 and 11 declare: "The LORD Almighty is with us; the God of Jacob is our fortress."

2. *The Shepherd*. Jacob had referred to the shepherd work of God once before in his final testimony (see Gen. 48:15), and he reintroduces the concept now—no doubt because this too stood out in his mind as one of God's chief characteristics. Jacob had been a shepherd himself. So he knew how difficult and unrewarding it is to care for sheep. Sheep are wayward, stubborn, helpless, stupid. They do not return affection, even when cared for faithfully. Jacob had been like this. At best he was God's "unprofitable servant." Yet God had performed a shepherd work for him throughout his long life.

3. *The Rock of Israel*. The third name that Jacob gives to God is "Rock," "the Rock of Israel." Maclaren writes, "The general idea of this symbol is perhaps firmness, solidity. And that general idea may be followed out in various details. God is a rock for a foundation. Build your lives, your thoughts, your efforts, your hopes there. The house founded on the rock will stand though wind and rain from above smite it, and floods from beneath beat on it like battering-rams. God is a rock for a fortress. Flee to him to hide, and your defense shall be the 'munition of rocks,' which shall laugh to scorn all assault, and never be stormed by any foe. God is a rock for shade and refreshment. Come close to him from out of the scorching heat, and you will find coolness and verdure and moisture in the clefts, when all outside that grateful shadow is parched and dry."[3]

In calling God "the Rock of *Israel*," Jacob did the same thing as when he called him "the Mighty One *of Jacob*." Israel is another name for Jacob. He was saying that God had shown himself to be *his* rock, not merely the rock of his forefathers Abraham and Isaac.

4. *Your father's God*. How could Jacob make his trust in God plainer than he does in this prophecy? He has called God "the Mighty One of *Jacob*." He has termed him "the Rock of *Israel*." Now he calls him "*your father's* God, who helps you." It is a wonderful thing that Jacob knew God so personally that

he could refer to him in this way, but it is no less wonderful that he could pass on faith in this God to his posterity.

Can you say to your children, "Your father's God (or 'your mother's God') has helped you, and will help you"? Can you speak of your faith and know that they will see it as real and want to trust the One who has been so real in your life?

5. *The Almighty*. The last name that Jacob recalls is *El Shaddai*, a name revealed for the first time to Abraham on the occasion of God's establishing the covenant of circumcision with him and his family (Genesis 17). Scholars have not always known how to render this name. It is often used in contexts implying might or strength, so they translate it as "God Almighty," as here. That may be right. But the name is actually based on the Hebrew noun *shad*, which means the female breast. Because of this, I believe that it really refers to God as the one from whom his people draw nourishment. I would even argue that the context of Genesis 49 requires this meaning, for the verse that begins "because of the Almighty, who blesses you . . ." goes on to speak of "the blessings of the breast and womb" (v. 25).

Thus it is that the names of God, which begin with a strong male image ("the Mighty One of Jacob") also embrace female characteristics and show God to be the source of *every* good and perfect gift for his people.

The Blessings of Jacob

The last verse of Jacob's prophecy about Joseph may be taken in two ways. Jacob may be saying, "The blessings that I have received in my life are greater than the blessings of any of those who have gone before me," that is, greater than God's blessings upon either Abraham or Isaac. If this is the case, Jacob was expressing gratitude for the mercy of God that had been poured out on him.

One commentator writes, "It was his acknowledgement that [he had] received in inverse proportion to his desserts. If he had had a New Testament, he would have put himself with the woman whose love the Lord illustrated with the parable of the two debtors. The one who had been forgiven the most, loved the most."[4] Instead of feeling cheated by life, as so many people do, Jacob looked back over his days and felt himself to be the most fortunate of men.

This verse can also be understood, however, as referring to the blessings Jacob was himself bestowing. These were greater than the blessings of his ancestors, for Abraham and Isaac could each bless only one son (or at most, two sons), while he had been fortunate to bless all twelve of his sons, each of whom was to become the father of a tribe of Israel. His blessings were also great in the sense that the legacy they bestowed was everlasting.

If this last possibility is the correct one, then these words must have had special meaning for Joseph, who undoubtedly possessed a noble's share of the considerable treasures of Egypt. Egypt was rich beyond the wildest imaginations of most of the peoples of that day. What is more, the Egyptians were intent on preserving their treasures even beyond death. Egyptians constructed intricate burial chambers and immense pyramids in which the wealthy were interred with their possessions. Contrary to our popular proverb, they seemed to think that you could indeed "take it with you."

Jacob was telling Joseph that the greatest blessings of God are spiritual because these alone really last. If Joseph had wished, he could have been buried in a magnificent tomb in Egypt. Perhaps Jacob could have had that apparent honor as well. But what would this have amounted to in light of eternity? A moment's honor? A few centuries (perhaps a few millennia) of peace and preservation of the body? Yes, but then nothing. If even heaven and earth will pass away, certainly the wealth of the Pharaohs was perishable. What lasts? Only God . . . and those who by grace are united to him forever.

That is why what we do for him lasts. It is not that you and I can do anything lasting. As I said earlier, in reference to Christ's statement in John 15:5, without Christ we "can do nothing." But when we are united to Jesus so that his life is seen in us, then our works are his works, and we can know that what God does through us is everlasting.

173

Benjamin: Call of the Wild

Genesis 49:27–28

"Benjamin is a ravenous wolf;
  in the morning he devours the prey,
  in the evening he divides the plunder."

All these are the twelve tribes of Israel, and this is what their father said to them when
he blessed them, giving each the blessing appropriate to him.

Judging from the last verse of Genesis 49, Jacob, the aged patriarch of Israel, was hours from dying. Yet he would not die until he had pronounced the last inspired sentence of admonition to his sons. Spurgeon said, "He was immortal till his work was done."[1]

Jacob is a magnificent figure in this chapter. There had been moments in his life when he was far from magnificent: when he had cheated his brother of his birthright, when he had fled from Esau's wrath, and later when he had tried to slip away from Laban. But Jacob had grown during these years, and at the end of his life he is seen as God's spokesman uttering prophecies that were to guide the destinies of the tribes of Israel for centuries.

What balance his words possess! He does not spare his sons for their faults, but neither does he condemn them utterly. It is said of Reuben, the firstborn, that he will no longer excel, because he had dishonored his father by sleeping with his father's concubine Bilhah. But Reuben is not cut off; he is still to be a father of one of the twelve tribes of Israel. Simeon and Levi are also criticized for their fierce wrath displayed in the slaughter of the Shechemites. But they are not disinherited; their punishment is merely that they will be scattered throughout Israel.

The prophecies of this chapter may be divided into two main parts: the first containing admonitions for the six sons of Leah, the second containing admonitions for the other six sons—four sons of the concubines and two sons of Rachel (Joseph and Benjamin). In the first section the dominant prophecy concerns Judah, from whom the Messiah was to come. In the second, the dominant prophecy concerns Joseph.

Little Benjamin

After the magnificent words about Joseph, in which Jacob seems to ransack heaven and earth for blessings, the prophecy about Benjamin seems quite insignificant. It is only three lines, and it reads like an anticlimax. It says, "Benjamin is a ravenous wolf; in the morning he devours the prey, in the evening he divides the plunder" (v. 27). Yet this is not too short for what was apparently the smallest of the tribes.

Achievement does not depend on size. Benjamin was small. Yet it is said of Benjamin that the people of this tribe would be bold, strong, and ferocious and that they would achieve victories over their enemies. We must point out that the comparison with a wolf is no more disparaging of Benjamin than Jacob's comparing Judah to a lion, Issachar to a donkey, or Dan to a serpent. Jacob chooses good characteristics of these animals for his comparison. Benjamin, the wolf, is to be fierce and ready always to take weapons in God's cause. Moreover, he is to be successful in warfare. "In the morning" he is to fight his enemies. "In the evening" he is to divide the plunder of his conquests. This unexpected prominence of Benjamin is captured in Psalm 68 in a description of the advancing tribes of Israel:

> Your procession has come into view, O God,
>   the procession of my God and King into the sanctuary. . . .
> There is the little tribe of Benjamin, leading them,
>   there the great throng of Judah's princes,
>   and there the princes of Zebulun and of Naphtali.
>
> verses 24, 27

Benjamin would be small, but a leader. It was to be a prominent tribe.

History bears this out. I pointed out in earlier studies that several of the tribes, although large in numbers, have nevertheless left very few names in history. In the entire Old Testament we learn of only a handful of descendants of the tribes of Reuben, Simeon, Dan, Naphtali, Gad, Asher, Issachar, and Zebulun. (Levi, Judah, and Joseph are exceptions.) But Benjamin, though it is small, has left records of many descendants and numerous outstanding men. For example, on "The Adam and Eve Family Tree," which I mentioned in earlier studies, I count a mere 7 names of descendants of Gad, 8 of Zebulun, and another 8 of Naphtali. But for Benjamin I count 101.

Benjamin could boast of such distinguished individuals as Ehud, the second of Israel's judges; Saul, Israel's first king, and his distinguished son Jonathan; Abner, the commander of Israel's armies under Saul; Mordecai, who lived in Babylon after the captivity and rose to power in the king's court; and his niece, who became Queen Esther.

The fierce courage of Benjamin is seen, for example, in Ehud, the judge, and Jonathan, the son of Saul.

In Ehud's day Israel became subject to Moab and its king, Eglon. Any Hebrew who came into Eglon's presence was searched for weapons. But Ehud was left-handed. So he fashioned a short sword, which he attached to his right thigh under his clothing. Presumably, when he was searched, the attendants of Eglon felt his left side, where the weapon of a right-handed man would be, and passed him in. Thus Ehud by a risky move gained access to the king and killed him while his attendants were outside the room. Ehud then made his escape, gathered patriots to his stronghold in the hills of Ephraim, and attacked Moab's armies. He killed ten thousand of the enemy, subjected Moab to Israel, and brought peace to his country for eighty years (Judg. 3:12–30).

Jonathan is a second outstanding example. In the early days of his father's reign the Philistines were the great enemies of Israel. They had confiscated Israel's weapons, so that only Saul and Jonathan had swords and spears. The Israelites fought with plowshares, axes, and other domestic tools. Jonathan believed God could deliver his people through some bold act. So he called his armor-bearer and challenged him to ambush an entire detachment of Philistine soldiers at the pass of Micmash. The Philistines taunted them: "Look! The Hebrews are crawling out of the holes they were hiding in. Come up to us and we'll teach you a lesson" (1 Sam. 14:11–12).

Jonathan said to his armor-bearer, "Climb up after me; the LORD has given them into the hand of Israel" (v. 12). The pair scaled a cliff, slew twenty of the soldiers, and routed the detachment. Their boldness turned the tide of war and led to a great victory for Israel.

The Bad Side of the Force

I said earlier that the description of Benjamin as a wolf is not pejorative. It is a praiseworthy reference to Benjamin's bold ferocity. But to be perfectly balanced, it is probably also true that the comparison is at least a warning. Properly directed, the chief characteristic of this tribe would be a good quality.

Misdirected, it could become destructive. Boldness would turn to arrogance. Strength would turn to cruelty.

This did happen. In the period described at the end of the Book of Judges, before Israel had kings, the descendants of Jacob were living according to their own moral standards, and things were done in Israel that were not done either before or since.

There was a Levite from Ephraim who had a concubine from Judah. She left him to return to her father's house, and he left Ephraim to find her and persuade her to come back. At last he prevailed, and the two set out from Bethlehem in the south to Ephraim in the north. On the first evening of their journey, they were approaching Jebus (an early name for Jerusalem, when it was still inhabited by Jebusites), but the Levite was unwilling to stay overnight in an alien city. Instead he turned aside to Gibeah, a city of the Benjamites. The people of this city were not hospitable. So he prepared to spend the night in the city square.

Late that evening an old man from the Levite's home area of Ephraim, who was living in Gibeah, came in from the fields, saw his countryman, and invited him to his house. While they were there, some wicked men of the city surrounded the house and demanded that the stranger be sent out to them so they could abuse him sexually, much as the Sodomites had demanded that the angels who had visited Lot on an earlier occasion be released to them. The host refused. But the Levite, probably to protect his host (and his daughter, who was a virgin), allowed them to have his concubine.

The story tells us that the men of the city abused her throughout the night, letting her go only at dawn. She managed to crawl back to the house where her master was staying, but she died there. The Levite found her on the front step the next morning.

The remainder of the story is even worse. The Levite took the body of the woman back to Ephraim. Then he cut her into twelve parts and sent one part to each of the twelve tribes to stir up their reaction. In this he succeeded. Four hundred thousand soldiers of eleven of the tribes of Israel gathered at Mizpah and solemnly set themselves against Benjamin. They demanded that the Benjamites surrender the offenders so they might be put to death. Benjamin refused, and the result was what is called "the Benjamite wars." In this first civil war in Israel, the Benjamites slaughtered forty thousand soldiers of the other tribes. Then the tide turned. The eleven tribes routed Benjamin, destroyed its cities, killing their inhabitants, and exterminated all but six hundred men of the tribe.

No disaster of this proportion had occurred before in Israel. An entire tribe was on the point of utter extinction, a result of that fierce but misdirected valor of the Benjamites. At last the people of the eleven tribes relented and made efforts to provide the six hundred survivors with wives "so that a tribe of Israel will not be wiped out" (Judg. 21:17). Purged of its sin, the tribe of Benjamin then reestablished itself and again rose to some prominence.

Overcome by Good

We have seen a quality given by God used for good. We have also seen this same quality perverted to wicked ends. The third thing we need to see about this fierce boldness is that the perverted gift of Benjamin could be turned about by God to become a blessing. The chief example is the apostle Paul.

Paul was a Benjamite, as he indicates at two points in his writings (Rom. 11:1; Phil. 3:5). In fact, in its original form his name was Saul, which means that he was named for his illustrious ancestor in his tribe, the first king of Israel.

Saul—that is, Paul—possessed the chief characteristic of this tribe in high measure. Early in life he was by his own admission "zealous" for the religion of his fathers, which he showed by his persecution of Christians. He had become a fanatical Pharisee, and in his judgment Christianity was a dangerous threat to true religion. He tried to stamp it out. The Book of Acts tells us he was present at the stoning of Stephen, the first Christian martyr. Later we find him on his way to Damascus with letters from the high priest giving him authority to find the Christians and bring them to Jerusalem as prisoners.

It was on this fierce errand that Jesus stopped Saul and turned him to his own service. As he neared Damascus, a bright light flashed from heaven, and Saul fell to the ground blinded by it. "Saul, Saul, why do you persecute me?" a voice asked.

"Who are you, Lord?" Saul asked.

"I am Jesus, whom you are persecuting," Jesus replied. "Now get up and go into the city, and you will be told what you must do" (Acts 9:4–6). When he reached the city, Jesus sent a disciple named Ananias to restore his sight and commission him to service. From that time on Saul displayed the same zeal in proclaiming the gospel that he had shown in persecuting Christians.

Saul, using his new name, Paul, continued to be a warrior, but it was no longer with the weapons of this world. He wrote to the Corinthians, "The weapons we fight with are not the weapons of the world. On the contrary, they have divine power to demolish strongholds. We demolish arguments and every pretension that sets itself up against the knowledge of God, and we take captive every thought to make it obedient to Christ" (2 Cor. 10:4–5). Alexander the Great had conquered the world by force of Greek arms, but he held it only a short time. Paul's conquests were spiritual. Because they were the conquests of Christ and not the conquests of a mere man, his victories were forever. At the final judgment many millions will confess Paul to be their father in the faith.

I wish Paul's experience could be that of every Christian. Left to ourselves, we use even the best of God's most gracious gifts wrongly—to destroy others and oppose Christ's kingdom. But when we are conquered by Christ ourselves, these gifts are turned to good ends and become a blessing.

Old Israel, New Israel

With the conclusion of Jacob's prophecies, we are told, "All these are the twelve tribes of Israel, and this is what their father said to them when he blessed them, giving each the blessing appropriate to him" (v. 28). This is the first time in the Bible that the phrase "the twelve tribes of Israel" occurs. It is a significant moment that should cause us to review what was said and apply it to ourselves who are the New Testament Israel by means of God's call of us to faith in Jesus Christ.

George Lawson has provided the most extensive commentary on the prophecies of Genesis 49 that I have found, and he reflects on each of these phrases wisely:

> *"And this is it that their father spake unto them, and blessed them."* How did Jacob bless Reuben or Simeon or Levi? He gives them a part in the inheritance of Jacob. Reuben was not to excel, but he was to have a part and a name in Israel; Simeon and Levi were to be divided and scattered, but not among the Gentiles that knew not God. We may add that their chastisements under the divine management were blessings to them. They were taught more effectually by the denunciations of divine pleasure than they would have been without them, seeing how evil and bitter their transgressions were for which their dying father laid them under a censure never to be forgotten. Those threatenings and reproofs and chastisements which do us good are needful blessings, and we ought to receive them with thankfulness.
>
> *"Every one according to his blessing he blessed them."* He did not give them all the same blessing. He could not have blessed any of them without divine direction, for it was impossible for him to know, unless God had told him, that any of them would live to inherit the blessing or that any of them should ever leave the land of Egypt. But he not only gave them all a common blessing, but he gave each of them his own peculiar blessing; what he said of any one of them could not be said of all or could not be said with equal propriety of any other of them. . . .
>
> It was a sublime source of joy to Jacob on his death bed that he could leave blessings to all his seed. The greatest evils that Jacob saw in his life were the wicked actions of some of his children. How rich was the mercy of God to himself as well as to them that after all that most of them had done to provoke the Lord to anger, he was authorized to bless them!
>
> Parents, mourn over the sins of your children, when you see them despising the instruction which you give them. Yet discontinue not your endeavours to reform them; what know you whether God may not give you reason for better thoughts of them before you leave the world? Or if you should leave the world without seeing any good effects of your parental admonition or any answer to the prayers you presented to God for your children, you are not sure that they will be lost to them, and you may be sure that they are not lost to yourselves.
>
> If God had given you such a father as Jacob or promised you such blessings . . . as those which Jacob promised from God to some of his children, would you not have reckoned yourselves very happy? Would you not have lived all your days in the faith of such gracious promises and in the hope of such precious

blessings? But all that believe in Christ are his spiritual seed. He bequeathed to them all the most precious blessings when he was leaving the world. The dying speeches and last words of Jesus may afford us far richer consolation than the best blessings of Jacob could afford to his sons. "Peace," said Jesus, "I give you; my peace I leave with you." With whom did he leave it? Not with the apostles only but with all that should believe on him through their word.[2]

These are our blessings. Indeed, all the blessings of the entire Word of God are ours if we are in Christ.

174

The Death of Jacob

Genesis 49:29–33

Then he gave them these instructions: "I am about to be gathered to my people. Bury me with my fathers in the cave in the field of Ephron the Hittite, the cave in the field of Machpelah, near Mamre in Canaan, which Abraham bought as a burial place from Ephron the Hittite, along with the field. There Abraham and his wife Sarah were buried, there Isaac and his wife Rebekah were buried, and there I buried Leah. The field and the cave in it were bought from the Hittites."

When Jacob had finished giving instructions to his sons, he drew his feet up into the bed, breathed his last and was gathered to his people.

The last chapters of Genesis are filled with deathbed scenes: first the protracted account of the death of Jacob, then the shorter account of the death of Jacob's beloved son Joseph. They remind us that everyone must die.

What Charles Haddon Spurgeon wrote of Jacob is true of everyone: "He who had journeyed with unwearied foot fully many a mile was now obliged to gather up his feet into the bed to die. His life had been eventful in the highest degree, but that dread event now came upon him which is common to us all. He had deceived his blind father in his youth, but no craftiness of Jacob could deceive the grave. He had fled from Esau, his angry brother, but a swifter and surer foot was now in pursuit, from which there was no escape. He had slept with a stone for his pillow and had seen heaven opened, but he was to find that it was only to be entered by the ordinary gate. He had wrestled with the angel at the brook Jabbok, and he had prevailed; at this time he was to wrestle with an angel against whom there was no prevalence. He had dwelt in Canaan in tents, in the midst of enemies, and the Lord had said, 'Touch not mine anointed, and do my prophets no harm,' and therefore he had been secure in the midst of a thousand ills; but now he must fall by the hand of the last enemy and feel the great avenger's sword."[1]

Everyone must die. Yes, but *how* we die—that is the matter of real importance. In Jacob's case we have a man determined to take charge of his death and bear a witness to the end. Earlier in this chapter he had spoken to each of his sons, rebuking sin, promoting godliness, and pronouncing blessings upon those who would descend from them. In these last verses Jacob spells out his own last wishes and is taken home.

When the celebrated English essayist and poet Joseph Addison was dying, he sent for his son-in-law, the Earl of Warwick, that he might see how a Christian could die. Jacob is like that. Jacob is an example of how we ought to die when the time comes.

No Earthly City

The first notable characteristic of Jacob's death is his focus on the next world. He speaks of it, saying, "I am about to be gathered to my people" (v. 29). In books by unbelieving professors there are attempts to minimize the meaning of this sentence. "To be gathered to one's people" means only to be buried in the same plot of ground as one's ancestors, we are told; it is only another way of saying, "I am dying."

But this is patently untrue. It is evident even from Jacob's own statements that this is untrue. Jacob first made the statement that he was about to be gathered to his people and then voiced the additional request: "Bury me with my fathers in the cave in the field of Ephron the Hittite." That is, whether he would be buried in Egypt or in Canaan, he would be gathered to his people. But in addition to that, he also wanted to be buried where Abraham and Isaac had been buried before him. The same meaning is also clear earlier when Jacob asked Joseph to swear that he would return his body to Canaan. He said, "Do not bury me in Egypt, but when I rest with my fathers, carry me out of Egypt and bury me where they are buried" (Gen. 47:29–30). This means that after his spirit had joined the spirits of his fathers in the next world, he wanted his body to be buried where their bodies were buried.

Ishmael was gathered to his people, according to Genesis 25:17, but he was not buried in the cave at Machpelah. The statement means rather that he died in faith and was gathered with the people who died in faith earlier.

So also had Abraham been gathered to his people (Gen. 25:8).

So was Isaac gathered to those who had died in faith before him (Gen. 35:29).

Although this exact phrase is not used in earlier cases, the same undoubtedly was true of the deaths of Adam, Seth, Noah, and other great saints of the earliest days of earth's history.

It is hard to overemphasize the importance of this faith, for it is not merely a deathbed faith. It is a life-transforming orientation of those who have learned the passing nature of this life and the overriding permanence and importance of the life to come. It is said of Abraham that he lived "like a stranger in a foreign country" and that he looked "to the city with foundations, whose architect and builder is God" (Heb. 11:9–10). That is true of all God's people; and if this outlook has not emerged, the individuals involved are not truly converted from sin to faith in God. Christians *are* otherworldly. So although a believer realizes that this is God's world and can enjoy all that God has given him in and through it, he nevertheless knows that it is a fallen world and is destined to perish. He does not set his affections on it.

The world does not like this orientation, of course. The mass of unbelieving men and women are utterly ignorant of spiritual things and are therefore 100 percent "this-worldly." When Christians profess faith in what they cannot see and, worse yet, exhibit a higher and ultimate loyalty to unseen things, the world resents it and heaps scorn on them. Christianity is regarded as useless, a "pie-in-the-sky" philosophy. It is termed an opiate. It is said to make us insensitive to real needs, real life, real problems. It makes us turn our backs on real duties.

Does it? Actually the opposite is the case, as I will show. But this much is true: Christians do believe that this world is not the end of all things. There is a world of the spirit, which is far more important, and it is sadly true that in an attempt to gain this world and its pleasures, many lose their own souls.

We say to our contemporaries: One day you will die and be swept into the bosom of eternity. We ask: How will you die? To what will your soul be gathered? We believe that there are two destinies and that being gathered to God's people depends on turning to God through faith in Christ while in this life. We urge all who are not believers in Christ to turn to him.

Earthly Concerns

One reason why unbelievers resent a Christian's commitment to unseen things is that they suppose Christians therefore have no concern for what is visible. But that does not follow. Because I am interested in *A* does not mean that I cannot also be interested in *B*. Because I care for God does not mean that I cannot also be concerned for my fellowman. In fact, when we are speaking of spiritual things, it is only a concern for God that motivates a proper concern for men and puts all other concerns in proper perspective.

This is where the next portion of Jacob's dying testimony comes in. The most striking thing about this section is the length to which Jacob seems to go in describing the cave of Machpelah in which his forefathers were buried: "Bury me with my fathers in the cave in the field of Ephron the Hittite, the cave in the field of Machpelah, near Mamre in Canaan, which Abraham bought as a burial place from Ephron the Hittite, along with the field. There Abraham and his wife Sarah were buried, there Isaac and his wife Rebekah were buried, and there I buried Leah. The field and the cave in it were bought from the Hittites" (vv. 29–32). Commentators have suggested that these details are provided because the place was unknown to the sons of Jacob, or that these are merely the garrulous ramblings of an old man.

The real explanation is that Jacob wished to speak precisely and seriously of this place and thus remind his sons of the way and the reasons for which it had come into the possession of his family. Machpelah was the patriarchal toehold in Canaan. The patriarchs had been living as strangers in the land of promise, but they believed nevertheless that God had truly given them this land. Their burial there was proof of their faith in that promise. One commentator says, "Jacob wished to live in a place which the inhabitants of the country knew to be the property of his family, and expected that his seed after him would still retain their hope and desire of living in a country so much valued by their ancestors, the land which God promised to give them, and where he was to dwell among them and bless them."[2]

This is also the explanation of the Christian's proper concern for this world's affairs. Only the concern of the Christian is greater even than the concern of the patriarch Jacob. God had promised the land of Canaan to him and his descendants. He was determined to be buried there in anticipation of the fulfillment of those promises. In the Christian's case it is not merely a segregated "land of promise," but the entire world that is his or her concern: because he serves the Lord Jesus Christ, and Christ is Lord of all. Ours is a world religion, and we possess a world concern. There is no part of human life or endeavor that we should not strive to bring into subjection to Jesus.

First Things First

But it is a concern for Christ and his kingdom that makes the difference. I said that just because I am interested in *A* does not mean that I cannot also be interested in *B*. That is true. But it obviously makes an enormous difference whether I am interested in *A* first and *B* only second, or whether I am interested in *B* first and *A* only to the extent that my concerns for *B* permit.

This distinction is reflected in Jacob's dying words. Almost the very last thing Jacob said is that it was in the cave of Ephron the Hittite, where Abraham and Isaac were buried, that he "buried Leah" (v. 31). This is important as we remember that Jacob had two wives and two concubines and that, though he was married to Leah first, it was actually Rachel he loved. Rachel had been on his mind earlier. We know this because, when speaking about blessing Joseph's two sons, he had broken into his train of thought to reminisce about Rachel's death: "As I was returning from Paddan, to my sorrow Rachel died in the land of Canaan while we were still on the way, a little distance from Ephrath" (Gen. 48:7).

If a modern storyteller were inventing the final scene of Jacob's life, he would have Jacob ask to be buried by Rachel, on the road to Ephrath, and not in the gloomy cave at Machpelah. This would be touching, romantic. But Jacob does not do this! Why? It is because, although he was greatly attached to Rachel and undoubtedly still loved her, he wanted to be buried in the cave of his fathers as a testimony to the fact that his faith was the same as theirs and that the meaning of life is to be found, not in this life alone, but in eternity.

It is only those who are interested in the things of God first and foremost who make any real difference in the world. This is because they alone have a perspective that is of any transforming value. Unbelievers criticize Christians, as I have said. They call us otherworldly while they concentrate on purely secular concerns. Much of the contemporary church has adopted this attitude and has become quite secular, using the world's methods while adopting its agenda. This changes nothing. The world remains the same, because what is needed is a change in the perspectives that have made the world what it is. What is needed is an outlook that desires God first and sees faith in him as being of greater importance than one's fate or finances.

In the first volume of his commentary on Ephesians, D. Martyn Lloyd-Jones illustrates from history how this happens: "The greatest benefactors that this world has ever known, the men who have brought the greatest good to this world, have been men who have emphasized most of all the importance of 'seeing the unseen.' One has but to read the eleventh chapter of the Epistle to the Hebrews to find proof of this. There we have a list, or a gallery as it were, of the greatest benefactors this world has ever known; that is why they stand out in history. And they are all people, we are told, who fixed their eyes not so much on this world as on the next. That does not mean that they ignored this world. They were not monks or anchorites living in monasteries or deserts; they did not subscribe to the false, ascetic Roman Catholic teaching which has so bedeviled this whole question. The alternative to the popular view which is being advocated today is not monasticism. The 'heroes of the faith' of Hebrews, chapter 11, started with the unseen world, and then in the light of that, they applied themselves to the present world."[3]

He speaks of Calvin, who reformed the social as well as the spiritual life of the city of Geneva. Calvin was more concerned with decent, proper living in this world than were others of his time.

He speaks of the Puritans, who laid the foundations for the greatness of England and that of her American colony, the United States. No one had a more otherworldly view than the Puritans, but this did not stop them from being benefactors of the common people. Indeed, their seeing of the unseen fired their beneficence.

He speaks of the Evangelical Awakening, which saved England from a revolution similar to the French Revolution. From such spiritual revivals the greatest secular improvements come.

Lloyd-Jones concludes, "When men forget the next world and concentrate only on this present life, this world becomes a kind of living hell, with confusion and lawlessness and immorality and vice rampant. It is only men who have a complete view of life who really know how to live in their world. The only man who really respects life in this world is the man who knows that this world is only the antechamber to the next world. It is only the man who knows himself to be a child of God, and who knows that this world is God's world, who is really concerned about decency in this world."[4]

How Shall We Live?

I suppose that somewhere, somehow there is a danger of talking too much about heaven—if heaven is used as an escape from the demands of this life. But that danger is not nearly so great as failing to think enough (and in a proper way) about it. For one day each of us must die, as Jacob did, and we must stand in the presence of the holy God of heaven. How shall we stand before him? As those who have lived for this world only and thus for self, and who are startled to confront him? Or as those who lived life in light of that which is to come and who therefore appear to give an accounting of how they served the Lord here?

In Genesis 49:33 Jacob dies: "When Jacob had finished giving instructions to his sons, he drew his feet up into the bed, breathed his last and was gathered to his people." He had lived 15 years with his grandfather Abraham (who was 160 years old when Jacob was born to Isaac, and who died when he was 175). He had lived with or near his father Isaac for 100 years (Jacob was 120 years old when Isaac died, but he had spent 20 of those years in Haran). Now Jacob has been living with both of them in a far better world for thousands of years, and he will continue to live with them for eternity—and with Christ, which is far better.

George Lawson concludes, "Live by faith, as the patriarchs did, and you also shall be gathered to them when you die. How wretched will we be if we see millions with Abraham, Isaac and Jacob in the kingdom of heaven, and ourselves cast into utter darkness! But how excellent will our joys be if we are admitted to those blessed regions where our fellowship with Abraham and Isaac and Jacob and with an innumerable multitude of saints and angels will make but a small part of our happiness!"[5]

175

A Time to Weep

Genesis 50:1–13

Joseph threw himself upon his father and wept over him and kissed him. Then Joseph directed the physicians in his service to embalm his father Israel. So the physicians embalmed him, taking a full forty days, for that was the time required for embalming. And the Egyptians mourned for him seventy days.

When the days of mourning had passed, Joseph said to Pharaoh's court, "If I have found favor in your eyes, speak to Pharaoh for me. Tell him, 'My father made me swear an oath and said, "I am about to die; bury me in the tomb I dug for myself in the land of Canaan." Now let me go up and bury my father; then I will return.'"

Pharaoh said, "Go up and bury your father, as he made you swear to do."

So Joseph went up to bury his father. All Pharaoh's officials accompanied him—the dignitaries of his court and all the dignitaries of Egypt—besides all the members of Joseph's household and his brothers and those belonging to his father's household. Only their children and their flocks and herds were left in Goshen. Chariots and horsemen also went up with him. It was a very large company.

When they reached the threshing floor of Atad, near the Jordan, they lamented loudly and bitterly; and there Joseph observed a seven-day period of mourning for his father. When the Canaanites who lived there saw the mourning at the threshing floor of Atad, they said, "The Egyptians are holding a solemn ceremony of mourning." That is why that place near the Jordan is called Abel Mizraim.

So Jacob's sons did as he had commanded them: They carried him to the land of Canaan and buried him in the cave in the field of Machpelah, near Mamre, which Abraham had bought as a burial place from Ephron the Hittite, along with the field.

Years ago a Presbyterian student went off to college, joined a fraternity, and made himself obnoxious to his fraternity brothers by talking about Presbyterianism. According to the student, Presbyterians were best. They had the best churches, the best form of church government, the best worship services, and above all, the soundest and most unshakable faith. Everything about Presbyterianism was in first place. His fraternity brothers were mostly Baptists, and they were not about to accept this. So they devised a plan. One evening they slipped sleeping powder into his coffee, and when he passed out they loaded him into a car and took him out of the city to a remote graveyard. They had placed an open coffin there, resting on a large flat tombstone, and they put him in it. Then they hid behind the nearby tombstones to see what he would do when he woke up.

For a long time nothing happened. Night passed. Dawn came. Then, as the long red rays of the rising sun began to pierce through the graveyard, casting gray shadows and causing the mist to rise slowly from the ground, they heard a sound from the casket. Their fraternity brother was waking up. "It won't be long now," they thought. "As soon as he wakes up and begins to look around the graveyard he'll scream, jump out of that casket, and tear off through the woods. We'll laugh about it forever."

As they waited, an arm slowly rose out of the casket and stretched itself. Then there was another arm. Finally the young man sat up and looked around. His friends thought, "This is it! He's going to scream now!"

Instead he suddenly shouted triumphantly, "Hallelujah! It's the resurrection morning, and the Presbyterians are the first ones up!"

Inevitably a person's religious convictions (or lack of them) bear fruit in the way he looks at death. But the tragedy of our time is that a society that used to approach death from the standpoint of Christian faith now increasingly approaches it in a purely secular spirit, with devastating results.

In the mourning of Joseph at the death of his father, Jacob, we have a reminder of what a believing person's proper response should be.

A Death-Denying Culture

Franz Borkenau is a historian who believes that cultures can be analyzed by their attitudes toward death. He says there are three basic attitudes. In ancient Greece he finds a *death-accepting* attitude. In the Judeo-Christian sphere he finds a *death-defying* attitude. In our own modern, post-Christian era he finds a *death-denying* attitude, the most inadequate of all.

We need not go far to find examples of this last view. The most obvious—and a very modern approach—are the death-denying views of Mary Baker Eddy and the religious movement known as Christian Science, which she founded. According to Mrs. Eddy, death is an error of the mind. It is not real. This attitude has worked its way into the editorial pages of the *Christian Science Monitor,* a well-respected newspaper, where the word "death" is never printed. The funeral industry does something similar. It renames death for marketing purposes. So does the insurance industry, whose chief product, "life insurance," is a misnomer if there ever was one.

Richard W. Doss explains in a book on death in America just how this happens. "A massive cultural conspiracy is at work in creating a 'new image' for death. We attempt to reshape our understanding of death by the language we use, particularly imaginative euphemisms we have invented to soften the reality of death. Consider what takes place when a person dies. If he dies in a hospital (and the odds are he will), it will be announced that the patient 'expired' and the attending physician will sign a 'vital statistics form.' No longer a 'patient,' the person enters a new state as a 'loved one.' The 'remains' of the 'loved one' are removed to the mortuary where the family arranges 'the memorial estate.' After 'preparation' the 'loved one' is placed in the 'slumber room' (sometimes called the 'reposing room'). If he is a member of a church, the minister announces from the pulpit or in the bulletin that 'Mr. Jones has gone home to be with the Lord' or 'passed to his heavenly home.' The newspaper states succinctly that 'Mr. Jones, beloved father, passed away. . . .' This is the accepted social practice for speaking of death. If you are so coarse as to mention in a matter-of-fact way, 'Did you hear that John Jones *died* last week?' people may think you to be in poor taste or indiscreet. Use of softened language indicates a strong need to deny the harshness of death."[1]

In his analysis of Western culture Doss finds three reasons why our society is death-denying. The first is *psychological.* Sigmund Freud, the father of modern psychology, spoke of death as a great unconscious fear of man. Consequently, the more one is faced with death, the more one denies it personally. America is bombarded with death. It stares at us incessantly from the television screen and leaps up at us from the newspaper. Through real-life pictures of death (as on television) or fictional death (as in violent television shows or movies) the average Western child sees more death before he goes to grade school than the average person of a previous age saw in a lifetime. Such persons deny the reality of death because they see so much of it.

The second reason is *cultural.* American society emphasizes youthfulness, vitality, and productivity. The worth of persons is measured by what they do. Wholeness is measured in terms of thinking and acting young. In America death is not the last enemy as the Bible describes it, but an enemy to be defeated now—through gyms, spas, facelifts, health foods, and other body-enhancing pastimes and procedures.

However, in Doss's judgment the chief reason for America's having become a death-denying culture is *religious.* "Religion has been a major force in shaping the ideas and life-style of the American people. Our forefathers came to this country with a clearly defined view of man and the world. From the Puritan settlement of New England to nineteenth-century life on the western frontier, a theological framework supported and interpreted man's place in society and his relationship with nature and God. Men believed and felt that God had a purpose for life, and more, that every man could know and understand God's plan. Death was one element within this religious framework and thus could be dealt with openly and treated as a natural part of life. Burial of the dead was carried out with religious rites which gave expression to this view of God's purposes for man. Burial rites supported the needs of the community to affirm not only the life of the one who died, but the life of the community as well. God, man and the community were integrally tied together in the funeral service."[2]

But this worldview has evaporated as Western man has rejected God and religion. Doss writes, "The twentieth century has seen a virtual abolition of the traditional Christian framework with no new proposal to take its place. Secularization has separated modern man from older understandings of man and society, and in so doing has separated death from the means by which it had been explained for so many years. As a result, death has been isolated and denuded. With no meaningful framework for understanding death, our culture has adopted a style of denial and avoidance."[3]

Of course, the reality of death cannot ultimately be avoided. We treat it as fiction. But suddenly death steps across the threshold of our home or into our neighbor's, and we tremble.

A Death-Accepting Culture

The ancient Greeks are an example of what Borkenau calls a death-accepting culture. The chief example—one of the best-known deaths of all time—is the death of Socrates. Socrates was the philosophical mentor of Plato, who records the story of Socrates' last hours in the "Phaedo." Socrates had been sentenced to death by the rulers of Athens for corrupting the city's youth by his "atheism"—he denied the literal reality of the Greek gods—and the moment approached when he was to drink the fatal draught of hemlock. His friends, the youth, were gathered about him, and some were weeping. Not Socrates! He used the occasion to reason with the sorrowing young men about death's significance. He did not shrink from it. When the cup at last was presented, quite readily and cheerfully he drank of the poison and thus perished.[4]

What gave Socrates power to die in this fashion? It was his commitment to reason. Earlier in the story, in a dialogue recorded in the "Crito," Socrates argued that he was then seventy years of age and that a man at that age ought not to shun death. But chiefly his reasoning was about the immortality of the soul. In the Greek system the soul was part of the spiritual or immaterial world and hence good and permanent, while the body was part of the material and evil world and thus perishable. Death is the only way an individual can be set free from bodily existence, which is evil, the Greeks believed. Hence, death is the soul's friend. Death frees the soul from a body that keeps it from functioning on the highest level.

The problem is that it is difficult to die serenely on the basis of a philosophical hope. And death is still a loss for the survivors! Plato was Socrates' star pupil. But in the "Phaedo" he confesses that when his mentor drank the hemlock, he, along with the others, burst into tears at having lost such a just and wise companion.

Is this the best we can do? Must we either accept death with philosophical stoicism, as Socrates did, or else deny its reality, which is the approach of our materialistic culture?

A Death-Defying Culture

Franz Borkenau does not think so, for he speaks in the third place of the Judeo-Christian or death-defying culture. It is epitomized in the defiance sounded clearly by the apostle Paul:

> Where, O death, is your victory?
> Where, O death, is your sting?

> The sting of death is sin, and the power of sin is the law. But thanks be to God!
> He gives us the victory through our Lord Jesus Christ.
>
> 1 Corinthians 15:55–57

The phrase "death-defying" is not, to my mind, the best way to encapsulate the biblical perspective. But it is close enough, because it embraces the acknowledgment of death's reality and horror on the one hand, while recognizing a life beyond death and a triumph over it on the other.

This is what we see in Joseph's reaction to the death of his father, Jacob. We see Joseph accepting death and grieving over it. But at the same time we also see a death-transcending hope that culminates eventually in the resurrection faith of mature Christianity.

The most striking feature of Joseph's reaction to his father's death is *grief*. In our culture, where death is denied so strenuously, it is considered improper to grieve, or at least to grieve visibly or long. Undertakers report that the trend in funeral arrangements is to "get it over with" as quickly as possible and that the survivors often prefer the arrangements to be made by some impersonal third party.

This is not how Joseph responded. Genesis tells us that Joseph "threw himself upon his father and wept over him and kissed him" (Gen. 50:1). Then he entered upon a formal period of seventy days of mourning while he and the brothers were still in Egypt, an unrecorded period of time (perhaps three weeks) while the funeral procession was on its way to Canaan, a week at the threshing floor of Atad, near the Jordan, where the Egyptians particularly grieved, and finally a period in which the sons carried the patriarch's remains across the Jordan to the cave in the field of Machpelah, where they buried him.

Can you imagine someone doing that today? If someone you know should act that way in response to the death of a parent, child, or spouse, you would regard him as mentally deranged and the mourning as intolerably morbid. You would give him a sedative to calm him down or even lock him in his bedroom and stand guard over him. Joseph was not deranged. On the contrary, he is a model of faith. He was what we would term one of the most self-possessed characters in all Scripture. Yet he grieves loudly and long.

Are we wiser than Joseph? I think not. I have a friend who lost her husband in a sudden plane crash some years ago. She is a woman of strong faith and great self-control. Yet she told me recently that it has only been lately, after the passage of perhaps a half-dozen years, that she has been able finally to recover from her loss and get on with life fully.

The second thing we notice about Joseph's response to the death of his father was *service* to his father's memory and to the physical parts of him that remained. In Egypt the prolonged and skillful process of embalming was an attempt to cheat death of its inevitable ravages and illustrate what was believed to be an undiminished exercise of life's functions and pleasures in the next life. The Egyptians were preoccupied with death, so much so that students of ancient Egypt have termed it "a culture of the dead." We are not to think that Joseph was motivated by any of these unworthy concerns. He did not think that preserving Jacob's body would somehow preserve him for the land of shades. But neither did he forego the normal decent preparation and honoring of the body that was customary in that culture.

In the same way, it is not wrong and is actually beneficial for us to have funerals and graveside services in which we honor the memory and serve the remains of the one who has died. These rites of passage are proper for the deceased and are helpful for us in working through the grief process.

Third, Joseph *honored the promises* that he had made to his father earlier. Jacob did not want his body to be left in Egypt and had made Joseph swear an oath that he would carry his body out of Egypt and bury him in the cave in the field of Machpelah in the land of his ancestors. This was an expression of Jacob's faith in God's solemn promises to Abraham and Isaac, and Joseph was not about to disregard them. On the contrary, this was also his faith. So when the time came for him to die, he likewise made his survivors swear to "carry my bones up from this place" (Gen. 50:25).

Can we think that this failed to have a strong beneficial impact on the Egyptians? If Joseph had not expressed grief over the death of his beloved father, the Egyptians would have concluded merely that he had not cared for him, that perhaps he was even glad to have the old man out of the way. If he had expressed nothing but grief, the Egyptians may have concluded that the hope of an afterlife by these Semitic people was no better than their own dark hopes and may even have been inferior to theirs. But what about this trip back to Canaan? What about this burial in the ancestral tomb of Abraham, Isaac, and the others? Are we to think that Joseph was silent during these many months concerning the nature of the God he served and the promises God had made to his people? I think Joseph took charge of these rites of mourning, as he took charge of almost everything else, and that he used them to testify to God's salvation promises.

So must we who believe in Jesus Christ. We grieve, but not "like the rest of men, who have no hope" (1 Thess. 4:13). We believe that Jesus rose and that because he rose, those who have died in faith in him will also live again. Death is defeated. The grave is robbed of spoil. Therefore, we "encourage each other with these words" (1 Thess. 4:18).

176

A Time to Cease from Weeping

Genesis 50:14

After burying his father, Joseph returned to Egypt, together with his brothers and all the others who had gone with him to bury his father.

Life must go on. The thought offers little comfort to one who is grieving over the loss of a parent, spouse, child, or good friend. It is true, nevertheless; and it is good that it is true. No one should grieve forever.

Joseph did not grieve forever. He had grieved with tears for three or four months. But the time for grieving passed, and Joseph at last returned to Egypt. The text in Genesis says, "After burying his father, Joseph returned to Egypt, together with his brothers and all the others who had gone with him to bury his father" (Gen. 50:14).

It must have been hard for Joseph to return to a land where he had experienced so much suffering, difficult to leave a place where his hope of God's promises was focused. He was seventeen when he had last seen Canaan. What memories the visit to old haunts, particularly the cave at Machpelah, must have had for him. Now he was leaving. One commentator wrote, "It is almost

1243

like a second selling to the Midianites, a second going down to captivity. It is as if he were a second time exchanging Canaan's bright promise for Egypt's dark and bitter slavery!"[1] Yet Joseph set out again for Egypt.

Those who have lost someone very close to them must do something similar. Perhaps not today, perhaps not next week or next month. Dealing with grief takes time. But life must resume in full someday, and the knowledge of that as well as consciousness of moving toward it is part of the healing process.

Death and Dying

In recent years there has been considerable study of the process of dying from which helpful, recognizable steps have been formulated. The person best known for this is Elisabeth Kübler-Ross, who has highlighted five stages:

1. *Denial.* In this stage the person's typical response is "No, not me!" According to Kübler-Ross, denial helps the person deal with the shocking news and begin to collect the necessary defenses for what follows.

2. *Anger.* This second stage is expressed in the response "Why me?" Anger can be displayed in many directions: toward doctors, nurses, family, friends, even God.

3. *Negotiation.* In this stage a person attempts to postpone what is now seen to be inevitable. This can take the form of trying to make a deal with God to serve him if more time can be given.

4. *Withdrawal.* This is a time of preparation in which a person begins to cut himself off from relationships that are going to be severed ultimately.

5. *Acceptance.* In this stage the emotional turmoil subsides and is replaced by what Kübler-Ross calls "a certain degree of quiet expectation."[2]

Today it is being recognized that there are also stages in the process of grieving. Unfortunately, this has not been so neatly spelled out or so widely recognized. Putting a number of sources together, I would say it goes something like this:

First, there is the *shock of death* itself. Sometimes, as in the case of a long illness where the outcome is not really in doubt, the shock extends from the time the survivor learns of the coming death of the other until death comes. Often, as in the case of an accident, the shock is sudden, intense, and shattering. Nothing so characterizes this stage as a turmoil of conflicting emotions, like having an eggbeater thrust into the mixing bowl of our emotional life, as one writer put it.

There may be fear. This was the emotion that most confronted C. S. Lewis at the death of his wife, Joy, though he said it was not fear, but only something like it. There may be anger. Wives have been angry at their husbands for leaving them. One accused her dying husband, saying, "You . . . you're not going to be there for me when I die." There may be guilt. Many feel that the death is their fault or that it would have been less painful if only they had shown more love, had more time, or displayed more understanding. Paul Tournier said, "There is no grave beside which a flood of guilt feelings does not assail the mind."[3]

Usually there is just bewilderment. "Where am I? What has happened? What should I do now?"

These feelings will pass; the emotions will settle down. But this takes time, and other people have a role to play in the transition. Statements of fact should be made: "Mary is dead, John. It's time to go home. We need to sleep. We need to get something to eat." Friends can encourage the shocked survivor to cry or begin to express his or her thoughts in words as much as possible.

Second, there is *numbness*, in which nothing seems quite real and the person who is grieving withdraws. C. S. Lewis's reactions were like that. He wrote on the first page of a journal he kept in the months following his wife's death, "There is a sort of invisible blanket between the world and me. I find it hard to take in what anyone says. Or perhaps, hard to want to take it in. It is so uninteresting. Yet I want the others to be about me. I dread the moments when the house is empty. If only they would talk to one another and not to me."[4] In this stage the person is aware of what is happening but is detached from it. The numbness is like that of a wound healing.

Third, there is *renewed activity*, an attempt to get back into things. This is what Joseph was doing in his return to Egypt. In this stage the threads of life are again picked up, and the work that had been properly interrupted goes on.

The last stage is *adaptation*. It is evident at this point that life will not be the same as it was formerly, but there is an acceptance of this and recognition that there are still good experiences ahead. One writer speaks of this time as bringing a sense of liberation ("The person feels free of the image of self as mourner"), new perspective ("The loss is now seen in a new light"), and a fresh focus on reality ("Earlier distorted, simplistic thinking gives way to rational reasons and biblical truth").[5] This last stage may be delayed. Some never reach it. But most people, particularly Christians, come through the grief process and find life enriched with the close presence of God and the joy of serving him again.

Help through the Valley

But the question is how? How does one who has lost a person dear to him or her, one who seems the very essence of life itself, get on with living? Knowing the normative stages may help. Friends, if one has them and if they are perceptive, count a great deal. But grief, like dying, is still a path that one treads alone. What is it that helps a person move from the initial shock of death to the fullness of life again?

I have been helped greatly on this account by Elisabeth Elliot, who has suffered the loss of two husbands. The first, Jim Elliot, was killed by Auca Indians in Ecuador while trying to reach them with the gospel. The second, Addison Leitch, was slowly consumed by cancer. What helped Elisabeth Elliot through the grief process? She cites six scriptural ideas.

1. *To be still and know that God is God.* This response to death or some other tragedy comes from Psalm 46, in which the writer thinks of the earth giving way, the waters roaring, and the mountains quaking and falling into the heart of the sea. This is not a bad description of the way one feels in the first shock of a loved one's death, Elliot notes. Everything that has seemed most dependable has given way. Mountains are falling, earth is reeling. In such a time it is a profound comfort to know that although all things seem to be shaken, one thing is not: God is not shaken. "God is our refuge and strength, an ever-present help in trouble" (v. 1). Therefore, it makes sense to "Be still, and know that I am God; I will be exalted among the nations, I will be exalted in the earth" (v. 10).

"Stillness is something the bereaved may feel they have entirely too much of. But if they will use that stillness to take a long look at Christ, to listen attentively to his voice, they will get their bearings."[6]

2. *To give thanks.* There is much we cannot be thankful for, or at least cannot see how to be thankful for: death itself, grief, loneliness. But we can be thankful for the promise of God's presence through the valley: "Even though I walk through the valley of the shadow of death, I will fear no evil, for you are with me; your rod and your staff, they comfort me" (Ps. 23:4). We can be thankful that in the face of life's terrors God is still in charge.

3. *To refuse self-pity.* Self-pity is one of the most destructive, paralyzing forces of life. "It is," says Elliot, "a death that has no resurrection, a sink-hole from which no rescuing hand can drag you because you have chosen to sink."[7] Self-pity must and can be resisted. When some great sorrow enters our lives we want to think that it is a greater burden than we should ever be called upon to bear, that it is a greater sorrow than anyone has ever borne. But that is not true. Death, suffering, and sorrow are the common lot of humankind.

Failing that line of thought, we argue that we do not "deserve" such suffering. But what are we saying when we voice an opinion like that? That we deserve better? That we deserve anything? No true Christian can think that way for long. We deserve nothing. We stand where we do solely by the grace of God. And if we suffer, well, it is only what our Master, the Lord Jesus Christ, endured in a far more intense manner before us. We were not called to escape life's sorrows, but to suffer as he did, following his steps.

4. *To accept one's loneliness.* This is one of the hardest things of all, because God has made us social beings and our hearts naturally long for social interaction. But loneliness has uses and graces of its own. It is a stage when we are aware of our own helplessness. It is a stage when we can become increasingly aware of God's presence and be drawn to him more closely.

5. *To offer one's loneliness to God.* Loneliness is not something a normal person chooses. But if it has been given to us by God, the only reasonable procedure is to offer it back to him to use and transform as he wishes, just as we would offer any other of his gifts back to him. "But my loneliness is so little. It is such a 'nothing' thing." True, but so is anything else we might

offer. What makes something useful to God is not the size or importance of the thing itself, but whether we place it in his hands. The small boy's five loaves and two fish were paltry enough. But in the hands of Jesus they were used to feed a great multitude. Think how many people have been helped in their grief by those who, like Elisabeth Elliot, have offered their loneliness back to God and have allowed him to work through their emptiness for the benefit of others.

6. *To do something for somebody else.* In my view Elisabeth Elliot speaks best on this point.

> There is nothing like definite, overt action to overcome the inertia of grief. The appearance of Joseph of Arimathea to take away the body of Jesus must have greatly heartened the other disciples, so prostrate with their own grief that they had probably not thought of doing anything at all. Nicodemus, too, thought of something he could do—he brought a mixture of myrrh and aloes—and the women who had come with Jesus from Galilee went off to prepare spices and ointments. This clear-cut action lifted them out of themselves.
>
> That is what we need in a time of crisis. An old piece of wisdom is "Dow the next thynge." Most of us have someone who needs us. If we haven't, we can find someone. Instead of praying only for the strength we ourselves need to survive this day or this hour, how about praying for some to give away? How about trusting God to fulfill his own promise, "My strength is made perfect in weakness"? Where else is his strength more perfectly manifested than in a human being who, well knowing his or her own weakness, lays hold by faith on the strong Son of God, Immortal Love.
>
> It is here that a great spiritual principle goes into operation. Isaiah 58:10–12 says, "If you pour yourself out for the hungry and satisfy the desire of the afflicted, then shall your light rise in the darkness and your gloom be as the noonday. And the LORD will guide you continually and satisfy your desire with good things, and make your bones strong; and you shall be like a watered garden, like a spring of water, whose waters fail not, . . . you shall be called a repairer of the breach, the restorer of streets to dwell in [or, in another translation, 'paths leading home']."
>
> The condition on which all these wonderful gifts (light, guidance, satisfaction, strength, refreshment to others) rest is an unexpected one—unexpected, that is, if we are accustomed to think in material instead of in spiritual terms. The condition is not that one solve his own problems first. He need not "get it together." The condition is simply "if you pour yourself out."[8]

This is what St. Francis of Assisi was talking about in his classic and much-quoted prayer.

> Lord, . . .
> Make me an instrument of your peace,
> Where there is hatred let me sow love,
> Where there is injury, pardon;

Where there is doubt, faith;
Where there is despair, hope;
Where there is darkness, light; and
Where there is sadness, joy.

O Divine Master, . . .
Grant that I may not so much
Seek to be consoled as to console,
To be understood as to understand,
To be loved as to love.
For it is in giving that we receive;
It is in pardoning that we are pardoned; and
It is by dying that we are born to eternal life.

Not only grief, but most of the troubles of our lives would be utterly transformed if we would only learn to think of others first and then serve them before ministering to ourselves.

Death and Resurrection

In Christianity the ultimate answer to death is resurrection, and we therefore rightly look forward to the resurrection of those we love and to reunion with them. It is a strong source of comfort:

Brothers, we do not want you to be ignorant about those who fall asleep, or to grieve like the rest of men, who have no hope. We believe that Jesus died and rose again and so we believe that God will bring with Jesus those who have fallen asleep in him. According to the Lord's own word, we tell you that we who are still alive, who are left till the coming of the Lord, will certainly not precede those who have fallen asleep. For the Lord himself will come down from heaven, with a loud command, with the voice of the archangel and with the trumpet call of God, and the dead in Christ will rise first. After that, we who are still alive and are left will be caught up together with them in the clouds to meet the Lord in the air. So we will be with the Lord forever. Therefore encourage each other with these words.

1 Thessalonians 4:13–18

The resurrection of believers at the last day is a great hope, as I said in commenting on this passage in the previous chapter. It is a comfort. But there is another kind of resurrection that is no less part of the Christian hope and no less a comfort. It is a resurrection we know now.

When a loved one dies, it is not only the person himself who dies. There is a sense in which the lover also dies, or at least a large part of him dies. Part of Joseph was buried in Machpelah's cave when he placed his beloved father next to Abraham, Sarah, Isaac, Rebekah, and Leah. Part of us also lies interred when we bury a spouse, child, or other loved one. Thus, we also need to be resurrected.

As we stand at that grave and hear the words of the service assuring us that the one who has died shall rise again, let us hear them not only as a promise for the deceased but as a promise for ourselves as well. Today a part of us is buried. But we shall live again. Grief will be overcome. Sorrow will be conquered. Why? Because God will see to it. He will yet unfold the riches of his blessing in our lives.

177

"God Meant It for Good"

Genesis 50:15–21

When Joseph's brothers saw that their father was dead, they said, "What if Joseph holds a grudge against us and pays us back for all the wrongs we did to him?" So they sent word to Joseph, saying, "Your father left these instructions before he died: 'This is what you are to say to Joseph: I ask you to forgive your brothers the sins and the wrongs they committed in treating you so badly.' Now please forgive the sins of the servants of the God of your father." When their message came to him, Joseph wept.

His brothers then came and threw themselves down before him. "We are your slaves," they said.

But Joseph said to them, "Don't be afraid. Am I in the place of God? You intended to harm me, but God intended it for good to accomplish what is now being done, the saving of many lives. So then, don't be afraid. I will provide for you and your children." And he reassured them and spoke kindly to them.

Years ago there was an elderly minister to whom God gave marvelous ability to minister to the sick and distressed of his congregation. He had an old bookmark he carried with him in his Bible. It was made of silk threads woven into a motto. The back of it, where the ends of the threads were knotted and tied, was a hopeless tangle. When he

1250

visited a home in which there was some great trouble—sudden sickness, sorrow, or death—and where the believers involved were puzzled by what God was doing in their lives, he would often show this bookmark, first presenting the side with the tangle of threads. After the befuddled parishioner examined it in vain, the pastor would turn it over. On the front side, standing out in colored threads against a white background, was the motto: "God is love."

So it is in life. We live through events that seem tangled and meaningless, but they appear that way only because we cannot see the pattern. When we see life from God's side, his message of love and providence shines through.

Fear of Reprisal

It was thus with Joseph. When Joseph's brothers came to Egypt to buy food and Joseph had at last revealed himself to them, all had been filled with fear. Suddenly they were in the power of this Egyptian prime minister, and their hearts rightly accused them of the wrong they had done to him so many years before. They thought he would kill them. Instead, they found Joseph to be moved by great love. They came to Egypt with their father, Jacob, and then lived there under Joseph's protection for nearly twenty years.

Jacob died. At first, their fears were probably dulled by mourning, maybe even shunted aside by the elaborate funeral arrangements. Still the fear was there, and eventually it began to feed upon them. "What if Joseph holds a grudge against us and pays us back for all the wrongs we did to him?" they wondered (Gen. 50:15). When his father, Isaac, died, Esau had planned vengeance on Jacob for stealing his blessing, saying, "The days of mourning for my father are near; then I will kill my brother Jacob" (Gen. 27:41). Perhaps Joseph's thoughts were like that. Perhaps he had been restrained only because of his affection for his father, to whom he did not wish to add more sorrow. If so, they could expect harsh treatment at his hands.

The brothers had reason to fear, for theirs had been a great crime. They had sold an innocent young man, their own brother, into slavery. But from Joseph's side their fears were unfounded. They came with their argument—that their father had told them to tell Joseph, "Forgive your brothers the sins and the wrongs they committed in treating you so badly" (Gen. 50:17), which Jacob may or may not actually have said—and to humble themselves, saying, "We are your slaves" (v. 18). But they found to their relief that Joseph was entirely forgiving. In fact, he had forgiven them long before, though they distrusted him.

Joseph reassured them in what is surely one of the great statements of Scripture. "Don't be afraid. Am I in the place of God? You intended to harm me, but God intended it for good to accomplish what is now being done, the saving of many lives. So then, don't be afraid. I will provide for you and your children" (vv. 19–21).

"You Meant It for Evil"

I once preached a sermon series on verses of the Bible that contain the words "but God." There is Ephesians 2:4–5 ("But God, who is rich in mercy, for his great love wherewith he loved us, even when we were dead in sins, hath quickened us together with Christ," KJV); 1 Corinthians 2:10 ("But God has revealed it to us by his Spirit"); Romans 5:8 ("But God demonstrates his own love for us in this: While we were still sinners, Christ died for us"); 1 Corinthians 10:13 ("But God is faithful, who will not suffer you to be tempted above that ye are able, but will with the temptation also make a way to escape, that ye may be able to bear it," KJV); 1 Corinthians 1:27 ("But God chose the foolish things of the world to shame the wise"); Acts 13:30 ("But God raised him from the dead").

Each of these texts depends for its effect on what goes before. Ephesians 2:4 speaks of God's love, but that is set against the background of man's sin. First Corinthians 2:10 speaks of God's revelation of himself in his Word, but that is contrasted with our inability to know God by human measures. And so for each of these texts. On the one hand, there is a dreadful, sinful reality; on the other, there is an aspect of the greatness of God that overcomes it.

This is the case with Genesis 50:20, which was also part of my "but God" series: "But God intended it for good." This is a great saying, a forceful testimony. But its strength comes from contrast with what precedes it, namely, the hurt intended by those who scorned or hated Joseph. This was real scorn, not apparent scorn. It was real hate, not playacting. It is only against the background of the reality of this evil that the good providence of God has real meaning.

Joseph suffered three forms of abuse from those who should have loved, honored, or remembered him.

1. The *hatred* of his brothers. Being a child, Joseph had perhaps acted naively and unwisely in telling his jealous older brothers of his two dreams in which sheaves of grain, representing themselves, bowed to his sheaf, and the sun, moon, and stars bowed to him. But at the worst this was a childish mistake. (It may also have been a divine revelation of the future that he was obliged to make known.) It was certainly nothing to merit the ill will and hostile actions of the brothers.

What caused the brothers' hatred was the fact that Joseph was not like them and was favored by their father because of the difference. They were cruel; he was gentle. They were faithless; he was faithful. They were worldly; he was spiritual. Joseph was a true man of God. So they hated him, as the world always hates those who exhibit God's character. They decided to kill him. As it turned out, they spared his life for sordid personal gain and sold him into slavery instead. It is one of the most inhumane acts in Scripture.

No wonder the brothers were fearful now, at the end. One writer says, "Though treated kindly by Joseph, an increasing sense of the awfulness of their crime made them wonder how Joseph could possibly have forgiven them."[1]

2. The *cruelty* of a prominent and influential woman. The brothers' hatred would be evil enough for one young life, but Joseph was not so fortunate as to have the hurts from others stop there. He arrived in Egypt as the lowest of slaves. He rose upward in the slave ranks through his own integrity, faithfulness, and hard work. His master recognized these qualities and placed him in charge of his estate. The text says, "He did not concern himself with anything except the food he ate" (Gen. 39:6). But even this was a snare. When Joseph was a lowly slave, his presence went largely unnoticed, except to his master Potiphar. But when he became prominent he attracted the amorous attentions of Potiphar's philandering wife. The woman was sensuous, direct, and persistent. She solicited Joseph. At last he fled from her, leaving his garment in her hands.

There is no fury like the fury of a woman scorned, and the fury of Potiphar's wife pursued Joseph with the result that he was thrown into prison. So it was not only his own brothers who caused harm. This woman harmed him greatly. She would have killed him if she could.

3. The *forgetfulness* of a friend. Sometimes harm is inflicted by neglect, and this was the case in the third incident of Joseph's most unfortunate years. In prison he made the friendship of the chief baker and chief cupbearer of Pharaoh. These were important positions, but these men had fallen into disfavor with Pharaoh and so were confined in the same prison as Joseph to face an unknown end. While there they had dreams. Joseph interpreted the dreams, showing that after three days the cupbearer would be taken from the prison and restored to his office and that the baker would be taken from the prison and hanged.

Joseph appealed to his friend the cupbearer, "When all goes well with you, remember me and show me kindness; mention me to Pharaoh and get me out of this prison. For I was forcibly carried off from the land of the Hebrews, and even here I have done nothing to deserve being put in a dungeon" (Gen. 40:14–15). No doubt the cupbearer promised to work for Joseph's release. But the story concludes, "The chief cupbearer, however, did not remember Joseph; he forgot him" (v. 23). The next chapter begins, "When two full years had passed . . ." (Gen. 41:1).

Joseph lay forgotten in prison for two full years—and that on top of his brothers' malicious hatred and Mrs. Potiphar's hot scorn. Few persons in history have suffered as intensely and as unjustly as Joseph. But it is precisely against this dark storm of evil that our text containing Joseph's testimony to God's providence shines most brightly. "Am I in the place of God? You intended to harm me, but God intended it for good to accomplish what is now being done, the saving of many lives."

Our Gracious God

What gave Joseph the grace to make this remarkable reply? There is only one answer: Joseph knew God. In particular, he knew two things about God. He knew that God is sovereign—that nothing ever comes into the life of any one of his children that he has not approved first; there are no accidents. And he knew that God is good—therefore, the things that come into our lives by God's sovereignty are for our benefit (and for others') and not for our harm.

What Joseph saw and spoke of in this next-to-last scene of his earthly life is what the apostle Paul wrote about eloquently hundreds of years later. It is a text often memorized by Christian people: "We know that in all things God works for the good of those who love him, who have been called according to his purpose" (Rom. 8:28). It is impossible to overestimate the wonder of this verse. It teaches three things, all of which are illustrated in the life of Joseph.

First, God is working for the *good* of those who love him. This is what Joseph saw. On the surface he saw much that looked bad. I think here of Elisabeth Elliot, who saw numerous reversals in her early years as a missionary and then endured the loss of two husbands, one murdered by Auca Indians and the second slowly destroyed by cancer. Reflecting on these experiences, this godly woman wrote "The experiences of my life are not such that I could infer from them that God is good, gracious and merciful necessarily. To have had one husband murdered and another one disintegrate, body, soul and spirit, through cancer, is not what you would call a proof of the love of God. In fact, there are many times when it looks like just the opposite."[2]

But this is not how a Christian judges things—by sight. Not at all! "My belief in the love of God is not by inference or instinct," she wrote. "It is by faith. To apprehend God's sovereignty working in that love is—we must say it—the last and highest victory of the faith that overcomes the world."[3]

Second, the text teaches that *all* things are controlled by God and therefore work to our good. In Joseph's case it would have been easy for him to say that the dream of Pharaoh, which he was enabled to interpret and which led to his being elevated from the prison to the throne, was of God. It was clear how that was used for good. But while that was obviously of God and was good, Joseph did not allow his testimony to stop there; he extended it to include even the hostile and damaging acts of his brothers. We can see that even sin works for good for those who belong to God.

Can you say that? Can you say with confidence that all things are working together for good in your life, whoever you are and whatever the circumstances of your life may be? Do you believe Romans 8:28?

If "all things" really mean "all things" and God is not a liar, then there is truly nothing in your life that can possibly be excluded. "All" includes the experiences of your childhood and whether they were affirming or destructive. It includes who your parents were (even if you did not know them) and where you were born. It includes your education, your present employment (or lack of it), the house in which you live, the furniture you have, the car you are driving, your friends, your church, even your appearance—the face that stares back at you from your mirror in the morning—and whether it is attractive, as the world measures attractiveness, or whether it is not. Every one of these things is included in that word "all." So are many more besides. Whether you can see it or not—and often we cannot—everything is being used of God for your good as well as the good of others.

Third, *we can know this* and live by it, as Joseph did. If all things worked together for our good without our knowing it, it would be a wonderful fact even though we might not find out about it until much later. But we do not have to wait until later. We can know it now. We can know that all that enters our lives is actually working for good now. This knowledge is by faith, as I indicated. It is not always by sight. But it is nevertheless certain, because it is based on the character of God, who reveals himself to us as both sovereign and benevolent.

Greatest Evil, Greatest Good

It is tempting to object at this point that although Romans 8:28 and the experience of Joseph, which preceded it historically, teach that God controls circumstances and undoubtedly overrules what happens for our benefit—although this is true—certainly the principle cannot be extended to cover deliberate sin in all instances. But this is precisely what the Bible does teach, and in proof of this conviction I submit the example of the greatest evil in all history producing the greatest good imaginable. I refer to the crucifixion of the Lord Jesus Christ.

It is parallel to the story of Joseph, because Joseph prefigured Christ in nearly every way. Jesus was our elder brother sent into a foreign land for our rescuing. He was the favored of his Father, but he became a slave (and later rose to the highest position of power) in order to seek us out and save us. Most significant, he was hated by his brethren, the very ones the Father was using him to save. He was innocent of any wrongdoing. "He was oppressed and afflicted, yet he did not open his mouth; he was led like a lamb to the slaughter, and as a sheep before her shearers is silent, so he did not open his mouth" (Isa. 53:7). Yet we hated him. Against him cruel and evil men poured out wrath. He was unjustly arrested, unjustly tried, unjustly convicted. Then he was killed without mercy. Never in the entire history of the world has greater evil been done—for this was an extreme of evil practiced against one who was not only innocent of crimes but was also actually sinless.

Yet, from this greatest of all evils—evils that parallel but infinitely exceed the abuse inflicted on Joseph—God brought forth the greatest possible good: the salvation of a vast company of people.

As long as the cross stands in history, no one who knows its meaning will be able to pronounce a limitation on God's providence. Christians will never say, "I am aware that *most* things in life are controlled by God and are good for me in some way, though I may not always see how." They will say, "We know that in *all things* God works for the good of those who love him, who have been called according to his purpose."

When people conspire to harm us and actually inflict wounds born of cruel hatred or indifference, we will not call their evil good. Evil remains evil. Sin is still sin. But we will testify before these and the world that in a universe ruled by a sovereign and benevolent God—our God—their evil will not succeed. We will say, "You intended to harm me, but God intended it for good." We will declare that in the ultimate assessment, nothing can be anything but good for God's people.

178

Blessings upon Children's Children

Genesis 50:22–23

Joseph stayed in Egypt, along with all his father's family. He lived a hundred and ten years and saw the third generation of Ephraim's children. Also the children of Makir son of Manasseh were placed at birth on Joseph's knees.

Approaching the end of this study of the Book of Genesis prompts some reflection on it. One profitable line for reflection is that Genesis is a book about families. It begins with a family, after all. When God had created the first man, he observed that it was not good for him to be alone. So he made Eve for Adam, and from their union children began to be born, among them Cain and Abel, the first brothers. In the story of the flood we find another strong family, Noah's. All who were around it were evil. Noah's family members were faithful servants of God, and when the flood came it was this family—Noah and his wife, his three sons, and their wives—that was saved. In later chapters Genesis introduces us to Abraham and his family, Isaac and his family, and finally Jacob and his family.

In the very last scene of Genesis we meet Joseph and the family God had given him. "Joseph stayed in Egypt, along with all his father's family. He lived

1257

a hundred and ten years and saw the third generation of Ephraim's children. Also the children of Makir son of Manasseh were placed at birth on Joseph's knees" (Gen. 50:22–23).

We think also of the recurring phrase "this is the account of..." or "these are the generations of...," which is used in Genesis to mark the major divisions of the text. In all it is found eleven times:

1. "This is the account of the heavens and the earth" (Gen. 2:4);
2. "This is the written account of Adam's line" (5:1);
3. "This is the account of Noah" (6:9);
4. "This is the account of Shem, Ham and Japheth" (10:1);
5. "This is the account of Shem" (11:10);
6. "This is the account of Terah" (11:27);
7. "This is the account of Abraham's son Ishmael" (25:12);
8. "This is the account of Abraham's son Isaac" (25:19);
9. "This is the account of Esau" (36:1);
10. "This is the account of Esau the father of the Edomites in the hill country of Seir" (36:9);
11. "This is the account of Jacob" (37:2).

When *we* think of Genesis we tend to outline it by episodes: the creation, the fall, the flood, Abraham's years without children, the birth of Isaac, and so on. This is not Moses' way of outlining the book, however. Because of the phrase "this is the account of...," it would be correct to say that the book really falls into two unequal parts. The first part runs from 1:1 to 2:3 and tells the story of the creation. The second part, from 2:4 to 50:26, is the story of the "generations." This latter portion—forty-nine of the fifty chapters—is the history of the major families God was blessing.

A Blessing of God

We live in an age of individualism and geographical mobility, and as a result we do not properly value families as being among the greatest of God's great gifts. Children go away to school, marry, and settle down—often hundreds of miles from where they were raised and where their parents still live. Or they work for a company that transfers them to distant parts of the country.

The French say that people who suffer this kind of move are "mutated." That word makes a good point. For whether we admit it or not, being separated from a family produces changes in the one moved, not all of which are good. It is easier to fall away from a parent's faith, for example. It is easier to adopt lower moral standards. In the context of a family these standards are preserved and society is helped to remain stable.

Besides, each of us has personality needs that are met chiefly in families. David wrote, speaking of God's grace and wisdom, "God sets the lonely in families" (Ps. 68:6). David knew that it is a hard thing to be alone, and he saw as one of the evidences of God's goodness that those who are alone in this world are often given another place to be. This is the why the church is so often described as a family. It is wonderful to be part of a natural, supportive family.

Many have never known this blessing. Some have been orphaned at an early age. Others are estranged from their families, sometimes for the gospel's sake (Matt. 10:35–36). What are they to do? They are to be taken into the bosom of the church and there they are to find new fathers and mothers and brothers and sisters. Our Lord spoke of that in his own case when he asked, "Who is my mother, and who are my brothers?" and then, pointing to his disciples, answered, "Here are my mother and my brothers. For whoever does the will of my Father in heaven is my brother and sister and mother" (Matt. 12:48–50).

God gave Joseph his own family again after many years. He had been torn from his home at the age of seventeen. He had spent many lonely years in Egypt. It was only when he was at last exalted by Pharaoh and given a wife with whom he had two children that Joseph began to forget his years of loneliness. When his first child was born Joseph called him Manasseh, which means "forgetfulness," because, he said, "God has made me forget all my trouble and all my father's household" (Gen. 41:51). He called his second son Ephraim, meaning "twice fruitful," because, he said, "God has made me fruitful in the land of my suffering" (v. 52).

We have the same kind of scene unfolded at the end of Genesis. In these last chapters Joseph loses his beloved father, Jacob. When Jacob dies, Joseph is 56 years old.[1] But Joseph died at the age of 110, which means that he survived his father by 54 years—long enough, we shall see, to know several generations of his descendants.

In Hebrew usage the phrase "the third generation of Ephraim's children" could refer to Ephraim's great-grandchildren (Joseph's great-great-grandchildren), beginning with Ephraim and counting three generations beyond that. Or it could refer to Ephraim's grandchildren (Joseph's great-grandchildren), counting Ephraim himself as the first generation. The parallel with Manasseh, whose son Makir placed his children on Joseph's knees, suggests that the latter is the case, that is, that only three generations beyond Joseph are intended. But there is time for the additional generation if each of the fathers was married and had children on the average before the age of twenty-six.

Whatever the case, God restored to Joseph the years the locusts had eaten. He was with his father for the last seventeen years of his father's life, and he lived many years after that to witness the beginning of God's multiplying his family in accord with the earlier prophecies (Gen. 12:2; 15:5; 17:2–16; 22:17;

26:4; 28:14; 35:11; 48:16; 49:22–26). If families are a blessing of God, as the Bible says they are, then Joseph had a generous share of this kindness.

Channels of Blessing

But there is something else here. Not only are families a blessing in themselves, so that it is a good thing to belong to families, it is also the case that families are the ideal structure through which the blessings of God in the gospel may be passed on. Exodus 20:5–6 says, "I, the LORD your God, am a jealous God, punishing the children for the sin of the fathers to the third and fourth generations of those who hate me, but showing love to a thousand generations of those who love me and keep my commandments." The promise at Pentecost, recorded in Acts 2:39, reads, "The promise is for you and your children and for all who are far off—for all whom the Lord our God will call." Even where only one parent is a believer, the promise remains firm. First Corinthians 7:14 indicates, "Otherwise your children would be unclean, but as it is, they are holy."

Some years ago when I was preaching from the first chapter of John, I was drawn to the fact that when Jesus began to call disciples, the gospel spread first within families. John the Baptist had pointed to Jesus as being "the Lamb of God" and "the Son of God" (John 1:29, 34), and two of his disciples, Andrew and probably the apostle John, followed Jesus. They spent the night with him. The next morning, so the text tells us, "The first thing Andrew did was to find his brother Simon and tell him, 'We have found the Messiah' (that is, the Christ)" (v. 41). His brother! The story tells us that the first real case of witnessing, after John the Baptist had identified Jesus as God's Son, was when Andrew found his brother Peter and brought him to Jesus.

So it has been in countless situations. Donald Grey Barnhouse wrote of family evangelism.

> Oh, it is true that the first generation of believers in any tribe come straight out of heathenism, generally by the witness of some foreigner who has brought the witness to that particular tribe. . . .
>
> Most of church history is the story of some alien who entered a tribe with little knowledge of the language and preached Christ in the power of the Holy Spirit so that people were saved. Paul, the Greek Jew, took the gospel to the tribes of Asia Minor, Macedonia and Greece. Irenaeus, a Greek, was the first to take the gospel to Gaul, which is now France. A Latin from Rome, the second St. Augustine, was the first missionary to England, while an Englishman, Boniface, was the first to carry the gospel to Germany. Young Patrick, of high family, was kidnapped by marauders and carried off to Ireland at the age of sixteen, later to become the instrument of the conversion of Ireland. In modern times the list of similar instances crosses the world. Henry Martyn took the gospel to Hindustan and to Persia. We have Adoniram Judson of Burma; Hudson Taylor of China; Mary Slessor of Calabar; Livingstone of central Africa

. . . and the list goes on until we have Betty Elliot of the Aucas, and Wycliffe Bible Translators in many another tribe.

But in spite of all this list, which grows longer every year, these pioneers win but a small proportion of those who come to Christ. The informant who teaches his language to that strange creature, the missionary, usually ends up by coming to know the missionary's Savior. He has seen Christ in the missionary first of all, and then the informant goes and finds his own brother! This is a first in countless tribes. The God of Abraham became the God of Sarah, Abraham's wife, and then the God of Isaac and the God of Jacob.[2]

This relationship works in two ways. On the one hand, the believer has a genuine concern for those of his family who do not yet know Christ—because they are dear to him and the Christian wants them above all others to know the joy he has experienced.

On the other hand, the unbelieving member of the family knows the one who is attempting to share the new life of Christ with him. He has known him before his conversion and is now seeing him after it. If there is no change, a brother or sister will know it immediately—long before anyone else will notice it. But by contrast, if there is a change, that will be noticed also. "Before, my brother was stingy; he never gave anyone anything. Now he has become generous with what he has. He is generous with me." Or, "Before, my sister never thought about anyone but herself; she spent all her time buying clothes and applying makeup. Now she takes time for me." Thousands of persons testify that they have found Christ in just this manner, praising God that he first called that other member of the family.

I do not believe the Bible teaches that in all cases each and every member of a family (or even each and every child of a believing parent) will necessarily come to Christ in salvation, though that may well be what happens. We remember that even in Adam's family, Cain went the way of the godless while only Seth remained godly. Isaac's son Esau gave no evidence of being regenerate. Only Jacob moved gently forward with God.

But although I do not believe that the Bible guarantees the salvation of other members of our family or even of our children, the presumption is on that side. The members of our family do not inherit salvation; salvation cannot be inherited. But they do inherit the benefit of a living, vital witness to the power of God in a converted person's life. They inherit his or her witness to Scripture and often an exposure to gospel preaching, Christian books, spiritually directed conversations, and Christian friends. The children of believers are even more blessed; they become members of God's covenant family and are thereby exposed to the collective witness, life, and prayers of God's people.

These are not negligible advantages. Instead, they are mighty advantages. They are grounds for encouragement as Christian parents try to raise their children in the love and knowledge of him who has first revealed himself to be their own Savior.

God's Faithful Family

If you are a parent, I want to encourage you by the scene of Joseph's taking the children of Makir, his grandson, upon his knees. Your children may be far from God at this moment. It does not mean that the day will not come when they return to the faith of their fathers and even bring their own children to you for your blessing.

You may be a young person who is alone in the world, who does not have a home. It does not mean that you will never have one. In the meantime, you should find a believing, caring church and there take an interest in other parents and other children. You may be a Joseph to some child who is as much alone in the world as you are.

But you must work at it. These are great promises and great possibilities, but they do not happen automatically. We must do at least these things:

1. We must be *faithful parents*. Not all of us are brilliant in our mastery of the Scriptures. Not all of us have exceptional wisdom in raising children or in dealing with their adolescent rebellions. We cannot all be of Joseph's stature. But we can be faithful. We can keep from sin. We can stay close to Jesus. We can be regular in our church attendance, Bible study, prayer, and good deeds, including those we do for our children. God works through such means, and he is especially close to those who want to be faithful to him. Joseph had exceptional gifts, but we can be sure he did not rely on these to the neglect of the lesser things. On the contrary, it was his greatness in large matters that made him faithful in details. Can we believe that he held the children of Makir on his knees without praying for them and instructing them in the knowledge of their fathers' God?

2. We must build *caring churches*. There has always been a need for caring churches, but there is a special need in our day. In the past, when the world was simpler and people were not torn from their home environments as often or as radically as they are today, the fundamental family supports for godly living were intact. That is not the case now. So the function of the visible body of Christ as a caring family in a particular place is of even greater importance. Our streets are filled with lonely, hurting people. Our pews hold the walking wounded. We must be supportive. We must reach out to these, and we must also help our families in their times of trouble and support them in what they are doing. Families need families, just as people need people. The church family must help the nuclear family to be all God intends it to be.

3. We must provide *open homes*. It is easy in our day for those with good homes to transform them into little protective units where the world is shut out and the members can live exclusively for their own interests. This ought not to be. Christian homes should be open homes. They should be places where those without homes (at least for the time being) can be brought into the larger, caring atmosphere that a family provides.

4. We must be *praying people*. If the blessings of Christian homes and the transfer of the gospel from generation to generation in this context were a

mechanical thing, so that the blessings followed automatically whenever certain preliminary things were done, we would not need to pray. But blessings are a matter of grace, and grace is not mechanical. Grace flows from God. So we must approach God prayerfully, asking him to enrich and stabilize our homes and use them to reach out to others. And we must pray for our children that the knowledge of God might pass from us to them and so on through generations of our descendants.

This was so in the case of Saint Augustine and his praying mother, Monica. In his youth Augustine was quite far from the Lord. But never did a son have a more prayerful mother. She prayed for him in his wildest days; she prayed for him as God began to draw him to himself. Monica was encouraged to keep on praying by Ambrose, the bishop of Milan. He said (overstating the case), "The son of such tears cannot be lost."

Thus, in time Augustine embraced the gospel and became a great defender of the faith. Some days before Monica died—at the age of fifty-six, when Augustine himself was thirty-three—the mother and son shared deep things about the faith, conversing among other subjects on the blessedness of the saints in heaven.

Brothers and sisters, fathers and mothers, let us also be praying people. The God who created families and who delights to answer prayers on behalf of them will bless us and extend the blessings we have enjoyed to our children's children.

179

The Faith of Joseph

Genesis 50:24–25

Then Joseph said to his brothers, "I am about to die. But God will surely come to your aid and take you up out of this land to the land he promised on oath to Abraham, Isaac and Jacob." And Joseph made the sons of Israel swear an oath and said, "God will surely come to your aid, and then you must carry my bones up from this place."

One day when he was very young, Dale Carnegie, the author of *How to Win Friends and Influence People*, wrote a letter to Richard Harding Davis. Davis was a highly regarded author at the time, and Carnegie was writing a magazine article about authors. He wanted Davis to tell him how he did his work. Sometime before this, Carnegie had received a letter from someone else that contained at the bottom the words "Dictated but not read." That sounded important. So when he wrote Davis, Carnegie added these words to the bottom of his letter. Davis never even troubled to answer. He simply returned the letter with a note scribbled across the bottom: "Your bad manners are exceeded only by your bad manners."

In telling that story later, Carnegie confessed that he had been foolish and that he had even deserved the rebuke. But he was hurt by it and resented it—so much so that ten years after, when he read of the death of Richard Davis, this was the memory that came first to his mind. He remembered Davis for the hurt he had given him.

It is strange what people are remembered for. A man can spend a lifetime building a company and amassing a fortune, but his children will remember him for the time he spent talking to them at night after dinner—or for the time he failed to spend with them. A woman will pour her time into charitable activities and benefits, but her co-workers will remember her for the harshness of her voice, the hats she wore—or perhaps for the gracious manner in which she deferred to others and saw that they got credit for the benefits.

In the next-to-last verses of Genesis we have a declaration of faith in God for which a very great man, Joseph, is remembered in the New Testament. But it is strange for two reasons.

First, it is the only thing for which the New Testament remembers and praises Joseph. This is peculiar because the Old Testament records so much about him. The story of Joseph begins in Genesis 37 and continues for thirteen chapters, about the same amount of space as is given to Abraham. But there are only four places in the New Testament where Joseph is even mentioned: (1) he is mentioned in an incidental way in John 4:5, where Jesus is said to have passed near a plot of ground Jacob had given to Joseph; (2) Stephen mentioned his name five times in Acts 7:9–18 in summarizing the history of the Jewish people; (3) Revelation 7:8 mentions twelve thousand persons from the "tribe of Joseph," along with an equal number from the other tribes; and (4) the closing of Genesis is cited in Hebrews 11:22 as evidence that Joseph lived by faith, as did the other Old Testament saints mentioned in that chapter. Of the four passages, it is only this last passage, in which Genesis 50:24–25 is cited, that commends Joseph. Hebrews 11:22 is the only New Testament text in which the actual words of Joseph are referred to.

The second strange thing about Genesis 50:24–25 is its content. Important *it obviously is*, at least to the author of Hebrews. But it is only a deathbed scene in which Joseph speaks of God's coming to the aid of the Jews at some future time and instructs them to carry his bones up from Egypt when that happens. We may not understand all that is involved in this passage, but it should teach us this at least: God does not always remember us for what we might consider to be of great importance.

Oaks and Mushrooms

We must try to understand these closing moments of Joseph's long life, and the place to begin is with the fact that Joseph had fewer spiritual advantages than his brothers and yet was stronger in faith than all of them.

Joseph's brothers were raised in their father's household and continued under his influence for many years. They would have been taught stories of God's dealings with the earlier patriarchs and would have been instructed in God's promises. They would have participated in the daily worship of God under the direction of their father Jacob.

Joseph's case was quite different. He had been taken to Egypt when he was 17 years old. Since he died when he was 110 years old, this means that he had lived in the hostile spiritual environment of Egypt for 93 years. Egypt was technically advanced but spiritually depraved. Its religion was the rawest form of polytheism, in which gods and goddesses took the forms of animals, snakes, and insects. The worship of these gods was often sexual in nature, and there were probably occult or demonic activities as well. Moreover, Joseph was not an obscure individual. He was second only to Pharaoh and must therefore have been under intense and continuing pressure to conform to Egypt's customs.

Under similar circumstances many a man would have capitulated easily and would soon have been indistinguishable from his environment. Joseph did not follow this pattern. His dying statement, for which he is praised in Hebrews, is proof that faith does not need to be destroyed by circumstances.

It also proves that faith can grow strong in adversity, for Joseph's dying faith was also strong, as we will see. God grows faith in difficulty, and the faith thus grown is a hearty faith. If you want to grow mushrooms, you can grow them quickly in protected conditions. But if you want to grow an oak tree, it must be in the open where it will stand against the storms of summer and the snows of winter. Adversity makes the oak tree strong.

Theology of Hope

Years ago the German theologian Jürgen Moltmann wrote a book entitled *The Theology of Hope*. Its thesis, which had a profound effect on many at the time, was that eschatology (the doctrine of the last things) should not be an appendix to Christian theology—something tacked on at the end and perhaps even dispensable to theology—but should be the starting point of everything. It is faith in what God is going to do that should determine what we think and how we act now.

This is the kind of faith Joseph had. It is interesting, when we compare the dying words of Joseph with the dying words of his father, Jacob, to find that this is the great point of comparison. Both men certainly believed in the same God, and they believed the promises given to the patriarchs. But Jacob's dying words have to do almost entirely with the past, while Joseph's have to do almost entirely with the future.

Jacob had prophesied concerning the future of his children. But when he died he spoke of the cave in the field of Machpelah, how it had been bought from a Hittite and how Abraham and Sarah, Isaac and Rebekah, and Leah had been buried there. He wanted his body to be taken from Egypt and buried with these others in his own land. By contrast, Joseph looked entirely to the future. He saw difficult times for his people, but he also predicted that God would see them through those times and would eventually come to their aid and lead them out of Egypt. In anticipation of that future deliverance he requested that his body remain in Egypt temporarily, but that it be taken up eventually and removed to Canaan.

This is a true theology of hope. It is a theology that fixes its gaze on what God is yet to do and disposes present affairs in that light.

When we read Joseph's dying words we see that he was aware of what was coming. Otherwise he would not have spoken of God's coming to his descendants' aid.

How did he know this? There are several ways. He would have known God's revelation of these future events to Abraham in the vision recorded in Genesis 15. In that vision God told Abraham: "Know for certain that your descendants will be strangers in a country not their own, and they will be enslaved and mistreated four hundred years. But I will punish the nation they serve as slaves, and afterward they will come out with great possessions" (Gen. 15:13–14). That revelation would have passed to Joseph through Abraham's son Isaac and Abraham's grandson (Joseph's father) Jacob.

Again, Joseph may have received a revelation of these coming events himself. He had been given dreams earlier in his life. He had shown that he was able to understand them. God may have warned him of the future by dreams.

Finally, Joseph may have seen the beginning of the coming dark ages in his lifetime. We are not told anything about affairs in Egypt during the last fifty or so years of Joseph's life; but it may be that events were even then beginning to move toward the grim circumstances seen in the first chapter of the very next book of the Bible.

Whatever the case, Joseph did not have high hopes for any schemes of human betterment and so did not allow his hopes to become rooted in Egypt's political life. He was in the world but not of it, just as we should be. Joseph knew what was coming, as we know what is coming, and for that very reason he fixed his gaze on God and what God would accomplish. If the hymn had been written then, I suppose they could have sung at Joseph's funeral:

> This world is not my home;
> I'm just a-passin' through.
> My treasures are laid up
> Somewhere beyond the blue.
> The angels beckon me
> From heaven's open door,
> And I can't feel at home
> In this world anymore.
>
> Oh, Lord, you know
> I have no friend like you.
> If heaven's not my home,
> Then, Lord, what will I do?
> The angels beckon me

From heaven's open door,
And I can't feel at home
In this world anymore.

A Sign of Hope

When we speak of Joseph's being oriented to the future, we might suppose that he therefore had very little interest in the present. But biblical hope does not work that way, and neither did Joseph's anticipations. Joseph knew that dark days were coming and that God would eventually intervene to rescue his people from them. But precisely because he believed that, Joseph did what he could to provide encouragement for those who remained behind.

This is why Joseph wanted his body to remain in Egypt for what was to be four hundred years rather than having it brought up out of Egypt and buried in Canaan, like his father's corpse. Joseph's fortunes may have been declining during his final years in Egypt, but it is hard to imagine that he could not have had his body returned to Canaan for burial if he had wanted that to happen. He did want to be buried there eventually. The fact that he allowed his body to remain in Egypt temporarily must be due to the benefit he supposed his uninterred remains would have for his descendants during the ensuing years. For *he was not buried!* His coffin was not deposited in some Egyptian pyramid or tomb. His coffin stood above ground, awaiting its removal to Canaan when the time should come. Therefore, all who looked at it would be reminded of that anticipated day and destiny.

F. B. Meyer writes well on this point. "What a lesson must those unburied bones have read to Israel! When the taskmasters dealt hardly with the people, so that their hearts fainted, it must have been sweet to go and look at the mummy case which held those mouldering remains, waiting there to be carried forward; and, as they did so, this was doubtless their reflection, 'Evidently, then, Joseph believed that we were not to stay here always but that we should sooner or later leave for Canaan; let us brace ourselves up to bear a little longer, it may be only a very little while!' Yes, and when some were tempted to settle down content with prospering circumstances and to feast upon leeks, garlics and onions, it was a check on them to think of those bones and say, 'Evidently we are not to remain here always; we should do well not to build all our hopes and comfort on the unstable tenure of our sojourn in this place.' And, oftentimes, when the people were ready to despair amid the difficulties and weariness of their desert march, those bones borne in their midst told them of the confident hope of Joseph—that God would bring them to the land of rest."[1]

That is precisely what God did, and when he did so, the bones of Joseph accompanied the people and eventually were buried in Canaan at Shechem. Exodus 13:19 tells us that when Israel left Egypt, "Moses took the bones of Joseph with him because Joseph had made the sons of Israel swear an oath. He had said, 'God will surely come to your aid, and then you must carry my bones up with you from this place.'" The Book of Joshua closes by saying, "And Joseph's bones, which the Israelites had brought up from Egypt, were buried at Shechem in the tract of land that Jacob bought for a hundred pieces of silver from the sons of Hamor, the father of Shechem. This became the inheritance of Joseph's descendants" (Josh. 24:32).

What do we have to bolster our faith in hard circumstances or keep us from too great contentment in the land of our pilgrimage—we who live so many thousands of years after Joseph? We do not have a coffin in Egypt. We have no bones for faith. *We have something better.* We have an open tomb, an empty grave, a risen Savior, a blessed promise: "I will not leave you as orphans; I will come to you" (John 14:18); "and surely I am with you always, to the very end of the age" (Matt. 28:20).

To Be a Pilgrim

The final reason why Joseph's dying words are exceptional and are therefore mentioned in Hebrews is that they declare whose side Joseph was on. I have noted that Joseph lived in Egypt ninety-three years. During that time he must have seemed to be conformed to Egypt in every outward way. He served an Egyptian king. He bore an Egyptian title. He had married an Egyptian wife. He would have shared in every honorable form of Egyptian court life, politics, and trade. Yet Joseph was no Egyptian, especially in his heart.

Alexander Maclaren wrote in this regard, "He filled his place at Pharaoh's court, but his dying words open a window into his soul and betray how little he had felt that he belonged to the order of things in the midst of which he had been content to live. This man, too, surrounded by an ancient civilization and dwelling among granite temples and solid pyramids and firm-based sphinxes, the very emblems of eternity, confessed that here he had no continuing city but sought one to come."[2]

Joseph was a true pilgrim. Abraham had lived in the highlands of Canaan, refusing to descend, as Lot did, to the cities of the plain. Isaac had lived in the grassy land to the south. Jacob had removed to Hebron, refusing to mingle with the people of the land. Joseph was in Egypt—a very different situation. He was in the midst of utter paganism; but it was where God had put him. And because God had put him there and he remained close to God, he was able to live in Egypt and be uncontaminated by it. He was on God's side.

Most of us are like Joseph. We do not have the luxury of a detached existence. We are in the melting pot of life, and we sometimes think that because our lives are busy and our environments secular, we cannot live for God as "spiritual" people do. If we are inclined to think that way, we should remember Joseph. Joseph was surrounded by every secular pressure. He was a citizen of the world. But his conduct throughout his entire life, as well as his dying words, proved that he did not live for the material things life can bring, but for God and his kingdom and glory. If Joseph lived like that in his circumstances, we can live for God in ours. We can endure and triumph as those whose eyes see things that are invisible.

This does not happen automatically. For every Abraham there is a Lot. For every Joseph there are millions who adopt the world's values. What makes the difference? What keeps one godly in a comfortable world? Two things!

First, the invisible must be often, if not always, in our thoughts. If we do not fill our minds with spiritual realities, secular dreams will take true religion's place and our horizons will shrink to what is now but will surely pass away. The sense of God's presence will recede. Prayer will become unreal. If we would triumph, as Joseph did, we must think of God and his kingdom often, and we must associate with and encourage others who think the same.

Second, the invisible must be always in our wishes. That is, we must look for God's kingdom and pray that it might come, as Jesus instructed ("Pray: . . . 'Your kingdom come'" [Matt. 6:9–10]). Joseph did this. All through the long years of his Egyptian service, though his body was in Pharaoh's country, his mind was in Canaan and he looked forward to that day when his bones should be carried out of Egypt and be buried there in anticipation of the final resurrection and fulfillment of God's promise. Should we do less, we to whom the promises have been made even clearer and who have in addition the sure and certain knowledge of our Lord's own resurrection? If that resurrection is uppermost in our wishes, we will live for eternity now and will make a powerful impact on earth.

Joseph was the prime minister. If he had wished, he could have had a magnificent burial in Egypt and perhaps one day have had his body discovered and placed on display for the admiring gazes of less privileged persons. Instead, he preferred burial in Canaan after four hundred years. There his grave was forgotten. He himself was certainly forgotten by the Egyptians. But Joseph is remembered in the Word of God, and he is with God today in glory.

180

A Coffin in Egypt

Genesis 50:26

So Joseph died at the age of a hundred and ten. And after they embalmed him, he was placed in a coffin in Egypt.

Acoffin in Egypt." What a way for a book as important as Genesis to end! It could have ended differently. Genesis could have concluded with a description of the lavish honors paid to Joseph as Egypt's savior. It could have ended with fresh revelation of the future of the Hebrews. Many things might have made for a more upbeat or optimistic ending. But this is *not* the way the book ends. It declares simply, "So Joseph died at the age of a hundred and ten. And after they embalmed him, he was placed in a coffin in Egypt."

This is not how Genesis began. What hopes we had then, as for two whole chapters we read how God brought all that we know into being, declaring after each stage that what he had created was good. In those opening chapters God made light and darkness, sky and earth, land and water, trees, plants, birds, fish, animals. Last of all he made a man and a woman, and all was good.

So chapter 2 concludes brightly: "The man and his wife were both naked, and they felt no shame" (Gen. 2:25).

Ah, yes! But that was before the fall of the human race, as recorded in chapter 3. Adam's sin brought death, and from that point nothing so characterized the history of the human race as the reappearance of this grim enemy. Chapter 5 is filled with it: "Adam lived 930 years, and then he died. . . . Seth lived 912 years, and then he died. . . . Enosh lived 905 years, and then he died. . . . Kenan lived 910 years, and then he died . . ." (vv. 5, 8, 11, 14). The chapter continues that way through the deaths of Mahalalel, Jared, Methuselah, Lamech, and Noah. All died! (Except Enoch, who "was no more, because God took him away" [v. 24].) So it is at the end, as we read about Joseph.

One commentator writes, "All his grandeur and riches and goodness could not save [Joseph] from the hands of the last enemy."[1] In his lifetime Joseph had been used to deliver most of the civilized world from starvation. Yet it could be said of him, as it was said in an improper way of one far greater than Joseph, "'He saved others, . . . but he [could not] save himself'" (Matt. 27:42).

All Must Die

In the previous study I said that the presence of Joseph's coffin in Egypt served to remind the Hebrews who would be living there between this incident and the deliverance under Moses years later of some important things. That was valuable, of course. But now I call your attention to the use of the coffin in reminding, not the Jewish people but ourselves of what we need to have constantly in our minds as we await the return of Jesus Christ. I would argue that this "coffin in Egypt" has the prominent place it has—as the very last phrase in Genesis—precisely for this purpose.

What does this "coffin in Egypt" teach us?

The first and obvious thing is what I allude to when I describe Genesis as recording nothing so consistently as the inevitable death of all people. It tells their stories, it is true. We are told a great deal about some of them; some, particularly those in the earliest chapters, lived a long time. Methuselah lived 969 years. Yet Methuselah, no less than Joseph, died. Abraham died. So did Sarah and Isaac and Rebekah and Jacob. The Bible says, "Man is destined to die . . . and after that to face judgment" (Heb. 9:27).

We are not greater than our fathers. So when we look at Joseph's coffin we must be reminded of our own pending death. We may be great, as Joseph was. No matter. We may have the world at our feet, looking to us for wisdom or lauding us for our achievements. No matter. As Joseph died, so must we. Fame and wealth cannot save us. We may be loved, as Joseph was no doubt loved by his family. We may have a spouse who says—and means—"I cannot live without you." People may depend on us for their jobs, their care, their comfort. No matter. All the love or dependence in the world will not give one minute of life when our turn comes to die. The English dramatist James Shirley wrote wisely:

> The glories of our birth and state
> Are shadows, not substantial things;
> There is no armour against fate;
> Death lays his icy hand on kings.

It was out of this awareness that Moses declared, "The length of our days is seventy years—or eighty, if we have the strength. . . . Teach us to number our days aright, that we may gain a heart of wisdom" (Ps. 90:10, 12).

"Let God Be True!"

The second lesson we learn from this "coffin" is that God speaks truth, even when it is something we do not want to hear or something that runs contrary to our perceptions.

A moment ago I wrote that the fall of man, recorded in Genesis 3, altered forever the state of purity and innocence portrayed in the first two chapters of the book. How did that happen? What was the nature of man's fall? It is described as the devil tempting Eve in the matter of the restriction from eating of the tree of the knowledge of good and evil. God had said, "You are free to eat from any tree in the garden; but you must not eat from the tree of the knowledge of good and evil, for when you eat of it you will surely die" (Gen. 2:16–17).

The devil asked the question, "Did God really say, 'You must not eat from any tree in the garden'?" (Gen. 3:1). This was a slur on God's goodness and was probably asked in an incredulous tone of voice. Could God really have said *that?* It was to put doubts in Eve's mind.

But Eve answered correctly. She said that God was allowing them to eat from all the trees of the garden *except* that one. Nevertheless, he had said, "You must not eat fruit from the tree that is in the middle of the garden, and you must not touch it, or you will die" (v. 3).

At this point the devil blatantly contradicted God's statement and confronted the woman with a crisis: "You will not surely die. . . . For God knows that when you eat of it your eyes will be opened, and you will be like God, knowing good and evil" (vv. 4–5). What was the woman to do now? To this point the only statements she had ever heard about the true nature of things were from God. She had never doubted them; she never had cause to. Now suddenly there was this very impressive serpent telling her that God was not truthful and was, in fact, deliberately withholding the experience of eating from that tree in order to keep her and her husband ignorant. Moreover, God had said, "You will surely die," and the serpent was saying, "You will *not* surely die."

Who could be trusted? Was Eve to listen to God? Was God speaking truth and the devil lying? Or was the devil speaking the truth and God lying? It was the ultimate question that confronts the human race.

We know what happened. Eve decided to trust neither God nor the devil implicitly, but rather to check things out for herself. She investigated the tree and saw that it was "good for food" (a pragmatic test), "pleasing to the eye" (an aesthetic test), and "desirable for gaining wisdom" (an intellectual test). When she was satisfied on each of these points, she took and ate the fruit, later giving some to her husband, who also ate.

Eve thought she could disregard God's word on the basis of her own experience. She was wrong! The fruit of the tree met her tests, yet her tests were not sufficiently comprehensive. They could not be, because she was finite and could not understand all that the Creator knew intuitively. She thought she could eat of the tree and live. She did not live! Eve died in spirit, soul, and body, and today her dust lies scattered in an unknown grave. The very thing that God said would happen did happen. God was true, and all contrary words were from liars.

Let us learn that lesson as we look at Joseph's coffin. You may find sin attractive—pleasing to the eyes, good, desirable. But "the wages of sin is death" (Rom. 6:23)—God says so—and sin will always lead to death. Learn that God always speaks truth and that his Word alone can always be trusted, in this and in all other areas.

Resting on the Promises

The third lesson that we can learn from this "coffin in Egypt" comes from the fact that it contained the remains of a believing man. Eve had doubted God, and her disobedience brought death on the race—including the death of Joseph. But Eve did not die in unbelief. She came to believe God again, and Joseph also believed God and testified to that belief as he died.

The Israelites must often have thought of Joseph's faith as they passed that coffin for those hundreds of years they waited in Egypt for God's promised deliverance. Joseph had said many things in his long life; but although his lips were now sealed in death, his descendants must often have remembered that as he lay dying he spoke of the promises God had made through Abraham so many centuries before. God told Abraham, "Know for certain that your descendants will be strangers in a country not their own, and they will be enslaved and mistreated four hundred years. But I will punish the nation they serve as slaves, and afterward they will come out with great possessions" (Gen. 15:13–14).

As he was dying, Joseph remembered this and said, "I am about to die. But God will surely come to your aid and take you up out of this land to the land he promised on oath to Abraham, Isaac and Jacob. . . . God will surely come to your aid, and then you must carry my bones up from this place" (Gen. 50:24–25).

I like the repetition of "surely": "God will *surely*, . . . *surely* come to your aid." Where did Joseph learn that? We do not know for sure, but let me suggest an idea. The Hebrew text does not have any one word for "surely," but it makes that emphasis by repetition of the chief verb—in typical Hebrew idiom. In Hebrew the text literally says, "to aid God will aid you." It means "God will surely aid you," which is what the translators say to get the idea across. This is important, because it is precisely the way God spoke to Abraham when the promise was first given. God said, "Know for certain," which in Hebrew is literally "to know you know."

I think Joseph remembered those words exactly and was patterning his own faith on them. God repeated his word for emphasis, so Joseph repeated his. He was being no more certain than God, but neither was he less certain. God said it. Joseph believed it. Joseph would die in that confidence.

God did do it, although it took long centuries. How long did that coffin, containing Joseph's body, remain in Egypt before the deliverance under Moses? There are differences of opinion concerning how the years of Egyptian bondage should be reckoned.[2] But the simplest way is to take the four hundred years of mistreatment literally and assume that the coffin remained visible as evidence of Joseph's deep faith for four centuries.

Four centuries!

"I am about to die. But God will surely come to your aid and take you up out of this land to the land he promised on oath to Abraham, Isaac and Jacob."

Four centuries!

How can you keep up a faith like that for four centuries? For five or ten years, maybe. Perhaps for fifty years. But not four centuries! Yet the promises were fulfilled. When the time rolled around for the deliverance of the people, the bush burned, God spoke, Moses went, and Pharaoh eventually responded to the demand to "let my people go." God is never slack concerning his promises. One writer has said, "God lifts his feet slowly, but he plants them firmly as he walks through the world."

So let us have patience, trust God, and refuse to give up. In his study of Joseph, Leslie Flynn calls attention to a sermon that George Mueller, founder of the faith orphanages in England, preached in his seventy-fifth year. Mueller said that thirty thousand times in his fifty-four years as a Christian he had received an answer to prayer on the same day the prayer was made. Yet not all his prayers were answered quickly. He waited weeks for some, for others months. He told of one prayer that he had brought to God about twenty thousand times over a period of eleven and a half years. One important prayer was for five individuals who were not Christians, but whom he had begun to pray for when he was about forty years old. He had seen the conversion of one after about a year and a half. Another came to Christ after five years, a third about six years after that. When he gave this sermon, the last were still not Christians, but Mueller said he was still praying. "I hope in God, I pray on, and look for the answer," he said. "Therefore, beloved brethren and sisters, go on waiting upon God, go on praying."

The end of the story is that one of these friends finally became a Christian just before Mueller's death. The last one became a Christian six years after Mueller died.[3]

Let us not lose faith in the promises of God. "The revelation awaits an appointed time; it speaks of the end and will not prove false. Though it linger, wait for it; it will certainly come and will not delay" (Hab. 2:3). God will answer our prayers and fulfill his promises to us no less surely than he fulfilled his promises to the ancient patriarchs.

A Cloud of Witnesses

I have one last point. I have spoken of the faith of Joseph and of the testimony he left behind to encourage his descendants. We must see that his testimony (and that of other believing men and women of that time) was not wasted but rather that God honored their father and brought at least a remnant to know him even during the ensuing dark ages of the nation's history. We do not know who these people were. We do not know the names of those who passed on the torch of the knowledge of the true God from hand to hand for those centuries. But we know they did. For on the very next page of the Bible we begin to read of a man and woman of the tribe of Levi, Amram and Jochebed (cf. Exod. 6:20), who were believers and who instilled knowledge of their fathers' God into Moses, whom God called to lead the people to Canaan.

I can state this truth another way. The only serious mention of Joseph in the New Testament is in Hebrews 11:22. It reads, "By faith Joseph, when his end was near, spoke about the exodus of the Israelites from Egypt and gave instructions about his bones." It is not much in words. But it is a record of faith, and it puts Joseph in the very center of that great cloud of witnesses spoken of in that chapter, a chain stretching backward to Adam through such saints as Jacob, Isaac, Abraham, Noah, Enoch, and Abel, and forward to Moses, Rahab, Gideon, Barak, Samson, Jephthah, Samuel, David, and others—even to those of our time, who are admonished:

> Therefore, since we are surrounded by such a great cloud of witnesses, let us throw off everything that hinders and the sin that so easily entangles, and let us run with perseverance the race marked out for us. Let us fix our eyes on Jesus, the author and perfecter of our faith, who for the joy set before him endured the cross, scorning its shame, and sat down at the right hand of the throne of God.

> Hebrews 12:1–2

Sometime ago I read of an Egyptian archaeologist who touched off a furor by claiming that a mummy in the Cairo museum, discovered in the Valley of the Kings in 1905, was the mummy of Joseph. His "discovery" was nonsense! Joseph's remains are not in Egypt, because when the time came for the people to leave the land of their oppression, those who were in this great chain of faith remembered Joseph and took his remains to Canaan as he desired.

All this means that "a coffin in Egypt" is not just the end of this great book of beginnings. More importantly, it is part of the beginning of the end. For it is the testimony of one, who like many others, looked for the coming of him who was to destroy death, crushing Satan's head. Egypt had the most magnificent coffins the world has ever seen, coffins of gold, lapis lazuli, and other rare stones. But they were still only coffins, monuments to death.

We do not raise monuments to death, because we have something better. We have a resurrection. We look to him who conquered death, and we anticipate the victory.

> Listen, I tell you a mystery: We will not all sleep, but we will all be changed—in a flash, in the twinkling of an eye, at the last trumpet. For the trumpet will sound, the dead will be raised imperishable, and we will be changed. For the perishable must clothe itself with the imperishable, and the mortal with immortality. When the perishable has been clothed with the imperishable, and the mortal with immortality, then the saying that is written will come true: "Death has been swallowed up in victory."
>
> > "Where, O death is your victory?
> > Where, O death, is your sting?"
>
> The sting of death is sin, and the power of sin is the law. But thanks be to God! He gives us the victory through our Lord Jesus Christ.
>
> 1 Corinthians 15:51–57

Notes

Chapter 121: A Man for All Seasons

1. Henry M. Morris, *The Genesis Record: A Scientific and Devotional Commentary on the Book of Beginnings* (Grand Rapids: Baker, 1976), 535.

2. C. F. Keil and F. Delitzsch, *Biblical Commentary on the Old Testament*, vol. 1, *The Pentateuch* (Grand Rapids: Eerdmans, n.d.), 334.

3. John Peter Lange, *Commentary on the Holy Scriptures: Genesis* (Grand Rapids: Zondervan, n.d.), 581.

4. Blaise Pascal, *Pensées*, trans. with introduction by A. J. Krailsheimer (Baltimore: Penguin, 1966), 223.

5. M. R. DeHaan, *Portraits of Christ in Genesis* (Grand Rapids: Zondervan, 1966), 162–85.

6. Arthur W. Pink, *Gleanings in Genesis* (Chicago: Moody, 1922), 340–408.

7. Leslie B. Flynn, *Joseph: God's Man in Egypt* (Wheaton: Victor, 1979), 5–6.

Chapter 122: Joseph's Early Years

1. The other expressions are (1) "This is the account of the heavens and the earth" (Gen. 2:4); (2) "This is the written account of Adam's line" (5:1); (3) "This is the account of Noah" (6:9); (4) "This is the account of Shem, Ham and Japheth" (10:1); (5) "This is the account of Shem" (11:10); (6) "This is the account of Terah" (11:27); (7) "This is the account of Abraham's son Ishmael" (25:12); (8) "This is the account of Abraham's son Isaac" (25:19); (9) "This is the account of Esau" (36:1); (10) "This is the account of Esau the father of the Edomites in the hill country of Seir" (36:9); and (11) "This is the account of Jacob" (37:2). For a discussion of the importance of this phrase, see *Genesis*, 1:91–92.

2. F. B. Meyer, *Joseph: Beloved—Hated—Exalted* (Fort Washington, Pa.: Christian Literature Crusade, 1982), 10–11.

3. "Joseph's brothers were justified in their resentment over their father's favoritism," writes Flynn, *Joseph: God's Man in Egypt*, 25.

4. *Luther's Works*, vol. 6, *Lectures on Genesis, Chapters 31–37*, ed. Jaroslav Pelikan and Hilton C. Oswald (St. Louis: Concordia, 1970), 320–21.

5. Meyer, *Joseph: Beloved—Hated—Exalted*, 15.

Chapter 123: Joseph and His Brothers

1. George Lawson, *Lectures on the History of Joseph* (1807; reprint, London: Banner of Truth, 1972), 13.

2. Donald Grey Barnhouse, *Genesis: A Devotional Exposition*, vol. 2 (Grand Rapids: Zondervan, 1971), 158.

3. For a fuller discussion of the problems at Rome, see James Montgomery Boice, "Christian Troublemakers" (Phil. 1:15–18), in *Philippians: An Expositional Commentary* (Grand Rapids: Zondervan, 1971), 65–71.

Chapter 124: Who Grieves for Joseph?

1. Meyer, *Joseph: Beloved—Hated—Exalted*, 21–22.

2. Barnhouse, *Genesis: A Devotional Exposition*, vol. 2, 161.

3. John Calvin, *Commentaries on the First Book of Moses Called Genesis*, vol. 2, trans. John King (Grand Rapids: Eerdmans, 1948), 267.

Chapter 125: God's Man in Egypt

1. *Encyclopedia Britannica*, 1967, s.v., "Egypt."

2. James H. Breasted, "Dedication Address," 5 December 1931. Quoted in Henri Frankfort et al., *The Intellectual Adventure of Ancient Man* (Chicago: University of Chicago Press, 1946), 119.

3. Robert Brow, *Religion: Origins and Ideas* (Chicago: InterVarsity Press, 1966), 11, 13.

4. For a more detailed discussion of Egyptian polytheism and the relation of the ten plagues of Exodus to the country's gods, see James Montgomery Boice, *Ordinary Men Called by God: Abraham, Moses and David* (Wheaton: Victor, 1982), 65–76. Originally published in 1974 as *How God Can Use Nobodies*.

5. Meyer, *Joseph: Beloved—Hated—Exalted*, 27.

Chapter 126: Man's Man in Canaan

1. H. C. Leupold, *Exposition of Genesis*, vol. 2, chaps. 20–50 (Grand Rapids: Baker, 1942, rev. 1979), 990.

2. Luther had a problem with this dating, because Genesis 46:12 lists two sons of Perez, one of Tamar's sons, as having gone down to Egypt with the migration of Jacob's family. This would mean that time for an additional generation must be included, the sons of Tamar needing to grow up, marry, and then have children of their own. Some of the church fathers (Augustine, for example) solved this difficulty by starting the events of Genesis 38 earlier, that is, when Joseph was still at home. Luther concluded that Judah was only

twelve years old when he married, that he had three sons in two years, that Er was likewise given in marriage when he was twelve, and so on (*Luther's Works*, vol. 7, 8–9). It is probably easiest to assume that the sons of Perez did not actually go down to Egypt at the time of Jacob's migration, but were born there, or that Perez' family joined the others later.

3. Robert S. Candlish, *Studies in Genesis* (1868; reprint, Grand Rapids: Kregel, 1979), 602.

4. *Luther's Works*, vol. 7, 11.

Chapter 127: The Women in Jesus' Family Tree

1. *Luther's Works*, vol. 7, 11. See the ending of the previous chapter of this volume.

2. Ibid., 44.

3. Donald Grey Barnhouse, *God's Glory*, The Book of Romans, vol. 10 (Grand Rapids: Eerdmans, 1964), 181.

4. Charles Haddon Spurgeon, "Rahab," in *Metropolitan Tabernacle Pulpit*, vol. 18 (Pasadena, Tex.: Pilgrim Publications, 1971), 398–99.

Chapter 128: Favored by God and Man

1. *Luther's Works*, vol. 7, 64.

2. Ibid., 66–67.

Chapter 129: When Temptation Comes

1. Charles Durham, *Temptation: Help for Struggling Christians* (Downers Grove, Ill.: InterVarsity Press, 1982), 15–16.

2. The debate was published as an occasional paper entitled "Christianity and Hedonism: A Clash of Philosophies," by the *Christian Chronicle*, Box 4055, Austin, TX 78751.

3. Flynn, *Joseph: God's Man in Egypt*, 49–50.

4. Meyer, *Joseph: Beloved—Hated—Exalted*, 31.

Chapter 130: Sin against Man, Sin against God

1. James Fixx, *The Complete Book of Running* (New York: Random House, 1977), 92.

2. Randy Frame, "Sex without Love," *Christianity Today* (22 April 1983): 24–28.

3. Luis Palau, *The Schemer and the Dreamer* (Portland: Multnomah, 1976), 94–95.

4. Flynn, *Joseph: God's Man in Egypt*, 54.

Chapter 131: What If I Do Sin?

1. Charles Haddon Spurgeon, "Repentance after Conversion," in *Metropolitan Tabernacle Pulpit*, vol. 41 (1895; Pasadena, Tex.: Pilgrim Publications, 1975), 304.

Chapter 132: It's a Bad, Bad World

1. Meyer, *Joseph: Beloved—Hated—Exalted*, 45.
2. Portions of this chapter have been recast from material appearing previously in James Montgomery Boice, *The Sermon on the Mount* (Grand Rapids: Zondervan, 1972), 56–69.

Chapter 133: Prospering in Prison

1. See "A Man for All Seasons" (Gen. 37:1–2), chap. 121 in this volume.
2. See "Joseph and His Brothers" (Gen. 37:5–24), chap. 123 in this volume.
3. The material on Paul has been borrowed with changes from Boice, *Philippians*, 62–64.

Chapter 134: "I Had a Dream"

1. Barnhouse, *Genesis: A Devotional Exposition*, vol. 2, 173.
2. Ibid., 175.

Chapter 135: Forgotten!

1. The sentence occurs in the reading of Psalm 105 for morning prayer, day 21: "Whose feet they hurt in the stocks: the iron entered into his soul."
2. Meyer, *Joseph: Beloved—Hated—Exalted*, 56.
3. Ibid., 57.
4. Ibid.

Chapter 137: Joseph, the Prime Minister

1. Meyer, *Joseph: Beloved—Hated—Exalted*, 62.
2. Pink, *Gleanings in Genesis*, 341–408. Cf. "A Man for All Seasons" (Genesis 37:1–2), chap.121 in this volume.
3. Meyer, *Joseph: Beloved—Hated—Exalted*, 63–64.
4. John Skinner, *A Critical and Exegetical Commentary on Genesis,* in *The International Critical Commentary* (Edinburgh: T. & T. Clark, 1956), 470; Gerhard Von Rad, *Genesis: A Commentary,* trans. John H. Marks (Philadelphia: Westminster, 1961), 373.

Chapter 139: God and the Conscience Part 1: The Pinch of Want

1. Flynn, *Joseph: God's Man in Egypt,* 93.
2. Cited in *Roget's International Thesaurus,* new ed. (New York: Thomas Y. Crowell, 1953), 630.

Chapter 140: God and the Conscience Part 2: The Pain of Harsh Treatment

1. Dale Carnegie, *How to Win Friends and Influence People* (1936; New York: Pocket Books, 1963), 27–28.
2. *Eternity* (November 1982): 59, 48.
3. *Eternity* (May 1983): 57.

4. Candlish, *Studies in Genesis*, 652.

Chapter 141: God and the Conscience Part 3: The Press of Solitude

1. A. W. Tozer, *The Pursuit of God* (Harrisburg, Pa.: Christian Publications, 1948), 28.
2. Ibid., 69–70.
3. Charles W. Colson, *Loving God* (Grand Rapids: Zondervan, 1983), 99–102.
4. Meyer, *Joseph: Beloved—Hated—Exalted*, 75.

Chapter 143: No One Loves Me, This I Know

1. Epictetus, *Discourses*, Bk. I, xxix, 48–49. The Loeb Classical Library, trans. W. A. Oldfather (Cambridge: Harvard University Press, 1961), 1:199.

Chapter 144: God and the Conscience Part 5: The Pattern of Necessity

1. Candlish, *Studies in Genesis*, 669.
2. Ibid., 672–74.

Chapter 145: God and the Conscience Part 6: The Power of True Affection

1. Donald Grey Barnhouse, *God's Wrath, The Book of Romans*, vol. 2 (Grand Rapids: Eerdmans, 1953), 25.
2. Ibid., 27.

Chapter 146: God and the Conscience Part 7: The Purge of Self-Confidence

1. Colson, *Loving God*, 24.
2. Joseph's cup is described as the one used "for divination" (v. 5), which makes one wonder whether Joseph actually practiced what was forbidden to Jews at later periods (cf. Deut. 18:9–13). We know from other sources that the ancients actually did use sacred cups for divination. Homer speaks of Nestor's cup. Spenser tells how Britomart found the mythical Merlin's cup and used it to uncover a closely guarded secret. Did Joseph actually use his cup in this fashion? It is possible he did, since the Scriptures had not yet been given; the God who spoke to Joseph in dreams was certainly capable of revealing his will to him through such mechanical devices. On the other hand, Joseph does not say that he used the cup himself. The words are spoken only by his steward. Not knowing Joseph's God, the steward may have assumed wrongly that Joseph gained his insights in a manner similar to that in which the kings and priests of the time claimed to gain theirs.
3. Meyer, *Joseph: Beloved—Hated—Exalted*, 86.
4. Ibid., 91–92.
5. Colson, *Loving God*, 25.

Chapter 147: Judah's Plea for Benjamin

1. Meyer, *Joseph: Beloved—Hated—Exalted*, 94.

2. Leupold, *Exposition of Genesis,* vol. 2, 1086.

3. Barnhouse, *Genesis: A Devotional Exposition,* vol. 2, 200.

4. I have borrowed portions of the stories of Moses and Paul from a longer treatment in Boice, *Ordinary Men Called by God: Abraham, Moses and David,* 99–108. Original title: *How God Can Use Nobodies.*

Chapter 148: "I Am Joseph"

1. Charles Haddon Spurgeon, "Joseph and His Brethren," in *Metropolitan Tabernacle Pulpit,* vol. 8 (Pasadena, Tex.: Pilgrim Publications, 1969, 1973), 267.

Chapter 149: "God . . . God . . . God . . . God"

1. Harold S. Kushner, *When Bad Things Happen to Good People* (New York: Avon, 1981), 148.

2. Barnhouse, *Genesis: A Devotional Exposition,* vol. 2, 203.

Chapter 151: A Day to Remember

1. Morris, *The Genesis Record,* 623.

2. *Luther's Works,* vol. 8, *Lectures on Genesis, Chapters 45–50,* ed. Jaroslav Pelikan and Walter A. Hansen (St. Louis: Concordia, 1966), 51.

3. Ibid., 54.

Chapter 152: Favor in Pharaoh's Eyes

1. The story of Carter's discovery is told in many places. I have taken it from *Everyday Life in Bible Times* (Washington: National Geographic Society, 1967), 116, 121.

2. Charles Haddon Spurgeon, *Spurgeon's Illustrative Anecdotes,* ed. David Otis Fuller (Grand Rapids: Zondervan 1945), 48–49.

Chapter 153: No Quarreling

1. Frank E. Gaebelein, *The Practical Epistle of James* (Great Neck, N.Y.: Channel Press, 1955), 88–89.

Chapter 154: What Can I Believe?

1. C. S. Lewis, *Mere Christianity* (New York: Macmillan, 1958), 107–8.

2. Tryon Edwards, comp., *The New Dictionary of Thoughts,* rev. C. N. Catrevas, Jonathan Edwards, and Ralph Emerson Browns (New York: Standard Book Co., 1960), 43.

3. Charles Haddon Spurgeon, "Jacob and Doubting Souls—A Parallel," in *Metropolitan Tabernacle Pulpit,* vol. 42 (Pasadena, Tex.: Pilgrim Publications, 1976), 293.

4. J. B. Phillips, *Ring of Truth: A Translator's Testimony* (New York: Macmillan, 1967), 75.

5. Spurgeon, "Jacob and Doubting Souls—A Parallel," 294.

6. Ibid.

Chapter 155: "Jacob! Jacob!"

1. Charles Haddon Spurgeon, "The Unchanging God Cheering Jacob in His Change of Dwelling Place," *in Metropolitan Tabernacle Pulpit,* vol. 35 (London: Banner of Truth, 1970), 641.

Chapter 156: Seventy in All

1. Paul Tournier, *A Doctor's Casebook in the Light of the Bible,* trans. Edwin Hudson (New York: Harper, 1960), 123–24.

2. Candlish, *Studies in Genesis,* 707.

3. There is an excellent discussion of this problem in Gleason L. Archer, *Encyclopedia of Bible Difficulties* (Grand Rapids: Zondervan, 1982), 378–79.

4. Candlish, *Studies in Genesis,* 710–11.

Chapter 157: Reunion

1. The story is told in George Lawson, *Lectures on the History of Joseph* (1807; reprint, London: Banner of Truth, 1972), 336–37.

2. Flynn, *Joseph: God's Man in Egypt,* 125–26.

Chapter 158: Jacob Blessing Pharaoh

1. Candlish, *Studies in Genesis,* 721.

2. Aleksandr I. Solzhenitsyn, *The Gulag Archipelago, 1918–1956: An Experiment in Literary Investigation,* I–II (New York: Harper & Row, 1973), 130.

Chapter 159: Joseph and the Famine

1. *The Interpreter's Bible,* ed. George Arthur Buttrick, et al. (New York and Nashville: Abingdon, 1952), vol. 1, 809.

2. John T. Brink, *Joseph of Egypt and His Managed National Economy* (Topeka, Kans.: Mid-Continent Publishing, 1954), 20.

3. Ibid., 30.

4. George Gilder, *Wealth and Poverty* (New York: Basic Books, 1981), 187.

5. Jacques Ellul, *The Political Illusion,* trans. Konrad Kellen (New York: Vintage, 1972), 222.

6. Meyer, *Joseph: Beloved—Hated—Exalted,* 101, 103–5.

Chapter 160: Prospering in Egypt

1. Abraham was 75 when he left Haran for Canaan and was 100 years old when Isaac was born. Isaac lived 60 years before he had Esau and Jacob, and Jacob was 130 years old when the family emigrated to Egypt. The total number of years in Canaan is 25 plus 60 plus 130, or 215.

2. Jonathan Chao, "The Place of Suffering in the Christian Life," in *Tenth: An Evangelical Quarterly* 14, no. 2 (April 1984): 12.

3. Ibid., 18.

Chapter 161: Jacob's Last Days

1. Barnhouse, *Genesis: A Devotional Exposition*, 218–19.
2. Lawson, *Lectures on the History of Joseph*, 389.
3. Tom Bethell, "Darwin's Mistake," *Harper's Magazine* (February 1976): 72.
4. There is a technical problem in this verse due to the fact that the Hebrew consonants in the word translated "staff" (NIV) can be pointed in two ways. The consonants are *m-t-h*, which can be read as *matteh* ("staff") or *mittah* ("bed"). The Masoretic Hebrew text, which adds the vowel points and which was developed in the eighth century A.D., opts for the second possibility. So the Hebrew texts we have actually say, "Israel bowed down at the head of (or upon the head of) his bed" (cf. NIV footnote). By contrast, the New Testament quotation of the text in Hebrews 11:21, being based on the Septuagint (or Greek) text of the third century B.C., says "staff." The difference is slight, of course, and the interpretation of Jacob's act does not depend upon the translation. Still, the idea of Jacob leaning on his staff is most probable and relies on the earliest reading. The Masoretic text should therefore probably be changed accordingly (cf. Archer, *Encyclopedia of Bible Difficulties*, 421).

Chapter 162: The Living Church

1. Barnhouse, *Genesis: A Devotional Exposition*, vol. 2, 221.
2. Ibid., 222.
3. Lawson, *Lectures on the History of Joseph*, 400.

Chapter 163: A Faithful Blessing

1. Candlish, *Studies in Genesis*, 741.
2. Meyer, *Joseph: Beloved—Hated—Exalted*, 126.

Chapter 164: The Lord Is My Shepherd

1. Philip Keller, *A Shepherd Looks at Psalm 23* (Grand Rapids: Zondervan, 1970), 20–21.
2. Portions of this study have been adapted from "The Chief Shepherd" in James Montgomery Boice, *The Gospel of John: An Expositional Commentary*, vol. 3, *John 9:1–12:50* (Grand Rapids: Zondervan, 1977), 106–12.

Chapter 165: God with Us

1. Charles Haddon Spurgeon, "Four Choice Sentences," in *Metropolitan Tabernacle Pulpit*, vol. 27 (1882; reprint, London: Banner of Truth, 1971), 647.
2. Ibid., 650–51.
3. Ibid., 652.

Chapter 166: Reuben: The First Shall Be Last

1. Charles Haddon Spurgeon, "Sermons from Saintly Death-Beds," in *Metropolitan Tabernacle Pulpit*, vol. 13 (Pasadena, Tex.: Pilgrim Publications, 1970), 670.

2. Ibid., 671.

3. Ibid., 672.

4. Lawson, *Lectures on the History of Joseph,* 487.

5. See James B. Pritchard, ed., *Ancient Near Eastern Texts Related to the Old Testament,* 2d ed. (Princeton: Princeton University Press, 1955), 320.

Chapter 167: Simeon and Levi: Brothers in Wickedness

1. Lawson, *Lectures on the History of Joseph,* 492.

Chapter 168: Judah: Pride of Lions

1. *The Greater Men and Women of the Bible,* ed. James Hastings (Edinburgh: T. & T. Clark, 1914), 113.

2. Charles Haddon Spurgeon, "Shiloh," in *Metropolitan Tabernacle Pulpit,* vol. 20 (Pasadena, Tex.: Pilgrim Publications, 1971), 85.

Chapter 169: Shiloh

1. Candlish, *Studies in Genesis,* 750.

2. Lawson, *Lectures on the History of Joseph,* 506.

3. Spurgeon, "Shiloh," 90.

4. Cf. Donald Grey Barnhouse, *Man's Ruin, The Book of Romans,* vol. 1 (Grand Rapids: Eerdmans, 1952), 44–48.

Chapter 170: Zebulun and Issachar: At Ease in Zion

1. H. C. Leupold, *Exposition of Genesis,* vol. 1, *Chapters 20–50* (Grand Rapids: Baker, 1942), 1185.

2. Barnhouse, *Genesis: A Devotional Exposition,* vol. 2, 235–36.

3. Lawson, *Lectures on the History of Joseph,* 516.

Chapter 171: Dan, Gad, Asher, Naphtali

1. Lawson, *Lectures on the History of Joseph,* 520.

2. Pink, *Gleanings in Genesis,* 329–31.

Chapter 172: Joseph: A Fruitful Vine

1. Charles Haddon Spurgeon, "A Boundless Benediction," in *Metropolitan Tabernacle Pulpit,* vol. 43 (Pasadena, Tex.: Pilgrim Publications, 1976), 397.

2. Alexander Maclaren, *Expositions of Holy Scripture,* vol. 1 (Grand Rapids: Eerdmans, 1959), pt. 1, 298–99.

3. Ibid., 303.

4. Barnhouse, *Genesis: A Devotional Exposition,* vol. 2, 243.

Chapter 173: Benjamin: Call of the Wild

1. Spurgeon, "Sermons from Saintly Death-Beds," 661.

2. Lawson, *Lectures on the History of Joseph,* 550–51.

Chapter 174: The Death of Jacob

1. Spurgeon, "Sermons from Saintly Death-Beds," 661.
2. Lawson, *Lectures on the History of Joseph*, 553–54.
3. D. Martyn Lloyd-Jones, *God's Ultimate Purpose: An Exposition of Ephesians 1:1 to 23* (Grand Rapids: Baker, 1979), 381–82.
4. Ibid., 383.
5. Lawson, *Lectures on the History of Joseph*, 556.

Chapter 175: A Time to Weep

1. Richard W. Doss, *The Last Enemy: A Christian Understanding of Death* (New York: Harper & Row, 1974), 8–9. This book was written under a grant from the Forest Lawn Foundation, a large West Coast funeral institution, which was interested in the Christian theology of death and funerals.
2. Ibid., 7.
3. Ibid., 8.
4. Plato, "Phaedo," in *The Works of Plato*, trans. B. Jowett (New York: Tudor Publishing, n.d.), 3: 270.

Chapter 176: A Time to Cease from Weeping

1. Candlish, *Studies in Genesis*, 793.
2. Elisabeth Kübler-Ross, *On Death and Dying* (New York: Macmillan, 1969), 34ff.
3. Paul Tournier, *Guilt and Grace*, trans. Arthur W. Heathcote (New York: Harper & Row, 1962).
4. C. S. Lewis, *A Grief Observed* (New York: Bantam, 1980), 1.
5. Charles M. Sell, *Grief's Healing Process* (Portland: Multnomah, 1984), 21–22.
6. Elisabeth Elliot, *Facing the Death of Someone You Love* (Westchester, Ill.: Good News, 1980), 8. First published as an article in *Christianity Today*, 1973.
7. Ibid., 10.
8. Ibid., 12–14.

Chapter 177: "God Meant It for Good"

1. Flynn, *Joseph: God's Man in Egypt*, 134.
2. Elisabeth Elliot, "Denial, Discipline and Devotion," in *Tenth: An Evangelical Quarterly* (July 1977).
3. Ibid.

Chapter 178: Blessings upon Children's Children

1. Joseph was thirty years old when he entered the service of the Pharaoh (Gen. 41:46). He was thirty-nine years old when he revealed himself to his brothers and arranged for them to bring his father to Egypt—after the seven years of good crops and two years of famine (Gen. 45:6). His father lived in Egypt for seventeen years after that (Gen. 47:28), making Joseph fifty-six when his father died.

2. Donald Grey Barnhouse, "He First Found His Brother," in *First Things First* (Philadelphia: Bible Study Hour, 1961), 15–16.

Chapter 179: The Faith of Joseph

1. Meyer, *Joseph: Beloved—Hated—Exalted,* 156–57.
2. Maclaren, *Expositions of Holy Scripture,* vol. 1, pt. 1, 319.

Chapter 180: A Coffin in Egypt

1. Lawson, *Lectures on the History of Joseph,* 475.
2. The revelation of God to Abraham recorded in Genesis 15 says that the people would be enslaved and mistreated for 400 years. But that is a round number and, in any case, Exodus 12:40 specifies that "the length of time the Israelite people lived in Egypt was [exactly] 430 years." Some have suggested that the people were in Egypt for the longer period but were afflicted 30 years less than that, the persecution therefore beginning about 13 years after Jacob died.

But it is not as simple as that. Galatians 3:17 also mentions the 430-year period, but it seems to indicate that the period involved was from the establishing of the covenant with Abraham to the giving of the law on Mount Sinai. If that is followed, then Genesis 15:13 and Exodus 12:40 should be understood in a more inclusive sense, which can legitimately be done. Genesis 15:13 could be understood as saying, "Your descendants will be strangers in a country not their own, and they will be enslaved and mistreated [by many people, not just the Egyptians] four hundred years." Similarly, Exodus 12:40 could read, "Now the sojournings of the Israelite people, who lived in Egypt, were [altogether, that is, from the time of the giving of the covenant until their settling in Canaan] 430 years." In this case, the length of time the people would actually have been in Egypt would have been approximately 215 years, subtracting the years of the patriarchs from the larger figure. The Septuagint version of Exodus 12:40 seems to support this view, for it substitutes the words "in the land of Egypt and the land of Canaan" for the Hebrew words "in Egypt."

It is hard to decide between these two positions. The shorter period makes better sense of the four generations that Genesis 15:16 says was to be the time the people were in Egypt. Each generation would be about 50 years. But since the people increased from seventy-five to approximately two million during the Egyptian years, the longer period seems preferable.

3. Flynn, *Joseph: God's Man in Egypt,* 146–47.

Subject Index

Aaron, 898, 1187
Abel, 859, 1144, 1276
Abimelech, 1218
Abraham, 858, 859, 865, 898, 901, 902, 904, 1009, 1016, 1069, 1093, 1102, 1103, 1107, 1109, 1123, 1140, 1159, 1174, 1197, 1200, 1210, 1211, 1221, 1235, 1242, 1249, 1257, 1258, 1261, 1266, 1269, 1270, 1276, 1135–37, 1231–33; burial of, 867; called by God, 1099; descendants of, 894; excused his sin, 929; faith of, 1136; hope of, 1144; meaning of his name, 1136
Absalom, 883
Abu Simbel, 1071
Acceptance, 1245
Acton, Lord, 1127
Adam, 859, 864, 872, 1135, 1136, 1144, 1176, 1232, 1261, 1272, 1276; and Eve, 1015, 1032, 1065, 1178, 1196, 1197, 1257; blamed Eve for his sin, 928, 929; fall of, 1273; meaning of his name, 976
Adam and Eve Family Tree, 1179
Adaptation, 1245
Adoption of Joseph's sons by Jacob, 1156
Adullam, 894
Advantages, loss of spiritual, 1178–80
Adversity, 857
Affection, power of true, 1028–34
Akhenaton, 1122
Alcibiades, 1044
Alger, Horatio, 906, 907
American dream, 907
Ammon, 1213
Amnon, 1183
Amram and Jochebed, 1186
Ananias and Sapphira, 1131
Andrew, called Peter, 1069, 1260
Angel of the Covenant, 1159
Anger, 1245
Animism, 888, 889
Anna, a prophetess, 1214

Asenath, Joseph's wife, 976, 1114, 1152
Asher, 1038, 1155, 1217, 1225; meaning of the name, 1213
Augustine, 1263; the second, 1260
Aurelius, Marcus, 1143

Babylon, 1137
Baker, Pharaoh's chief, 890, 942, 964, 965, 1058, 1060, 1253
Banowsky, William S., 915
Barak, 1205, 1214, 1276
Barnhouse, Donald Grey, 861, 862, 874, 902, 952, 970, 972, 1032, 1033, 1043, 1062, 1174, 1260
Bathsheba, 899–905, 1144
Bayly, Joseph, 993
Beersheba, 1099, 1112, 1219
Benjamin, 858, 987, 1011, 1012, 1014, 1023–25, 1031, 1036, 1039, 1043–45, 1051, 1053, 1056, 1072–74, 1082, 1087, 1107, 1114–16, 1155, 1192; bad side of, 1225, 1226; birth of, 867, 1151; cup found in his sack, 1038; Jacob's dying prophecy about, 1223–29; prominent descendants of, 1225; small yet prominent, 1224, 1225; tribe of, 1187
Benjamite wars, 1226
Bethel, 866, 1009, 1101, 1136, 1137, 1149, 1156, 1172
Bethell, Thomas, 1142
Bilhah, 867, 875, 882, 994, 1001, 1203, 1210
Birth, advantages of, 1177, 1178
Bitterness, birth of, 867–69; fruit of, 875; root of, 873, 874; shoot of, 874, 875
Blessings, upon children's children, 1257–63; faithful, 1154–60; families a channel for, 1260, 1261; thanksgiving for, 1150, 1151
Boaz, 902, 1179
Boniface, 1260
Bonivard, Francois, 934

1290

Scripture Index